MOXIE

How I Learnt To Harden the F♥ck Up!
Foreword by Dr Tererai Trent

JUSTINE MARTIN

Copyright © 2026
First published in Australia in 2026
By Morpheus Publishing Pty Ltd, Geelong, Victoria 3216
www.morpheuspublishing.com.au

All rights reserved. No part of this publication may be reproduced, stored in a retrieval system, or transmitted in any form or by any means, electronic, mechanical, photocopying, recording or otherwise, without the prior written permission of the publisher or author.

Paperback ISBN: **978-1-923650-10-7**
Hardback ISBN: **978-1-923650-12-1**
Ebook ISBN: **978-1-923650-11-4**

Author:	**Justine Martin**
Editor:	Lynette Reurts
Cover Graphics:	Lynette Ingles
Typesetter:	Oseyi Okoeguale
Cover Photo:	Adrienne Dillion

A catalogue record for this book is available from the National Library of Australia.

DISCLAIMER
This book is a personal memoir based on the author's lived experiences. The events, medical journeys, emotions, and reflections shared are true to the author's life, but they are not intended to replace medical, psychological, legal, or professional advice. While the author speaks openly about illness, trauma, resilience, and recovery, every person's body, mind, and circumstances are different. Readers should always seek guidance from qualified health professionals or appropriate specialists regarding their own health, wellbeing, or personal situation. Some names, identifying details, and circumstances may have been changed to protect privacy. The views expressed are those of the author at the time of writing. The purpose of this book is to share a story, offer connection, and provide hope — not to diagnose, treat, or prescribe. The author and publisher accept no liability for any loss, damage, or consequences arising from the use or misuse of the information contained in this book.

PHOTOGRAPHS
Many of the photographs in this book were taken years ago and the original photographers are unknown. Justine Martin is deeply grateful to those who captured these moments, as the images help tell her story, and she acknowledges their contribution with sincere thanks.

COPYRIGHT
All original material in this book is the sole property of the author and Morpheus Publishing.

DISTRIBUTION
This book is distributed by Morpheus Publishing and is available through authorised distributors, booksellers, and the Morpheus Publishing website.

COPYRIGHT PERMISSIONS
For copyright permissions or any other inquiries, please contact:

PUBLISHER: Morpheus Publishing
www.morpheuspublishing.com.au | hello@justinemartin.com.au | +61403 564 942 |

AUTHOR: Justine Martin
https://www.morpheuspublishing.com.au/authors/justine-martin

TABLE OF CONTENTS

Dedication v
Introduction 1
Preface 5
Foreword: Dr Tererai Trent 8

PART ONE 13
   Chapter 1: How It All Began 14
   Chapter 2: The Dungeon 32
   Chapter 3: Those Junior Teenage Years 48
   Chapter 4: Those Mid-Teenage Years 63
   Chapter 5: Gutter Slut 74
   Chapter 6: The Gap Years 87
   Chapter 7: Herbs and Spices 102
   Chapter 8: Z for Zakariah 112
   Chapter 9: Mum 123
   Chapter 10: One Small Voice 133
   Chapter 11: Princess Pain's Birth 145
   Chapter 12: She Was Supposed to Live Forever 152
   Chapter 13: Waiting for God to Give Me a Sign 165
   Chapter 14: Choices I Made 176
   Chapter 15: Breaking The Arrow 184
   Chapter 16: I Bought My Own Lawn Mower 193
   Chapter 17: I Love a Good Pull 204

Chapter 18: One Plane Trip 214
Chapter 19: Wake Up Call 229
Chapter 20: The Sex Party 242

PART TWO **251**
Chapter 21: Returning Full Circle 252
Chapter 22: Not JUZT a Hobby 263
Chapter 23: Broken Heart 298
Chapter 24: Curve Ball 310
Chapter 25: The C Word 318
Chapter 26: Happy New Fucking Year 328
Chapter 27: VAD 339
Chapter 28: Their Voices 349
Chapter 29: It Didn't Just Come Off 358
Chapter 30: Spock 367
Chapter 31: Laying Down The Baton 376
Chapter 32: You Were Not Supposed to Go First 386
Chapter 33: Finding My Voice 394
Chapter 34: Same Same But Different 403
Chapter 35: Adapt and Modify 415
Chapter 36: Fair Weather Friends 425
Chapter 37: The Canvas of Life 433
Chapter 38: The Elephant in the Room 440
Chapter 39: Shame 447
Chapter 40: The Weight of a Blue Rosette 452
Chapter 41: I Forgave Her 470
Chapter 42: More Than My Fair Share 478
Chapter 43: What If 496

Justine Martin Contact Details 516
Bring Moxie to Your Stage 517
Publish Your Story Through Morpheus Publishing 518

DEDICATION

To my children and grandchildren, who are my why, my light, and my reason to keep getting back up no matter how hard life hits. You are the greatest gift of my life.

To my mum, who lives in my heart, my memories, and the story of who I am. Our journey was not simple, but it shaped me in ways I now understand with more compassion and grace.

To the younger version of me, who carried more than she ever should have had to, and still kept going.

And to anyone whose body, heart, or life has felt like a battlefield.
May you find your own strength, your own voice, and your own moxie.

INTRODUCTION

> **Trigger Warning:**
> This book contains references to childhood trauma, abuse, sexual assault, domestic violence, and medical trauma. Please take care while reading. Pause when you need to, breathe, and return when you are ready. These words are not meant to shock but to show truth and survival in their rawest forms.

It's the middle of the night again. My house is silent and dark. I wake to the familiar burn deep in my legs and the ache that has settled into my bones. For a few seconds, I lie still, hoping it will pass, but it doesn't. It never really does.

I sit up and push my feet into the floor, steeling myself against the pain, reminding my body that I am still here. It has become my ritual, a quiet battle between what hurts and what heals. I breathe through it, eyes closed, swearing on the inside with each inhale until the edges soften.

This is where moxie lives for me now. Not in the big moments, not on a stage or in a spotlight, but in the stillness of 3 am when no one is watching and giving up would be easy.

I wasn't supposed to make it this far.

Not according to some of the people who tried to break me. Not according to the doctors who wrote my body off. Not according to the voices in my head that whispered I would never claw my way out of the darkness. But here I am. Still standing. Still breathing. Still writing. Still fighting.

People see the woman I am now and think they understand strength. They see the smile, the awards, the businesses, the laughter, and the public face. What they don't see are the nights that nearly swallowed me whole. They don't see the quiet moments when pain becomes so loud it fills the room. They don't see the years it took to build a life out of what was left.

Moxie isn't something I was born with. It was forged. In hospitals, in heartbreak, in silence, in survival. It grew out of moments that stole the air from my lungs and left me with nothing but the choice: to lie down or get up.

That's what this book is about.

For over six years, I have been writing, rewriting, and wrestling with these words. It has taken time because this story demanded honesty, and honesty takes courage. It has meant pulling apart every version of myself I have ever been and deciding which truths to leave bare.

Writing *Moxie* hasn't been a project. It has been a process. A long, uncomfortable, necessary reckoning with who I was, who I became, and how I learned to survive when life refused to play fair.

I thought it would be easy to write about my past. I thought I could sit down, type out the stories, close the laptop, and feel finished. But telling the truth, really telling it, means going back to the places you have spent a lifetime trying to escape.

There were days I stared at the screen and couldn't type a single word. Not because I didn't know what to say, but because the memories came too fast. Some chapters reopened wounds that had never healed. Some made me laugh at the absurdity of it all. And some reminded me how far I've come.

For years, I questioned if anyone would care about my story. Would it matter? Would it help anyone? Would it even be good enough? I asked myself those questions so often that they became a kind of white noise in the back of my head. But I've come to understand that this book isn't about being good enough. It's about being real enough.

So this is it. My truth. My history. My life.

This book gives you the backstory, the parts that shaped me into the woman I am now. It explains the moments that broke me, the moments that rebuilt me, and the reasons I keep getting back up when most people would have stopped. It's not a straight line from pain to peace. It's a zigzag through fear, laughter, heartbreak, and hope.

I've been through things that have left permanent marks. Some physical. Some invisible. I've faced abuse, illness, and loss. I've been told I wouldn't walk again, wouldn't work again, wouldn't survive. I've had doctors shake their heads, people underestimate me, and others pity me. None of them knew that I wasn't asking for their approval. I was building my own kind of strength.

The word *moxie* found me later in life, but it fits like a second skin. Moxie is courage when there is no applause. It is the stubborn fire that says, 'Not today.' It is the quiet power that turns pain into purpose.

INTRODUCTION

Every story you are about to read was lived, not imagined. I remember them vividly. My long-term memory is a filing cabinet that never forgets. My short-term memory, though, is another story. It is like a goldfish: blink and it's gone. So if the stories jump or loop, that's me being real. That's how my mind works after everything it's been through.

Some names have been changed, some replaced with numbers. This isn't to protect them, it's to protect me and their families.

Before you go any further, I should warn you that there's swearing in here. Not the polite, once-in-a-while kind, but the kind that slips out when life hits you too hard to stay quiet. Because sometimes 'oh dear' just doesn't cut it. This book is raw, unfiltered, and written exactly as I lived it. If you are here for perfection, you won't find it. But if you are here for the truth, welcome.

This isn't a self-help book. It's not a guide to happiness or a list of steps to success. It's a story about survival. About getting up again and again, even when there's no strength left. It's about losing everything you thought defined you and finding something better in its place: yourself.

There were years I could barely function. Days when I was too tired to eat, too broken to talk, too lost to care. But I kept going. Because sometimes survival isn't dramatic. It's just showing up. It's putting one foot on the floor, then the other. It's doing the next thing, however small, until momentum returns.

Moxie isn't about being fearless. It's about feeling the fear and doing it anyway. It's about crying your eyes out, swearing under your breath, and then getting back up because you refuse to let life win.

Every chapter in this book is a piece of me. Some pieces are light. Some are dark. All of them are true. I've learned that you can hold pain and joy at the same time. You can be grateful and grieving, brave and terrified, healing and hurting. They can all exist together.

I don't want this book to be read as a tale of tragedy turned to triumph. It's not that neat. It's about the messy middle, the part most people skip. The hours, days, and years between falling apart and standing tall. That's where the real work happens.

If you've been through trauma, you'll understand what I mean when I say the past never really leaves. It lingers in your body, in your dreams, in the way you flinch when someone moves too fast. Healing doesn't mean forgetting. It means learning how to live with it and still find joy.

And joy does come back. Slowly, gently, sometimes unexpectedly. It returns in small moments such as a smile, a sunrise, a deep breath that doesn't hurt. I've learned to look for those moments and hold them close. They are proof that moxie works.

When I began *Moxie*, I thought it was a book about resilience. Now I know it's about something deeper. It's about reclaiming power after it has been taken. It's about finding your voice when it has been silenced. It's about choosing yourself every single day, even when the world tells you not to.

And before we start, I want to make something clear. What you're about to read is my version of the truth. My memories. My feelings. My perspective. The world looks different through everyone's eyes, and this is how it looked through mine. I know there are always three sides to every story: yours, mine, and the truth that sits somewhere in between. These are my memories as I lived them, shaped by pain, love, confusion, and growth. They are honest. They are imperfect. They are mine.

You can't survive what I've survived and come out untouched. You come out carved open, rebuilt from the inside out. You come out changed. You come out awake.

If you are reading this, maybe you've faced your own battles. Maybe your scars look different from mine, but they still ache when it rains. Maybe you are tired of pretending you are okay. Maybe you are ready to start again. I hope these pages help you see that starting again is always possible.

You don't need to be unbreakable to have moxie. You just need to keep showing up.

This is my story. My truth. My reminder that even when life knocks you down, you can rise.

Welcome to *Moxie*.

Welcome to how I learnt to harden the fuck up.

Or, as my therapist likes to say, how I learnt to soften the hell down.

Both are true. Both saved me.

And maybe, just maybe, they'll help you find your own moxie too.

PREFACE

When I look back at the person I was fifteen, ten, even five years ago, I recognise someone struggling to find her backbone. Someone who at times seemed brittle, fragile, vulnerable. Someone who thought vulnerability was weakness. But this book is about a different truth. It's about the realisation that hardness isn't about armour, it's about truth. Hardening up is not shutting down. It's opening up under pressure and refusing to break. It's finding your steel, your backbone, your voice and using them when the world says you should whisper.

I titled this book *MOXIE: How I Learned to Harden the Fuck Up* because I didn't want niceties or euphemisms. I wanted blood, sweat, honesty and the kind of language that matches the fight. I wanted the word moxie because it captures guts, nerve, resilience and audacity. Because every time I had to fight the cancers, chronic illness, loss, invisible diagnoses and setbacks, what got me through wasn't a polite version of courage. It was raw, it was fierce, and yes, I hardened up. But I also softened because real toughness and softness can live together.

My journey started long before I knew the word moxie. It started in the quiet of the hospital waiting room, in the moment I heard the words 'Multiple Sclerosis'. It started when I learned my body could betray me, when I discovered that 'normal' is a lie and 'health' is a gift and 'control' is a myth. I started when I realised that if I didn't harden up, I would get hardened out. That life would bend me into something unrecognisable. That moment taught me that I have to choose who I become, even if I didn't choose my circumstances.

I grew up hearing things like 'just get on with it' and 'you'll be right' and 'pull yourself together.' I absorbed them without questioning. And when the shit really hit the fan, I discovered that those phrases don't reach far enough. 'Get on with it' is easy when you still breathe without effort. But when your veins conspire against you and your body betrays you in subtle and gross ways, when you watch your children cry because you are weak, when you fear that you might run out of time, then the phrase becomes sour. It offers no solace. It demands a posture you cannot maintain. It creates shame rather than strength.

So I had to rewrite the narrative. I had to say: I will feel this. I will wrestle with it. I will survive it. I will stand my ground even if standing means trembling. I will harden myself not by shutting off but by leaning in. I learned that to harden up is to drop the pretence of being invincible and to acknowledge I may be scared and still act anyway. To harden up is to dig in, dig deep, and say, 'Okay world! Show me what you've got!'

Over the years, I have walked through pain and fear and loss. I have been certified sick with multiple diagnoses, and I have had to make peace with the fact that sickness and strength are not opposites. I have felt humiliation when I couldn't do the things I used to do. I have felt rage that my body wasn't on my side. I have felt grief at the life I thought I'd have and the one I ended up with. And through all of that, I discovered that what looked like weakness on the outside was often the birthplace of ferocious resilience. I found new muscles in corners of me I didn't know existed. I learned that hardening up is less about building walls and more about building wings.

When I wrote this book, I didn't set out to tell a sanitised version of my life. I didn't aim for inspiration porn or feel-good sound bites. I wanted the truth. Raw, visceral — at times unflattering — truth. I wanted to give you something that grips you by the throat and whispers: you are stronger than you think. I wanted to share stories, not to say 'look at me', but to say 'look at us'. Because if you have ever felt small, silenced, diminished, sidelined, left behind, invisible, then this book is for you. And if you have ever thought, 'Maybe I'll just give up?' then you and I need to talk.

Moxie doesn't come from perfection. It doesn't come from never falling down. It comes from getting up when you shouldn't be able to. It comes from saying 'yes' even when the 'no' feels louder and sometimes easier. It comes from recognising that the world will test you, and you're allowed to answer back. This book is a walk-through of how I found that answer. I don't claim to have all the answers. I claim to have looked at the devil at the door and said, 'Not today'. I claim to have been knocked down and gotten up again, thinking, 'You know what, this time I'm fighting for me'. I claim to have discovered that the only person I needed to harden up for was myself.

Now in my life today, the word 'moxie' still hums in my veins. It shows up when I'm on stage speaking to a room full of people about resilience, when I'm sitting in a hospital clinic listening to yet another test result, when I'm home with my family and thinking about what kind of example I want to be. It shows up when I create plans

PREFACE

with purpose, when I rise before dawn to write, when I let myself cry and then wipe the tears and pick up the pen again. Moxie is not a one-time event; it's a muscle. And the more I use it, the stronger it becomes. The more I use it, the more it grows. And I want you to grow yours too.

Because if you're reading this, you have your own fight. It might be quiet. It might be loud. It might be blatantly obvious or layered behind smiles and routines. But it's there. And I promise you this: you will emerge from it. The person you become will not just bear the scars, the losses, the battles, the diagnoses and the fears, but will carry them as proof. Proof you were alive. Proof you showed up. Proof you did not give in. That's the gift of moxie.

As you dive into these pages, you might recognise yourself in the mirror of my stories. You might see your own tears in mine, your own knock-downs in mine, your breath-catching in mine. And that is the goal: to hold up a mirror so you recognise not only what you've been through but what you still carry. And to invite you to say: I am done being small. I am done being silent. I am rising. I am hardening up. I am stepping into the life I am meant for, even if parts of me are still tender, still healing, still raw. Because tenderness is not the opposite of strength, it is its companion.

So welcome. Welcome to this journey. Welcome to the climb. Welcome to the messy, beautiful, brutal, hopeful path of moxie. Thank you for being here. Thank you for choosing to open these pages. Because by opening them you are already saying 'yes'. Yes to yourself. Yes to your story. Yes to the fact that you matter. Yes to the fact that your voice matters. Now let's begin.

— **Justine**

FOREWORD

Dr Tererai Trent

Dear Beloved Sahwira,

Come near the fire and sit with me. The story you are about to read belongs to one of the most courageous women I have ever met. In my culture, when we honour the sacredness of a story, we gather close. We listen not just with our ears but with our hearts. Today, I invite you to do the same.

Her name is Justine Martin, and her journey will move you, excite you, and awaken something powerful within you.

I met Justine in November of 2023 beneath the heavy skies and timeless stones of Crom Castle in Ireland. We had both come to a writer's retreat, two women from opposite sides of the world, drawn together by ink, intention, and spirit. When I first saw her, tall and commanding, with raven-dark hair and a strong, chiselled jawline, I felt something ancient stir within me. Perhaps I recognised her — not from this lifetime but from the soul's knowing. A Sahwira. A sacred sister.

There was a quiet power about her — a mystery. When I saw the tattoos peeking out from beneath her jumper sleeves, I knew this woman carried stories not only in her mind but also across her body and deep within her bones. Stories she had lived and survived.

Later that evening, in a dimly lit room adorned with heavy tapestries, she began to speak. The air was thick with anticipation, making each word feel monumental. A profound ceremony followed — a sacred soul exchange that transcended the physical realm. Her voice resonated with certainty, weaving together stories and emotions that invited the listener to explore the essence of their being.

Justine opened her heart to me with raw truth, and I listened, not as a mentor or fellow writer but as a witness. And oh, what a story she told.

She spoke of illness — life-altering, body-breaking illness. Multiple Sclerosis. Cancers. A heart weakened by stress and battle. An acquired brain injury. Pain layered upon pain, and yet, she did not speak as a victim. She spoke as a warrior. She spoke as a mother walking barefoot through fire for her children. She spoke as a woman who had faced her mortality not once, but many times, and chose to rise again and again.

As she wove her narrative, vivid images unfurled before me: the ink swirling on her arms, each marking a testament — a tribute to a son's brave enlistment, a chapter etched in the hardship of chemotherapy, a haunting memory of hair surrendered to the bathroom floor, a dream both shattered and beautifully reborn. Her body, far from being merely a vessel, emerged as a sacred scroll, intricately inscribed with stories of resilience and the depth of her journey.

Justine doesn't hide her scars; she wears them boldly. She paints them into art and transforms them into language. This is what you will discover in the pages that follow. This book, MOXIE, is more than a memoir. It is a declaration and a rebellion against everything that says, 'you can't'. It is a middle finger to limitation and a roadmap for those who have felt broken, silenced, or pushed aside.

The word moxie means determination, courage, and spirited grit. And if there is anyone who embodies that word, it is Justine. However, you will quickly learn that her version of moxie isn't just about toughening up; it's about softening into truth. It's about owning every part of your story, even the messy, brutal, heartbreaking bits.

Justine has learned to harden the f*ck up — but not in the way the world tells us to, not by closing off or pretending to be invincible. She has done it by being vulnerable. She allowed herself to fall apart and chose to rise again and again, becoming stronger in her cracks, softer at her centre, and fiercer in her truth.

Let me share this with you: this remarkable woman is not here to play it safe or fade into the background. She is not interested in offering mere platitudes or superficial inspiration. Instead, she is on a bold mission to challenge the very foundations of our understanding. She fearlessly confronts our perspectives on disability, illness, trauma, and the strength inherent in femininity. With a powerful presence, she makes her voice heard, paints vivid stories, writes with passion, and lives her truth in a courageous and unapologetic manner. In doing so, she invites all of us to embrace our authenticity and live boldly alongside her.

This book is dedicated to the woman who has been told to 'calm down' or 'be less,' to stifle her spirit and silence her voice. It serves as a lifeline for those weary from the relentless struggle for survival, those longing for someone to see their pain and affirm, 'Sawubona, I see you, and you are not alone.' It is for those who have navigated through the darkest depths of despair, clawing their way back with blood under their fingernails, yet still harbouring a fragile whisper of hope within their lungs.

You, beloved reader, my Sahwira, are on the brink of stepping into the extraordinary world of a woman who has risen from the ashes of adversity. With unwavering resolve, she has transformed her disability into a source of purpose, turning personal loss into a beacon of leadership. Through the ink of her pain, she has crafted a powerful new legacy that extends beyond herself, touching the lives of her children, uplifting her community, and now reaching out to you.

Allow her words to ignite a flame deep within your soul. Let her unwavering resilience break the barriers surrounding your heart. Let her fierce courage serve as a poignant reminder that, no matter how many times life tries to knock you down, there is always a path to rise anew. Always.

I honor you, Justine. Your story is sacred, your fire is fierce, and your moxie is unstoppable.

With deep love and unshakeable belief in your calling,
Dr. Tererai Trent

FOREWORD

2023 Dr Tererai Trent and myself at Crom Castle Northern Ireland

Dr. Tererai Trent is a renowned scholar, educator, humanitarian, and motivational speaker, celebrated as Oprah Winfrey's 'All-Time Favorite Guest.' She founded Tererai Trent International (Tinogona Foundation), advocating for children's quality education, women's empowerment, and leadership. Dr. Trent holds a doctorate in interdisciplinary evaluation from Western Michigan University and teaches Global Health at Drexel University. She has authored the award-winning 'The Awakened Woman: Remembering and Reigniting Our Sacred Dreams.' The Statues for Equality Project of Gillie and Marc recognised Dr. Trent as one of the ten most inspiring women in the world. Alongside notable figures like Oprah Winfrey and Jane Goodall, a life-size bronze statue of her was unveiled on Women's Equality Day, August 26, 2019, in the United States.

PART ONE

CHAPTER 1

How It All Began

I was born on a Wednesday in March 1971 at Baxter House, a maternity unit at Geelong Hospital in Victoria, Australia. I arrived into a shotgun marriage, the kind that was never spoken about but sat quietly in the room with everyone. My mother, Marian Martin, née Londish, was twenty two. My father, Norman Martin, was twenty three. Young. Unprepared. Doing what people did back then because they thought they had to.

They met at the Carlton Hotel in Geelong in 1968. If you went looking for it now, you would only find the facade. The rest of the building has long been demolished. In its place now sits the National Office for the Agency of the National Disability Insurance Scheme. The NDIS. The irony is not lost on me. Decades later, I am an NDIS participant due to my disabilities. In some strange, circular way, my life is still tethered to the place where my parents met. I started there, and I came back there, just in a different form. Talk about coming full circle.

My conception story is one that has been argued over for years. I was conceived in a car. That part is not up for debate. The rest is. I always thought I was a Holden girl. It felt right. Solid. Reliable. Very Australian. Then a few years ago Dad casually dropped into conversation that it was actually a Ford. That rocked me. More recently, he revised his story and said it was a Holden after all. The details are hazy. It could have been the front seat or the back seat. No one seems quite sure. And honestly, at this point, your guess is as good as mine.

What I do know is this. My life began in a car, not a bed. A car.

There is something oddly fitting about that. I did not arrive into softness or stability. I arrived into movement, into uncertainty, into something that was never meant to be permanent. A car is not a place you are meant to begin life. Maybe that says everything about how unstable the start of my world really was.

Maybe that explains more about my life than I ever realised until now.

From the very beginning, nothing about my story has been neat or conventional. It has been layered, complicated, sometimes uncomfortable, often ironic, and rarely predictable. I did not come into the world wrapped in a bow. I came in sideways, into a situation already moving faster than anyone involved could control.

And yet, here I am.

My parents married quickly, without an engagement, and seven months later I arrived. It was 1.30 in the afternoon. I weighed 7 pounds 10.5 ounces, or 3.45 kilograms, and I entered the world with jet-black, spiky hair that refused to lie flat. The nurses nicknamed me the bottlebrush kid. They would actually wet my hair down before visiting hours in an attempt to make me presentable. Even then, it still tried to stand to attention.

Mum kept everything. Every tiny detail of my early life was carefully recorded and preserved. She saved pieces of hair from my first eight haircuts. She wrote down what my first meals were and the first words I spoke. She documented the day I took my first steps and how much I weighed at different stages. There was nothing casual about it. It was meticulous, almost reverent.

She also created a scrapbook. Newspaper cuttings announcing my birth. My hospital wristband. Congratulatory cards. Sections of wrapping paper from the many gifts they received. Telegrams. Even the labels from the champagne bottle they used to wet my head at the Bateford Hotel. I still have all of it. Every piece. These are the treasures I return to in the moments when doubt creeps in and I question whether my mother loved me. The evidence is there in her handwriting, in the care she took, in the way she preserved my beginnings.

Dad was not there when Mum went into labour. He was out buying a washing machine. That detail has always stayed with me. At the time he was a service repairman for National Cash Registers. Mum was working as a secretary at one of the Valley Mills woollen mills in Geelong. The mill building still stands, though its purpose has changed. It is now Little Creatures Brewery, a place I often visit for drinks with friends. When I sit there, glass in hand, surrounded by noise and laughter, I feel strangely close to Mum. I know she once walked those same floors. That her working life passed through those walls. It grounds me in a way I cannot quite explain.

Our first home was in Church Street, Herne Hill, Geelong. A small house tucked in behind a butcher shop. Mum always said it was haunted. She told me that one day, when she was checking on me in my cot, she felt the pressure of a man's hand slide slowly down her arm. When she turned around, there was no one there.

I have driven past that house in recent years. I can still feel something unsettled just sitting outside it. An unease that sits heavy in my chest. I have never gone back inside. I do not need to. Some places hold memories that do not belong to us alone, and that house is one of them.

From the very beginning, my story was layered with detail, care, mystery, and things no one could yet see. I entered the world loved, watched, and recorded, but already carrying more inside my body than anyone could have imagined. Not just personality. Not just potential. I was carrying genetic threads, weaknesses, and future illnesses quietly woven into me, lying dormant, waiting their turn. The kind of things that do not show up in baby photos or birth announcements. The kind of things that sit silently in your cells, biding their time.

I was the first born child, daughter, grandchild, granddaughter and great granddaughter on both sides of my parents' families. I arrived carrying a lot of firsts before anyone realised the weight of expectation, responsibility and projection that came with them, or how early those things would shape my life. I was spoiled endlessly by my father's mother, Nanna Violet, or as we called her, Nanna in Geelong. She adored me in a way that felt instinctive and unquestioning, the kind of love that wraps itself around you without asking anything in return.

Mum used to say that Nanna Violet had always wanted girls, but instead she had three sons. Mum would then add, without much subtlety, that she ended up with bitches as daughters-in-law. They did not like each other. There was no pretending otherwise. My Nanna Violet had hoped my father would marry someone else, and that tension sat quietly in the background of our family life, unspoken but ever present.

My parents did not wait long before starting on baby number two. My brother Simon was born ten months and three weeks after me, arriving six weeks early in January 1972. He was due just one day after my birthday. We should have been twelve months and one day apart. Instead, he was impatient to enter the world.

Simon was very sick when he was born. He had hyaline membrane disease, which meant his lungs were not fully developed. His early arrival shaped more than just his first weeks of life. For six weeks of every year, Simon and I are the same age. That small quirk has confused people our entire lives. We were born in different years, yet share the same age for part of each one.

People often thought we were twins, or assumed we had different mothers. The reality was far less neat. When Simon was born, I was still in nappies. I was not even crawling yet and was still being bottle fed. I never learnt to crawl at all. Walking came late for me. Up until I was eighteen months old, I got around by scooting on my bottom. I know this because Mum documented it all meticulously in my baby book.

Sometimes I find myself wondering if that delay had less to do with physical development and more to do with circumstance. The only time I consistently received my mother's full attention was when she had to pick me up and carry me. Babies adapt quickly. They learn how to survive within the environments they are given. They learn how to get attention when they feel it slipping away.

Mum often commented that it would have been easier if Simon and I had been born twins rather than so close together. That observation stayed with me. It hints at just how stretched she must have been. Two babies, both so young, one fragile and premature, the other still very much a baby herself.

From the beginning, Simon and I learned to exist side by side in a world that was already demanding more than our parents knew how to give. And in ways I would only understand much later, those early dynamics quietly shaped the woman I would become.

At that age, I spent a lot of time with Mum's sister, Lynny. She would drop off my cousin Matthew, who was close to Simon's age, swap us over, and take me grocery shopping with her. Those outings became a small pocket of consistency in a life that already felt unpredictable.

Apparently, if she parked me in my trolley too close to the shelves, I would quietly add extra groceries, which she only discovered when she reached the checkout. This is a habit I am fairly certain I still have to this day, quietly adding things to my basket at Officeworks, which now occupies the building that used to be our local supermarket more than fifty years ago. I like to tell myself it has nothing to do with the fact that I love shopping, but the truth is probably somewhere in between.

Simon was a small child because he was born prematurely, while I was always above average in both height and weight. Mum was 5'1". Dad was 6'1". I inherited my father's height and my mother's body shape, particularly her legs. That combination shaped more than just my physical appearance. It shaped how I was seen and how I learned to see myself.

I believe the size difference between my brother and me played a significant role in my body image issues, through no fault of his. I was known within my family as the garbage truck. I was always hungrier than Simon. My meals were twice the size of his. Food became something more than nourishment. It became comfort. It became safety. It became a way to protect myself from a world that already felt overwhelming. By my teenage years, food had become armour, cushioning me from pain and from feelings I did not yet know how to name.

As a child, I could never seem to do anything right, while my brother could never do anything wrong. He was the golden child. That was simply how it was. I did not know any differently at the time. It was only years later, when I became a parent myself, that I began to understand how profoundly unequal that dynamic had been. I could not reconcile why Mum treated me so differently, and that realisation cut deeper than I expected. It forced me to question not only my childhood, but the beliefs I had carried about myself for decades.

In September 1974, everything shifted again. Mum found a lump the size of a golf ball in her right breast and was diagnosed with breast cancer. She was just twenty seven years old. She underwent a full mastectomy of her right breast, something that was almost unheard of at the time. Against the odds, she survived.

I was three and a half.

My Nanna Marie, or Nanna in Sydney as we called her, drove down from Sydney to collect Simon and me so we could live with her and my grandfather, Parpa, for six months while Mum recovered from surgery and radiation. We spent that time with our cousins, surrounded by family who loved us.

But I was far too young to understand what was really happening. I did not understand cancer. I did not understand recovery. All I understood was that I had been sent away. In my young, literal mind, I believed I must have done something wrong. I believed I was being punished. I felt abandoned by both of my parents at an age when safety should have been unquestioned.

After six long months, Mum was well enough to care for us again. I can still vividly remember the drive back down the Hume Highway with Nanna, waiting to see my parents after what felt like an eternity. That reunion carried hope, relief and confusion all at once. It would not be the last time Simon and I lived with our grandparents. It happened three times during my childhood, and each time reinforced the belief that had quietly taken root in me, that I was not truly wanted.

Mum recovered fully from the cancer and went on to become a founding member of the Mastectomy Association of Victoria, serving as their secretary. She channelled her experience into advocacy and support for other women. But while her body healed, the emotional scars remained.

Dad never saw her the same way after the surgery. Mum felt she was no longer a whole woman, now that she only had one breast. There was no counselling back then. No one told her that her worth was not measured by her body. No one reminded her that she was still complete, still desirable, still enough.

And in that silence, both of my parents carried wounds they did not know how to heal. Those unspoken wounds filtered down into our family, shaping the emotional landscape of my childhood in ways I would spend much of my adult life unravelling.

I was a very young child, no more than three years old, when my uncle took me into the family shearing shed on our farm in Teesdale. My memories are not clear pictures, but flashes. Sensations. A sense that something was wrong long before I had words to describe it. I remember him touching me. I remember confusion. I remember fear.

What I remember most clearly is my pop walking into the shed.

He caught him in the act. He yelled for my nanna to come and get me. He grabbed my arm tightly and walked me straight out of the shed. Nanna came running from the house and took me from him. No one explained anything. No one said the words. But something shifted forever in that moment.

The next day, Nanna took me to Geelong and bought me a brand new television so I could watch Humphrey B Bear. It was meant to be a kindness. A distraction. A way of smoothing something over without ever naming it. That television sat in the corner of the room, bright and cheerful, while something very dark settled quietly inside me.

For the next few years, whenever we visited the farm, I would not go anywhere near the two men. I would walk as far away from them as I could. I did not need to be told to do that. My body already knew. My pop died when I was six. My uncle died when I was seventeen. But my trust in adults died when I was three.

There was also a family friend. I remember him touching me in a similar way when I was about seven. Again, confusion. Again, fear. Again, silence. When I was sixteen, I saw him again and felt an overwhelming urge to run. My heart raced. My stomach dropped. My body reacted before my mind could catch up. Three men who were meant to protect me did not. That shaped everything that followed.

I accepted things in my life that should never have been acceptable. I endured horrific situations because somewhere deep inside me, a very young part of me believed that this was normal. That this was what adults did. That this was what I deserved. I never told my parents. I was threatened. I was told terrible things would happen if I spoke. I carried that secret for decades. A secret I never should have had to carry. A secret I will not carry anymore.

That is where my moxie began, not as confidence, not as courage, but as endurance. As survival. As a tiny child finding a way to keep breathing in a world that no longer felt safe.

I was three and a half when I started at Highett Kindergarten. I made friends, including one who is still a Facebook friend today, more than fifty years later. At our Christmas concert, I was an angel. I wanted to please Mum. I wanted her attention. I wanted to be good enough. Later, in prep at primary school, I played the Virgin Mary in the Christmas pantomime, with my Baby Alive doll as Jesus. Mum bragged about it to everyone. For a brief moment, I felt loved. But it was love for what I did, not for who I was. And even then, it was conditional.

That became a pattern. Perform. Please. Achieve. Be useful. Be impressive. Maybe then I would be safe. Maybe then I would be loved.

Simon often got me into trouble. He was rough when we played. He would hit me. And I would get smacked for hurting my brother. I was no saint, but I was punished far more than I deserved. One day Mum told me that if I screamed one more time, she would not come running. I was about five.

Not long after that, she brought home a free calendar from the butcher for Simon and I. I was walking into Simon's room with the calendar tucked against my left side. I was wearing shorts. The calendar had a metal strip along the top. It caught in the door jamb and flung back, tearing a large chunk out of my leg. I screamed louder than I ever had in my life.

No one came.

I stood there with blood pouring down my leg and onto the floor. Simon ran outside to get Mum. I hobbled into the kitchen sobbing, waiting. When Mum finally came in, she sat me on the kitchen table. She poured undiluted Dettol into a bowl. She dipped cotton wool into it and cleaned my open wound. She cut the hanging skin off my leg. She told me off for blubbering. She reminded me that she had warned me she would not come running.

I should have had stitches. Years later, Mum admitted she should have taken me to hospital. I still have the scar. A centimetre wide. Five centimetres long. A permanent reminder etched into my skin.

That was the moment something hardened inside me.

Nobody is coming.

From that day on, my moxie became something sharper. Quieter. More determined. If no one was coming, then I would have to survive on my own. I would learn not to scream. I would learn not to need. I would learn not to expect comfort. I would learn to endure pain silently and keep going.

That belief carried me through childhood, through trauma, through illness, through relationships that mirrored what I had been taught was normal. It made me strong in ways people praised, and broken in ways no one saw.

But moxie is not just about hardening up. It is about surviving long enough to one day soften down again. It is about recognising that the strength that saved you as a child does not have to rule you forever. Writing this now, naming it, breaking the silence, is moxie too.

Because the bravest thing I have ever done is not to endure. It is to tell the truth.

The people who were closest to me were not there for me.

She did not come.

She was not there.

The person who was supposed to love and protect me more than anyone else in the world did not come running. That moment damaged me far more deeply than I understood at the time. In truth, it shaped the next forty five years of my life.

From that day on, my decisions were made by the five year old girl living somewhere deep inside me. Decisions I did not consciously make, but lived by all the same. I will do it myself. I cannot rely on anyone. If I need something, I must make it happen alone. That belief sat beneath every choice I made. It influenced my relationships, my tolerance for pain, my endurance, and the way I navigated illness after illness. Everything I have survived medically, I have done largely on my own. I relied on systems. I relied on doctors. I relied on procedure and protocol. But emotionally, I stood alone. Get up. Keep going. Do not expect comfort. Do not wait for rescue.

That was the day I learnt to harden the fuck up. Not because I wanted to, but because I had to. That little girl whose mum did not come running learned that the only person she could truly rely on was herself. That belief became my armour. It kept me alive. It also cost me dearly.

There is another memory from childhood that has stayed with me, one that seems small on the surface but carried enormous weight. One night Mum, Simon and I drove to Tullamarine Airport in our V8 HK Holden Kingswood to pick up my grandfather who was visiting. Simon and I were strapped into racing harnesses in the back seat. Seatbelts were not standard then, and we could not undo them ourselves. Mum had locked the doors before leaving home, worried someone might grab us while stopped at traffic lights.

She got out of the car at the airport, shut her door, and realised she had locked the keys and her children inside. Panic set in quickly. Her panic became our panic. Simon and I cried, trapped in the back seat, unable to free ourselves. Mum left us in the car to find help and collect my grandfather. Time stretched. Fear grew. We did not understand what was happening. We only knew she had gone.

Eventually she returned with my grandfather and a wire coat hanger. They bent it, slipped it down between the window and the rubber seal, and clicked the door open. We were told off for crying. No one acknowledged how frightened we were. No one reassured us. No one named what had happened. I am certain now that this is where my claustrophobia began. Another moment where I felt trapped, powerless, and abandoned. Another piece of evidence quietly filed away by a child who learnt not to expect rescue.

These moments may seem insignificant when told decades later. They were not. They shaped my nervous system. They shaped my sense of safety. They shaped how I learned to move through the world. I have spent years in counselling working to rewire those pathways, to teach my body and mind that not every moment of vulnerability ends in abandonment.

Even as a child, I was deeply caring. That part of me was always there. When I was around four, I found a sparrow in our backyard. It was struggling to fly, clearly unwell. Like children everywhere, I wanted to fix it. I found a container and made a small bed from an old rag. I placed the bird inside, wanting to nurse it back to health. Wanting to save it. I put the lid on to keep it warm and took it to Mum, who was still in bed.

I had no idea that by doing so, I had suffocated it.

When I realised the bird was dead, I was horrified. Truly horrified. I had killed a living thing. The shock of that moment still sits in my chest even now. Mum laughed at me. Fifty years later, I remember that laughter. I remember standing there devastated, ashamed, and confused, while the person I needed comfort from dismissed my pain. Once again, the message landed quietly but clearly. You get it wrong. You do not do things right. Your care causes harm.

Those early experiences did not make me weak. They forged my moxie long before I knew the word. They created a woman who could endure extraordinary pain and keep moving. A woman who could survive abandonment, illness, and trauma without collapsing. But they also created a woman who struggled to ask for help, struggled to believe she deserved care, and struggled to trust that someone might stay.

Understanding this now does not place blame. It brings clarity. It brings compassion. It allows me to see that the strength I once needed to survive does not have to be the strength I live with forever.

As Simon and I grew older, life continued to move at a pace that required independence long before either of us was truly ready for it. By the age of six, we became Junior Jet Setters with TAA and later Ansett. Our parents would put us on planes unaccompanied and fly us to Sydney to spend school holidays with our grandparents. From there, we were often sent on again to stay with my aunt and uncle, where we spent weeks playing with our cousins. In many ways, those cousins became more like siblings. We grew up together across state lines, and that bond has lasted into adulthood. Even now, they live not far from me, and those early connections remain some of the safest relationships in my life.

At the time, it was simply practical. It was cheaper to fly us interstate than to pay for a babysitter. I have fond memories of those holidays, but when I look back through adult eyes, I see how early independence became normalised. Being sent away was not unusual. Being self sufficient was expected. My moxie was being built quietly, again and again, through necessity rather than choice.

Mum obtained her motorbike licence in 1975 in Melbourne. Anything Dad did or wanted to do, she followed alongside him, including learning how to ski. She taught me, through example, that anything a man could do, a woman could do too. These are some of my most positive memories of Mum. She was strong in her own way; determined, capable, and unafraid to step into spaces that were not traditionally welcoming to women. That lesson stayed with me and became one of the foundations of my own resilience.

Unfortunately, I was a sick child. I seemed to catch everything that circulated through the community in the seventies. Around 1977, Simon and I both suffered years of recurring tonsillitis. Every six weeks, without fail, we were back at the doctor and back on antibiotics. So many rounds of antibiotics that I often wonder how they impacted on my gut health and long term wellbeing. We missed large amounts of school. It was during this time that my penicillin allergy became apparent.

Mum eventually had enough of us being constantly unwell and demanded that we both have our tonsils and adenoids removed at the same time. We went into Sandringham Hospital together. On the day of the surgery, the hospital staff placed a pink blanket on Simon's bed with the name Simone written on it, and a blue blanket on my bed with the name Justin. I turned to Mum in tears and blurted out that if they could not even get our names right, how would they get our operations right.

I woke up vomiting large amounts of blood. Over the following months, my hearing changed, and I began to think people were yelling at me. The chronic infections had caused permanent hearing loss in my left ear, damage I still live with today. I also struggled with speech. My voice sounded nasal. It turned out that too much tissue had been removed when my adenoids were taken out. I spent the next twelve months seeing a speech therapist, blowing a ping pong ball across a table with a straw and relearning how to form sounds properly. Even now, when I am tired or speaking quickly, some words still come out through my nose. I have to consciously think about how I speak.

So yes, when they got our names wrong, my intuition was spot on.

For several years after that, I was in and out of hospital with severe abdominal pain that no one could explain. It was not until many years later that I learned I am lactose intolerant. Mum used to let me drink a full six hundred millilitre milk bottle every day, with a straw shoved through the foil lid, believing she was doing the right thing. I still remember the thick cream sitting on top of the milk. Once I removed dairy from my diet as an adult, the improvement was immediate. It is astonishing how long pain can go unexplained when no one is looking in the right place.

Between the ages of four and six, there were multiple moments that quietly shaped my nervous system. Both of my parents raced speedboats, and weekends were often spent at lakes and dams around Victoria watching them compete. It was an incredibly dangerous sport. They eventually stopped after Dad narrowly escaped a potentially fatal accident at Albert Park Lake. Even now, remembering that incident triggers a stress response in my body. Fear does not always need words. Sometimes it settles into the bones.

Another time, we had been shopping at Southland Shopping Centre in Moorabbin. We were probably around six years old. Mum had bought a barbeque chicken for dinner and we were in the lift heading back to the car when it suddenly stopped. The doors would not open. The phone in the lift did not work. Mum managed to pry the doors open a few centimetres and scream for help. The panic in her voice is something I have never forgotten. Simon and I were terrified. Mum tried to joke that at least we would not starve because we had a hot chicken for dinner. It took an hour to get us out. That was my second clear experience of claustrophobia. I have never looked at a hot chicken the same way since.

Not long after that, at the same shopping centre, I wandered off while Mum and Aunty Marg were walking to the car. I was distracted by the lights, the shops, the movement. I stepped onto an escalator and realised too late that they were heading in another direction. I screamed as I was carried up to the next level. No one noticed I was missing until they reached the car.

I was terrified. A kind woman took me to centre management, where they made an announcement over the PA system. Mum came to collect me, apologising publicly, giving me that look that told me what was coming later. When we reached the car, and again when we got home, she smacked me hard. There was no comfort for being lost. No reassurance. No acknowledgement of fear.

That was the era we grew up in. We rode our bikes to school. We played in the street until dusk. We ate simple food. Meat and three vegetables. Apricot chicken. Homemade fried rice. Roast meat. Corned beef and white sauce. There was no takeaway except on special occasions. Chinese food for birthdays. Mum's special Chinese chicken wings. We ordered lunch once a term when Mum worked in the tuck shop, and those days felt like a treat.

Looking back now, I can see how these experiences layered on top of one another. Moments of independence mixed with moments of fear. Responsibility mixed with abandonment. Love mixed with pain. Each experience quietly reinforced the belief that I needed to be strong, adaptable, and self reliant. That is where my moxie was forged. Not in confidence, but in survival. Not in bravado, but in endurance.

These early childhood moments still ripple through my life today, influencing how I travel, how I handle anxiety, how my body responds to stress, and how I relate to others. Understanding them has not erased their impact, but it has allowed me to soften toward myself, and to view myself with kindness and compassion. To recognise that the strength I developed was never accidental.

It was necessary.

1945 Pop and Nanna Violet

1968 Mum

1969 Mum and Dad, Geelong, Victoria

1969 Mum and Dad

1970 Mum and Dad's Wedding

1971 Me at Queenscliff, Victoria

1971 Mum pregnant with Simon, Dad and me at Church Street Geelong West, Victoria

1972 Dad, Simon and me at Queenscliff, Victoria

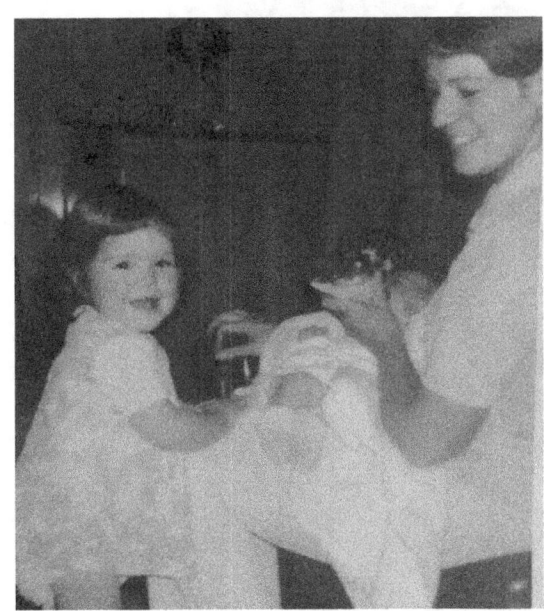
1972 Mum, Simon and me

1972 Simon and me, with just 10 months and 3 weeks between us

1973 Mum, Dad, Simon and me. This is one of my favourite family photos

1973 Mum, Simon and me in Church Street Geelong West

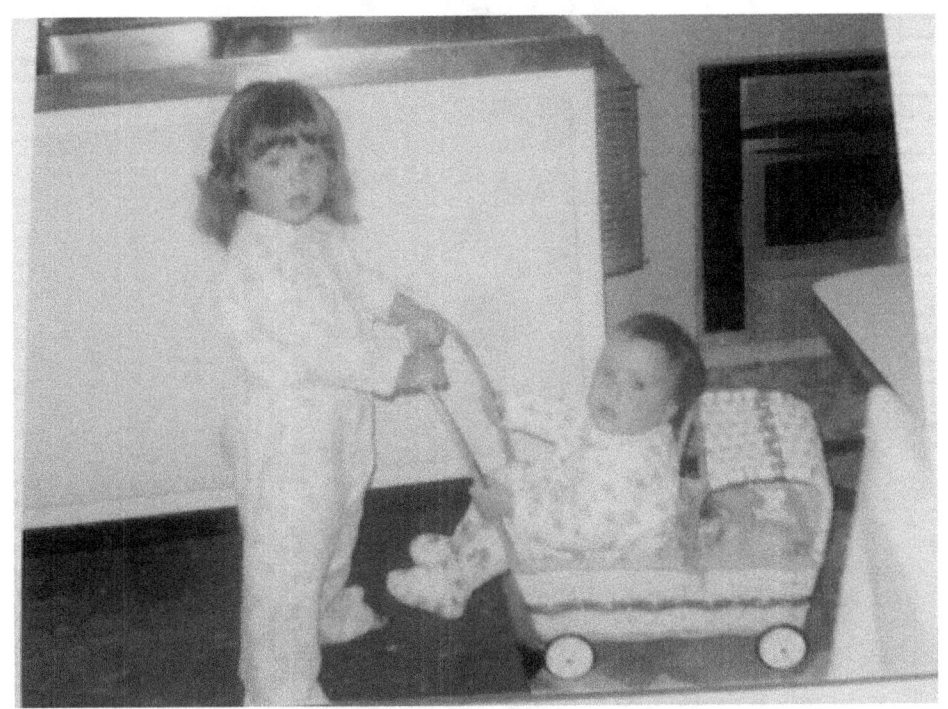

1973 Simon and me

1974 Mum, Simon and me. The first time we had seen her in 6 months, after her breast cancer

1974 Noonoo, Simon and me, Darling Point Sydney

1975 Highett Kindergarten

1976 Mum pumping fuel at their Golden Fleece Service Station, Kings Way Melbourne

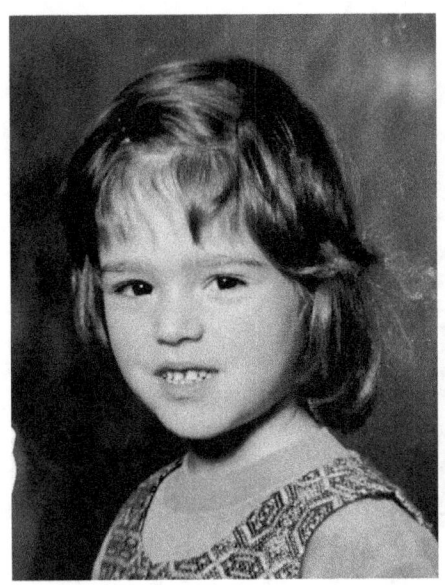

1976 Worthing Road Primary School

1977 Mum, Simon and me, taken with a Polaroid camera at Southland Shopping Centre

1978 The Murray River

CHAPTER 2

The Dungeon

Mum would often take Simon and me to the South Melbourne Markets. It was one of the few places where she seemed lighter, less weighed down by the world. She would buy us the now-famous steamed dim sims, handed over in paper bags, drenched in soy sauce and eaten hot with fingers that always smelled of it for hours afterwards. The stall she bought them from is still in the exact same spot today. Sometimes I stop there on purpose and buy one, not because I want it, but because it feels like a way of visiting her. The last time I did, I took one bite and immediately spat it out. They are not the same. But standing there, even with the disappointment, Mum felt close to me then, in a way that surprised me. Some foods are tied to memories, and those memories have a way of waking up grief.

One particular day on our way to the markets is etched into my body, not just my mind. We were in our white HR Holden station wagon, a car with no seatbelts, because back then no one thought twice about things like that. Simon and I were in the front seat with Mum. She gave way to a tram and then started across the intersection. Out of nowhere, a drunk man appeared and suddenly he was sitting on the bonnet of the car. Mum had hit a man. I can still feel the jolt, the shock, the split second where the world stopped making sense. He slid off the bonnet, walked straight up to Mum's window and abused her viciously, before staggering off into oncoming traffic and nearly getting hit again, this time by a tram. I remember freezing, watching an adult world I did not understand erupt right in front of me.

My parents owned a lunch room at the Golden Fleece service station on Kings Way, and that is where Mum drove us afterwards. The lunch room had one-way windows, the kind where you can see out but no one can see in. People would stand right in front of the glass, fixing their hair or checking their reflection, completely unaware that Simon and I were inside watching and laughing. It was such a small thing, but it amused us endlessly. We spent a lot of our childhood at that service station, especially on weekends, playing in chemical soaked soil without any idea of the danger and eating far too many lollies from the shop counter. It was our normal.

Mum was shaken and upset but she held it together long enough to get us back there. The dim sims never eventuated that day. Guilt got the better of her and she decided to take herself to the police station to surrender. The police took her details and told her they would be in contact if anyone reported the incident to them or to a hospital. They suspected the man had simply walked straight out of the pub on the corner. He must have been alright because we never heard another word about it. Mum was relieved. Then she blamed Simon and me for distracting her, for arguing in the car and for being the reason she was not paying attention to the road. That part stayed with me even longer than the man bouncing on the bonnet.

Mum used to take us with her when she went to the warehouses to buy lollies and chewing gum for the service station. We would sit in the back of the mini panel van, which not only had no seatbelts, but didn't even have seats. We rolled around back there as the van moved, thinking it was fun, not knowing how vulnerable we were. I remember going to the Red Tulip chocolate factory just across the road, the smell of chocolate thick in the air. Those trips were some of the happier moments of my childhood. Time with Mum when she was not angry with me. Time when I felt included instead of in the way.

As a child, for reasons no one ever fully explained, I had weak enamel on my teeth, which resulted in fillings at a very early age. My first lot of fillings were done under happy gas. I experienced claustrophobia again, and this is also when I began to understand that anaesthetics do not work properly on me. I had six fillings done that day on my baby teeth, and the experience was anything but happy. I remember feeling like I was floating above my own body, watching from somewhere outside myself as the dentist worked. It felt unreal, disconnected, frightening. We lived just down the road from the dentist, so Mum carried me home afterwards. The whole experience stayed with me. Even now, decades later, I still sweat when I go to the dentist, my body remembering something my mind would rather forget.

My teeth continued to be an issue as I grew. I have large teeth and a small mouth. In an attempt to manage this, I was taken to an orthodontic clinic on Little Collins Street in Melbourne. I wore a plate in my mouth for several years. Mum and I would catch the tram in from the service station, and I would spend the day with just her, without Simon. For brief moments, I felt special, chosen, almost spoiled by having her attention to myself. Looking back though, I cannot recall her hugging me or telling me she loved me. The closeness was practical, not emotional, and I learnt early to take what I could get and not ask for more.

We spent a lot of time riding motorbikes and camping around places like Walhalla and Bacchus Marsh, often travelling with family friends. We drove all around Victoria, New South Wales and South Australia on long weekends and during some school holidays. One particular trip stands out, a minibus packed with six adults and six children. We drove up to Broken Hill, down to Wilpena Pound and then back home again. We saw native animals everywhere. The first emu was exciting and strange. After the hundredth, we barely looked at them. Those trips were fun, and they gave me memories of being part of something, of belonging, even if only temporarily.

In 1976, Mum enrolled me in calisthenics. She must have sewn hundreds of sequins onto my performance costumes. One year, I was a little geisha girl. I won several silver medals. Mum told me I had not tried hard enough and said they should have been gold. I remember the sting of that comment more clearly than the applause. It planted something deep inside me, a belief that effort was never enough and that I was always falling short. Simon did judo, and Mum celebrated every new level he achieved. The contrast was never spoken about, but I felt it keenly.

Alongside the service station, Mum started a party plan business in 1977, selling handmade macramé made by her mother, my Nanna Marie, and her younger sister, my Aunty Lynny. The three of them had a neat little system. Mum took the orders and sold the items, while they made pot plant holders and decorative pieces. Mum also bought knick knacks from warehouses around Melbourne to sell at the parties. I began collecting them, and my collection grew and grew.

My entire bedroom wall became a shadow box filled with trinkets. Many of them were broken. When Mum could not sell something, she would give it to me. Without realising it at the time, that reinforced the message that I was worthy of leftovers, of damaged things, of what no one else wanted. They looked bright and cheerful all together, but they gathered dust. It would take me an entire day to take them down and clean them, standing on my bed, carefully placing each one back in its spot.

It also explains why, even now, I still buy a small knick knack when I travel somewhere new, adding to a collection that continues to gather dust, although thankfully these days I have a house cleaner to deal with that part.

Simon and I were often dragged along to Mum's party plan evenings and made to sit in the old HR Holden station wagon in the driveway while she hosted, no matter how hot or cold it was. We fought, coloured in, drew pictures and waited. By today's standards, it would be considered neglect. Back then, it was simply how things were done. I still have a couple of the macramé pot plant hangers in my home today, including one that hung in my bedroom more than forty five years ago. It even has a

THE DUNGEON

matching turquoise lampshade, which now lives in my granddaughter's room, a small thread of continuity woven through generations.

Over the years, I have held on to many objects and trinkets that carry memories of my great grandmother, my nannas and my mum. I have tried more than once to pack them away, and I have talked to my counsellor about my attachment to things. What I have come to understand is that after a childhood marked by unpredictability and emotional absence, those objects represent the moments of warmth, the people who loved me in the ways they could. Holding on to them is not weakness. They are anchors to the better moments, reminders that not everything was hard, and I am allowed to keep what brought me comfort.

In 1977, I came down with the mumps, which was yet another way I became an inconvenience to my mother. We were right in the middle of moving house, only a kilometre up the road in Highett, from Highett Road to Panorama Avenue. My being sick was the last thing she needed at that moment. Illness did not pause life in our house. It simply got in the way of it.

Mumps generally affects males. Mum decided that since it was dangerous for grown men to get it, as it can affect fertility, it would be best if Simon caught it too, as a child. She put him into bed with me so he could get it. He never did. Somehow, once again, I failed. I could not even pass on a contagious disease properly. Instead, I developed complications and ended up with encephalitis. I was extremely unwell. I could not lift my head off the pillow, my body heavy and unresponsive. More antibiotics followed, and it took weeks before I began to recover. I was still a child, but already learning that being sick was something to be endured quietly, without fuss or sympathy.

As if that was not enough, by the end of 1977 I brought home a severe case of chickenpox. I was covered head to toe in itchy sores. Even now, decades later, I still carry a couple of scars on my body from that time, small physical reminders of how thoroughly it took over my body.

Around the corner from Mum and Dad's service station was Bunratty Castle, a medieval-themed restaurant where diners sat at long rough tables and ate with their hands. Not long after I had recovered from chickenpox, we went there for dinner with Mum, Dad, Simon, Nanna Marie and Parpa. The night was noisy and chaotic, with people laughing, eating and drinking. At one point, a conga line formed and everyone got up to dance around the tables.

A man sitting near us lifted Simon onto his shoulders. Simon was only five and not very well. The next day, he broke out in chickenpox. It turned out that this illness I had passed on. He then passed it on to Dad. It was just before Christmas, and both of them spent Christmas Day in bed together, sick and miserable. Mum often wondered aloud how many other people might have caught it that night. The story was told like an amusing anecdote, but I carried the weight of it quietly, aware once again of how my body seemed to create chaos wherever it went.

In 1978, Dad brought home a puppy. Someone owed him money for work done at the service station and paid him instead with a pedigree corgi named Beau. Beau had won seconds and thirds in shows but never a first. In the breeder's eyes, he was never quite good enough. I understood that feeling immediately.

I was terrified of dogs. In 1974, when we lived in Brighton, Mum had been out walking with Simon in the pram and me beside her when a dog attacked and bit me on the mouth. Even now, despite owning a dog of my own, I am wary of most dogs and have been bitten again in recent years. Fear, once learnt that young, settles deep.

Beau, however, slowly became part of our family. We could never keep him contained. Somehow, our small but determined corgi could climb a six foot trellis fence. When we moved to New South Wales in 1981, my grandparents arranged for him to stay with one of Mum's friends. We thought it would be temporary. It was not. Two years later, we finally got him back.

As strange as it sounds, Beau made me feel closer to Dad. He was one of the few living connections I had to him during those years. Beau lived a long life and died in 1990 at sixteen years old. In his later years, he lived up the road on Meade Street with an elderly woman who spoiled him with fresh chicken, unlike the Pal dog food Mum had fed him when he lived with us. I found out he had died in the middle of a pub, told casually by the woman's son. The grief hit me unexpectedly hard. It felt like I had lost a piece of my father.

At that point, I had not seen Dad in seven years. I did get to visit Beau's grave once. Standing there, saying goodbye properly, mattered more than I realised at the time. It is something I still hold close, even now.

Mum had a fantastic work ethic and would do anything for her family. She worked various secretarial jobs while raising two children, and although affection was not something she gave easily, dedication was. I know without question that my own work ethic comes from her. She showed up. She kept going. She did what needed to be done, even when she was exhausted. I may not have felt nurtured, but I learnt early that work was survival, and effort was non negotiable.

Some of my happier memories with Mum and Simon were simple ones. On Saturday mornings we learnt how to roller skate together, the three of us taking lessons side by side. Those mornings sit gently in my memory. Simon took to skating effortlessly, gliding along with confidence, while I moved carefully, hesitant and slow. That difference followed us into many areas of childhood. When we got bikes for Christmas, Simon received a brand new push bike. I received my mum's old childhood bike, the same one my uncle had learnt to ride on years earlier. The only new things were the seat and the basket on the front. It was heavy, rusty and intimidating.

It took me nearly ten months to be brave enough to ride it, even with training wheels. Simon needed a crate just to climb onto his bike, and off he went without a second thought. I cried endlessly trying to ride that old bike, scraping knees, wobbling, failing and feeling stupid. It became another quiet lesson in how effort did not always equal reward.

Years later, I was offered that same bike, lovingly kept by my grandfather. I was told it would make a wonderful garden ornament in front of my house. I declined. Some memories do not need preserving.

There are darker memories that still sit heavy. One night my parents were out, and our babysitter, who I refer to as F1, was staying over. She also worked at my parents' Golden Fleece service station on Kings Way. She took Simon and me to see Star Wars, which felt magical at the time. Later, in the middle of the night, I woke to the sound of quiet voices at the end of my bed. I opened my eyes and saw my father standing there with F1. She was naked. I saw them kiss. Then he went back to my parents' room. I did not move. I did not speak. I lay frozen, confused and frightened, knowing instinctively that I had seen something I should not have.

Around that time, Mum would often load Simon and me into the car late at night to go looking for Dad. One night, bundled up in the back seat, we found him near the corner of Worthing Road Primary School. Mum asked him where he had been. He said he had fallen asleep in the tea room at the service station. Even then, I knew it was a lie.

There were nights I would get out of bed to try to comfort Mum when she was crying. Each time, she would scream at me to go back to bed. One night the arguing escalated so badly that Mum threw a chair at Dad. There was shouting, chaos and fear filling the house. Dad walked out and did not come home for days. My behaviour at school deteriorated, not because I was naughty, but because my world felt unsafe and unpredictable.

For months, Simon and I believed Dad was simply working long hours. We would see him at the service station on weekends when Mum worked, and that seemed to confirm the story we were telling ourselves. The truth was that he was not coming home at all. He had moved in with F1. This went on for over a year before anyone told us.

We had to move house from Panorama Avenue in Highett to Spring Road in Dingley because the owners wanted their home back. It was not until that upheaval, and the need to change primary schools, that Mum finally told us the truth. It was January 1981 when she said they had separated months earlier. By then, she had already started seeing the local butcher, Terry, the same butcher whose calendar had once torn my leg open.

Dad was not coming with us. They were getting a divorce. And the woman he was now with was our babysitter. My world collapsed. She was someone we were meant to trust. I could not tell Mum what I had seen the year before. I carried that alone.

I did not cope well with the changes. I became defiant, angry and deeply confused. I felt rejected by my father, who chose another woman over his family, and by my mother, who chose another man over me. I caught Mum in bed with Terry more than once, something no child should ever see, and each time it chipped away at my sense of safety.

Around this time, a travelling amusement fair was set up across from Southland Shopping Centre. I wanted desperately to go on the Superloop, a small ride that went around in a circle and flipped upside down. Mum refused to come on with me, joking that her fake breast, filled with birdseed, might fall out. She joked often about it sprouting if it got wet in the rain. I understand now how much humour she used to survive her own pain.

I was just tall enough to ride alone. I sat next to a teenage boy, around seventeen, and the seatbelt was loose. When the ride flipped upside down, the belt failed and I began slipping through it. There was a cage around us, but I remember screaming in terror, convinced I would fall through the gaps in the roof. The boy grabbed my arm and held me until the ride stopped. He saved my life.

I got off that ride shaking, nauseous and in shock. Mum did not fully understand what had happened. She took me home as I cried uncontrollably, unable to articulate the fear. I went to bed with the world still spinning. It took years before I could ride anything more intense than the Wizzer.

These moments, layered one on top of another, quietly shaped who I became. They taught me vigilance. They taught me fear. They taught me to rely on myself long before I should have had to.

Looking back now, I can see that I was a child entrepreneur long before I ever knew what the word meant. Fair warning, this next part is revolting. Even as I write it, I am slightly horrified by my own nine year old logic, but it is part of who I was and how my brain has always worked. We were living in Dingley, Victoria, having just moved to the suburb in the January of 1981. I had been quietly collecting the end bits of soap for years. Every sliver. Every remnant. All of it carefully saved. Yes, it is disgusting. I know.

I dissolved them with Lux soap flakes and created my own homemade cakes of soap. Not to use. To sell. I set up a stall out the front of our house with a large hand written sign that proudly declared SOAP FOR SALE 20 CENTS. We did not have lemons for a lemonade stand, so I adapted. That has always been my way. You work with what you have. You see an opportunity and you act on it.

I convinced Simon to help me, along with a couple of kids from the neighbourhood, and we stood there like tiny business moguls waiting for customers. The police pulled up, got out of their car and asked what on earth we were doing. I explained my business model with full confidence. They laughed, threw twenty cents out the car window and drove off. They did not want the soap. But to me, that twenty cents felt like a fortune. I had made my first million, at least in my own mind. That instinct never left me. By thirteen, I had upgraded from soap to babysitting. The seed was already there.

Around this same time, everything else in my life was falling apart.

In January 1980, when my mother was thirty three, her health declined dramatically again. Doctors in Melbourne believed she had a tumour in her brain, a secondary cancer from her earlier breast cancer. She suffered violent headaches, pain in her legs, shaking in her hands and disturbances in her vision. She could barely walk. My grandparents intervened and refused to allow exploratory brain surgery. They arrived, took control, and put Mum on a plane to Sydney in a wheelchair. My Great Uncle Sid, who sat on the board of Sydney Hospital, arranged for her to be treated by a neurologist, Professor Raymond Garrick.

With Mum gone to Sydney, our lives unravelled at speed. Nanna and Parpa took over packing the house. They sold everything. All the furniture. The television. The fish tank. Everything that made the house feel like home disappeared. We had only been at our new school for three weeks. The instability was crushing. I understood enough to know that I would not be seeing Dad any time soon, and the fear of that sat heavy in my chest.

All our personal possessions, including every toy we owned, were packed into forty tea chests and stored in Parpa's sheds in Woodend. Forty. That number still lands hard. It felt like my entire childhood was being boxed up and erased. I clashed constantly with my grandfather. I was defiant, angry and terrified. I did not want to leave. I did not want to lose any more than I already had.

One argument with my grandfather stands out more clearly than any other. Everything was packed. The house was hollow. In my bedroom, he held me down on the bed during a heated confrontation. He had a lit cigarette in his hand and held it close to my face. I screamed and fought with everything in me, pushed him away and ran out of the house and down the street. He chased me, caught me at the end of the block, dragged me back inside and hit me. I was told to stay in my room. I sobbed for what felt like days.

Simon and I later watched as my grandfather ripped up and burned most of the photographs of my parents together in the backyard. We managed to save a few. Watching those memories go up in flames was horrifying. My grandfather believed my mother had married beneath her. According to him, Simon and I were a product of our father. He referred to us as the arsehole's children. He said it to our faces. More than once.

Being called that as a child does something permanent. Words like that carve themselves into places that never quite heal. It is something neither Simon nor I could ever forget. It shaped how we saw ourselves and how we believed the world saw us. It created wounds that would take decades to understand, let alone tend to.

Those years were brutal. Chaotic. Defining. And somewhere in the middle of the fear, the instability, the cruelty and the loss, a fierce part of me was forming. A part that would not lie down. A part that would adapt. A part that would look at rubble and quietly begin to build something anyway.

That was the beginning of the grit. The beginning of the resilience. The early formation of the moxie that would one day carry me far beyond those tea chests, far beyond that house, and far beyond the names I was called.

We started at Boronia Park Primary School in New South Wales in March 1981, which made it our third primary school across two different states in a matter of months. I was nine years old. Simon was nine years old. And yes, I was a deeply confused child. My world kept shifting beneath my feet before I had any chance to find my balance.

We were finally reunited with Mum weeks after she had left us. She was in a ward at Sydney Hospital with seven other patients, and we visited her every second evening. I remember my tenth birthday clearly because I spent it sitting beside her bed. I made her flowers out of folded tissues, sticky tape and straws, arranging them carefully as if they were real. Every visit ended the same way, walking away from her bed and returning to what we had come to call our dungeon. That dark space became our normal.

THE DUNGEON

My aunt organised a surprise birthday party for me. My cousins and a few friends were there. All the food was healthy. Carrot sticks. Celery sticks. No cake. No treats. She thought I needed to lose weight. I felt humiliated and ashamed, even though I know now her heart was in the right place. I love her for trying, even if it hurt at the time.

My grandparents were doing their best, but they had not planned on becoming parents again at fifty nine years old to two nine year old children. Their house was not built for children. It was a two storey house set into a hill. Upstairs was the living area, kitchen, bedrooms and bathrooms. My mother's youngest brother Christopher still lived at home. He was twenty three.

Simon and I were put downstairs. Not in a bedroom. Not even in a proper room. When the house was built, too much earth had been removed from the hill, leaving a void, and that void was boxed in to create a space directly off the garage. That space became ours. There were no doors for privacy. Half of it was filled with my grandfather's junk, things he had collected and never thrown away. His office and workshop were part of the same space. The cars were parked only metres from where we slept.

There was also a door from that space into the cellar, whose walls were literally the hill itself. There was no carpet. The floor was cold outdoor patio tiles with a couple of old mats thrown down. Our beds were relics from my mother's childhood, complete with thirty year old mattresses. My grandfather never threw anything out.

There were no windows. No natural light. During the day, the only glimpse of the outside we could see was through small holes in glazed terracotta air vents near the ceiling, which we could peer through if we stood on our beds. At night, we lay listening to every creak of the house above us. Every footstep in the kitchen sounded like it was right on top of our heads.

And then there was the smell.

On the other side of our dungeon was a double garage that housed the laundry, the toilet and a massive workshop at the back where my grandfather worked. He bought items from auctions, refurbished them and sold them. Many were galvanised. The fumes, the chemicals, the fuel, the exhaust, all of it seeped into where we slept. There were times we were literally gassed out. People ask me now if I have ever been exposed to chemicals. The answer is yes, over and over again, from childhood.

Around this time, my body began to change early. I developed quickly and grew a forest of body hair that I was deeply ashamed of. Sharing a space like that with my younger brother was unbearable. I had no one to talk to. I ended up developing impetigo under both arms, blistered, oozing and painful. I was miserable. Eventually

I told Nanna, and she took me to the doctor for cream. It was one of the few times someone noticed I was struggling.

Mum remained in hospital for five months, and then she was transferred to a rehabilitation centre to learn how to walk again. After another three months, she finally returned to us, moving into the third bedroom upstairs. In August 1981, she was officially diagnosed with Multiple Sclerosis. She was thirty three years old.

That night we had corned meat, cauliflower in white sauce, peas and carrots for dinner. I know how strange it sounds that I remember that, but I do. We were all sitting at the table. Nanna. Parpa. Uncle Chris. Mum. Simon. Me. Simon refused to eat his cauliflower. Something in Parpa snapped. With Mum's diagnosis hanging heavy in the air, he lost his temper and kicked the three of us out of the house that evening.

Mum put Simon and me in the car and drove around for a long time. Parpa had always blamed my father for Mum's cancer and now for her MS, which was completely irrational, but that blame sat like poison in him. Eventually we returned that night, with Mum promising us she would get us out of there as soon as she could. Parpa never apologised.

Mum regained enough strength to take a job eight hours north in a small mining town in the North Tablelands called Emmaville, near Glen Innes. Parpa's brother Sid owned the Loloma tin mine. Mum was sent there as an office secretary, still using her married name, effectively acting as a spy to investigate missing money. She found it. She always did.

Simon and I were left behind again with my grandparents. The third time in our young lives. I hated school. The system was different. I missed my friends. I missed my Dad. We had started school young in Victoria and were younger than our New South Wales classmates. I had lost my home, my friends, my sense of stability, and the mum I knew. All contact with my father had stopped because Parpa had blocked it.

Each night we were allowed a short time upstairs to watch television before being sent back down to the dungeon. One night the show Special Squad was on. Right there on the screen was our father. Acting. In the show he was shot and fell into the water. It was the first time we had seen him all year. We were never allowed to say his name. Simon and I waited until the credits rolled to confirm that it was him. We were excited. We were punished for it and sent straight to bed.

Mum uncovered where the missing money at the mine was going and was offered a twelve month contract. December 31st 1981, closed one of the most chaotic years of my life. Moving to Glen Innes was only supposed to be for 12 months. Just Mum, Simon and me. Eight hours north. A fresh start.

Life, as it always does, had other plans.

1977 Panorama Avenue, Highett

1978 Beau, our pet corgi

1978 Dressed as a geisha girl for calisthenics at Panorama Avenue, Highett

1978 Mum and the Monaro at Panorama Avenue Highett, Victoria

1979 Mum at Glossodia NSW

1979 Simon and me

1980 Me at Panorama Ave Highett, Victoria

1980 Nanna, Simon and me with my cousins, Matthew and Myalie, in Leawill Place, Gladesville, NSW

1980 Year 4 Worthing Road School Report

1981 Mum with Julia, Dingley Village, Victoria

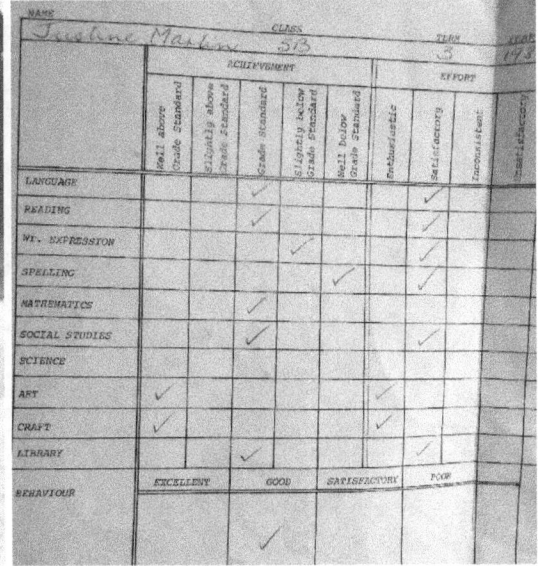

1981 My school report from Year 5 Boronia Park Primary School

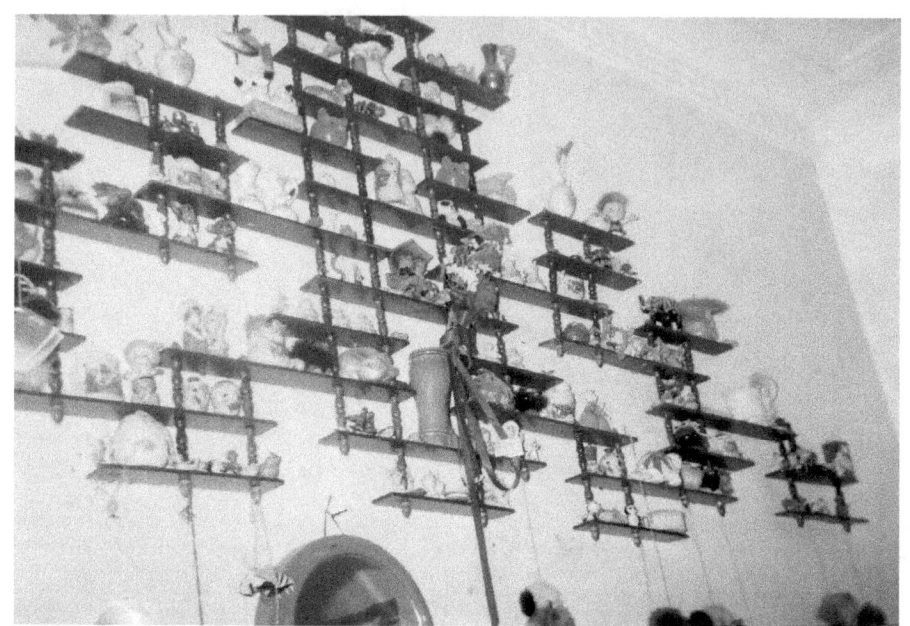
1981 My shadow box on my bedroom wall

1981 Spring Flowers - my painting

THE DUNGEON

1981 The Dungeon was located in the room behind the front steps, at Leawill Place, Gladesville

1982 My cousins Matthew and Myalie with Simon and myself at Glossodia, NSW

CHAPTER 3

Those Junior Teenage Years

On New Year's Eve 1981, we drove to Glen Innes to start our new lives. That phrase sounds hopeful, almost romantic, but at the time it was more about survival than reinvention. The first night we stayed in the same motel Mum had lived in for the previous three months without us, and just being back together as the three of us felt like relief. The constant conflict with my grandfather had worn us all down, and the quiet of that motel room felt like letting out a deep breath after holding it in for far too long.

Opening boxes of toys and clothes that had been packed away for over twelve months brought an unexpected sense of grounding. Familiar objects have a way of anchoring you when everything else feels uncertain. Looking back now, I can clearly see how traumatic my childhood had already been, but at the time this life was all I knew. Familiarity was comforting, even when it was flawed. Stability, however fragile, was something I craved.

We moved into a double red brick house at 33 Torrington Street in Glen Innes. It had three bedrooms, one bathroom, a plum tree in the yard and one very noisy possum that made its presence known most nights. It was modest, but it was ours. What we did not understand yet was just how cold Glen Innes could be. Cold does not even begin to describe it.

That first winter was brutal. We were completely unprepared. Our only source of heat was a small Warmbrite wood heater that barely warmed the lounge room, let alone the rest of the house. Inside temperatures often dropped below zero, with snow and deep frosts outside. At night I would pile on five blankets, a doona, flannelette pyjamas, socks, gloves and even a beanie just to make it through until morning. The pipes would freeze overnight, leaving us without water for drinking or showers. Mum learned quickly to fill a large jug with water before bed so we would have something in the morning, and showers became an evening luxury rather than a morning routine.

Despite the cold, that first year living back with Mum felt good. It was just the three of us again, learning how to live together after so much separation. But Mum was not the same woman she had been before her diagnosis. MS had changed her in ways none of us fully understood yet. She was exhausted most of the time, and her temper was short. She grieved deeply for the loss of her marriage, her health and the life she had imagined for herself. I tried to help as much as I could. I tried to be good. I tried to make things easier for her. But it never felt like enough.

Every day, Mum drove Simon and me forty five kilometres to school. I was placed in a composite class of Years Five and Six, which meant Simon and I were in the same classroom. It felt strange but comforting at the same time. We made friends easily, and some of those friendships have lasted a lifetime. I still hold deep gratitude for those connections. Years later, being asked to return as a guest speaker at Emmaville Central School's 150th birthday felt like a full circle moment I could never have imagined back then.

Mum had to apply for special permission for Simon and me to attend Emmaville Central School because we lived outside the zoning area. The school catered from kindergarten through to Year Ten and had only around 120 students. We were told very clearly not to tell anyone who we were or why Mum was really there. Our connection to the mine was to remain secret. Mum feared that if things went wrong, we could become targets. It helped that Simon and I carried our father's surname rather than Mum's maiden name. It offered a layer of protection we did not fully understand at the time.

After school, the office girl would often pick us up, or we would catch the school bus to the front gate of the mine. From there, our afternoons became something most children would never experience. We rode around in fifty tonne Terex trucks like it was the most normal thing in the world. It was thrilling. Completely illegal by today's standards and a complete breach of every workplace safety rule imaginable, but at the time it was simply life.

We learned to drive Mum's Commodore around the mine site, weaving past office buildings and along dirt roads where the only vehicles we needed to watch for were the massive Terex trucks. School holidays were spent at the mine too, and boredom quickly became a creative force. Like most kids our age, we were far more concerned with excitement than legality. This often involved taking Mum's car. I would drive while Simon hung off the windscreen wipers on the bonnet, then we would swap. How we survived without serious injury is something I still cannot explain. Mum could see us through the office windows, driving past without a care in the world, and yet she never stopped us. Boundaries were loose in our world, sometimes almost non-existent.

That lack of boundaries shaped us. At the time, it felt like freedom. Looking back, it was also neglect dressed up as trust. But we adapted. We always did. Glen Innes became the place where independence was forged early, where responsibility arrived long before it should have, and where childhood blurred into something far more complicated.

We arrived thinking it would be temporary. Just a year. Just a contract. Just enough time for Mum to get back on her feet. But life rarely sticks to the plan. Glen Innes quietly became the backdrop for the years that would shape who I was becoming, teaching me resilience.

And so our new life began, not with certainty, but with cold mornings, long drives, unspoken secrets, and a family doing the best it could with the tools it had.

Christmas 1982 saw us return to Melbourne to visit Dad. It had been twelve long months since we had last spoken to him, and the gap felt enormous to Simon and me. We stayed at his mother's home in Bannockburn, the house we always referred to as Nanna in Geelong's place. There was a strange mix of excitement and awkwardness hanging in the air, the kind that comes when you are reunited with someone you love but do not quite know how to be around anymore.

Dad let us choose what we wanted for Christmas. At the time, it felt magical. We felt spoilt and special, not understanding that he was trying to buy closeness, to compensate for his absence with things. He bought us an Atari game console with Space Invaders, which felt impossibly exciting. I chose Chocolate Starfish and Kiss records, along with a copper art kit and a Crayola crayon caddy. I still have both records to this day. I treasured everything he gave me, not just for what it was, but for what it represented. Those gifts became physical proof that he loved me, something I could hold onto in the months when he was not around.

Dad also took us camping with family friends down to Cape Otway. It was one of those holidays that sits softly in memory, full of laughter, tents, sand and freedom, until it abruptly changed. I fell down a steep sandbank and badly injured my right ankle. The ligament damage took months to heal, and it was the beginning of a pattern of injuries that would follow me through my life. Even then, my body seemed determined to betray me.

In 1983, I started Year Seven, moving onto the high school side of Emmaville Central School. For the first time, Simon and I were no longer together in class. That separation made me feel exposed and untethered. Not long into the school year, I woke one morning with a stabbing pain in my right side. Mum did not believe me and sent me to school anyway. I spent the entire day curled up in sickbay, ignored and dismissed, while the pain intensified. Mum refused to pick me up. This went on for three days.

Eventually, she took me to see Dr Early, a man who was, ironically, always late. After examining me, he turned to Mum and asked whether I would like my cut diagonal or straight across. That was how he told us I had appendicitis and needed urgent surgery. I remember being sent home to have a bath before going to hospital, my appendix close to bursting as I soaked in the tub. Then came the injections, straight into my backside, delivered by an old nursing sister who seemed to use me as target practice. It was terrifying, painful and confusing, and once again I felt like my body was something happening to me rather than something I inhabited.

Around this time, things at Emmaville began to unravel further. Word had spread about who Mum really was and why she was there. We became known as the rich kids, despite the fact that our life felt anything but. Men were being sacked from the mine as Mum uncovered who had been stealing money, and resentment followed us everywhere. Simon and I were bullied relentlessly. An angry boy in my Year Seven class threw a hole punch at my head. I did not feel safe. I did not want to go to school.

For our safety, Mum pulled us out of Emmaville Central School at the end of Term One. Simon was transferred to Glen Innes Primary School and I was sent to Glen Innes High School. Another move. Another fresh start. Another attempt to outrun trouble.

At the same time, my body began changing in confusing ways. I started developing breasts and felt deeply uncomfortable and self conscious. Mum never spoke to me about puberty or sex. Nothing was explained. I gathered fragments of information from friends and television and filled in the gaps myself. It took every ounce of courage I had to ask Mum for a training bra. When I did, she laughed at me and told me I did not need one. I was the only girl among my friends not wearing one, and at the same time the only one who truly needed it. Shame settled into my bones.

My new school was a shock. At Emmaville, my Year Seven class had consisted of just seven students. At Glen Innes High School, there were 130 of us. Three days after starting, we were sent across the road to the cow paddock for PE hockey practice. I tried to explain to the teacher that I had injured my foot and ankle over the summer holidays, but he refused to listen. He made us run laps of the paddock anyway. I fell again, reinjuring my ankle badly, and ended up in plaster.

That teacher and I would develop a complicated relationship over my six years of high school. A constant push and pull of frustration, misunderstanding and resentment. To me he was another adult who did not listen, another authority figure who assumed I was exaggerating or weak, another reminder that my body was not something others trusted.

By the time I settled into Glen Innes High School, I had already learned too much about instability, silence and survival. I had learned that pain was often ignored, that explanations were rarely given, and that moving on was expected whether you were ready or not. These were lessons I would carry with me far beyond my school years, shaping how I saw myself, my body and the world around me.

Year Eight was 1984 at Glen Innes High School. I sat in the middle class of the five Year Eight groups for most subjects, invisible enough not to be noticed, but never quite safe from attention either. On Wednesdays, sport meant swimming lessons at the town pool so we could earn our Swim and Survival Certificate. From memory, it must have been early in the year, because Glen Innes winters were brutally cold and the outdoor pool was emptied once the weather turned. In winter, the water might as well have been ice.

That day the pool was overcrowded. Too many bodies crammed into a thirty three metre pool, limbs everywhere, noise and chaos echoing off concrete. We were doing the treading water component in the deep end, fully clothed. Somewhere in the confusion, I was hit hard in the back of the neck by either an arm or a leg. I felt a sharp, searing pain and knew instantly something was wrong.

I told the teacher, who instructed me to get out of the pool. I realised then that I could not properly move my left arm. The pool and the hospital sat diagonally opposite each other at the same intersection. An ambulance was called, and I was taken straight across the road to Glen Innes Hospital.

I was thirteen years old and utterly terrified. The fear that I had done something permanent settled into my chest immediately. Paralysis. Lifelong damage. Losing control of my body completely. Those thoughts looped relentlessly. I spent weeks in hospital undergoing pinprick tests, lying flat, pumped full of painkillers and steroids. Two discs in my neck had been squashed together, forcing spinal fluid out. The only option was time, rest, and waiting for the fluid to return. Eventually, it did. I healed. Mum was not impressed. And once again, she did not come running.

That year, I also decided I wanted to learn to play musical instruments. Looking back now, I can see that this had very little to do with music and everything to do with wanting Mum's attention. She had played piano and guitar when she was younger, and I wanted to share something with her, or at least be seen through it. I asked her for a piano. She told me to ask my father.

Dad was meant to pay the six hundred dollars. He never did. Six hundred dollars was a lot of money back then. Despite that, Mum bought a beautiful pianola with one hundred rolls. I started lessons with a piano teacher, wanting simply to play, not to do grades or exams. Just to play. After twelve lessons, I asked Mum to sack the teacher and let me teach myself. She was delighted she no longer had to pay for lessons. The teacher would only let me play a C scale. I wanted music. That very first weekend after he was gone, I taught myself Chariots of Fire. It was Mum's favourite piece. Once again, I was reaching for approval.

I also developed a teenage crush on the drummer in the school band, so I auditioned. After trying flute, clarinet, saxophone and trumpet, I ended up playing the E flat tuba. I loved it. Heavy, loud, unapologetic. I have been known over the years for being full of hot air, so it felt fitting. Carrying it to and from school was no small feat, but I did it proudly.

That year, at thirteen, I got my period.

Like so many girls, I had an accident at school. Blood soaked through my clothes without me realising. Mortified, I wrapped my jumper around my waist for the long walk home, though it did little to hide the stain at the front. I was too scared to tell Mum. I did not want to be laughed at again. So I told no one.

For over two years, I used folded tissues as pads. Day after day. Month after month. I felt ashamed, dirty, wrong. It was not until Year Ten, while in Sydney for work experience and staying with my grandparents, that my Nanna noticed blood in my washing and gently asked if I had my period. I denied it. She worked it out anyway. She saw what I was using and took me to the supermarket to buy my first packet of pads. She told me to take them home just in case.

That one packet did not last long.

When I ran out, I went back to tissues. Nanna eventually told Mum. It took another six months before Mum would buy me more pads. I hated my life.

Midway through Year Ten, I finally gathered the courage to ask Mum to buy me tampons. It should never have been that hard. I made a promise to myself then. If I ever had a daughter, she would never go through what I did. I kept that promise. My children know they can ask me anything, at any time, without judgement.

Mum never gave me the birds and the bees talk either. But by then, I already knew far more than any child should have.

The only time Mum would drive Simon and me to school was if it was raining. If it was snowing, we still walked. If it rained in the afternoon, most of the time we walked home as well. Mum knew that if we arrived at school soaked through, the office would ring her and insist she come and collect us so we could go home and change into dry clothes. It was a system she relied on, and one we quietly endured.

For sport, I chose golf. No other girls played golf, and I was told I was not allowed to either. I challenged that immediately, calling the sports teacher sexist for excluding girls. After a letter from Mum and some upheaval, I was finally permitted to play. I did not play properly, though. I hid down the back nine of the golf course whenever I could, because I hated sport and everything it represented for me. My body never felt like it belonged in those spaces.

So there I was, day after day, walking to school in Glen Innes, a rucksack covered in my artwork on my back, a massive tuba case in one hand, and dragging behind me an old golf buggy loaded with clubs that Mum's boyfriend had lent me. It must have been quite a sight. Looking back now, I have no idea how I managed it physically, but I did that walk hundreds of times, in all weather, carrying far more than any teenager should.

Music became my refuge. Early on, I decided I wanted to know everything about it, and it consumed me completely. After school, I practised the piano for hours every single day. Then I practised the tuba, which Mum forbade me from playing inside the house. I would trudge outside to the garage or the backyard, even in the dead of winter, wrapped in a beanie, duffle coat, leg warmers and gloves. The metal mouthpiece would turn my lips blue, but I did not care. I wanted to be the best tuba player in the world. Music was the only place I felt any sense of control or belonging.

As high school progressed, my musical world expanded. My best friend Ali and I joined the choir and the stage band. In my senior years, I began tutoring younger students. I learnt the basics of multiple instruments including saxophone, clarinet, flute and trombone, and took lessons in violin and drums as well. I had a dream that lived quietly but fiercely inside me. I wanted to be a classical composer and conductor. Music was not a hobby. It was a lifeline.

A typical week consisted of Simon and me attending school while Mum worked. Weekends were not for rest. They were spent helping Mum do the grocery shopping and cleaning the house. For a couple of years, I played netball as a goalkeeper on Saturday afternoons, though I hated every moment of it. I hated sport. I hated exercise. My body always hurt, particularly my legs. At the time, I believed this was just weakness or laziness. It would take decades to learn the real reason.

Simon had more of a social life than I did. Mum relied heavily on me, and because of that, she rarely agreed when I asked to stay at a friend's house over the weekend. I learnt how to cook at eleven years old. When Mum was too sick to get out of bed for days at a time, I stepped into the role of caregiver, cooking meals and keeping the house going. Looking back at some of the strange food combinations I created, it is a miracle Simon and I survived, but at the time I did what needed to be done. I do not think Mum realised how dependent she had become on me, or perhaps she did and simply had no other option.

In 1984, Mum began going out with friends on Saturday nights. Simon and I would sit up late watching Rage on television, waiting for her to come home. One night, I was lying on the lounge room floor in my flannel pyjamas when Mum arrived home drunk with one of my male school teachers. The embarrassment was overwhelming. The idea that he had seen me like that, and that he was involved with my mother, filled me with shame and confusion. I never told any of my friends. It did, however, grant me a certain unspoken leeway at school in the years that followed.

Not long after, Mum began dating our next door neighbour, who became a surrogate father figure to Simon and me for a few years. Those were gentler times. We went camping down Old Grafton Road and at Copeton Dam, moments that remain some of my happiest memories of feeling like part of a family. As Mum's Multiple Sclerosis progressed, she ended the relationship, unwilling to let him become her carer. It was a deeply painful decision for her, and one that spoke to both her strength and her fear.

At the age of 14, I found my mother's porn collection of about half a dozen VHS videos. Not something I should have seen. I became addicted to watching them over the next couple of years, and I watched them any chance I could. This warped my understanding of what love was and should be. I carried this perspective through life for decades.

High school was a massive struggle for me. Throughout my entire schooling, reading and spelling were constant challenges, and it was not unusual for my English report cards to be filled with Cs, Ds and Es. At the time, it was framed as a lack of effort or ability, but looking back, there were many factors stacked against me. The loss of hearing caused by repeated bouts of tonsillitis when I was learning phonetics, the ongoing trauma of the childhood we were living through, and the ADHD I have only discovered much later in life all conspired to put me at a significant disadvantage. None of it was recognised or supported back then. I am deeply grateful for modern technology now. Spell check and writing tools have made it possible for me to write books, including this one, something that once felt completely out of reach.

Because of this, I found myself placed in the lower academic levels of my year for subjects like English, even though I excelled in others. Maths and music were my strengths, and in those areas I was placed in the higher levels, which created a strange disconnect. I was capable and confident in some classrooms and made to feel inadequate in others.

Socially, high school was divided into unspoken groups, as it is in most places. There were the popular kids, the ones who were good at sport, the thin girls in designer clothes with perfectly styled hair and confidence that came from knowing they belonged. There were the academic high achievers and the wealthy students, many of whom would go on to boarding schools in later years. There was the middle ground, where I mostly sat, friends with everyone but never fully anchored in one place. And then there were the students from lower socio economic backgrounds, often placed in the lowest academic streams and judged accordingly.

I floated between these worlds. In terms of status, I was usually somewhere in the middle, but academically I slipped into the lower levels for subjects like English. Being placed in level four for English while succeeding elsewhere quietly shaped how I saw myself. It taught me early that worth was measured narrowly and that being different often meant being underestimated. It is something that stayed with me far longer than it should have.

Our school uniforms were unmistakable. Royal blue skirts, yellow dress shirts, gold and blue ties, and matching school jumpers in winter. If your family had money, you could also wear a blue blazer. I desperately wanted one of those blazers. They symbolised belonging, sophistication, and being one of the kids who mattered. Mum refused. She thought they were a waste of money. Instead, she gave me her old duffle coat from when she was a teenager. It swallowed me whole and made me feel even more out of place.

As I grew, my summer tunic became too small. Rather than buying a new one, Mum had Nanna sew fabric inserts up each side to make it wider. The problem was the fabric was a slightly different shade and pattern, and it stood out horribly. Everyone could see it. I could feel their eyes on me. The embarrassment was crushing. It fed directly into the body issues I would carry for most of my life, the sense that my body was wrong and inconvenient and something that needed to be patched rather than cared for.

To complete the look, I had a short spiky haircut with a long bleached rat's tail. Yes, really. Even now I cringe when I think about it. I am not entirely sure why I chose that haircut. Maybe it was rebellion. Maybe it was a way to control something when so much felt out of control. Maybe it was just the 80s. I also wore bright green, blue and pink hairspray and carried a handbag that had been sewn into the shape of a chicken, complete with dangling legs. In a small conservative country town, I stood out like a neon sign. Looking back, this was probably the first of many times I deliberately shocked Glen Innes. At the time, it felt like armour.

Outside of the core subjects, I discovered a real aptitude for technical drawing in Years Eight to Ten. For a while, I thought I might become an architect. I loved drawing and had a natural ability for it. What I wanted just as much, though, was acceptance. I wanted to be liked. I wanted to be loved. If I am honest, I wanted a boy to notice me.

The technical drawing class consisted of eight boys and three girls. Most of the time, the teacher would set up the lesson and then disappear into the staff room for the entire double period. I would often complete not only my own work but also the work of the two boys who sat behind me. Despite this, they consistently received higher marks than I did. Not once did I receive a merit award. Our teacher made it very clear, both subtly and directly, that women did not belong in his class or in the design industry at all.

Three of the boys in that class tormented me relentlessly. They would hit me with the dusting pads used to stop drawings from smudging, leaving my royal blue skirt covered in white powder. When that stopped being amusing enough for them, they escalated. They threw plastic set squares into the ceiling fan. I would dive under a desk to avoid them, but not all missed. Some connected. Bruises became part of my normal. This went on for three years. I never told anyone. I did not complain. Somewhere deep inside, I believed I deserved it. Worse still, that attention, even cruel attention, meant I was seen. And being seen felt better than being invisible.

For every school social or Blue Light disco, Mum would take me shopping for a new outfit. Partly because I was growing so quickly that nothing fit for long, my height and weight constantly changing, and partly because it reflected well on her. That habit has been hard to break. Even now, a new occasion triggers the urge to buy something new. Back then, I had no choice but to shop in the women's sections at Fosseys or Kmart. Nothing in the junior departments fitted my body. Occasionally, Mum would take me into a store called Something Else. The only thing I ever remember fitting me there was a pair of jelly sandals.

Life has a funny way of looping back on itself. Years later, I would come full circle and buy that very store. But that is a story for later.

Three times a year, Mum would take Simon and me to Armidale, one hundred kilometres south of where we lived, and for those trips the rules changed completely. We were allowed to choose new clothes and anything else we wanted. We would fill two trolleys to the brim, usually spending around five hundred dollars. In today's money that would be closer to fifteen hundred. It felt extravagant and unreal. The day always included takeaway lunch at McDonalds or Kentucky Fried Chicken, followed by an all-you-can-eat dinner at Pizza Hut before the long drive home in the dark. I can still remember the heaviness in my body from too much food, the blur of headlights on the highway, and the strange mix of indulgence and exhaustion that came with those days.

Around that time, my personal style could only be described as bold. I coordinated my glamorous chicken handbag with fluoro hot pink tights, a grey fleece short dress and elf boots. It was a look. Years later, when I bought Jangles Fashion Hut, Ali laughed at the irony of me selling fashion to the town after my truly questionable dress sense in high school. She was not wrong.

At home, there were things I heard that I should never have had to hear. The walls were paper thin, and I could hear Mum entertaining various men in her room. There was very little left to the imagination. Paired with my accidental education from her porn collection, I was far more aware of what was going on than any teenager should have been. At times, she would make me sit in the car at the IPEC changeover depot while she went inside for what she called a cup of coffee with a truck driver passing through town. These experiences lodged themselves deep inside me. They hardened my resolve that my own children would never be exposed to the same things. Some lessons are learned by example. Others are learned by harm.

Late in 1986, Mum stopped working at the mine and instead took a job at the local video store. One Saturday night, when Mum was not at work, Ali and I rented a movie without having any idea what it was about. We sat up late watching it, increasingly wide eyed and unsure what we had stumbled into as Frank N Furter strutted across the screen. We were terrified Mum would find out we had watched The Rocky Horror Picture Show. She never did. It remains one of my favourite movies to this day.

By then, we had lived in a string of houses around Glen Innes. Torrington Street, then 248 Meade Street which was the Loloma mine manager's house, then 5 Robinson Avenue, and eventually back to Meade Street again. When we returned to Meade Street, Uncle Sid gave the house to Mum. Or so we believed. Mum renovated parts of it, including putting a pergola out the back. It sat on a huge block of land. We heated the house with two wood heaters, and I learnt to swing a blockbuster axe at a young age. Every day involved hauling wood inside. Cold was never optional in Glen Innes. You earned your warmth.

We lived in that house for eight years and never paid rent. Mum believed it was hers. Unfortunately, the title was never transferred into her name. In 1987, when the global financial crunch hit, Uncle Sid lost his millions, including the house we had called home. It was never legally ours. I was forced to leave that house in 1994. Losing it felt like another rug pulled from under my feet, another reminder that stability was always an illusion in my life.

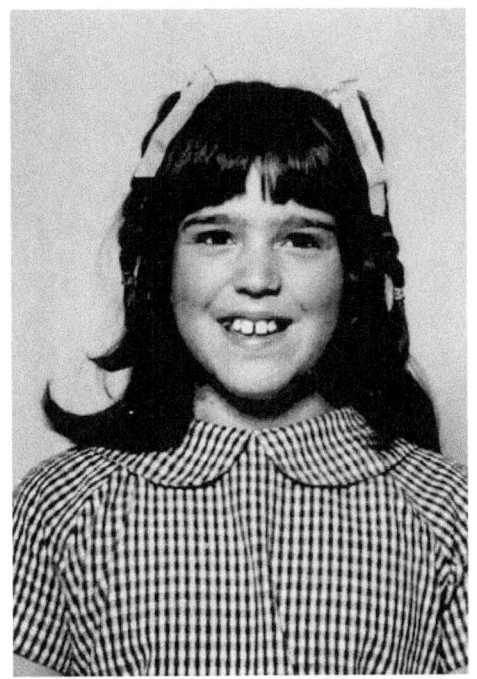

1982 At Emmaville Central School, NSW

1982 Torrington Street, Glen Innes

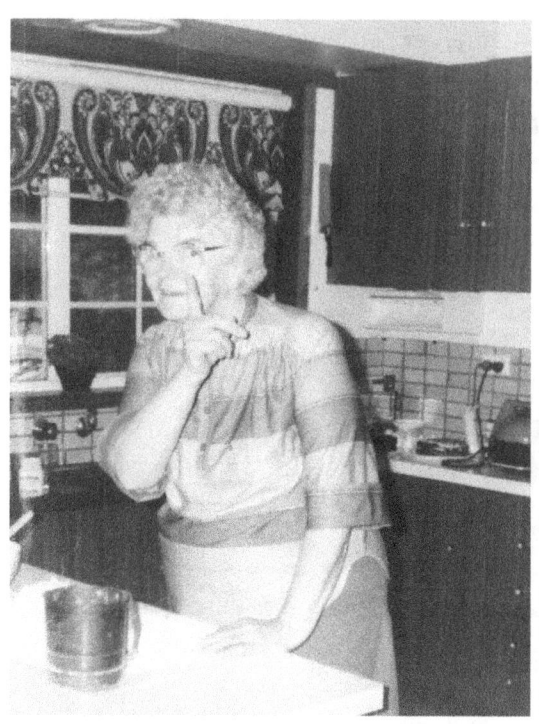

1983 Nanna Violet telling me off for taking her photo. This was the last time I ever saw her.

1983 Sovereign Hill, Victoria

1983 Visit with Dad in Geelong

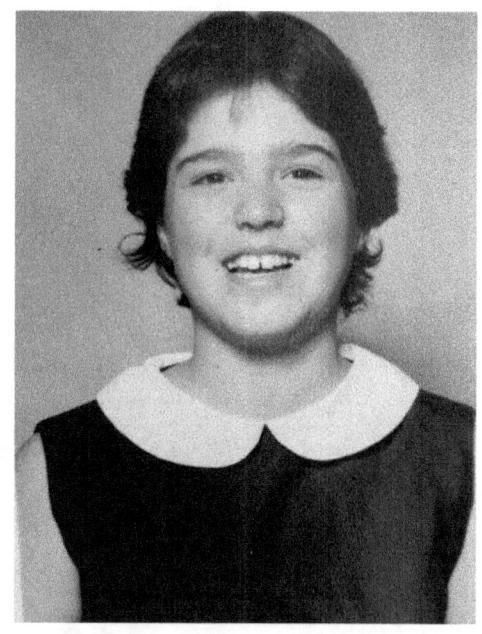

1983 Year 7 Emmaville Central School

1984 Meade Street, Glen Innes

1984 Year 8 Glen Innes High School

1985 Tech Drawing Class Glen Innes High School

Meade Street, Glen Innes, NSW

Robinson Avenue, Glen Innes

CHAPTER 4

Those Mid-Teenage Years

In 1986, at fifteen years old, I entered one of the hardest years of my teenage life. It began with my body once again demanding attention in ways I did not understand and could not control.

I had developed a lump on the top, dead centre of my scalp. Mum assumed it was a pimple and tried more than once to lance it with a needle and squeeze it. It was not a pimple. We were in Sydney staying with Nan and Parpa when the lump continued to grow, becoming more painful and more alarming. Parpa contacted my great-uncle Sid, a man with deep connections in the medical world, and everything suddenly moved very quickly. Before I had time to process what was happening, I was sitting across from Professor Fred Stephen, being told I needed emergency surgery to remove the growth.

The following day, I was admitted to the hospital. My biggest fear was not the surgery itself, but my hair. By then, I had long moved on from the spiky punk phase and rat's tail. My hair was shoulder-length, something I had grown carefully and fiercely guarded. For many women, hair is tied to identity and femininity, and at fifteen I clung to it as something that was mine.

They struggled to insert a cannula. They tried the backs of my hands first, five times in my left hand and three in my right. When that failed, they moved to my feet. It was painful, humiliating and frightening. I felt like a pincushion. Eventually, they succeeded, and I was taken into surgery.

When I woke in recovery, I was exposed. My chest was bare, heart monitor leads attached, my gown pulled down. I panicked and tried to pull it back up over my exposed breasts, only to discover that the eight cannulas were still in my hands. They hurt. I felt violated, though I couldn't articulate it. No teenage girl wants strangers standing over her while her body is uncovered. Today, there would be conversations about dignity and consent. Back then, there was nothing.

As I turned my head, still groggy, I noticed what I thought were coloured pillowcases. I remember thinking how modern the hospital looked. Then I reached up to feel my hair and a thick clump came away in my hand. I touched my scalp, and my fingers filled with blood. The coloured pillow slip was not a design choice. It was soaked through with my own blood.

They had cut a six-centimetre incision straight down the middle of my scalp. To access the lump, they had shaved a large circle of hair, twelve centimetres across, leaving me looking like a friar monk. I cried. How was I supposed to go back to school like this?

The results came back and we were told they had removed everything. It had been a far more extensive operation than anticipated. I had ten thick stitches in my scalp that could not be removed until we returned to Glen Innes. When we arrived back at Nan and Parpa's, Nan stood me over the laundry tub and gently sponged my hair, doing what she could while I cried.

And yes, we slept in the dungeon again. The same cold, dark room. Fresh linen on the beds, but even more items stacked around us. Nothing had changed.

A week afterwards, we travelled home by train because Mum's mobility was limited by her MS. My hair was stiff with dried blood. I went to our local doctor to have the stitches removed. The nurse remarked that cutting them was like slicing through ten-pound fishing line. They were thick and unforgiving. I returned to school with the most humiliating haircut imaginable, even worse than my earlier punk phase. The teasing was relentless. I cut my hair short to make it less obvious and waited impatiently for it to grow.

Forty years later, the scar is still there. A section of about two and a half centimetres has never grown hair again. There is a permanent dent in my scalp from what was removed. These days I know how to style my hair to hide it, and being tall helps as well. Very few people can see the top of my head.

But I can feel it. Every day. A reminder of that year. A reminder that my body has always had its own agenda.

My body was changing - slowly at first - but then more rapidly, in ways that terrified me. I did not notice the dark facial hair at first. It crept in quietly, until one day I became aware that I had coarse hair growing on my neck and chest, some of it a couple of centimetres long. I was mortified. I remember standing in front of the mirror, staring at myself, panic rising in my chest, genuinely wondering if I was turning into a man. My anxiety was relentless and consuming. I felt freakish and wrong, as though my body had betrayed me yet again.

Mum also struggled with facial hair, so she took me to a beautician. That was the beginning of decades of waxing and plucking, bleeding skin, ingrown hairs and shame. It became part of my routine, something I managed in secret, something I obsessed over daily. In 2002, desperate for a permanent solution, I underwent IPL treatment. I walked out of that appointment with second-degree burns across my face. The pain was excruciating, but the emotional damage cut deeper. For a long time after that, I would not let a man touch my face. I was terrified of being judged, of being seen, of someone discovering what I worked so hard to hide. I lived with constant ingrown hairs and inflammation, and my self-esteem took hit after hit. It affected how I saw myself every single day.

It took another fifteen years before I found the courage to try again, this time with laser hair removal. Even walking into that clinic took everything I had. After the first session, the results were extraordinary. I continued, session after session, fourteen in total, and for the first time since puberty, I was free of it. The hair never grew back. The lift to my self-esteem was profound. It felt like reclaiming a part of myself I had spent decades battling.

The year was 1986, and my home life continued to deteriorate. Mum was struggling to cope with her disability and the anger that came with it, and I was the closest target. If something was out of place, if something did not meet her expectations, I bore the brunt of it. She lashed out verbally and physically. As an adult, I can recognise her behaviour through the lens of illness, grief and frustration, but as a teenager, I internalised it as proof that I was fundamentally lacking. That I was the problem.

By then, I was already taller than her. She knew she could no longer hit me with her hand, so she adapted. She would take off her shoe and use that instead, or she would grab her walking stick and belt me with it. She had long fingernails, and one night when I raised my arm to protect myself, she clawed into my left arm and tore a chunk of skin away. I bled. I never hit her back. I yelled, I cried, I defended myself only by shielding my body, but I never struck her. Even then, some instinct in me knew that crossing that line would cost me something I could never get back.

Her outbursts were becoming more frequent, and so were the fights between us. Home no longer felt like a shelter. It felt like a battlefield I could never leave. I was under constant stress, carrying a weight far too heavy for a fifteen-year-old. I felt unloved, invisible and worthless. I hated school because of the relentless teasing, and I hated home because it was unpredictable and unsafe. I could not see a future beyond the pain I was living in, and I could not see a way out.

In my teenage mind, the only escape I could imagine was not being here at all.

One morning before school, I swallowed caustic drain cleaner. Drano. Two small mouthfuls. I was not dramatic about it. There was no grand plan. I just wanted the pain to stop. Nothing happened except a vile metallic taste that burned my mouth and throat. I stood there waiting for something, anything, to happen. When it did not, I took it as a sign that I had to carry on. Only years later did I learn just how horrific and painful that method would have been if it had worked. At the time, I was not trying to die so much as trying to be heard. I needed someone to notice how much I was hurting. I was crying for help in the only way I knew how. No one saw it. No one knew. No one came.

So I did what I would do for decades after. I hardened the fuck up. I swallowed the pain and I ate my feelings instead, building armour layer by layer around a heart that was already bruised. That was the beginning of my moxie, not the glamorous kind, but the raw, survival version. The kind that keeps you breathing even when you do not want to be.

In October 1986, I went to Sydney for two weeks of work experience. For the first week, I stayed with Nanna and Parpa, and for the first time, I was allowed to sleep upstairs in the third bedroom instead of the dungeon. I had dreams of becoming a musician and had arranged my placement at the Sydney Conservatorium of Music. In my mind, this was the doorway to a future that made sense to me. Nanna would drop me at the ferry on Sydney Harbour; I would cross the harbour to Circular Quay, then walk through the city to the Conservatorium, feeling grown-up and hopeful.

The reality crushed me. I spent the week in an office stamping envelopes. That was it. No music. No instruments. No inspiration. Just endless disappointment. I was devastated. It felt like another door slammed shut, another reminder that my hopes did not matter.

The second week could not have been more different. I went with my Aunty Lynny to her workplace at The Land newspaper in the graphic arts department. I loved it instantly. I was engaged, stimulated, and felt alive in a way I had not felt in a long time. I helped design an advertisement and felt capable for the first time in weeks. It showed me how much proper planning and care can change a person's experience. Aunty Lynny noticed that I was working very close to the page and suggested to Mum that I needed my eyes tested.

My vision had been deteriorating, and I was referred to an ophthalmologist in Armidale, one hundred kilometres away. I have always suffered from severe car sickness, and that trip was no exception. By the time we arrived, I was pale and nauseous. The ophthalmologist looked into my eyes and asked if I was feeling all right. I told her I was not. She advised Mum to take me straight home and let me rest.

Instead, Mum decided not to waste the trip and took me to Kmart to buy things we couldn't find in Glen Innes.

I slept the entire way home, my body heavy and disconnected. The next morning, I woke with intense pain on the right side of my chest. When I opened my pyjamas, I saw a rash wrapping around my body from my sternum to my spine, thin angry lines tracing their way along my skin. Mum sent me to school anyway. By afternoon, I was in the sick bay, and the office rang Mum to collect me. The doctor confirmed it. Shingles. I was fifteen years old.

I was stunned. Shingles were something old people got, not teenagers. I was in agony and terrified. I was only days away from sitting my Year 10 School Certificate exams. The blisters followed my nerve lines deep beneath the skin, and the pain was relentless. I lay in my room and sobbed, convinced the world hated me and that I was a waste of space. Mum was instructed to keep me isolated and not touch the blisters.

The school and Mum decided I could still sit my exams. I would be placed alone in the library, isolated from everyone else, with thick pads stuck over the blisters and a cubicle separating me from the rest of the world. I felt like a freak. I remember thinking that my life could not possibly get worse. I looked at my friends and wondered why none of them seemed to suffer like I did. I know now that everyone carries their own battles, but at the time, it felt deeply unfair.

It is well documented that childhood stress and trauma leave imprints on both the body and the mind. My body was already keeping score.

Through all of this, I kept going. Not because it was easy, and not because I was strong in the way people like to celebrate, but because I had learned to harden up when no one came running. That was my moxie being forged in real time. Not shiny. Not inspirational. Just survival.

By the end of that year, my four years of junior high school were over, and with them came a strange mix of relief and exhaustion. Every year, without fail, Mum would relapse in late summer. Her Multiple Sclerosis followed a cruel rhythm, as predictable as the seasons. She would deteriorate, then be admitted to Glen Innes Hospital for high-dose steroids, and sometimes she would be flown back to Sydney Hospital for more intense treatment and rehabilitation. This pattern shaped my adolescence.

She was in hospital for my tenth birthday, my thirteenth, my sixteenth, my eighteenth, my twenty-first, my twenty-third, my twenty-fourth and my twenty-fifth. Birthdays came and went like administrative details rather than celebrations. Simon and I would fend for ourselves until a family member could make the long drive up from Sydney to take over. Once I turned eighteen, the rescues stopped. We were simply expected to cope. Looking back now, it is staggering. If this had happened today, child protection would have been knocking on the door without hesitation.

By then, I saw myself as an overweight, ugly girl with no self-worth, living in a house where nothing I did was ever good enough. Mum and I fought constantly. I was allowed to have friends stay over, but I was deeply embarrassed by Mum and how she treated me. My best friend's mother would drop her off at our place each morning so we could walk to school together, but I never let her come inside. I did not want anyone to see how things really were.

I never ate breakfast before school. Mum stopped making our lunches when we were still in primary school. If we wanted food, we made it ourselves or went without. Most days, we survived on devon and tomato sauce sandwiches. Mum kept a stash of Violet Crumbles and Scorched Peanut Bars in the pantry and counted how many were in each packet. If one went missing, we were in serious trouble. It was not worth it. Our diet was awful. We rarely ate fruit. Dinner was usually meat and deep-fried chips. We did not drink water. We lived on soft drinks or powdered orange drinks like Tang, loaded with sugar and chemicals. It was fuel, not nourishment.

For years, I asked Mum why she never had an engagement ring and why her wedding dress had a yellow ribbon stitched across the top. She would not answer. She would change the subject or laugh it off. I did not understand why it bothered me so much until I was fifteen. In 1986, I was looking through my parents' wedding album when I noticed a handwritten message from my Aunt Lynny dated August 1970. I stared at it for a long time, counting backwards. There were not nine months between August and March.

When I asked Mum about it, she ran out of the room giggling.

That moment hit me like a sledgehammer. I realised my parents had married because of me. I believed for a very long time after that that I had ruined their lives. If I had not been born, they would not have had to marry each other. Their lives would have been different. Easier. Happier. I carried that guilt quietly for years, asking myself endless what-if questions over something I had no control over at all. As if I had chosen to arrive. As if I could have stopped them from having sex in that car.

Those thoughts lodged themselves deep inside me and became another layer of armour I carried into adulthood. Another reason to harden up. Another reason to believe that love was conditional and that my existence came at a cost.

That belief shaped more of my life than I ever realised at the time.

Mum walked with a stick and had a disabled parking permit. That was my first real exposure to how cruel and intrusive people can be about disability. Strangers stared openly as she walked, her gait uneven, as if she were drunk. Simon and I developed a look we would give people who stared too long. It was a look that said 'mind your business', without a word needing to be spoken. Very little was understood about Multiple Sclerosis in those days. Most people assumed she had been in a car accident. Strangers felt entitled to ask. They would walk up and demand answers, as though her body existed for public explanation. This was also the beginning of her cognitive decline. Years later, I learned that MS can cause a form of dementia. I believe this is what happened to my mum.

As her disability progressed, home became harder to live in. In late 1986, completely out of the blue, Dad contacted us. He was working in Sydney on a movie as a stunt double. I had not seen him in four years. He had not paid a single cent in child support. He rode his motorbike eight hours north from Sydney to visit us. Mum was over the moon and invited him to stay. It was one of the strangest times of my life. He slept in what we called the office on a fold-out bed and stayed only a few days. We went out for dinner together at the Gum Wah Chinese restaurant. That was the last meal we ever had as a family.

While he was there, Mum confronted him about money. What would he leave us if he died? I do not believe she was worried about Simon and me. I think she was more concerned with what she could get out of him.

At my Year Ten farewell, everyone had a date except me. I wanted a boyfriend desperately. I needed someone to love me. Someone to see me. Someone to choose me. I felt completely unwanted as a teenager. Looking back now, I understand something I could not then. I do not need a man to make me whole. I never did. I am enough.

In the January holidays of 1987, Simon and I travelled from Glen Innes to Melbourne by bus on our own to visit Dad. It was only the third time we had seen him in seven years. Mum was terrified we would not come back. I was fifteen. Simon was fourteen. The trip took eighteen hours, with a long stopover at an ungodly hour at the Dubbo bus exchange. We left Glen Innes in 16-degree weather and arrived in Melbourne on a 42-degree day. Dad had no air conditioning. He was seeing a woman we will call F2.

They took us to Brighton Beach in her pink convertible Volkswagen Beetle. Simon and I were in the water when we realised she was sunbaking topless. We stayed in the water for a very long time, not wanting to return to the sand. I did not want to look like a beached whale next to her. More than that, it felt deeply inappropriate to be exposed to that as children.

Over the following weeks, F2 would come over, say hello briefly, then she and Dad would disappear into his bedroom and have loud sex. Simon and I both had

Walkmans. Mine had flat batteries. Of course it did. It seemed I could never escape hearing my parents having sex. Both of them. Different houses. Same lack of boundaries.

Before we left to return home, he gave us the two treasures he had from his past. I was given my great-grandfather's button accordion. Simon was given his gold pocket watch. Those objects carried more weight than any words he ever offered us.

I tried to continue life as normal. For years at school, I lived on cheese buns and sausage rolls for both recess and lunch. Yes, at the same time. Back then, I could eat those foods. Now, I cannot eat any of them. In Years Eleven and Twelve, I started to put on more weight. I would buy my best friend a cheese bun and a sausage roll, but she would not eat hers, so I would eat both. This went on for a long time. I was gaining weight. She was losing it. We both had eating disorders, just at opposite ends of the spectrum.

I wanted to be like her in every possible way. From the outside, her life looked perfect. A nuclear family. Two parents who loved her and were still together. A slim body. A boyfriend. Everything I did not have. Looking back now, I can see that her eating disorder was a silent scream for help too. At the time, I was too consumed by my own pain to recognise hers. I was jealous. Deeply. And underneath that jealousy was the belief that I simply was not good enough.

A month before my sixteenth birthday in March, I went to see Crocodile Dundee with friends. Movies were a big deal for us, even though they arrived months later than they did in the city. That is country town life. My best friend was there with her boyfriend, and once again I was the third wheel. They had been together for a year. A boy in my year had shown me a little interest, and with some encouragement from those two, we sat next to each other. We held hands. Later, around the back of the RSL club, we kissed.

It was nothing like I had imagined. He shoved his tongue into my mouth and poked it around. I nearly gagged. Still, I could say I had been kissed before my sweet sixteenth. The next day at school, we avoided each other. We never spoke about it. I never spoke to him again. That was that.

Two weeks before my sixteenth birthday, Mum had Simon and me christened. She was terrified we would die and our souls would not make it to Heaven. I think she was thinking a lot about her own mortality and what would happen to us if she was gone. From a young age, Aunty Lynny and Uncle Gra had told us that if anything ever happened to Mum, they would never allow us to be separated and would make room for us in their home.

The priest told us not to touch the holy water, to let it flow where it would. Where it landed told a story. If it went in your eyes, you would see no evil. In your ears, hear no evil. In your mouth, speak no evil. Mine missed all of those and went straight down my top.

To this day, I still wonder what that meant. Because what happened just one month later, under the house of the Lord, changed my life forever.

Later that year, Dad rang Mum and told her he thought he had contracted AIDS and Hepatitis C from F2. After that phone call, he disappeared from my life entirely for the next twelve years. I thought he was dead.

Another abandonment. Another silence. Another reason to harden up and keep going, because stopping was never an option.

1986 Year 10 Farewell concert

1986 Year 10 Farewell Dinner at the Glen Innes Bowling Club

1986 Year 10 Winter uniform, Glen Innes High School

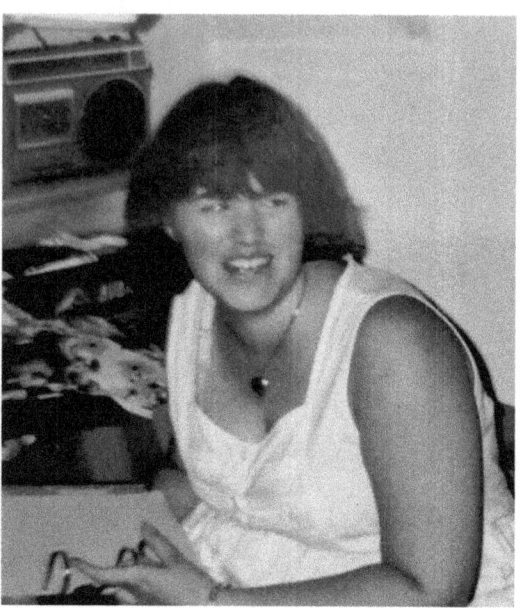

1987 Me sitting on my bed

1987 Me with a bad perm

1987 Sitting in Grey Street, Glen Innes

THOSE MID-TEENAGE YEARS

1987 Timbertown NSW

Glen Innes High School

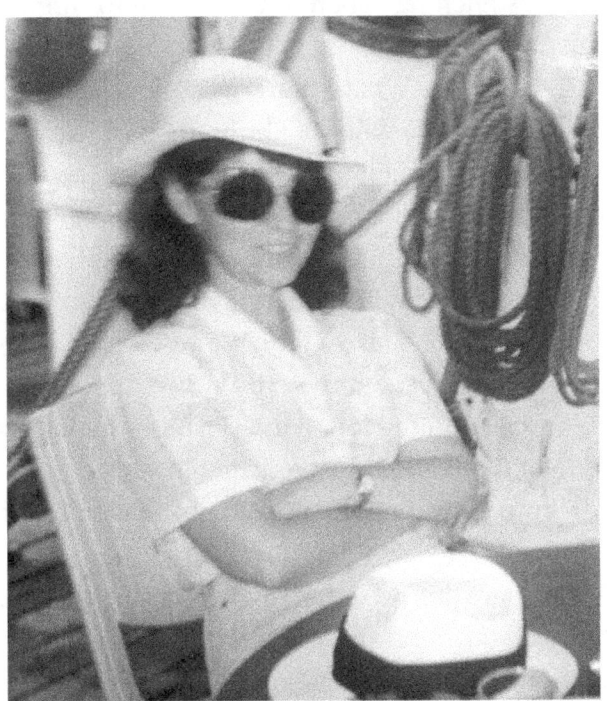
Mum in 1985

CHAPTER 5

Gutter Slut

When I turned sixteen, Mum's pension was cut. I began receiving Austudy, which was $60.13 per week. Mum did not see this as my money. She saw it as household money. I was required to pay her board of $30 per fortnight, which left me with around $30 to cover everything else. Clothes. Socialising. Movies. Anything beyond survival came out of that small remainder.

Once I got my licence in 1988, Mum introduced another system. She kept a logbook for her car. Every time I borrowed it, I had to record the kilometres driven. She then charged me ten cents per kilometre, which came out of my already limited money. Austudy did not stretch far. There was no room for impulse or indulgence.

Some people might say this was cruel. Others might say it was practical. The truth sits somewhere in between. What Mum was doing, whether consciously or not, was forcing us to learn to survive within tight limits. We learnt how to budget. We learnt how to go without. We learnt how to keep going even when it felt unfair.

This was where my resolve hardened. Not loudly. Not dramatically. Quietly, deep inside. I had already been through enough to know life was not going to hand me anything, but this was where it became crystal clear that no one was coming to rescue me. If I wanted something, I would have to earn it. If I wanted freedom, I would have to fight for it. If I wanted more from life, I would have to drag myself towards it, even when I had nothing left in me. That is what moxie looks like in real life. Not confidence. Not motivation. Just refusing to stop.

It was the 4th of April 1987, and my life did not change for the better. It became a lot worse.

I have struggled to share this period of my life, unsure whether I should ever tell the world. I have thought long and hard about whether this belongs here. In the end, I came to the conclusion that if I am sharing my life, I am sharing it warts and all. Somewhere, someone reading this needs to know that the terrible decisions we make, or the terrible things that happen to us, do not have to define who we are forever. We can get through them.

At that time, I used to go for walks every evening on my own. It was the only way I knew how to escape the house and get away from Mum. I would walk as far as the Catholic school, about a kilometre down the road, letting the quiet and the movement calm my racing thoughts. Walking gave me space to breathe.

On one of those evenings, four boys from my school were drinking under the trees on the school grounds. They called out to me, laughing, telling me to come over and join them. One of them was a boy I had a crush on, M1. I wanted so badly to be his girlfriend. I wanted to feel chosen. I wanted to feel wanted. At sixteen, I would have done almost anything to feel loved.

So I went over.

After a few drinks and flirting, I just wanted to be liked. I wanted to feel loved. I wanted everything I wasn't getting at home. Then, one thing led to another, and before I knew it, I was losing my virginity, to not one boy, but to all four. Otherwise known as 'gang bang'. One after the other, on the bare, cold concrete. I ended up bleeding, covered in not just hickeys all over my neck as their trophy, but also bruises on my body from one of them holding me down. M1 whacked my head hard on the concrete and gave me a mild concussion. I was only 16 years old when I encountered that violent assault. It was not ok.

When the four had finished with me, they discarded me like trash, and they just left. I dressed myself and walked home. When I got home, I took a long, hot shower and put myself to bed in shock. The cold night air sobered me up. This was not the fairy tale romance I had pictured I would lose my virginity to. It was vile and disgusting and set me up for years of pain and heartache, with traumatic flashbacks. I accept my responsibility for putting myself in that position. I had zero boundaries. However, I will never forget how they treated me before, during and after that night. I now recognise this act as rape as I did not consent to the full extent of what I was subjected to.

When I went to school the next day, they bragged about it. It spread through the school like wildfire. I do not know why I thought they would keep quiet. I hated my life. I wanted to crawl into a hole and disappear.

It did not take long before my brother's friends' mothers told Mum what had happened. I came home from school to find her and Mum sitting in the kitchen, waiting for me. I was interrogated like a criminal. I denied it. I said that one of them had given me his so-called badges of honour all over my neck. I still sometimes wonder what would have happened if I had told the truth. What would Mum have done? Would she have protected me, or would it have made things worse?

I was already being punished at school. The reputation followed me everywhere. I knew it would stay with me for a very long time. The guilt was unbearable. The shame was even worse. I carried it quietly and alone.

To this day, I do not know if that was what they had planned. I do know that it happened. I have chosen not to name them. Their names are not important in telling my story. I do not feel the need to punish their families for something that happened so long ago. What matters is that it happened, and that I lived with the consequences long after they walked away.

I was labelled a gutter slut by some, a slag, a hooker, a tart, a whore. The list went on. They were labelled studs. The difference was appalling. I just wanted someone to love me.

After what happened, it was almost impossible to find a partner for my debutante ball later that year. In desperation, I asked a boy in the year below me who was gay. He agreed and came to the first practice, but he could not cope with being the only homosexual surrounded by openly homophobic boys. He quit, telling me it was not his scene.

I remember sobbing for hours. Even a gay guy had rejected me. That was how low my self-worth had fallen. I was not just carrying the shame of what had happened; I was carrying the judgment of an entire community that saw me as disposable while excusing the boys who hurt me.

That double standard carved itself deep into me, and it stayed there for a very long time.

My brother agreed to partner with me under one condition. I paid him. I do not blame him at all for that. Mum had no idea.

So I saved my Austudy allowance and agreed to pay him one hundred dollars, which would be close to three hundred dollars in today's money. It took me three months to save the money.

My Nanna came up for the ball. My grandfather stayed in Sydney as his mother, Noonoo, was unwell.

Noonoo was Russian. She was about five feet tall and six feet round. She cooked traditional Russian food for us, especially piroshki — deep-fried Russian meat pies. She spoke Russian much of the time. She had travelled the world and would give us gifts of Italian glass statues. Most of them had chips in them. I still have them today.

She immigrated to Australia in 1926 from Tientsin, China, at the age of 19. Her husband was in his forties. She had married him through an arranged marriage in

China when she was just fourteen. A child. She had my grandfather Ivan at 15 and my great-uncle Sid at 17.

When I visited her as a 13-year-old, she would ask me when I was getting married. It added even more pressure to the already heavy weight I carried about not having a boyfriend or being loved by someone.

I wore a white dress to the ball. Mum would not buy me a new one or have one made, so we borrowed one. A debutante ball is meant to mark a young woman coming out into society, a formal declaration of adulthood. I was not a virgin. I felt I should not have been wearing white, and I felt everyone knew it.

In hindsight, many of the other debutantes were not virgins either. But shame does not work on logic.

It was one of the rare occasions Mum appeared proud. I believe it was more because Simon was doing it than because I was, even though he had been paid to be there. As I was presented on stage, I felt exposed. I felt like everyone was looking at me for the wrong reasons and talking behind my back.

At the time, I thought I was extremely fat. When I look at the photos now, I realise I was not. I was simply taller and broader than my shorter friends, Mum and Simon. I had to duck to walk under Simon's arm during our official dance.

My Parpa wrote a letter saying how proud he was of Simon and me, and how sorry he was that he could not be there. I still have that letter today. It meant more than he could ever have known.

And in that letter, he did not call us the arsehole's children.

That mattered.

Noonoo passed away the day after my debutante ball.

In Year Eleven, I studied two units of Maths, Veggie English, two units of Society and Culture, two units of Biology, and two units of Music by correspondence. My subject choices reflected exactly where I sat in the system. Academically underestimated in some areas and quietly excelling in others.

Around that time, Mum was dating a man who was part-owner of a local service station. He would arrive with brown paper bags filled with chocolates for Simon and me. The irony was not lost on me, given that my parents had owned a service station a decade earlier. I am grateful to him for one thing in particular. He gave me a job.

I started working part-time in the kitchen and on the front counter, and when the driveway was busy, I would also pump fuel. Simon worked there too. I stayed for about six months. It was another step in learning responsibility and survival, even if it came far earlier than it should have.

During Years Eleven and Twelve, I poured myself into music. It became my refuge. I was in the stage band, concert band and choir, and I also tutored younger students. Somewhere along the way, I discovered that our music teacher was married to our sports teacher. I quickly realised that if I made myself indispensable in music, I could avoid sport altogether.

I hated sport. Truly hated it.

Whenever sport came up, I would go to the sports teacher and tell him his wife needed me. In a school of six hundred and eighty students, I always came last in the cross country. Every single time. My legs simply would not work the way they were supposed to. No matter how hard I tried, they burned and tore as if the fibres themselves were failing me.

At the time, I thought this was another personal failure. Another reason I was not good enough. It never occurred to me that my body might be telling its own story.

What I was learning, without knowing it, was moxie. Not the glamorous kind. The quiet kind. The kind where you keep showing up even when your body hurts, your confidence is shredded and your dreams feel just out of reach. I was hardening up in the only way I knew how. Not by choice, but by necessity.

Music gave me somewhere to stand when everything else felt unstable. It was the one place where I felt capable, seen and strong. Even then, this persistence, this refusal to give up on myself, was shaping the woman I would become.

I had many run-ins with the female PE teacher. I tried to explain to her that there was something wrong with my legs, that running caused pain I could not push through. She responded by yelling louder, as if volume alone could fix my body. Her belief was simple. If I tried harder, I would succeed. If I failed, it was because I was lazy.

One PE lesson in Year Ten stands out clearly. She announced that if I came in last during the warm up run around the oval, I would be required to continue running through my entire lunch break. I came in last. Again. My friends were horrified. Without hesitation, they stopped running altogether and walked in solidarity with me. None of them would leave me alone to be punished. It was one of the few moments at school where I felt protected. It would be years before I would finally understand why my body could never do what was demanded of it.

My body already made me feel different. I had a larger bottom than all my friends, which made the short pleated sports skirts humiliating to wear. They barely covered me. I felt exposed and judged every time I moved. Eventually, I asked Mum to write a note giving permission for me not to do sport unless I was allowed to wear long shorts. It went against the uniform policy, but the school approved it.

Without realising it at the time, I paved the way for future generations of girls to wear shorts for sport. It was a small act of defiance, but it mattered. It was moxie in its earliest form. Quiet. Practical. Protective. I was learning to advocate for myself, even when my voice shook.

Towards the end of 1987, the NSW Corrective Services Band toured through the region. I was asked to join them as their tuba player. I was beyond excited. It was not just a band. It was a possible passport out. There was talk of touring, even travelling overseas, doing what I loved most.

Mum would not let me go. I had to finish Year Twelve before I was allowed to do anything with my life. I often wonder how different my path might have been if I had gone. When I finished school, my dream was clear. I wanted to be a classical composer and conduct an orchestra. More than that, I wanted to get as far away from Glen Innes as possible.

By the end of 1987, at sixteen years and nine months old, I could not wait to get my learner plates. Driving represented freedom. Control. Escape. I passed the test on my first attempt. Mum picked me up from school that afternoon so I could go for my very first drive.

All I wanted was to cruise up and down the main street and do what every country kid dreams of doing. A legendary lap.

Despite my first traumatic sexual encounter, I was sexually assaulted again later that same year. It was no better. I was riding my pushbike when two men approached me and gained my trust. They lured me into the back of a panel van behind the town hall in the car park, and took turns with me.

I was still searching for love, validation, and affection in all the wrong places, because I was not receiving it at home or anywhere else. I did not yet understand boundaries. I did not understand my worth. They did. And they exploited that.

They were both much older than me. I was a child. They saw vulnerability, not consent. They treated me like I was nothing. Like an object. Like something disposable.

Do I blame them? Yes, for what they did.

Do I forgive them? No, I do not.

But I do forgive myself.

That forgiveness did not come quickly. It took years. Decades, even. I carried shame that was never mine to carry. I believed I was broken, damaged, and unworthy of real love. In truth, I was traumatised and desperately trying to survive with the tools I had at the time.

I never spoke to either of those men again. I trusted that karma would find its way to them. Years later, I learned they had both died in accidents. That knowledge did not bring me satisfaction or closure. What mattered more was that I finally stopped punishing myself for choices made by a frightened teenage girl who was craving safety and connection.

This was not recklessness. It was survival.

And survival takes moxie, even when it looks messy from the outside.

I hardened up in the only way I knew how back then.

Now I know better.

And now I tell the truth.

In January 1988, we spent time in Sydney staying with Nanna and Parpa, back in what we always called our dungeon. Australia was celebrating its 200-year bicentennial, and for once, there was a sense of collective joy in the air. Mum's entire family gathered on the Sydney Harbour foreshore for the day. We watched the tall ships sail into the harbour, and later that night, the Sydney Harbour Bridge hosted its first massive fireworks display. It was spectacular.

That day marked the last time my whole family would ever be together. Many have since passed away, and others no longer speak to each other. It is deeply sad. Time is far too short to waste on grudges.

I completed Year Twelve in 1988. I hated the work. I struggled to understand much of it and felt constantly overwhelmed. My career adviser told me to drop two units of Biology and pick up an extra unit of Music. I was fourth in my Biology class, so it was terrible advice. It might have made sense if I had an actual Music teacher and classroom, but I did not. Instead, I sat alone in the library doing correspondence music for sixteen periods a week, with no guidance and no support. I didn't understand the work, so eventually, I stopped doing it altogether and didn't submit anything. No one followed up with me. I hid under the radar.

I could not wait for school to end. The constant sense of failure was humiliating and reinforced the belief that I was not good enough. I have never liked failing at anything. Very few people knew what life was really like at home. What we were carrying was invisible to the outside world.

Simon could no longer cope with the fighting between Mum and me, nor the pressure she placed on him. He moved out and went to live with older friends, leaving me alone with Mum. Suddenly, it felt like all responsibility for her survival had landed squarely on my shoulders.

I hardened up a little more, because I had to.

There was no other option.

That quiet resolve, that unspoken determination to keep going even when I felt like I was drowning, was moxie taking shape long before I had a name for it.

Mum worked as a volunteer for the MS Readathon. When she was too unwell to present, I would skip school and do the talks on her behalf at local schools. At the time, it just felt like another responsibility added to my load. Who would have thought I would need those public speaking skills decades later or that I too would one day work for them?

Reflecting on these experiences has not been easy. Writing them has required honesty, courage and a willingness to sit with uncomfortable memories. If you have lived through experiences like mine, I want you to know this. You will be ok. You are a good person, even if you made poor choices along the way. Those choices do not define you. Healing is possible with the right support. Please reach out to a mental health professional if you need to. Do not carry it alone.

I spent decades believing I was never good enough. That belief shaped many of the decisions I made and not in a good way. When you are taught through words, silence and actions that you do not matter, you look for validation wherever you can find it.

Then came M2.

I had been seeing a guy who was nineteen. At the same time, he was carrying on with one of my so-called closest friends. Both of our mothers were disabled, which we believed connected us in some way. One night, we went for a drive in his brown EH station wagon with red and white gingham curtains. We ended up out near Beardy Waters, about ten kilometres east of Glen Innes.

We were not having sex. That was not something we had done. He did not need it from me. My so-called friend was providing that.

I confronted him about her. It turned into a yelling match. Then, without warning, he smacked me across the face. The sting was immediate. The handprint burned against my cold skin.

I was stunned.

Is this what dating was meant to be like? Is this how men treated women who cared about them?

I had no role models to show me otherwise. My father had been absent for seven years. Those were the years when a father should be teaching his daughter what respect looks like and how she deserves to be treated. Instead, I learnt to harden up in all the wrong ways.

But buried underneath the pain, confusion and fear, something else was forming. A quiet, stubborn resolve. The early beginnings of moxie. The kind that does not announce itself, but survives anyway.

I refused to get back in his car and instead began the 10-kilometre walk home.

He drove slowly beside me, begging me to get back in. My guess is it was not concern for the damage he had done to my face, but fear about what I might say when I got home to Mum. I ignored him and kept walking.

By the time I reached home, both my cheeks were burning red from the cold night air. I was exhausted. I walked through the house, called out a quiet goodnight to Mum, went straight to my room and crawled into bed. I cried into my pillow until there was nothing left.

The next day, M2 rang the house phone. I told him I never wanted to see him again and to leave me alone. I knew what he had done was wrong. That part was clear.

What was not clear was who I could tell.

I was too frightened to tell Mum. She was not my safe place. She was not the person who would wrap me up, protect me or tell me it was not my fault. I had already learnt that lesson well.

So once again, I hardened up. I swallowed it. I carried it alone.

That was how I survived back then.

On Christmas Day 1988, Nanna Marie was visiting. I cannot remember why Parpa did not come. I was in the lounge room when the phone rang in the kitchen. It was Parpa wishing us a Merry Christmas.

I heard Nanna Marie and Mum whispering in the kitchen about keeping something quiet so it would not spoil Christmas Day. I overheard them and asked, "What secret?" So they had no choice but to tell me.

Parpa had received a phone call from my great Aunty Margaret, my Pop's sister on my father's side. She and her family were close friends with my mum's parents. Aunty Margaret mentioned how sad it was about Violet, my father's mother. We had heard nothing.

It turned out that in April of that year, my great Uncle Jack, my father's uncle, had died. In October, Uncle David, my father's brother, who was only thirty-eight, had died. And at the beginning of December, my Nanna Violet had died from motor neurone disease (MND).

I had sent Nanna Violet a Christmas card. She had been dead for three weeks.

We did not know.

My father's family assumed Dad would have told us. He did not. I thought he was dead. To find out on Christmas Day that three family members had died is something I never want to experience again. I hardened the fuck up that day.

Who does that to their children, to not tell them?

To make it worse, he did not even collect his own mother's ashes from the crematorium. She remained there for close to twelve months. My Aunty Diane, David's widow, eventually organised for Nanna's ashes to be placed in Pop's grave at Teesdale in Victoria. That cemetery holds most of Dad's family, buried in that hard red dirt.

I know without question that I do not want to be buried there. When my time comes, I want a tree planted over me, somewhere green and alive. Given my love of plants, that feels right. Life continuing from death.

At the time, the only explanation I could come up with for Dad not telling us was that he must have been dead himself. We had no idea where he was. We did not know if he had AIDS. We did not even know if he was alive. It never occurred to me that he simply had not bothered to tell us.

We did not know Nanna had been placed in a nursing home. We did not know she had MND. No one told us anything. We had no way of finding out. That silence sparked a deep anger in me that stayed for many years. I grieved again for the father I did not have and also for what he had done.

I received one thousand dollars from Nanna Violet's will, held in trust until I turned twenty-one. I combined some of that with money from Nan and Parpa for my twenty-first birthday and bought my first piece of gold jewellery, a purple amethyst ring. I have worn it every day since. It is thin now, worn down by time, just like so many things from that era of my life.

My HSC results arrived, and I was terrified of Mum's reaction. I failed. I scored 175 out of 500. I qualified for nothing. No university. No pathway forward.

In my mind, I was a complete failure. Mum reinforced that belief. She compared me to Simon, pointed out how well he was doing, and told me I had wasted my life.

I applied to Goulburn TAFE for an Advanced Diploma in Music, majoring in composition with a minor in piano. There was no one there who could teach tuba. I knew more than they did. My career adviser failed me yet again, telling me I had to attend an audition in Goulburn that same week. There was no way to get there in time. I missed the opportunity entirely.

And just like that, I was stuck in Glen Innes.

My dreams felt shattered.

1987 Letter from Parps for my debut

1987 My Debut with Mum and Simon

1987 My Debut with Mum

1987 My Debut with Simon

1988 Attending World Expo

1988 Bicentennial Australia Day, Sydney Harbour

1988 Green Valley Farm NSW

1988 My Year 12 Farewell

1988 The jumper I knitted instead of studying for my HSC

CHAPTER 6

The Gap Years

My mum was never a healthy woman. She never exercised, lived on fried food, and smoked like a chimney. I never once saw her drink a glass of plain water. Her body had been under strain for years, and by this stage, it was showing in ways far beyond her MS.

She hadn't been well for some time outside of her usual symptoms and finally went to the doctor. The diagnosis was cervical cancer. She was forty one years old.

I was a teenager then, old enough to understand what cancer meant, old enough to feel the fear properly, and old enough to be expected to cope.

I cannot remember the exact procedure they initially performed, but I do remember Nanna coming up to help after Mum returned home from the hospital. Mum had only been home a few days when everything went terribly wrong.

She began haemorrhaging.

There was blood everywhere. Along the hallway. Across the floor. In her bedroom. It was shocking and confronting, and something that no teenager should have to witness. I knew instantly this was serious. This wasn't something that could wait.

I called 000. My hands were shaking, my heart pounding, but I spoke clearly enough to get help on the way. The ambulance arrived quickly and took her straight back to the hospital for emergency surgery.

Watching your mother bleed out like that changes something inside you. It hardens you in a way nothing else quite can. It teaches you that you cannot rely on life being stable or safe, and that at any moment, you may have to step up and handle the unthinkable.

She required a hysterectomy.

In time, she recovered physically, but nothing truly returned to normal. Her body had endured yet another trauma, and so had I. By then, crisis felt familiar. Hospitals were part of the landscape of my life. Emergencies were no longer shocking, just something to manage.

This became the rhythm of my teenage years. Adapt. Cope. Harden up. Keep moving forward.

And I did.

I bought my first car in 1989.

To do it, I asked Mum to cash in my life insurance policy. She had been paying into an AMP policy since I was born. It was worth $3000, which was a lot of money back then. I wanted independence. I remembered thinking how ironic it was that I wanted my own car so I would not have to keep a log book for every kilometre driven. These days, I still keep a log book, only now it is for the ATO.

While Mum was away one time, Simon took the speedometer cable off her car so we could drive as many kilometres as we wanted without it recording anything. Just before she came home, he put it back on. We made sure we had driven a couple of hundred kilometres over our allowed limit. She never knew. That felt like a small win in a life where wins were rare.

I bought a muscle car.

A white 1972 HQ Belmont Holden.

She was a beast.

She had been converted from a bench seat to bucket front seats, with a four on the floor Aussie box gearbox and extractors. She had 19 inch rims with fat tyres, tinted windows, and a stereo that absolutely rocked. She had been repainted white from her original bright yellow.

She had faults. Just like me.

When it rained, the windscreen leaked. Water pooled on the floor and inside the doors. Eventually, I had to put holes in the floor pan to let the water drain out. Rust holes, really. But she kept going, and so did I.

I loved that car fiercely.

I cannot tell you how many laps I chucked in her, up and down the main street of Glen Innes, but it was a lot. She gave me something I had been craving my entire life. Freedom. Control. Independence.

That car was moxie on four wheels.

She did not fix my life, but she gave me room to breathe. And sometimes, that is enough to keep you moving forward.

In 1989, I found myself with a forced gap year to fill before I could reapply to Goulburn at the end of the year.

I enrolled at Glen Innes TAFE and started an Advanced Certificate of Commerce. I hated it. Absolutely hated it. It felt like yet another year of my life being wasted. I did not want to be there. I wanted to be doing music, and I wanted to be as far away from Glen Innes as humanly possible.

Instead of sitting in class, we spent most of our time at the pub. A few of us would drive out to different pubs around the region, never in town, always the little village pubs, just in case someone we knew saw us. We were young, restless, and running from lives we did not want to be living.

Around this time, a group of my friends and I decided to drive to Tamworth to see the international male stripper group, The Chippendales. I was not feeling well at all. I had a lump on the right side of my neck that was the size of a golf ball. It was huge. I was exhausted, constantly tired, and felt off. But I went anyway.

We laughed. We drank too much. For one night, I forgot everything.

The next morning hit me like a freight train. I was stuck in bed and could barely move. Over the next few days, I deteriorated rapidly. Until this point, Mum had rarely believed me when I said I was unwell. For some reason, this time she did. She insisted I go to the doctor.

Blood tests were taken. The results came back quickly.

I had glandular fever. And on top of that, the Epstein-Barr virus. A double whammy.

I spent the next six weeks at home, mostly confined to bed. I completed a 2000-piece jigsaw during that time and watched endless, mindless television because I did not have the energy to do anything else. I could not go to TAFE. Chronic fatigue had flattened me completely.

It took more than a year for me to feel anything close to normal again. Even then, I pushed myself through it. I did what I had been taught to do my whole life.

I hardened the fuck up.

Towards the end of the year, the computer room flooded, and they passed all of us because we couldn't finish that subject. Even though we didn't attend most of it. I would not have guessed it then, but a few years later, that certificate would help me get a full-time job when I needed it.

When I reapplied to do music, it turned out that I hadn't needed to go to Goulburn to audition after all. I just had to send down some copies of my composed music. I composed my first symphony at the age of 15. They accepted me straight away. I was so angry. I could have gone that year! Life has a way of working out in unexpected ways. One of my favourite songs was Tracey Chapman's 'Fast Car'. I felt like she had written it for me. Maybe I would need to change a few of the words, but the sentiment was spot on: I just wanted to drive out of town as fast as I could.

Mum was in Sydney again in the hospital. It was at the end of Summer. Why would this birthday be any different to the previous five? My 18th birthday fell on a Friday and was a night to remember. I started in the afternoon with a bubble bath in our pink bath and at the same time drank cocktails, such as a Brandy Alexander. My Nanna Marie's favourite drink. Thinking I was sophisticated! Ha!

Then, we went to the local Glen Innes Returned Services League (RSL) Club. A week before my birthday, I had seven moles removed, two from my lower right arm. They were sent away for testing for cancer and came back clear. I had the stitches out that day — yes, on my birthday. I was told to be careful with the newly formed scars.

I was with my friends, and I couldn't wait for a night of drinking and dancing. It was my first time out legally being allowed to drink. By that stage, I'd had a fair bit to drink. I wore a grandpa-style, cream long-sleeved T-shirt that buttoned up the front and an emerald green cable knit tube skirt nearly to my ankles. It was a hideous green colour and my shoes were brown, yes, brown snakeskin pumps (oh groan, it was the late 80s!)

I was asked to dance by a guy who was a schoolteacher at the local Catholic school. The dance floor was big and empty. There was no one up dancing. I didn't want to get up. I told him no several times. He grabbed my arm, and I didn't move. He then stood on a chair to get more leverage and pulled me to get up. I felt something pop as I got up, but I didn't pay much attention to it. By this stage, I'd started drinking Bacardi and Coke. I was out dancing on the dance floor. I remember looking down and seeing a substantial puddle of blood on the RSL floor. My hand felt wet. It was blood! I looked at my hand and arm and realised that he had reopened the wounds from the removal of the moles on my arm.

I was so embarrassed.

I had moved my arm across my bottom while dancing, as you do, and the white shirt had soaked up some of the blood. It looked like I had my period and was leaking! I was horrified. My friend took me to the bathroom. We got a paper towel and wrapped it around my arm, and she washed the blood off my top and dried it with the hand dryer. She then took me to the front desk. They wanted to call an ambulance to take me to the hospital. There was no way I was going to the hospital on my birthday. I said no and to patch me up. They got the first aid kit out, put a large pad over it, taped it up, and off I went to continue the party. I'd deal with it the next day.

The night was huge — two bottles of Bacardi, the second one from Mum's alcohol stash. I had decided to have the first of many after-the-pub parties at home when Mum was away, also known as an after-party. That second bottle went down straight without a mixer at the party around the fire in my backyard. The police liked to pop in, say hello, and get us to turn the music down at about 3 am.

I woke up the next day, extremely hungover, with a man in my bed, with my arm throbbing and a huge mess to clean up, not just with the house and the backyard, but also with my arm. When I took the pad off, I saw holes cut deep into my arm with all my flesh exposed. I knew I needed it stitched again. I went to visit Dr Early, who, ironically, was again late — the same doctor who took my appendix out. He went to give me a local anaesthetic, but I told him I didn't want it.

I was well and truly still drunk and didn't want to add drugs to the mix. So he stitched me back up without painkillers. Before they were ripped open, I had two nice, minor scars. Now I have horrible-looking scars on my right forearm — a permanent reminder of that night. I knew I didn't want to dance that night, especially with him. He never apologised for the damage he caused to me. Looking back, it was an assault. No means no in all contexts.

I would spend a lot of time at night with my girlfriends. I hated being at home. During the week, we would either be parked in the centre of Grey St or 'chucking laps' up and down that street. I can't tell you how many laps I've 'chucked' in the past 35+ years. Even now, when I return to Glen Innes, the first thing I do is 'chuck' a lap!

Glen Innes had a hotel on every corner of Grey Street, the main street. Each pub had a different clientele. One was for cow cockies (aka farmers), one for rugby union players, one for rugby league players, and so on. On Thursday nights, we would be at the New Tattersalls Hotel; on Friday nights, we would start at the RSL and do a pub crawl down to the Royal Hotel, then head to the Ampol Roadhouse service station for a feed before heading home. Saturday nights found us at the Royal Hotel, where we would catch live music at the local pubs, followed by a Sunday session at the Royal or Tatts. This was our life every single week.

The next month was April, and ANZAC Day, which saw all of us go to the pubs to watch the game two-up. We started at the RSL with a crowd of a few hundred people, and ended the night at the Royal Hotel. I had a couple of drinks, but I wouldn't say I was drunk that night.

There was a crowd of men that you would call the popular guys. The guys who drove the 'done-up' muscle cars and dressed cool. The gym junkies, muscles, tan bodies and sly smiles. They had mullet haircuts and hung around as roadies for rock bands. They could have any girls they chose. Their egos were bigger than Ben Hur and their '80s hairdos!

Mum was still away in Sydney in hospital; she had been there for nearly two months. I took the leader of the pack home, M3, who had that look of Thor. I was in shock that M3 wanted to come home with me! I was so naive. I had no self-confidence. I still thought I wasn't good enough. I was easy prey. I had a vagina and a name for myself. All I just wanted was someone to love me.

I knew what we would do when we went home. Have sex. Again, I hoped it would lead to more than just one night. It didn't, and I'm glad it didn't. We started having sex. M3 was in total control. I had no power. None. He held me down on my belly. His weight was on top of me. I said "No!" There is no way to say this nicely. He raped me anally. I screamed for him to stop. I screamed "NO!" He had his hand over my mouth, muffling my screams as he pushed my head into a pillow.

I tried to get out from under him. I was trapped. M3 told me that no one would believe me if I told them what he had done, as everyone had seen us leave the pub together, and everyone knew I was a slut. It would be his word against mine, and they would believe him and never someone like me.

He finished, got up and left. I sat in my room sobbing and bleeding. Me taking him home did not give him the right to do what he did. I was disgusted with myself, was bleeding and stood in a long, hot shower, trying to get clean. If only I could have washed my mind. I didn't ask to be raped. I screamed for help, but no one came running. Just as Mum said all those years earlier, no one would be there for me. She was right.

Years later, I learnt the term 'date rape'. I had been date-raped. He was a nasty, vile, evil man. This has affected me for close to 30 years. Something I've always been ashamed about. It is no longer my burden to carry. It is his! Karma took care of him, as he is now an overweight hermit with no one in his life and has let himself go.

Life moved on and I tried to put a smile on my face, yet I had so much anger building inside me.

Mum and I joined Amway. We were promised we would make millions. I became a business owner at the age of 18. Was that to be my ticket out of Glen Innes? We bought the $7 tape of the week and the $20 book of the month. We went to meetings. We bought the toothpaste and the washing powder and started selling them to everyone we knew. We didn't keep up the momentum and, after 12 months, stopped buying it and stopped doing the business. We had become failures. That was how I always saw myself.

Sundays in Winter saw us follow the local rugby league team, the Magpies. My friends and I would rug up and go and watch at least two football games. The reserves would play first, followed by the A grade, either at a home game or travelling 100km to a neighbouring town.

I wanted to fit in. My friends were dating the players, and I was always the third wheel. They would hold their annual footballers' ball. We didn't have formal dress shops in town. We would pick fabric from the local material shop and find a dressmaker to make our gowns. I wore an electric blue taffeta dress with a sweetheart neckline, puffy sleeves with bows on each shoulder, a yoke waist, a bow adorning my bottom and a full skirt that finished at ankle length. I wore white pumps with little blue bows from the same fabric that I 'Blu Tacked' onto my shoes. My hair had grown to shoulder length. I wore diamond heart earrings, pink eye shadow and pink lipstick. I thought I looked like a princess! No one even noticed me.

1990 came around fast, and Simon was selected for the Australian Army as a diesel mechanic. Mum was over the moon. She had wanted him to enlist. I was accepted for Goulburn TAFE. I was so excited I started packing straight away. Simon had his farewell party for his 18th birthday. We had been fighting more and more. Not just verbally but physically as well. Two large fights come to mind. I don't even know what started them. We had a punch-up in the sunroom, and I managed to get him to the ground and then sat on the beanbag on his head. The next thing, a fist came from under the beanbag and connected with my lip. I bellowed in pain. No one came running. Mum was outside. She ignored the yelling. The other time was in the kitchen when Simon chased me with a knife. He didn't get me. I, however, waited for him to be sitting in the lounge room and went up behind him and whacked him over the head with a Chinese cooking wok. He had to go through a few different tests to get into the Army because he had sustained a concussion. We were both as bad as each other.

I was so jealous of the relationship he had with Mum. Growing up, he could never do anything wrong in her eyes. Until he got a girlfriend. Mum didn't like my brother's girlfriend. It wouldn't have mattered who she was. She was jealous of their relationship.

Mum was getting harder to live with. She would argue with everything I said or did. I was unaware that she had a form of dementia caused by her MS. It wasn't until 2022 that I was even aware that that was possible. Everything then made sense about memory and how nasty she became in her final years.

Simon left for the army three months before I commenced my studies. Goulburn was located 10 hours south of where I lived. As Simon was marching out of basic training in a huge parade, Mum thought she would travel to Albury on the train and conveniently have me hop off the train at Goulburn to start my studies. It was something I'll never forget.

We left Glen Innes, and I had three very large blue, red and white striped bags full of everything I would need until I could get home to bring more belongings. The first leg of the trip saw us go from Glen Innes to Strathfield Station, where my grandparents picked us up, and we stayed the night at their home. The next day, Mum, Nanna and I boarded the train south. After just over two hours, we pulled into Goulburn railway station, and I quickly said my goodbyes and hopped off the train. I didn't know where my luggage was. I started to panic.

As the train pulled away, I could see the stripes of my bags on the other platform. I gathered my belongings, more scared and alone than I'd ever been, and caught a taxi to the campus that was about to become my home. I had organised my accommodation before leaving. But it turned out that I was a day early, and I stood there all alone with the doors locked shut. My anxiety was massive. How could she have left me all alone in a strange town where I knew no one? When all my friends started studying, their parents took them and their belongings to settle them in. To make sure they were safe. But I wasn't good enough. The 'golden' child always came first. Years later, my nanna apologised for leaving me at the station. She felt equally horrified.

I managed to find the caretaker of the accommodation. He was a man in his mid-70s who clearly had a drinking problem, but I was so grateful that he let me into my room. I locked myself in and put the desk and the chair in front of the door. I had no phone and no food. There was no one I could call. I was too far away to walk into the town for food. I knew no one. I was so scared and cried myself to sleep the first night.

Mum finally made contact weeks later when she was back home. I took the train home after about 4 weeks to pick up my HQ Holden. On this return trip home, I noticed Mum wasn't looking after herself very well. After that, I would call her on Sundays, and she would comment that she had been in bed for days. I started going home every second weekend. This was taxing on my body and was affecting my studies. I would make sure that Mum always had enough food and was ok, then leave on Sunday by 2 pm to be back home at midnight for classes the next morning. A 20-hour round trip.

I got a job at McDonald's in Goulburn as an 18-year-old, which at the time was considered old to start working there. One of my first tasks was cleaning the pickles off the windows. People thought it was funny to throw them up as high as they could and watch them slide down, leaving a big mess of mustard and ketchup. While working on the burgers, I would reach into the pickle bucket full of pickles and brine, with a plastic, food-safe glove on, and bring out the pickles. I could never see the point of the glove, as it would be full of pickles that got trapped inside it with my hand. Disgusting. If I worked a 4-hour shift, I was allowed to eat a junior meal, which was a junior burger or cheeseburger, small fries and a small drink. If it was a 6-hour or longer shift, we were upgraded to a larger burger and chips and a drink. While working there, my eating disorder developed even further. My mental state was suffering. I hated working there.

I was torn between wanting to follow my dreams and my passion, and knowing Mum wasn't well. Her MS was progressing. After nearly 10 months, I made the gut-wrenching decision to return home and stay there. I promised myself that I'd return to studying music one day. I broke that promise to myself — I never returned to it. I am still sad about that even today. I have recently tried to learn the drums again and play my piano. That part of my brain is damaged. What I did manage to do on my return was start up a little business teaching piano, and I did that for the next 10 years. I needed a job that I could do around my caring duties.

I got a job at the Ampol Roadhouse as a short-order cook, with my past experience at the other service station when I was 16 years old. I would mostly work the midnight shift and every weekend. My social life was non-existent. Here I was serving all my friends on a Friday and Saturday night from the opposite side of the counter. Seeing them all drunk turned me off drinking — well, for a few years. Working nights meant I was mostly home for Mum during the day if something went wrong, even if I was sleeping, and I could tuck her into bed at night before I had to start my shift.

My girlfriend, who lived over the road, knew of my struggle with Mum and saw where I was working. She worked at a pharmacy and had heard that another was hiring a bookkeeper/pharmacy assistant. In small country towns, most jobs weren't advertised, as word-of-mouth was enough to spread news of the vacancy.

I applied for the position and had an interview with the head pharmacist. I was offered the job. It turned out my advanced certificate of commerce did come in handy. I had to have my white uniform dress custom made, as I couldn't find anything in town that was long enough or wide enough to fit me.

My job was to pay all the accounts and handle the pharmacy staff pay, and if it got really busy in the shop, to serve as well. I had to make sure the accounts were paid before their due date, as it meant thousands of dollars in discounts. This was before electronic bank transfers, and so I had to handwrite all the cheques and get them in the post so they could be postmarked before the due date. It was a very stressful job, but I eventually came to enjoy working with numbers.

I excelled at maths in school. I was in 2 unit math in senior school but the homework level was an issue, and I dropped a unit and went back into what was called general maths, or the politically incorrect term we used to use was 'veggie' maths. English was my worst subject all the way through high school, so I was in veggie English too in my senior years.

I worked hard at that job. Our head pharmacist used to come in and joke that we were the fattest pharmacy in town. This did nothing for my self-esteem. Nowadays, he would be breaking the law by doing that.

A few weeks later, there was an incident at work. We could not leave to go on our lunch breaks until the person before us had returned from theirs. If they were late returning, it made the rest of us late. The girl before me was 20 minutes late. So I left late and I came back to work early, cutting my lunch break by 10 minutes. The Pharmacist was angry that I was 'late' back to work from lunch, even though I wasn't. I tried to explain what had happened. He cut me off and yelled at me. His reply was, "If you don't like working here, you can leave!" It was a Friday afternoon. I was in the middle of doing everyone's pay. The shop was busy. I packed up my things, including my typewriter, and walked past him, then walked out.

He asked another senior employee if she thought I'd be back. Her reply was, "Not likely, not after the way you treated her!" She rang me over the weekend and told me that if I apologised, I could have my job back on Monday. I was gobsmacked. I had to apologise for coming back to work early from lunch. My reply was no way. I was done. Which also meant I was unemployed!

I joined Amway for the second time. I was going to be rich! I joined a branch called IDA, also known as the International Dream Association. I have joined Amway four times in my lifetime, and yes, I'm currently a distributor, but I don't actively go to any meetings. Let me explain what that means.

As a distributor, I paid Amway a yearly membership fee, which then gave me the right to resell their product. I had an up line, the person who sponsored me into the business, and then they had someone, right up to the top with the person who actually owned Amway . In order to keep someone motivated to sell any multi-level marketing business and sponsor people under you, you need to have a good motivational program attached to it. This is where IDA comes in. They tell you that in order to make it big in the business (I never made it big in Amway), there were certain things you 'should' do:

1) Tape of the week: This little tape was purchased every week on a subscription, filtered down through our upline for $7 a week/tape. What was on these tapes, I hear you ask? There were recordings, mostly of

Americans in the business at 'pep rallies', what we would call 'conferences' in Australia. Each one had a different theme, and we were always reminded that there was no difference between those on the tapes and us. Yeah right! They were the ones who were making money, and we were the ones handing it out to our up line.

2) Book of the month: These books were about $20 a month, and I still have some of them today. Great reads by authors like Zig Ziglar, Dale Carnegie and Brian Tracy.

3) Weekly meeting: usually on every Monday night.

4) A monthly seminar, which was held three hours away from me.

5) A 6-monthly rally/conference in a major capital city. The biggest one I attended was at the Brisbane Entertainment Centre, with over 15,000 people in attendance. Zak was a baby, and you were not allowed to bring children to these events as they recorded them for Tape of the Week. I was so fixated on the 'cult' (did I say that out loud?), that I paid for a nanny to come away for the weekend to look after him while I went to the conference. He was about 4 months old. I thought I was creating a better future for both of us.

I learnt a lot of my foundations in the business marketing world from my time in Amway in the early days:

- Discipline.
- Self-marketing.
- Budgeting.
- Cash management.
- Goal setting.
- Dream building.
- Vision boards.
- Team building.
- How to think big.
- How to turn family and friends against you when they didn't see your big dream.
- How to apply make-up and face care, and sell it to everyone I knew.

- How to dress for business.
- How to use business cards. My first one read J.D.Martin and Associates.
- How not to tell someone you sell Amway, which had by then become a dirty word.
- How to keep a diary.
- How to upsell.
- How to burn through cash and not make much.
- How to use cleaning products
- Time management skills.
- How to sell above your own budget.
- How to not make much money yet not show the world.
- How to network.
- How to be brainwashed.
- How to sell your soul to the devil and come back from it.
- How to make friends.
- How to avoid meetings.
- How to think you were going to be rich one day.
- How to think on your feet.
- How to draw circles.
  AND
- How to eventually say no!

I stayed in IDA until 1995. I never made any money once I took all the expenses into account. I went back to using store-bought washing powder and toothpaste.

In 1991, Simon and Marissa got engaged and returned home from the Army for their engagement party on her family's farm at Pinkett. Mum refused to attend. I felt so sorry for Simon and Marissa. I was his only family member who attended. When the photos returned from the evening, there were a couple of nice shots of Simon, Marissa and me. Mum cut up the photos. She cut my sister-in-law out of every one.

After everything that happened, I was turned off drinking for a while and I barely had a social life. But it did not last. I did not have the tools to cope, and eventually I slipped back into old habits. I started going out again, three nights a week, chasing distraction and pretending I was fine.

I was going out three nights a week. I met a guy at the pub M3, and for about 6 weeks, we would go home drunk together on a Friday or Saturday night. I wasn't on any birth control. I stopped 'seeing' him, and then discovered I was pregnant. I plucked up enough courage to go and visit him to tell him. I was terrified, not of telling him, but of telling my own mother.

I knocked on the door and said we needed to talk. He didn't invite me inside. We instead sat on the front step of his house. I told him I was pregnant, and he replied after a long pause that he would support me in any decision I would make. Ok, I get the whole 'my body, my rights'. However, I felt that he would never be there to support me, especially when I needed it. I saw a flash of what my future would be like, and it wasn't good.

Telling Mum still haunts me. When I told her, the first thing that came out of her mouth was that she wasn't old enough to be a grandmother, and I had to get rid of it. Mum didn't talk to me for days, convinced that I was wrecking her life. I didn't realise until years later that my mum was a narcissist. I didn't even know what a narcissist was, or that I was a magnet attracting them.

I made the tough decision and booked in for a termination. I paid the $200 and never returned to the father of the unborn child to ask for help. My best friend and I drove to Tweed Heads the Friday night after work. We stayed in a cheesy hotel up the street from the clinic, and on a Saturday morning, we went to walk in. It was situated in what looked like a four storey office building. Downstairs at the front door were protesters with placards. I felt bad enough about what I was going through, let alone having to fight our way through that. Once inside, my nerves tripled. I felt so scared.

I remember having a cry and feeling so torn and alone, even though my best friend was sitting in the waiting room waiting for me. I had the procedure done, we left and drove the five hours back home. When I got home that night, Mum did not even ask how I was. She only asked if I had got it done. I was heartbroken. I never saw the guy who impregnated me again.

That was one of those moments where I did not get the comfort I needed, so I learnt to survive without it. I hardened the fuck up on the outside because I had no choice. But what I did not realise then was that something else was forming underneath the shock and grief. That was MOXIE. Not confidence. Not bravery. Just the raw determination to keep going when no one was holding my hand. The kind of strength you build when you have to carry the pain quietly and still show up for your own life.

1986 Work experience at The Land Newspaper, NSW

1989 Mum and me in the kitchen in Meade Street, Glen Innes, NSW

1989 Partying at the Royal Hotel, Grey Street, Glen Innes, NSW

1990 Mum at Simon's Farewell and 18th Birthday Party

1990 Mum, Simon and myself in Meade Street, Glen Innes.

1990 My dorm room at Goulburn TAFE

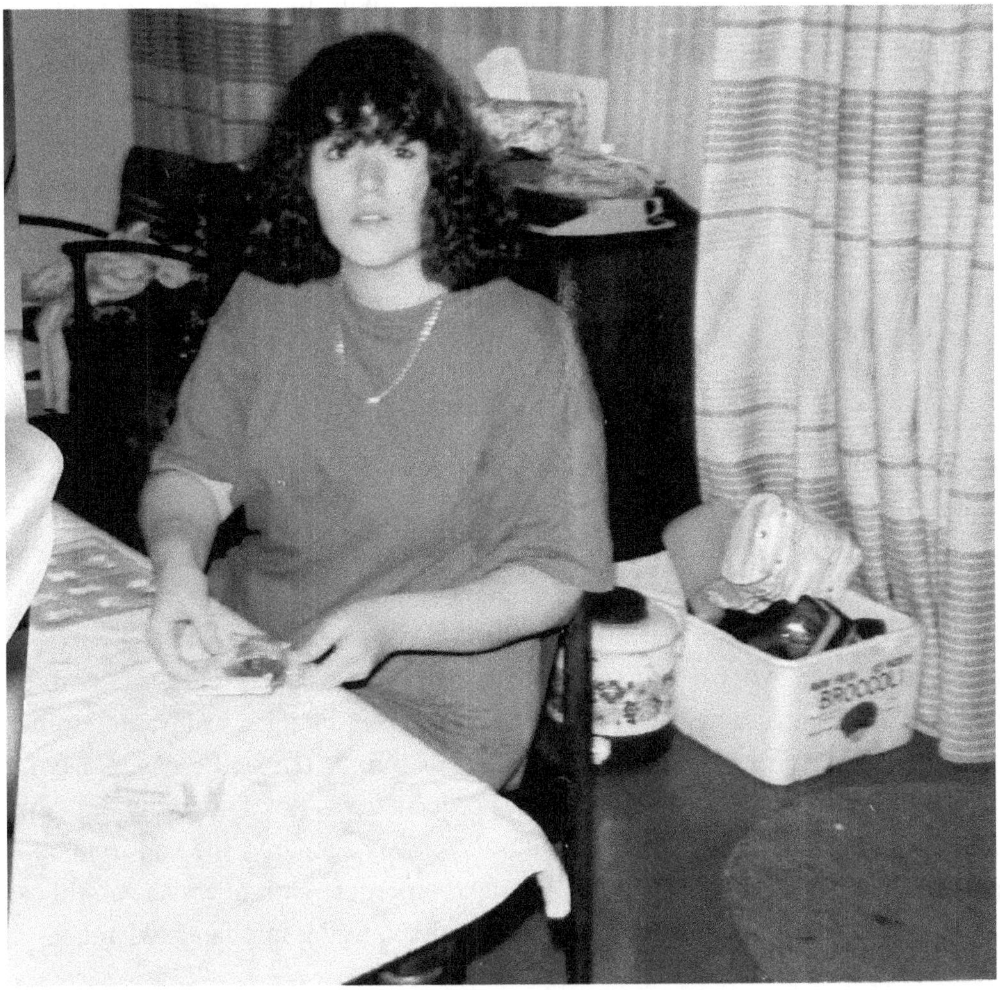

1992 Making lamingtons

CHAPTER 7

Herbs and Spices

I met M4 in 1992 at the Central Hotel in Glen Innes. We locked eyes, and he took my breath away. He told me not to look at him with those eyes. I laughed at his pickup line.

M4 was from out of town but was best mates with a guy I went to school with. We hooked up that night and spent the whole weekend together.

From that weekend, we kept in contact. He would call me from the phone booth up the road from the caravan park where he lived at Katingal, one of the outer suburbs of Tamworth. This was years before mobile phones. M4 was recently discharged from the Australian Navy, where he started as a boiler maker and then transferred to a clearance diver. He was divorced, and had a 4-year-old daughter who lived in Perth.

M4 would come up and stay for the weekends, or I would drive the two hours south to be with him. I was in love — my first true love and genuine relationship. I was 21 years old. I had never had anyone love me. Mind you, he never told me that he loved me. Not once. I chose to ignore that fact. Red flag! I had convinced myself that he loved me. After all, he was ringing me to ask me to visit him. It didn't worry me that he lived, of all places, in a caravan park. That should have been another red flag.

I would drive the two hours south like a love-sick puppy. He was involved in drugs, and I chose to ignore each and every one of his red flags. I just wanted someone to love me and take me away from the life I was living. The hell I was in. My mum and I fought all the time. Having our roles reversed was not something either of us wanted. To parent your parent is not natural. I always ensured she had food cooked for her for the two nights I was away. She had emergency numbers she could call if she needed help. I welcomed the short breaks away, living in a fantasy land.

M4 said he was going to take a four-week trip to Perth to see his daughter. In his previous relationship, his ex-wife got caught having an affair with his best man from their wedding when M4 was apparently deployed out at sea.

I was on the pill but had recently taken a course of antibiotics for a nasty chest infection. Before I knew it, I was pregnant again. I was so excited; over the moon. I so wanted this baby. We would be a family. M4 wasn't impressed and still planned to go away. I was 13 weeks pregnant when he left, and he told me to get rid of 'it' as he kissed me goodbye through my car window from the service station car park across the road from the caravan park. I chose to ignore his request. I wanted his baby, and thought he would change his mind when he came back. Hindsight is an amazing thing. He told me that he would be back in four weeks' time.

I waited those long four weeks. I didn't hear a word from him. The old saying 'out of sight, out of mind' was so true for him. He didn't return, and I didn't have another termination. I wanted this baby. It would be mine to love. I stood up to Mum and told her I was pregnant and keeping it. Besides, by the time I told her I was too far along to abort. I can't remember what my mum said in response, but it didn't matter because my decision was made.

I had some spare time on my hands while being pregnant. Rather than let boredom overcome me, I volunteered to care for the first ever Aboriginal quintuplets. I worked 3 to 4 shifts a week. Helping feed, change nappies, bathe and play with all five babies. It was so much fun. I gained so much experience that when people would ask me how I was going to cope with being a single mum, I could reply confidently that it was going to be a breeze, at least for the first few years, as I had knowledge and experience that a lot of other first-time mums didn't.

I had taken up a hobby of creating slip ceramics, also known as hobby ceramics, that year. We would buy the greenware, which had been cast in a mould into an item. It could be a knick-knack or a kitchen item, such as bowls, mugs or even plates. Then we would use underglazes or paints, depending on the item, to create the final product, and it would be fired in a kiln.

I loved doing it and had become so good at it that I won many awards for my work. In late 1994, I had a side business supplying five gift shops in the New England region — the money I was making helped supplement my income. I continued to supply shops until 1998, and then still created items for my personal use until 2004. I walk into my children's homes nowadays and can see the handful of items that I made for them both. I often wonder whose homes or op shops all the rest sit in.

1992 saw my neighbour Nelly, who worked at the Commonwealth Employment Services (CES) recommend me for a job. A mystery shopper for a Sydney-based company. They were looking for people to pretend to be shoppers in clothing stores such as Suzanne Gray, take-away venues such as Pizza Hut and KFC and banks like Westpac, Commonwealth and St George Building Society. I was paid for each survey I did, about $10, and that money I then had to declare to Centrelink. I was also paid 55 cents per km I travelled to do the survey. Doesn't sound much — and it wasn't! However, they would pay me to drive from Glen Innes, NSW, to Texas, Queensland, which was a 450km round trip, and that money I didn't have to declare. I had a little blue Barina, and it ran on the smell of an oil rag.

I would put Mum in the car, her wheelchair in the back, and off we would go. My area went from south of Uralla to North of Stanthorpe, Texas and Moree out west and sometimes Grafton to the east and every little town in between. It was a saving grace giving me that extra income. So Amway and mystery shopping were keeping me alive.

I didn't have an easy pregnancy. I spotted blood for months, praying I wouldn't lose the baby. I also had horrible morning sickness for the whole pregnancy. I couldn't hold down much food; however, it was all worth it knowing I would have someone who would love me.

I went to Tamworth at the end of January for Country Music Week and stayed with one of M4's sisters, T. She said she would stick by me and my baby. It was so hot and humid. I was so sick, vomiting in the gutter; people were thinking I was just drunk, but I was far from it. I would still be ill, even a month after I gave birth. It was a horrible pregnancy, with a few trips to hospital thrown in as well to help with the morning sickness.

I was sitting in the Tamworth RSL club. T was out dancing, and a guy was chatting with me. He seemed very nice, yet very familiar. His name was Lee. I felt fat, uncomfortable, and tired as it was very late at night. Lee's sister Tania was up dancing, and we chatted about the festival.

We had been to many different venues, so I explained all the good and the bad I'd seen. The next day, I was walking through the Kmart mall, and there he was — the man I was chatting to the night before — only bigger and hanging from the ceiling on a large life-size cardboard cut out! I had been talking to the famous Australian country music singer Lee Kernigan and didn't even realise who he was.

Despite the morning sickness, I loved being pregnant and feeling my baby's movements, growing more in love with them every day. I was five and a half months pregnant and had been volunteering at the Glen Innes Show at the show society at the BBQ at the bar. The smash-up car derby was underway, and we all made our way to the show ring to wait for the cars to collide with each other.

It is always the highlight of the end of the show. We were standing on the benches to get a better view when a really drunk guy tripped and pushed me from behind. I flew into the air. My belly ended up being pushed into the post of the fence of the main ring of the showgrounds. I screamed. A large crowd was around, all standing on the benches, unaware I had been injured.

My friend Michaela was with me; she raised the alarm and said that I needed emergency help. I was transported to the hospital via ambulance. I spent 48 hours under observation in the Glen Innes Hospital. I had luckily avoided any significant injury to me and the baby, just a large bruise on my belly from the fence post. We were very, very lucky.

I bought a bassinet for $20 and set it up in my bedroom. It was a tight fit. I bought a little electric heater. We had a wood heater in the lounge room, which kept that room warm, but not the rest of the house. We had diesel central heating, but Mum would only run it a few times during winter as it was so expensive to operate. We froze the rest of the time.

Our hot water system also ran on diesel, and it would freeze in winter, or the pilot light would go out, and I would have to go outside in minus degrees in the morning to light it. How I never blew up myself, or the house, amazes me even today. The house was freezing throughout winter.

I was due to give birth at the end of May 1993. I had kept Nanna and Aunty Lyn updated on regular phone calls about my pregnancy. I knew I would have someone who would love me and be mine. I couldn't wait to be a mum.

My pregnancy concluded without further drama. I fell pregnant at 100kg. I went to have the baby at 99kg. I was lighter at 41 weeks pregnant than before I fell pregnant. The one upside to having morning sickness for nine months!

I had massive cravings for two unusual items of food for me. Raw meat — steak, to be precise. I would stand at the meat counter in the supermarket wanting to rip the plastic cling film off and bite into it. The other craving was Caramello koalas. I loved them; I would buy a bag of them. Mum would have to hide the bag as she would hear me eating lots of them at night. That was back when I could eat chocolate, unlike nowadays with my intolerances and allergies. Mum was getting excited about becoming a grandmother.

I asked Nanna and Parpa to come up and look after Mum while I went in to have the baby. I was due on 28th May 1993. They had come up a few days before I was due, in case I went early. I was so grateful that they were there, as I wasn't sure what I was going to do with Mum otherwise.

The stress I was under was massive. I had not heard from M4 since he left in October of the year before and had no way of contacting him in Perth. None of his family had heard from him either. I was fearful of being a sole parent. I wondered how I would handle having a baby and looking after Mum as well. I wondered where he was, hoping that he would come back to us, as I was still madly in love with him.

My support partner for the birth was the mother of one of my school friends, Diana, whom I had become very close to. She was good friends with Mum and was one of the few who knew how hard things had become at home.

She had seen the psychological changes in Mum over the previous 18 months. Diana had become a second mother to me.

At my 40-week mark, I wasn't feeling my usual self. I had a doctor's appointment, scheduled on Monday 31st May. It was freezing. Glen Innes is the coldest town in the country on average. I had been wearing opaque stockings and tube skirts. I hadn't had a bikini wax or shaved since M4 had left. I had a forest of growth. I thought maybe i was being chaffed from the stockings and the hair. But something didn't feel right. I had an itch and pain. I thought maybe I had thrush or chaffing.

I told my doctor of my concerns. He had been my doctor since I was 14 years old. I couldn't see past my huge belly, even if I tried to use a mirror! I had a patch about the size of a 50-cent piece that was so painful and wasn't getting better. I'd had it there for a few days. I was feeling so uncomfortable with the pregnancy and wasn't sure what was happening.

My doctor took a swab of it and sent it to pathology. He then explained that he thought it was genital herpes — WTAF! I couldn't believe what he was saying. He went on to explain that if I went into labour before the results had come back, it would result in me having a caesarean, as having an active outbreak of genital herpes is extremely dangerous for the baby during birth. It can cause the baby to go blind, cause brain damage, or even cause death.

Just like when a person kisses a baby with a cold sore on their mouth, which can lead to the same symptoms. I was told the results would be back the next day. My world was spinning.

I drove straight to Diana's house and told her what was happening. I was a mess. Crying and shaking. Unsure what was going to happen. Diana calmed me down, and I headed home to where Mum, Nanna and Parpa were. I had to act like everything was okay. It wasn't. I was under pressure from Parpa. He wanted to go back home to Sydney, and it was an inconvenience having to look after Mum, his own daughter.

Tuesday afternoon had come around, and I had no signs of labour. I went in to find out the results. It was negative. A massive sigh of relief came over me. My doctor then explained that I could have a natural birth. However, if I hadn't started labour by Friday morning, I would have to be induced. I showed no signs of labour at 41 weeks.

Each day passed, and nothing happened. There were no signs of labour. It was a very long wait. Friday morning at 8 am, I got dropped off by my grandfather at the Glen Innes Hospital and walked in by myself, alone and scared. No one was there for me, just like my mum had warned me 15 years earlier.

I had my observations done by the nurse — I went to school with her sons. It's a small town where everyone knows each other; she put the gel in to ripen my cervix and bring on labour. Now, I just had to wait for it to work. I sat in my room and cried. I was doing this by myself. This is not what I had thought would happen. Where had the happy family picture I had imagined gone? M4 still didn't make contact.

I'm never a patient person. I was so excited and scared to meet my baby and start my new life as a mum. At 10.30 am, my doctor came in and did an internal. My baby was fully wedged down my birth canal. He decided to hurry things along and break my waters at 1cm dilated by putting on a finger glove with a hook on the end. It's a bit like a crochet hook.

I have a posterior cervix, and it was excruciating. But things started to happen. I wore nappies folded in my undies and walked up and down the hallway and up and down the hospital stairs by myself. This was not how I thought I'd have my first child, as a single mum. I had dreamt of getting married and being in a loving, committed relationship like many of my friends and my brother. But I wasn't.

At around 12.30 pm, the nurse came in and told me that my test on Monday had returned. I was confused as I had already had the results. It turned out that the results were wrong. It was a false negative.

Pathology had stuffed it up.

How the hell does that happen?

I stood in the hallway when she told me the results were positive. No privacy. No support. I had genital herpes. The world was spinning. I burst into tears and started shaking. My fears turned to my unborn baby. I had several internals, and they had broken my waters, all while having an active outbreak. That was extremely dangerous for my baby.

The nurse explained that I would have to have an emergency cesarean. I asked her to call Diana for me. I returned to my room and cried. I was so scared and felt dirty. Dirty and ashamed.

What would people think of me when they found out?

What would Mum say?

I was worried that the town would find out — oh, the embarrassment.

The shame.

Who had given it to me? Was it M4, or had it happened before him?

It's taken me 33 years to write this openly. I have told a few people over the years. Long-term partners. It's incredible how many people actually carry the herpes virus in all its different types. Here are some facts on Herpes.

HSV-1 and HSV-2 are two types of the herpes simplex virus. HSV-1 usually causes cold sores around the mouth and lips, but it can also cause genital herpes through oral sex. HSV-2 mainly causes genital herpes and is spread through sexual contact. Both types are lifelong infections that can stay dormant in the body and sometimes flare up again. While there is no cure, antiviral medications can help manage symptoms and reduce the risk of passing the virus to others.

To calculate the combined prevalence of HSV-1 and HSV-2, we must be careful not to double-count people with both types. But for a simple estimate, here's a rough idea:

- HSV-1: 67% of people
- HSV-2: 13% of people
- Some people have both, so the total combined rate is around 70–80% of the global population.

So what does that mean?

If we use the lower estimate of 70%, then:

- 1 in every 1.4 people has some form of herpes.

Or more simply:

- About 7 out of 10 people have herpes (either HSV-1, HSV-2, or both).

It's much more common than most people realise — and many people never have symptoms or even know they have it.

It is socially acceptable for people to have cold sores on their mouths, faces and noses. You wouldn't kiss someone with a cold sore. The only difference with genital herpes is that it's at the opposite end of the body. A place most people are too embarrassed or ashamed to talk about.

Well hang on, because I'm about to talk about it.

When having an outbreak, you cannot have sex. I have to take pills called Valtrex when I feel I am having an outbreak to help suppress it. When I was going through Chemotherapy, I had to increase my dose to twice daily.

It's taken many, many years to come to terms with it. Not least due to the way people talk and make jokes about it, like it's some vile and shameful thing. It's not pleasant to have, for sure. Can someone please explain to me why it's so different? Why one is accepted, and one isn't, when it's the same virus?

Yes, it's painful. I've learnt what my body does when it's about to have an outbreak. I get nerve pain from the back of my left leg from my knee to my thigh. It runs on a nerve line. So, as soon as I feel that intense pain, I don't have sex and increase the medication Valacyclovir (Valtrex). I take this daily to reduce the outbreaks and the risk of passing the virus on. I take responsibility for not passing it on. It's agony for 48 hours. Then, a tingling and itch. It can happen anywhere around the genitals and anus and is extremely painful at the same time when the outbreak occurs. Then it blisters, and then it crusts up, just like on the mouth. The length of time it lasts depends on your own body. Without medication, it can last for 2 weeks. With Valtrex, it heals a lot sooner. It doesn't tend to leave scars. But it will repeat in the same places. Stress, lack of sleep, lack of exercise, and poor diet, such as highly processed foods, cause more frequent outbreaks, and more pain.

I have in the past told casual partners about having it, only to be told, 'Oh, I've got that too', in such a blasé way, as if it's unimportant. Um, when were you going to tell me you had it? If I hadn't broached the subject first, would they have told me? Probably not — I often didn't tell people I was casually sleeping with. If a relationship was to become serious, I always made sure they knew I had it. I have never passed it on to any long-term partners. Using condoms doesn't always stop the spread, as it depends on the location of the blisters and skin-on-skin contact.

You can also contract it through oral sex. If a person had cold sores on their mouth and they performed oral sex on you, violà — transferred. As simple as that. Do I know who gave it to me? Maybe, but I can't be entirely sure. Researching after Zakariah was born, I discovered that I had probably had it for at least a few years.

It doesn't show up in females first as blisters but as a little split or crack on the vulva, and that had been happening for some time. The stress of the birth had caused it to flourish. My next partner, M5, gave it the nickname 'Herbs and Spices', as he couldn't stand the word Herpes.

Zakariah, at the age of 10, had chickenpox. A virus from the herpes family causes chickenpox and shingles, but it's a different type.

- Chickenpox is caused by the varicella-zoster virus (VZV).
- After you recover from chickenpox, the virus stays dormant in your body and can reactivate later in life as shingles (also called herpes zoster).

So, while HSV-1 or HSV-2 doesn't cause chickenpox and shingles, they are part of the herpes virus family — just a different member.

To break it down:

- Herpesviridae is the virus family.
- HSV-1 – usually cold sores
- HSV-2 – usually genital herpes
- VZV – causes chickenpox and shingles.

These viruses can stay dormant in the body and reactivate later — a key feature of herpes viruses. Zakariah had chickenpox on his eyeballs. He was given an eye ointment to help treat the blisters on his eyes. There was some leftover, and I was having an outbreak, so I thought I'd try it. It worked! It alleviated the itch and pain of the blisters and accelerated recovery. It's been a game-changer.

Now, that's just been my experience. It may not work for you. But since 2002, I have told every doctor about my discovery to help more people. You ask for Aciclovir 3% eye ointment.

It turns out I am one of those rare people who doesn't have antibodies for herpes, which explains why I got a false negative. I also get cold sores and have had shingles twice.

With all the advances in medicine, there has been no advancement in treating the herpes virus in over 30 years. As I've mentioned, they now estimate that 7 in 10 people carry the virus. That's a lot of the population. I often stand in a crowded room and try to guess the ones who have it, as it doesn't discriminate.

It was a wake-up call for me. The next step could have been AIDS. I started using condoms, and my friends will tell you I've often talked about safe sex, especially to my children when they were teenagers. I never want anyone to go through what I've experienced.

I was only 22 years old. Alone, scared and ashamed. More shame than you could ever imagine. It is more acceptable for guys to have it. They are studs, and girls are sluts when they contract it. Regardless of your sex, no one deserves this.

Every year, Zakariah's birthday is a painful reminder of the day I was diagnosed. The day a false negative test became positive. The day my life changed forever.

I have lived with the shame for far too long. I now release all that shame and the weight of carrying it.

It has caused me to make decisions throughout my life — decisions I regret.

One thing HSV taught me was how to harden the fuck up. Not in a cold way, but in a survival way. It shaped my moxie because I had to learn how to keep going even when I felt ashamed, scared, and completely alone.

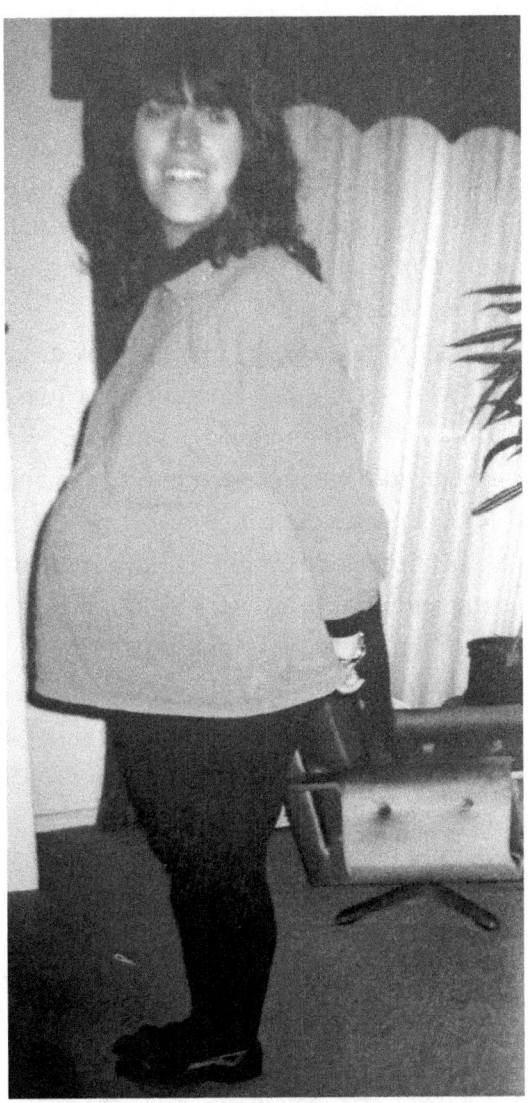

1993 The night before I gave birth to Zak, at 41 weeks pregnant, Meade Street, Glen Innes

CHAPTER 8
Z for Zakariah

The nurse called Diana. Within 20 minutes, she was up there with me. Things were happening so fast. They took Diana away to scrub up for the theatre. She was a nurse and knew what to prepare for. Another doctor came in and spoke about the epidural and the risks involved. I have low blood pressure at the best of times, which was a concern for the doctors.

My contractions were getting stronger. I had a shower and was put in a lovely dull blue hospital gown. I was so big that I had to wear two, with one facing each way to cover me. I had to sit very still on the edge of the bed, hunching over in a ball, and not move, while a long needle was inserted into my lower spine in between two vertebrae, all while I was having contractions.

The anaesthetic was then injected straight into my spine in between contractions to deaden me from chest level down. I lay back on the bed, waiting for the effect to start. Moments later, something didn't feel right. I had trouble hearing; the room was closing in. The anaesthetist took my blood pressure, and it wasn't good. 70/50. I started to panic. I thought I was dying. I was given some medication, and my blood pressure started to rise. At the same time, the nurse was inserting a catheter into my bladder.

I was then moved into the operating theatre. Everything was happening so fast. I had lost control. Life would never be the same again. I would be responsible for another little human. I had tears forming in my eyes. I had herpes! WTAF!

The anaesthetist then did a pinprick test across my big pregnant belly. Asking me if I could feel it. I said I could; his reply was "No, you don't!" I had the surgeon and my normal doctor start the cesarean with a cut across my lower belly. It hurt. They then proceeded to cut through the next layers. I screamed and held onto Diana's hand! My doctor turned to me and asked if I could feel them cutting. "YES!" I screamed in horror. I could, and it was the most painful thing I'd ever experienced.

My doctor then asked the anaesthesiologist to top up the epidural, but he was hesitant to do so, due to my low blood pressure.

They paused, and I was given the option of being put fully under anaesthetic — which would affect the baby as well as increase my recovery time — or to continue, and they would endeavour to get the baby out as quickly as they could; then they could give me something for the pain.

I chose to harden the fuck up, and chose the latter.

I was scared beyond belief. I had nurses holding down my legs to stop me from moving. My left hand squeezed Diana's hand so hard that I nearly broke her fingers, and my right arm was strapped down onto a board so I couldn't move it. It was horrific and terrifying.

I screamed for what seemed like forever. I had nightmares for a very long time after the birth. I felt the cuts; I felt them pull the skin back to make the hole bigger to pull the baby out of me. I felt terrible pain.

At 1.40 pm, I heard a tiny cry.

The little human growing inside of me was a boy! I had a son! Zakariah Michael Paul Martin-Taylor was the name I had chosen before giving birth. If he had been a girl, he would have been Jordyn Mickaela. As they pulled him out of me, Zakariah urinated on me and on both doctors. Everyone laughed. I remember lying there in complete shock and disbelief at what had just happened in a few hours, and the amount of pain I was in.

The nurse brought Zakariah up to my face. He was covered in blood and quite blue. I saw him for no more than 1 minute. She then took him away to get him checked, and my doctor gave me something for the pain; then they took their time stitching me back up. They cleaned up the theatre around me. I could hear my son crying for me as I cried, overcome with grief and shock when I should be the happiest I'd ever been. I felt so alone.

After about an hour, I was taken back to the ward and reunited with Zakariah. I got to hold him for the first time. He was perfect. 8lb 6oz, or 3,620 grams, 50 cm long and a head circumference of 36cm. Diana stayed with me for quite a while. I couldn't move. I lay flat on my back for a long period of time. Diana rang home to tell them that I had had a boy, and how the birth had gone. Nanna and Parpa visited briefly later that afternoon.

They both had cuddles with Zakariah and promised to bring Mum the next day to meet him. I didn't even have my mum there on that first day. She didn't come running, just like she said she wouldn't.

That evening, I was made to get out of bed and walk to the toilet. I thought the nursing sisters were cruel, but they were just doing their job. I tried to feed Zak, but my milk was taking forever to come in. No one explained to me that it would take longer after a C-section for your milk to come in.

The next day, Nanna brought Mum up in her wheelchair to see us. She had a cuddle with Zak, her first grandchild. Then she handed me a piece of paper. It had Zak's full name on it. M4 and I had picked out Zak's name before he had left in the previous October. Before he told me to abort the pregnancy. We both had read a book at school called Z for Zakariah, who was the last man left on earth.

- Zakariah would be his first name.
- Michael after M4's brother. At the time, Michael was dying from Hepatitis C.
- Paul was after my brother Simon's middle name.
- Martin-Taylor is a combination of both M4 and my last names. Hyphenated names were all the rage back then.

It all had a nice rhyme to it. However, my mum didn't think so. She had crossed out Michael and Taylor on the piece of paper and told me I was not to call him those names! I was so angry and upset. I told her to hand my son back, and asked Nanna to take her home because I didn't want to see her. He wasn't her baby, he was mine. I could name him whatever I wanted. His name wasn't changing! I felt so alone and upset. Fast forward 17 years, when Zak joined the Army, he rang me and cursed me for giving him five names, because of the number of times he had to write them all. Maybe I should have listened to her, although not for the reasons she wanted.

How was I ever going to cope at home with Mum the way she was, and protect my child? When she was trying to control everything.

On day 3, I developed a pain under my right ribs. To move, lying down or trying to sit up was excruciatingly painful. I could barely breathe. My doctor examined me. He thought maybe my gall bladder needed removing. I was being sent 100km south to Armidale for a CAT scan as our hospital didn't have that equipment. The only relief I got was when I walked. So I went up and down the hallway. It turned out to be a pocket of air trapped under my diaphragm from the surgery, which was a huge relief. It eventually passed.

I had lots of visitors in the hospital. Mum didn't come back to visit the whole week I was there. I felt so disappointed, and again as though I was not good enough. I didn't know what she would say or do when we went home.

I spent a lot of time crying that week. I was terrified of the world finding out my dirty little secret. I had to come up with a story as to why I had an emergency

Caesarean birth. I decided just to tell people that Zak got stuck and went into distress. A simple, plausible story that no one questioned.

A week after giving birth, I was allowed home. I walked out of the hospital with the lightest body weight I had in years. Nine months of morning sickness meant I hadn't put on any weight during my pregnancy. Parpa came to pick me up. It was snowing. I was under strict instructions not to lift anything heavier than Zak for six weeks or drive my car. I agreed just to get out of there, but I worried about how I would do things at home without any support.

When we got to the car, I asked for the car keys from Parpa. He was known as a terrible driver, and there was no way he was going to drive my newborn son home. Did I mention I wasn't allowed to drive? After I had been home a few hours I realised I needed things from the supermarket and chemist. So I put Zak in the car and drove us to the shops. Did I mention I wasn't allowed to drive? Did I mention I wasn't allowed to lift anything?

The next day, Nanna informed me that Parpa needed to get back to Sydney, which was an eight-hour drive south, and they would be leaving the next morning! I was terrified. How would I do everything? I went to my room and cried. I was so angry.

They departed in the early hours of the following day and left me with Mum in the wheelchair, a newborn baby and me recovering from being cut from hip to hip. So much for no lifting. I felt so alone. I hardened the fuck up.

You do what needs to be done. I had no choice. I had no help in looking after Mum and putting Mum in and out of the wheelchair, changing and washing her sheets after she soiled them every night, cooking and cleaning, grocery shopping, taking Mum to doctor appointments, breastfeeding and driving my car. I had to do it all. I had no help.

I took one week off from mystery shopping. A week later I put Mum, Zak and her wheelchair in the car and drove the 450km round trip to Texas to do a 5-minute survey at the NAB bank. I did what needed to be done to keep alive. I had moxie before I knew what it was.

At my six-week post-delivery checkup, my doctor explained to me that my name had been submitted to the Notifiable Diseases Database (NDD) for sexually transmitted diseases. I was horrified. I felt like a criminal. I was so ashamed and embarrassed, and I could tell no one. Nowadays, herpes is not included. I agonised over this for years.

Zak was never a good breastfeeder. He was always hungry. He fed for an hour, then was off for an hour. I fed him for 17 weeks. It was a nightmare. I was so tired and felt I was losing my sanity. I just didn't produce good milk, and looking back now, it was probably because of the stress I was under.

I didn't know where M4 was living, only that he was in Perth. I sent M4 a letter via his brother in Tamworth. In the letter were photos of Zak, a note asking M4 to please sign Zak's registration of birth and the official registration form.

I received the letter back about a month later. M4 had opened it and sent a letter back stating that he wasn't going to sign the registration forms as the baby wasn't his, and he refused to pay child support. He returned all the photos. At first I was gutted. I felt so alone and stupid. I felt the pain for Zak. Then I became furious.

During the relationship with him, I had not slept around in any way, shape or form; unlike him, who had been seeing a woman named Wendy, though he swore he wasn't. Every time I questioned him about her, he would say there wasn't enough beer on the planet for him to touch her. Yet every time I returned home during the week, they were sleeping together.

There was no way I was putting the father as 'unknown' on Zakariah's birth certificate when I knew exactly who his father was. I wanted M4 to take responsibility for his actions. I was trying to hold my shit together and put on a brave face when my dreams — ok, they were fantasies — came crashing down. He wasn't coming back to us. How could anyone walk away from their child?

I had Centrelink breathing down my neck to state who the father was and register the baby, or they weren't going to pay me any money for us to live on. I sat in disbelief. I was on the sole parent's pension, and I hated it. It was such a stressful, lonely time.

I sought legal advice through a solicitor. He gave me contact details for a private investigator. If they found out M4's details, I would have to pay $100 for their service. If they couldn't find him, it would be free. After what seemed like a lifetime, they sent me a letter with all the information on where M4 worked and lived, as well as his new girlfriend's name, Darlene, and where she also worked in Western Australia. Think of Dolly Parton's song Jolene and swap it to Darlene. She even fitted Dolly's description.

I had to write to the NSW Births, Deaths and Marriages to ask for special permission to not register Zak's birth within 28 days, but to wait until his father could be located. I was granted the exemption.

I was still friends with one of M4's sisters; he was from a family of 11. T was going out to visit M4's parents in Baradine, NSW. T asked me if I wanted to come to meet their parents so they could meet their grandson. Of course, I said yes. I was so nervous travelling the 5 hours to Baradine. I spent the weekend there. I have some precious photos of Zak and his grandparents together. While I was there, his mum rang M4 in Perth and told him we were there visiting. He wasn't impressed. She also told him to come home, sign the birth certificate and meet his son.

M4's brother, Michael, was disgusted that M4 did not take responsibility for Zak, and he offered to sign the certificate as Zak's father. I didn't want to do this, so I declined the offer. Michael died six months later. That was a sad day. If only M4 had compassion like his brother did.

I sent a letter again to M4 at the address I was given by his mum with a new registration form. It was returned signed, but it was not his signature or handwriting, it looked like a female's. His girlfriend had forged his signature, breaking the law. If I had submitted it knowing that, I would have committed fraud.

My solicitor drafted a letter to M4 stating that he was to sign the enclosed registration form, or we would have his and her arses in court. Hers for fraud for signing the birth certificate, and his for DNA tests at his cost. I should not have had to go through all of that.

Zak was eight months old, and on the 27th of January, I drove my girlfriend Karen, Zak and me to Tamworth Court House, where I met M4 and Darlene. I was shaking from head to toe with nerves. I wore a white blouse and a black pencil skirt to my ankles. I had continued to lose weight after having Zak and was looking fit and healthy despite everything that was going on at home.

I was so nervous about seeing M4 face-to-face for the first time in over 15 months and wondering what Darlene would look like. I stood tall and proud, and I knew I looked a lot better than the last time he had seen me, crying and pleading for him not to leave me.

We walked into the office at the Tamworth Courthouse early. I wanted to be there first. I wanted to be in control of the situation. M4 and Darlene walked in, which was the first time M4 had seen his son. All we had to do was sign the registration form in front of a Justice of the Peace. I went first and handed Zak straight to M4 to hold while I signed.

Then M4 passed Zak back to me and finally signed Zak's registration. It was such a relief not only for me and the pressure I was under with Centrelink but also for my son, who now had a legal name.

We were civil towards each other under the circumstances. Zak looked like a miniature version of his father. There was no mistaking who his father was. It was such an awkward situation to be in. There was minimal conversation amongst the four of us. I just wanted to get out of there.

I thanked the court officer, nodded at Karen, and walked straight towards the door. I did not look back, as it hurt too much. I held it together until I got to the car, then broke down sobbing. I knew that M4 signing would never mean we would get regular maintenance. I would have to do this all on my own, but at least Zak had a name. It was an uncomfortable, awkward situation. It was a long drive back home. I learnt to harden the fuck up.

A friend introduced me to Le Reve Cosmetics. A multilevel party plan perfume business. Nowadays, they sell aromatherapy and skincare, but back then, it was just perfume. We had perfumes that were supposedly created in the identical perfume houses as the top fragrances in the world. This was the ultimate upselling experience; everything I had learnt in Amway I used, plus some additional skills I learned through this business.

I was now a single mum, and making money was a matter of survival. The threat of starvation and homelessness are great motivators to create an income and not to be fussy about what you do. I was always told growing up that it was easier to get a job you liked if you had a job already, regardless of whether you liked it or not. What I did like was my pay at the end of the week.

We were living on the sole parents' pension, which didn't go far, and I swallowed my pride and went to the Salvation Army for vouchers for gas and electricity. It was very humbling and embarrassing as everyone knew each other in a small town.

I didn't have anyone who could help me out of the pickle I had found us in. We weren't getting any maintenance from Zak's father, and Parpa had still isolated me from the family. We had no one I could turn to for financial support. I did have Diana, who would often babysit Zak. She and her husband, Alan, thought of Zak as their own grandchild, and I am so grateful to have had them in our lives. I really don't know where I'd be in life if they hadn't been there.

I also had Kathryn, who was my sponsor and up-line into Le Reve. She and her husband owned a farm a few hours away. When she came to visit, as we didn't have a phone, she would bring chunks of home-killed fatty lamb for us to stock the freezer. That meat kept us alive for a long time. Many meals I would go without so Zak could eat. I was in survival mode. Forced into that mindset, I was always thinking outside the square of ways to make money. Neither Zak or myself are big lamb eaters nowadays. I often wonder if it's because it kept us alive for so long.

For Zak's second Christmas, I couldn't afford to buy him a new toy. I had a friend whose neighbour was giving away a small trike. It was pink. I bought a cheap spray can of black paint and painted it for Zak as his Christmas present from Santa that year. I vowed to myself I would never be in that position again.

I did very well with Le Reve, as we had limited options to buy expensive French fragrances in the bush. Le Reve had thought hard about their range. They introduced us to the concept of layering, which was, in effect, up-selling on steroids. Each layer was the same scent. First you would start with a cream, then silk talc, then keep layering products, with the perfume last. Then of course the atomiser to carry in your purse. I would do Le Reve parties in the same area I would travel to for mystery shopping, meaning I was being paid to drive to my perfume parties. I wore two different badges, well, three if you counted being a single mum.

In the space of 12 months I drove thousands of kilometres selling fragrances and doing mystery shopping. 1994 saw me travel to Sydney for the Le Reve conference for their first ever Founders' Day Away. I sold close to $70,000 worth of Le Reve across the New England area, with a population of 6000 people in Glen Innes. Let's just say everyone smelled great! Things were going incredibly well for me, until Le Reve changed their return policy. You see, if you bought the product, you had a 30 day change of mind policy. This was fine, until Le Reve started taking months to give refunds. As the demonstrator, it was my responsibility to refund the customer's money, and then I had to wait to get my money back. I had to return the goods at my own cost. I had some parties where the whole order, over $1000 worth, had to be refunded on day 29. This happened a few times and left me with zero money to live on. I couldn't afford to keep selling it. Orders like this were eating into my profit and it reached the point where it was costing me money to sell their product.

I knew then that it had run its course.

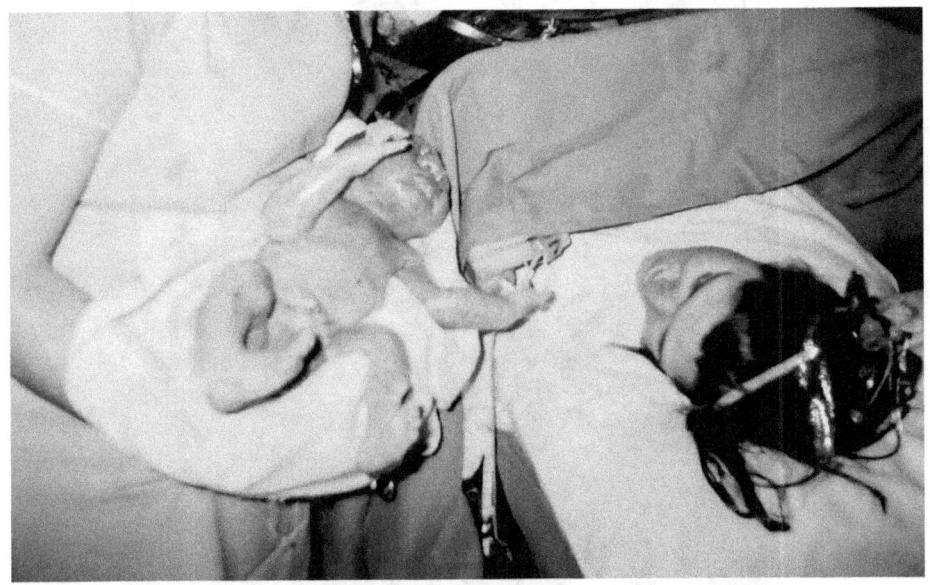

1993 Zak's birth by C section

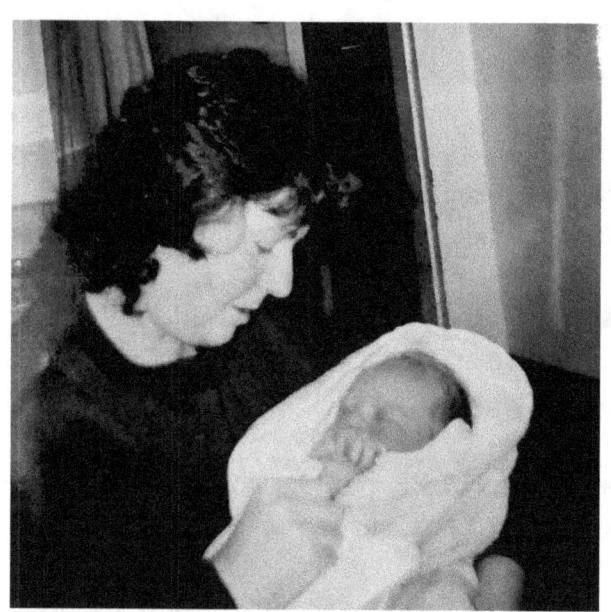

1993 Mum with Zak, 1 day old, when she told me to change his name.

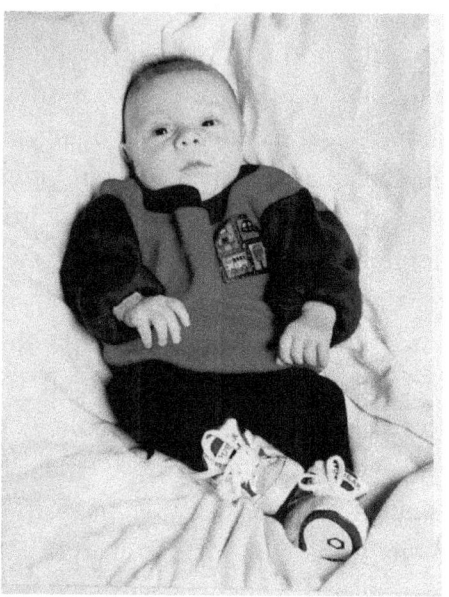

1993 Zak at 8 weeks old

1993 Zak 8 weeks old and myself off to an Amway function in Coffs Harbour

1993 Zak and me at an Amway conference in Brisbane

1993 Me and Zak, 6 months old

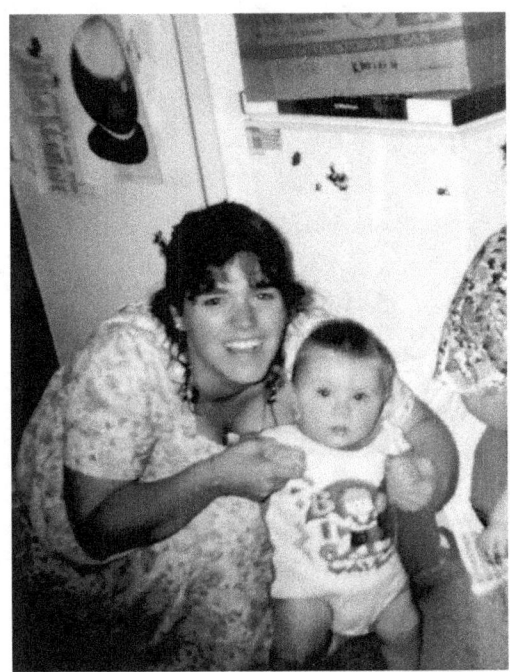
1993 Me and Zak, 7 months old

1994 Zak at 11 months

1994 Zak's first birthday at Church Street Glen Innes, NSW

1995 Zak and me in Lawrance Street Glen Innes

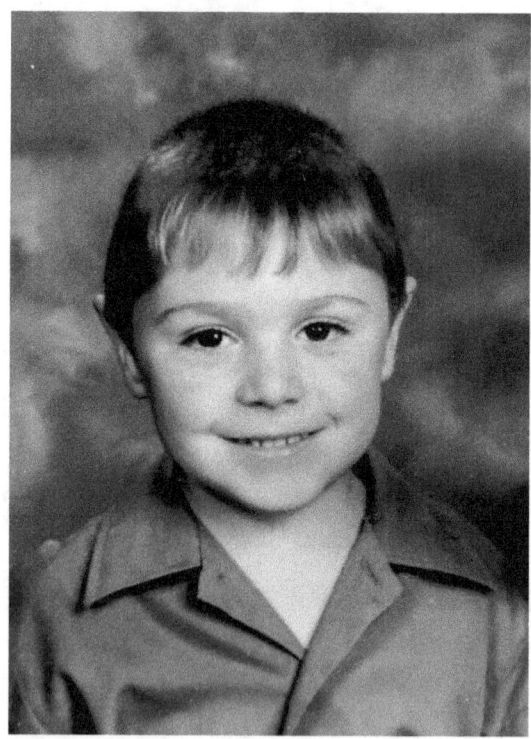
1998 Zak in Kindergarten, Glen Innes Primary School

CHAPTER 9

Mum

While all of this was going on, I was still caring for my mum. We had done a complete reversal of roles for several years leading up to this point. I did all the cooking and cleaning. We did have a home care lady who would come in once a week to wash Mum's clothes, vacuum the floors, and clean the kitchen floor. Every second day, they would help shower her. I had to do the rest.

Diana knew the pressure I was under. So, to give me a few hours' break, she and her husband Alan would babysit Zak on a Saturday night so I could meet my friends at the local pub. So that I could do things other people my age were doing. I very much looked forward to that time. I would make sure Mum had dinner, and she would be in the lounge watching TV when I'd leave the house at about 8 pm. I would then drop Zak off and head out. I would only have a drink or two, till about 10.30 pm. I would then have to go home and put Mum into bed.

Then I could go back out till 1 am, when the pub would shut, and I'd pick up Zak and go home. One particular night, it had gotten to about 12 when I suddenly realised I had forgotten to go home and put Mum to bed. I drove straight home, and found Mum slouched over in her chair in the middle of the hallway. She made me feel so guilty for forgetting about her and not coming home to put her to bed. I put her into bed and picked up Zak. I never forgot about her again.

Nanna and Parpa came to visit when Zak was about 3 months old. Zak was out of his bassinet and was sleeping on the cot mattress on the floor. Parpa had brought up an old rusty cot, which was mine when I was a baby. I was going to restore it for Zak. Parpa never threw anything out. Nanna and I had to go up the street to get groceries, but we knew we wouldn't be there long. Mum was in her wheelchair in the lounge room, and Parpa was also watching TV.

Zak was asleep in my room. We were gone for under an hour. On our return, Parpa was sleeping in front of the TV, snoring, and Mum was nowhere to be seen. I walked to my room, and Mum was sitting on my bed holding Zak! She had managed to push herself up the winding hallway, get herself out of her wheelchair and get Zak off the mattress from the floor. Yet only weeks earlier, she had made me feel guilty for leaving her in the hallway to fall asleep. I discovered that she could still do many things for herself, but was jealous of the amount of time Zak was taking up, and no longer being the centre of my universe. She made me feel guilty for everything I did and didn't do.

She was becoming more defiant in everyday tasks such as brushing her hair and teeth, getting dressed and changing into clean clothes when she had soiled herself. We had many yelling and screaming matches with each other, to no avail. I hated it and what my life had become. I wanted my mum back, to parent me and not the other way around.

Throughout this time, I picked up some casual work as a salesperson at the local Glen Innes Show in the pavilion, collecting names for a company selling a maths tutoring program. Years later, in 2005, I ended up buying that maths tutoring program for my own kids, who never used it. That job was hard work, standing there trying to get people's phone numbers so the company could call them. We had to dress in a business-like manner. I remember going for that job and telling them I could talk with a mouth full of marbles underwater. I was hired. Who knew decades later I'd be making a living out of my voice as an international keynote speaker.

Approaching people taught me a lot about myself and my self-esteem. I had to set aside all my fears and failures and focus on the task at hand and the bigger picture. The bigger picture being the paycheck at the end of it to provide for my family. It was always about the paycheck. I couldn't be fussy about the job at hand. I just got in and did it. I knew it wouldn't be for long. But it was a job, and it gave me money. A lot of the jobs I worked made me uncomfortable, but until you get uncomfortable with your situation, you won't do anything to better yourself or the pickle you're in. And that's not just for jobs, but any life situations that you are in.

At about the same time, in May, M4's father passed away, and we went with T to Coonable for his funeral. Everyone there knew who we were, and T ensured we sat in the front row. I saw M4 and Darlene. Looks were exchanged, but we did not speak. We drove the five hours straight home after the service, not going to the wake. I stood proud at the funeral, knowing Zak and I had every right to be there. I learnt to harden the fuck up.

Five months had passed when Nan and Parpa came through for a visit on their way to see Nanna's sister Ruth on the Gold Coast. They were both remarkable for the amount of driving they did at their ages.

It was early December. I had made sure Mum had her breaky of Weetbix, and that there were clean sheets on the double bed in Simon's room for them to sleep in. I was heading out to my girlfriend's farm for lunch for a few hours. Nan and Parpa would be arriving about the time I was to be home. They beat me home by half an hour.

When they arrived, Mum was sitting on the kitchen floor, covered in Weetbix. She had had a fall and didn't get up. She could have if she had really wanted to. But she knew that they wouldn't be far away. So, to get me into trouble, she sat there. When I arrived home, I no sooner had gotten Zak out of the car than Parpa lashed at me for leaving Mum.

I tried to explain what had happened and what she was doing, but he refused to listen. I grabbed Zak. I was in tears, so I drove to Diana and Alan's, which was only about a five-minute drive from my place. I told Di what had happened. She was well aware of how difficult it had become with Mum. For me to get her to do anything, I would, unfortunately, have to threaten to put her into Roseneath, which was the old-age nursing home. Not somewhere someone of 46 would want to live or should live. I still, 30 years later, feel bad about our relationship. I am angry at what MS took away from my brother and me.

Diana went around home and sat down with Nan and Parpa and told them some home truths about what had been happening and how I was coping, or more to the point, how I wasn't coping.

I returned home, and Parpa took me aside, apologised, and said he would take care of things. Mum, at that stage, had been diagnosed with MS for 14 years, and not once in that time had he ever done anything in regard to stepping up as a parent in his own daughter's health care.

Parpa had a meeting with her doctor, and they had organised for Mum to go into the MS home, which was situated on the grounds of Lidcombe Hospital in Sydney, eight hours south of where we were living. Nowadays, the MS home is still there, but the hospital was pulled down to build accommodation for the 2000 Olympic Games.

I went back there in 2013 and visited the home. I walked in, and the smell was overwhelming. It has the most disgusting odour, one that brought back very sad memories of having to leave her there. We could never give her anything good, as people would steal her things.

The only way we could get Mum to go was to say that it would just be a trial for four weeks and that she would be home for Christmas. She went, and it was just Zak and me for the first time. I had so much extra time. I felt guilty for the extra time.

Simon and Marissa brought Mum home for Christmas. That would be her last Christmas in her home. She thought that she was going to live in her home forever.

It was gut-wrenching having to pack up her clothes, knowing that she would never live in her home again. I stood in the driveway and waved goodbye as Simon and Marissa drove Mum back to her new room in Sydney. I burst into tears from the guilt I felt for not being able to care for her. It was one of the hardest decisions I've had to make.

We had lived in that house for seven years and never paid rent, as it was assumed that the house was given to Mum by her Uncle, her father's brother. However, the titles were never put in Mum's name, and when my great-uncle lost a lot of money in the global financial crisis (GFC) in 1987 he never recovered, and the liquidators wanted to take possession of the house, our home.

My grandfather worked for my great-uncle and then for the liquidators, who wanted me out of the house so it could be sold.

Simon and I had packed up all ours and Mum's belongings in the house and had divided them between the two of us, what I wanted and needed and what he wanted.

Simon had all of his stuff on a tandem trailer owned by Parpa, and it was parked in the garage waiting for Simon's next trip home to tow it back to Sydney.

Parpa wasn't impressed with the way that Simon had packed the trailer and with the stuff that Simon and I were taking, so he made sure that he took it back to Windsor to store in his worksheds there — things like Mum's good cutlery, dinner sets, limited-edition statues, anything that was worth money— regardless of the sentimental value to Simon and myself.

I was left to pack up the rest of Mum's clothes that no longer fit her. Mum was a yo-yo dieter for as long as I could remember. She had sizes 8 to 16 in her wardrobe. She would count calories, eat off small bread and butter plates, and then go through times of gorging. Little did we know that she also had another genetic disease called Lipoedema. Seeing her struggle with her weight didn't help me at all with my own weight challenges.

I had to find somewhere to live. I found a little two-bedroom house on the New England Highway, which is also known as Church Street, Glen Innes. It looked like a doll's house. The woman who owned that house was someone I went to school with. She was a year younger than I. She had won it by entering a competition on the Nescafé coffee label. Years later, I discovered that she also was diagnosed with Multiple Sclerosis.

I didn't have any money to pay for the bond. Parpa said he would loan me the money, and he did, but it came with conditions. Interest. He handed the cash over to me in the middle of aisle six of the Bi-Lo supermarket without anyone in sight. He wanted 25% back in interest! He demanded his own granddaughter pay 25% interest to put a roof over her and his great-grandson's head.

I had been really sick with tonsillitis and got septicaemia from it, even though I'd had my tonsils out when I was 6. At that time, they removed them by ripping them, and fragments remained. As I grew, so did the fragments, and enough remained to cause major issues. I was on high doses of antibiotics, but couldn't go to the hospital as I had no one who could look after Zak for more than a few hours. Doing the housework at that time and trying to pack up what was left of the house were not high priorities. Added to that, I was trying to look after Zak and get better. My grandparents had gone to Queensland for a few days, and on their return, I had organised to pick up my piano.

I treasured that piano. It held all my dreams, and I had to walk away from them. I was still teaching piano and had organised four men to pick it up. We met at the home, and Parpa wouldn't let me inside and informed me that he was keeping the piano — anything that held any dollar value, he wanted so he could sell it.

We had a screaming match at the door. I called him a silly old 'see you next Tuesday', as he yelled back at me that I was exactly like my father, and never to contact him or my nanna again.

I was heartbroken. How could he do this to me? His own granddaughter. Out of greed.

I went and rang Mum. I could call her at the MS centre. Many times I'd ring and she wasn't there, and they couldn't find her. She would often, in her motorised wheelchair, scoot down the road to the corner shop so she could buy her smokes. Thank goodness this wasn't one of those occasions. I told her what Parpa had done with my piano. She told me to call her oldest brother, Jeff, and he would help. I called Uncle Jeff, and he told me he would help no matter the cost. He didn't get along with his father. I'm sure he was helping out of revenge. He advised me to get legal advice. So I did. I went and saw my solicitor, who had dealt with my grandfather when my family owned the tin mine at Emmaville.

The solicitor drafted a letter, which we faxed to Uncle Jeff, who then took it to Mum to sign and then faxed it back. I then had the signed letter from Mum stating that I owned the piano and it was to be returned to me. I went and knocked on the door and served the document to Parpa. I organised the same four men to take my piano, and we did it that same day.

I will never forget the disgust on Parpa's face and the sorrow in my Nanna's eyes as I walked out of my family home. I found out through the solicitor that I should never have moved out of that home. I actually had squatter's rights in it. The house went up for auction and sold for $77,000 — a lot of money in 1994.

I really was all alone now, just Zak and me. For the next few years, I would get letters in the mail from Nanna with a $50 note in it and a few short lines that she was thinking of us, and she loved and missed us. Oh, and not to tell anyone about the money as she had had a win on the pokies. I didn't care where the money had come from. It always helped pay a bill or put food on the table.

I went back to teaching piano, and I still have that piano today. I have shipped it across the country twice. I can no longer play like I used to. That all left my brain when I got MS. But I do remember how good I was at playing and can still hear the songs I composed.

It took a few years before I was game enough to call and speak to Nanna and be allowed back to visit them.

When going through all of mum's things, that I had packed up without looking at, I found this speech that she had written: she must have been talking at an event, or maybe it was submitted to be printed.

My life with MS by Marian Londish, Your Mum (13.11.89)

I was first diagnosed as a 'sufferer' of MS in 1981. When I was 33. Since then, I have learned to live with it. I will admit it has been very hard. Both mentally and physically.

I have tried the 'Transfer Factor', and that failed; so did the 'Interferon' trial, and the ACTH injections (strong doses of cortisone) given in hospital. This cortisone is to replace your natural cortisone made by the 'Pituitary' gland, which is the gland on top of your head.

The only thing that works is yourself.

I do not have any pain, but that is very common with M.S. FATIGUE is my killer. It is shocking in the hot weather; you go to bed tired and rise the same way.

My front is different to my back, and my LHS is different to my RHS, so I have massive trouble having a shower or a bath. I also have to have the weather temperature at an even 20 degrees, so needless to say I have an air conditioner in the car and at home.

Sun – if I am in the sun, I shake, but as soon as I am in the shade or in front of a fan or air conditioner, I am ok. Cold weather is just as bad. I dare not stay in bed all day; at times, I force myself to get out of bed.

When I came to Glen I was Stage 2. Now I'm at 3 — by the time you reach Stage 8, you are dead. You do not die from M.S. but from complications; your life span is 80 per cent of a normal life.

The only medication I take now is 'Bachloflen' for the muscles in my legs, 'Nortabs' for the pins and needles in my right hand, and I have B1 (for energy) and B12 (for depression) injections monthly.

I do everything I should not. I smoke and drink. I have given up smoking several times; at the moment, I am only smoking out of boredom. If I drink too much, I make sure I am at home; I also consume very little dairy, even 'Shape' milk or 'Lite/White'.

Diet does take a major role in this disease; we are supposed to revert back, say, 100 years, when everything was natural.

Now you are saying what a hypocrite. I know.

Only a very few people in this town are aware that I have MS. As far as people are concerned, I have had a car accident, as people find that easier to accept than if I say I have MS. People just do not know about the disease, and offer you sympathy. Yuk! If someone really asks, then I will explain.

I have enclosed my X-rays for your interest. Head and spine after a car accident in 1983 (whiplash neck.) Mammogram – yearly and CAT scan.

After my last stay in hospital, it's clear that the nurses do not know how to deal with MS. This is because there are not enough of us here — only two. They are taught at college but have no practical experience. MS patients who go to hospital and are on cortisone need physiotherapy as soon as possible, otherwise you take longer to recover, as now I am doing all my exercises at home.

You ask what I miss the most? Before I divorced, it was a case of if you cannot 'lick' him, join him. I took up motorbike riding, both road and trails, speed boat racing, snow skiing, and roller skating with my children. But that does not answer the question. The answer is my health.

My last healthy day was on the 28 January 1974, the day before I had my cancer operation.

You can have all the money in the world, but you cannot buy your health; but you can have good fun spending it.

I have to admit I have come very close to suicide, but then you say to yourself, there are people in this world worse off than you.

There are five of us in Glen Innes District, and I would say I would be about the second worst case.

Please do not feel sorry for me; I've lived through cancer. Just learn to understand this disease, the same way as I am learning.

So please remember we were all born equal; it's just that my life took a different road to yours.

===========================

After doing research over the last 8 years:
Victoria is leading the way (see Video).

There are so many theories:

QLD: is following drugs (Qld MS Dec '89) also 'Posterior sinus infection' (George Dick and Derek Gay) researchers(Qld MS 89), this goes with Roger McDougall's theory (Judy Graham's Book – England) and Dr. Kousmins (French Dr, Living in Switzerland). Translated into English — I have a copy.

WA: Believes in cats and measles, which I believe in, as we had 2 cats (Peter and Paul). I never had the measles but became a carrier S.M.H. (11/11/89). And as for cold weather, I grew up in Victoria in the Great Dividing Range with weather similar to G.I.

NSW: is working on remyelinating the myelin sheath. MS 89

Vic: are working on the 'T-Cells' of the brain (Quatom 6/11/89)

All States are working on different things; I only wish they would get together.
Then you have the other theories:
Pritikin – Viral Infection.
Ross Horne 'The health revolution' – viral infection
Mercury (60 mins – Oct 89), which could be possible as I have a 'metal mine' in my mouth. Costly way to find out (only 2 machines in Aust., both in Melb.)

Rock formation under the soil – lead see 'Minerals kill or cure'.
Adele Davis 'Let's Get Well' is different again and believes we are lacking in Lecithin in the brain.

Quatom (video) says it all.

I have condensed my History but will explain more should you wish to know.
Signed
M Londish 13/11/89

After reading this letter decades later, and with my own health battles, my heart ached for what she went through so alone. With very little help from anyone. I just wanted to give her a hug and tell her how sorry I was. But I couldn't.

1989 Mum at Meade St, Glen Innes

1994 Mum and Zak at the MS Home in Lidcombe NSW

1994 Mum, Aunty Lynny and myself at Simon's Wedding

1994 Mum, myself and Simon at his wedding

1995 Mum and Zak at the MS Home in Lidcombe NSW

1995 Mum at the MS Home in Lidcombe NSW

CHAPTER 10

One Small Voice

It was a struggle living on my own. I didn't receive any child support, and I had no contact with my family. I felt totally abandoned by those who were supposed to love me. Life was tough.

The little doll's house we were living in was on the busiest road in town, a major highway to Sydney and Brisbane. The house was on a huge block, which was a pain to mow. We didn't have secure fences around the property. The owner had erected sheep wire fences. That is a wire fence with large holes all along it, that a small child can easily fit through. Zak was a bugger for escaping. He would get up in the middle of the night in stealth mode and had worked out, at the age of two, to unlock the back sliding door and sneak out into the backyard without me hearing, then climb through the wire fence and out onto the highway! A parent's worst nightmare. I had to have a bolt put in the top of the door to stop the little Houdini from escaping.

I had an emergency line for my phone as I couldn't afford to ring out, but people could still call me. When I wanted to call my mum or Aunty Lyn, I would go to Diana and Alan's to call. I still wasn't allowed to contact my Nanna. I owned a little blue Barina, which I had bought in 1992 for $5000. I was struggling to make the repayments on it, let alone the registration. I got caught driving it with no rego. It was a $750 fine. I didn't know what to do. How was I going to pay for it? I called my Aunty Lynny, she lent me the money, and I paid her back over a 12-month period.

It was about this time that M4 came back into our lives. I was back to driving down to Tamworth on a Friday afternoon and picking him up, and then driving back to my place. A 400km round trip. He would classify it as a 6-pack drive and measure the distance by how many beers he could consume on the way. I would never let him drive. He came in and out of our lives for months. No commitment and no maintenance either. He would stay for two nights, and then I would have to drive him the 400km round-trip home. I was young and naive, and just wanted to have a happy, loving family. This 'arrangement' went on for over 12 months.

I applied for a Department of Housing home in 1994 and only had to wait a little over 12 months for a house. Zak and I moved into our new home in the middle of 1995. It made life easier at the time, with the reduced rent and the security of not having to move. It was a very old two-bedroom home, built in the 1950s, with asbestos sheeting on the outside walls and a red iron roof. It had no curtains. The backyard had a tall pine tree in it, and was a lot smaller than the two previous homes I had lived in. The gas stove was an old, green enamel stove from the 1950s or 60s, with a long vent right through the middle of it. Many a Tupperware container, named a 'season serve', I melted on the top of that stove as it dripped through to the grill. It was a secure place for both of us. I made it our home. I had no family around to help, and I relied on the generosity of friends to help us move.

In December 1995, Zak's father came for a visit before Christmas. After he had unprotected sex with me, he proceeded to tell me that he had Hepatitis C and HIV, and that Zak and I needed to be tested. The 19th is a day I will never forget, as he then stole my car and left Zak and me abandoned at a friend's Christmas party. I was so embarrassed. I had worked hard for that car and was still paying it off. I had kept the secret that he had told me only 2 days earlier, but I knew I had to tell Diana; she was livid when she found out. I was ashamed and embarrassed. How could he do that to us?

Diana and Alan drove us home that evening. My mind was racing. How was I going to cope without my car? Where was he? M4 had been drinking quite heavily that day, and I had no idea where my car was or if he had crashed it in his drunken stupor. I felt abandoned. I was sad and angry at the same time. Did I have Hep C and HIV too? Did Zak have it? It was bad enough having herpes, let alone throwing these two into the mix. Was I going to die? Who would look after Zak? Was he going to die too? So many questions were running through my head.

The front of my home had four steps. They were high-gloss, glazed, and slippery. There was no handrail. I was in flat shoes. We carried everything inside, and I came out to say goodnight to Diana and Alan. The next thing I knew, I had slipped down the steps. I had torn all the ligaments in my right ankle and foot. I sat there sobbing. What else could go wrong? Why me?

I was supposed to drive to Sydney later that week to spend Christmas with my mum and extended family. How was I going to drive now, with a sore ankle and no car? Had I broken it? Alan grabbed a bag of peas from my freezer to put on my ankle; Diana put Zak to bed and made sure I was okay. She said she would be back the next morning. This was years before I owned a mobile phone, and I couldn't afford a house phone.

It's scary to think about not having a phone to communicate in emergencies nowadays. But at the time, it was a considerable expense, and it was one I just couldn't afford. I didn't get maintenance at the time from M4, and I was on the sole parent's pension for Zak. The extra I earned from mystery shopping and selling hobby ceramics was indeed a blessing that saved us many times. Diana took us to the doctor the next day and then to the hospital for X-rays and blood tests.

The police came up to the hospital to interview me as I had to report my car stolen — M4 hadn't returned overnight. I was gutted. The man that I loved, the father of my son, had done this to us, to his flesh and blood. It was heartbreaking to see and hear Zak have his blood test. His screams still haunt me today. What was I going to do if the bloods came back positive? Who would look after Zak and raise him if his mother and father were dead? The Grim Reaper campaign was so vivid in my head. Every question was bouncing around. I kept repeating the same questions over and over. How would I get to Sydney to spend Christmas with my family when I no longer had my car?

After two very long days, the police contacted me to say they had found my car. It had been abandoned in a paddock two hours away, still with the keys inside. M4 was charged with stealing a motor vehicle. I was shattered. My foot and ankle had turned black as I hobbled around in immense pain, both physically and mentally. Diana and Alan drove me to Moonbi to pick up my car. M4 had left his wallet under the mat in the back seat. I knew his PIN number. I went to the ATM and withdrew $400. I bought Zak the best Christmas presents for his 3rd Christmas without any guilt. If this was to be his last Christmas, it was going to be a good one!

I was determined to spend Christmas with my family, particularly my mum. I headed to Sydney two days later with my right foot heavily bandaged, which, in hindsight, was probably highly illegal. The 8-hour drive was excruciatingly painful. I cried a lot of the way, but as I pulled up to my Aunty Lynny and Uncle Gra's house in Glossodia, I was relieved. That evening, I told my aunt about the blood tests and my concern that Zak and I had AIDS and Hep C. We decided not to tell the rest of the family, but to keep it a secret until the results came in. Why worry the rest of the family and spoil their Christmas? Because of the festive season, it would take longer for the results to come through.

That Christmas lives on in my memory; I spent it soaking in the treasured moments. We didn't realise at the time that it would be the last Christmas I would have with my mum. As I am writing this I am flooded with a wave of emotion. The anger of what I was living with, and the secrets. What should have been a joyful family occasion was instead overshadowed by fear and grief. The memory still leaves me angry.

On the way home, I called into M4's caravan in Tamworth to collect my belongings from him. It didn't end well, but rather with a slap across my face.

Early in January 1996, I rang the NSW Department of Housing to report the steps and my injury. I was told someone would come out to fix them. No one came.

April Fool's Day, 1st of April of the same year at 12.30 pm. Zak and I were heading out, and I pulled the front door shut. I had flat shoes on. There was no moisture, and it was a sunny day. The next thing I knew, I had slipped down the front steps again, the same way I had slipped down four months earlier. This time, I heard something snap in my right leg as I landed hard. I let out an almighty scream. The pain was so intense, nothing like I'd ever felt before.

Zak came up to me and put his arms around me as I sat there crying and screaming for help. I still didn't own a phone to call anyone. Of all times, this is one when I really needed it.

My elderly neighbours came out to see what all the noise was. Everything hurt, including my pride! I'd landed hard on my bum on the steps. They convinced me that nothing had broken and that I just sprained my ankle again. They had a home phone, and I begged them to ring an ambulance. They didn't.

I knew deep down that it was more than a sprain. It hurt a lot more than it had in the previous fall. I went into survival mode.

They convinced me to stand up, and that all I had done was reinjure the injury from December. I managed to hobble to the car, holding onto Zak's hand. He looked so scared. He knew something terrible had happened. How I picked him up and put him into his car seat beats me, but I did. I closed his door and, in agony, hobbled around to the driver's side.

Once in the car, I thought of where I should go. Driving was going to be an issue. My little blue Barina was a manual. I had to use both feet! How the hell was I going to do that? I thought about where the closest doctor's surgery was, as putting my foot on the brake was excruciatingly painful. I didn't know how I would get to my normal doctor's surgery across the main street in town as I was worried about hitting someone and killing them when I couldn't brake, let alone killing us.

I chose to go to the medical centre in Bourke Street, saving lives by avoiding the busier streets in town. I managed to park the car, hop out, go around, get Zak out of the car and then hobble inside. The receptionist, whose sons I happened to go to school with, took me straight into a consulting room as I was crying and could barely walk.

The doctor examined me, and she said she didn't think I had broken it because I was still walking, and that I had just sprained it again. I explained to her what I had done the previous December. She wrote a referral for me to go to the hospital to have X-rays taken. I hobbled out of the room, and the receptionist helped me put Zak in the car. Oh, how was I going to drive up to the hospital? I didn't do myself any favours by being 'strong' and pushing through the pain. I should have asked for help and said that I couldn't drive.

I managed to drive very slowly, under the speed limit, and avoid using the brake pedal, and got to the hospital car park, which was on a hill. When I got out of the car, I walked around and got Zak out. I managed to get about three steps from the car and just couldn't walk any further. The pain was excruciating.

I felt like I was going to vomit; I had the sweats, and the world was spinning.

Mrs Gallagher, who worked at the hospital, saw me struggling and came out with the wheelchair and met me in the car park. She pushed me up the hill into the hospital with Zak following beside us. I was so grateful and relieved for her help.

My strength and pain tolerance have often created more work for me in the long run, or caused me to be overlooked. It's something I have had to be aware of over the years.

I was taken to have an X-ray with the technician, and she made Zak sit outside the door by himself while she X-rayed my leg and foot. I was beside myself. Zak was only two and a half years old. What if someone took him, or he ran off? I asked for a vomit bag and started throwing up.

The technician came out of the cubicle in radiology and said that I'd broken my leg as she let Zak back into the room. He was standing at the door with a scared look on his little face. She then proceeded to tell me that I had a 5 cm diagonal fracture of my fibula. I burst into tears again. I asked them to call Diana, as I didn't know what else to do. They took me to the plaster room where the physiotherapist plastered my leg. I had gone into shock, which then had also brought on a migraine. I was not well at all.

I had been running on adrenaline until they told me it was broken.

Zak and I went home with Diana yet again. I really don't know where I'd be in life if it weren't for the friendship and the generosity of Diana and Allan Sharman. I thank you both from the bottom of my heart. Diana is mentioned a few times throughout this book. She was there for me when no one else cared. I can't stress this enough: I don't think I would be here without the love and support she gave me and my children, particularly in times of great need. They went above and beyond normal friendship. They became my family. Friends really are the family we choose.

We spent the next few days at their place until everything could be arranged for us to return home. I wasn't allowed to put my foot on the ground for eight weeks. How was I going to look after a two-year-old by myself? I was so scared and so angry to be in this position.

Five days after breaking my leg was my 10-year high school reunion. I was on the organising committee with my best friend Ali and another classmate, Suellen. They had joked 12 months earlier that they would both be pregnant at the reunion, and I said, "Yeah, and I'll break my leg!" Well, they both were pregnant, and I did, in fact, break my leg. Be very careful what you put out to the universe, as it can come back to bite you!

Diana organised for Zak to go to Gumtree Glen, which was the local childminding centre, meals on wheels for us, and home and community care to come and pick Zak up every morning to take him to daycare and drop him home. I spent the days lying on the lounge watching TV, gaining weight and slipping into depression.

It was during this time that Diana's daughter and son-in-law lent me a mobile phone, swapping it for my car as I was unable to drive, while theirs was off the road, and they lived out of town. The deal was I would pay the phone bills, and they could use my car, but it was to be returned in the same condition as they borrowed it, clean, full tank of petrol and with nothing broken.

I was confined to the house for 8 weeks. The only place I would go to was Hobby Ceramics a couple of times a week, when Diana would pick me up. Having that hobby was vitally important to building resilience. Again, I had no choice but to harden the fuck up.

After eight very long weeks, I finally had the plaster removed. I had to go to physiotherapy for my ankle. Something still didn't feel right. I still had a lot of pain on the top of my foot. I had trouble wearing shoes. It turned out that after four more sets of X-rays, I had also broken the top of my right foot! I had discovered this by looking through the X-ray films. Someone had circled a small bone on one of them, yet it hadn't been reported. I took the X-rays to my doctor and asked what that circle meant. It too was broken, but it had been set in the wrong place. It's never been corrected.

I rang the Department of Housing again and explained that I had slipped down the front steps again and this time broke my leg and foot. I was worried that a support worker or friend would do the same. They finally sent someone out to look at the front steps months later, and they put a handrail up and grip tape on the steps. By doing so they were acknowledging there was something wrong with them and admitting liability.

I wanted them to admit that they had failed in their duty of care to me, their tenant. Here was a 25-year-old single mum who was struggling in life. They were a huge government organisation. I sought legal advice on how to recover my costs of childcare, home care, and a doctor's visit, as well as to get an apology from the department.

After two long months of being in plaster and not putting my foot on the ground, I finally had the heavy plaster removed. I had to go to physiotherapy to learn to use my leg and ankle again. The pain was horrendous, with lots of exercises to build back my strength. I had started going out again on a Saturday night when I met M5. He was new to town but had family history in Emmaville. He said all the right things to start with. Nowadays I know this is love bombing.

Suing a government department took a lot of time and money. I tried to carry on with my life as best I could. My ankle continued to give me trouble, and I would fall over without notice. I couldn't go for long walks, and I started to gain a lot of weight.

I started going out with friends again to the pub on a Saturday night. One night I met a guy, M5, who swept me off my feet. I fell pregnant only two weeks after meeting him. I had no boundaries. He was a stranger, and here I was, trying to build a life with an imperfect stranger. We got engaged with a fake diamond, gold-plated ring, which cost him $49.99. He was constantly lying about everything. I ignored so many red flags. I knew on the inside I should have been running as fast as I could in the opposite direction. But I didn't. For a few reasons. I didn't want the town to talk, judging me for being a single mum to two different fathers, for not being good enough and for fucking up another relationship.

What I didn't realise then was that they were talking about me anyway.

I was learning to live with M5, which wasn't an easy task. A bigger reason for staying was that M5 had loving parents, who opened their home and lives to me, and more importantly, Zak as their grandson. We were part of a family. I hadn't had one in a very, very long time. I longed for that connection. Here was a man telling me that he loved me, and I believed him. I thought I loved him; but I didn't, not in the way I should have. Let me explain. I loved the idea of him, the idea of having someone love me despite my colourful past. I loved being part of a family. But because I never really loved him, the crack turned into big holes at a rapid rate.

Being pregnant, the added weight and swelling were horrendous on my leg. It swelled nearly twice its normal size for over two years. I struggled to walk and was in so much pain.

When my daughter Ally was born, she had a blocked tear duct. It was horrible. I would have to massage the pus out of it throughout the day and night to release the pressure. She constantly cried from the pain. I had postnatal depression. When Ally was 4 months old, she had her duct operated on in Brisbane Children's Hospital. We decided to spend a day at Dreamworld with Zak, who was 4, on the way home. We were in the IMAX theatre and I was carrying Ally up the long staircase when my ankle just collapsed and we hit the floor. I thought I had killed her; how I didn't, I'll never know. I weighed about 117 kg, and I fell hard on those steps. The mum-guilt of falling with her was huge, and the ear-bashing I got from M5 for nearly squashing his daughter was unbearable and uncalled for. I was taken to the first aid room for assessment. Ally was not hurt. I then sobbed for the entire 5-hour drive home.

I stopped breastfeeding Ally at 14 weeks as I had to have a scan on my right ankle that involved being injected with a radioactive dye. I was only allowed limited contact with her in the first 24 hours, and then for the next 24 hours, a little bit more. It took 3 days for the dye to leave my body. This injury was robbing me of so much.

A few months later, my right leg swelled up even more than it already was, and it hurt to bend. Something was wrong. I went to the doctor's as I thought my skin would split from the amount of fluid I was carrying. I couldn't get into my usual doctor, but I saw another one in the same practice instead. He booked me in for a chest X-ray, then an ultrasound that day. I felt nauseous.

I went and had the X-ray, then went through to the ultrasound at Glen Innes Hospital. It was when the technician was doing the ultrasound that she asked me if I could be pregnant. I said no. I was on the pill. Ally wasn't even 9 months old. She then showed me the monitor, and sure enough, there it was on the screen — a small dot that I had seen only three times in my life. I burst into tears and said I had just had an X-ray, and I knew instantly what that would mean.

The technician called my regular doctor and got me in for a visit right away. I sobbed all the way as I drove myself to the doctor's. Being exposed to full radiation in the first trimester of pregnancy causes major deformities to the unborn fetus. I was told I had two options. To continue with the pregnancy and have a copious amount of tests and procedures, that in itself would also risk miscarriage, or aborting the pregnancy. I sobbed some more. I had spent years looking after mum, I knew at the time I was in no head space, nine months after burying her, to even think about bringing a child with severe disabilities into this world. I knew M5 would blame me for everything. I decided before I left the doctor's surgery to terminate the pregnancy. I then had to go home and tell M5, which was going to be even harder to do. As I predicted he blamed me for what was happening and wasn't impressed that he had to drive me the four hours north to Tweed Heads for the termination. He never told his family as he was disgusted with me and ashamed. There was no compassion.

It was and still remains one of the hardest decisions I've ever had to make. All I know is that I did the best I could for my other children at the time. I sometimes think, normally in January each year, of what could have been, if only they had given me the ultrasound first. I would have had my third child. I always thought I'd have three.

Some months later, I was scheduled for an arthroscopic procedure in my right ankle. They discovered that I had small fragments of bone floating around in the ankle joint, and that's what was causing me to fall over all the time. After the procedure, I looked like I had two bullet holes in my ankle. It took me a long time to walk normally and reduce the pain. It was predicted that one day, when they were available, I'd have to have an ankle replacement, something that you don't want to hear at the age of 27. At 54, as I write this book, I'm still holding off for as long as possible.

I was sent to so many doctors and specialists by the Department of Housing about my ankle. They discovered that I have a 23-degree loss of movement in it, which has never improved. It's something that I still live with even today.

It took another nine months of letters from their solicitor to mine. On the 3rd March 1999, my birthday, nearly three years after breaking my leg, I received an offer of $60,000 as compensation from the department. If I had taken that money, it would not have gone down on public record that they were at fault. I saw this as hush money. 'Let's give the poor single mum money to keep her quiet.' The amount wasn't the issue, as I only ever wanted enough to cover my costs from it. That was more than enough, 10-fold.

My answer was 'no deal'. We went to court.

I was put in the witness box for nearly three hours of gruelling questions by their barrister. I did not crack or break. I wanted justice not only for myself but for every other person who had been pushed aside and had not been able to fix their homes. At one point near the end, their barrister handed my barrister a handwritten note. My barrister then asked for a 15-minute recess. I was taken into a back room and told I couldn't discuss anything about my testimony, only what was written on that piece of paper. They had doubled their offer. $125,000! It was A LOT of money — especially to someone who was living on government benefits. I knew if I had taken the money, it still wouldn't be on public record. I declined and walked back into court. I had found my moxie, and I was not backing down now. I figured that if they had doubled their offer at that point, they knew I was going to win, and that meant my case would become public.

Within 20 minutes of returning to the courtroom, the judge asked for a break. When we came back in, I sat there in disbelief. When he read out that I had been awarded over $217,000, I cried. The department had picked on the wrong single mum. As a result of this case, the NSW Department of Housing changed the way repairs were reported for its homes. We were given reference numbers, and urgent repairs were done a lot faster. I recently drove past my little two-bedroom home on Lawrence Street, Glen Innes, and the same glossy tiles are still on the steps; the handrail they had installed is still there. I don't know if the grip tape is.

Out of that payout, I had to pay Medicare and Centrelink back from the date of the accident, my barrister $17,000 per day, plus other expenses. I bought myself a car, and I bought M5 an old Land Cruiser ute. I also bought three-quarters of an acre to build a house on, and I bought a shop. I had $60,000 left to build a house.

I learnt a lot from that period in my life. To stand up for what is right. To be that one small voice. That the little person can win against the government and change things for the better. And I learnt to harden the fuck up.

1995-1996 Lawrance Street Glen Innes, NSW, where I broke my leg

1996 In a wheelchair for my broken leg at my ten year school reunion, at Glen Innes RSL Club

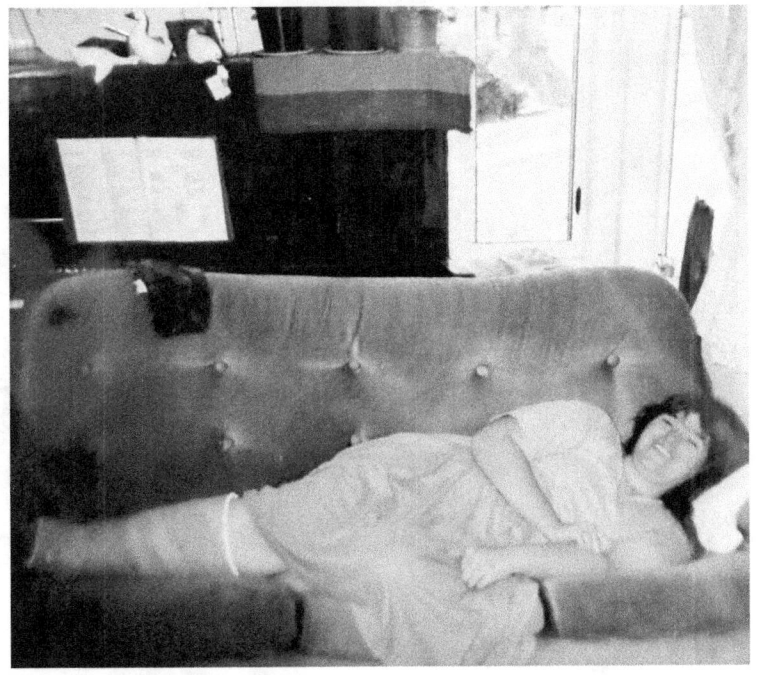

1996 Lawrance Street, Glen Innes with a broken leg

1996 The steps where I broke my leg, Lawrance Street, Glen Innes, NSW

CHAPTER 11

Princess Pain's Birth

Back in 1996 I tried to go to Sydney every six months to visit Mum. I would have loved to visit more often, but we were in no financial position to travel there. I called as often as I could.

It was the end of 1996, and M5, Zak, and I made the trip to Sydney for my cousin Matt's wedding. We visited Mum. We decided to take her out for the day, and took her to Taronga Zoo in the mini bus that we had hired from where Mum lived.

Mum was such a terrible wheelchair driver. I spent all day panicking that she would drive it straight off the gutters, a repeat of her rolling her scooter off the gutter in 1993 onto the New England Highway. At this stage I was five months pregnant. It was hot. We still managed to have a great day with some fond memories and a few photos. Mum loved Zak's expressions when he looked at the animals.

It was very tiring for me; I was exhausted by the end of the day. Her wheelchair didn't have enough zoom for it to get up a lot of the hills at the zoo, so I had to help push her chair.

Mum got cranky with me several times when it looked like she was going to drive the chair off the gutter again, and I would panic. But I'm glad that we made the trip. Mum spent a lot of the time with Zak on her lap, giving him rides. She really did love him.

We returned home to Glen Innes after being away for a week. It was so hard saying goodbye to Mum and leaving her in such a depressing place. Each time we left, she would make me feel guilty for leaving her there.

My pregnancy was going well. The baby was growing bigger, and I had no complications at that stage. I had cravings, but not as bad as when I had Zak. With this pregnancy, it was salt and vinegar chips. Packet after packet, until I made myself sick. But the morning sickness wasn't anywhere near what I experienced with Zak. This time, I actually put on weight, and hated my body even more.

I wasn't doing much work while I was pregnant. The odd mystery shop, while Zak attended childcare at Gumtree Glen a couple of days a week, enabled me to still go to hobby ceramics. Over the previous three years, I had been supplementing my income by making and selling hobby ceramics. I supplied five shops with my work, and I won many awards. I would help teach at Blue Iris studio to help out Diana, who owned the studio. She would pay me with credit to use in the studio. It suited us both.

It was just after my birthday in early March 1997 when Diana's son-in-law came marching into the studio in a manic rage, screaming and demanding that I give him money for a telephone bill for eight months earlier, when I had borrowed their phone. At the same time, my car was supposed to come back fully detailed, serviced, not to have been driven on any dirt roads, and if anything was broken on it, they had to repair it. It came back with a quick wash, a broken window visor, not serviced, and having been driven on dirt roads. They had broken our agreement.

I told him I wasn't going to give him any more money until I saw the bill, which he couldn't produce. I'd already given them $150. He then stood and screamed at me within a couple of centimetres of my face that he was going to kill me and Zak and burn down my house. It was horrific. We had a room full of students. I was seven and a half months pregnant, and thinking that Zak and I were about to die. I had seen the damage that he had caused over the years with his bipolar episodes, and now I stood in full force of one.

Dana was in the kitchen when this happened, but she could hear him, and she came in and told him to get out. I was shaking, and it wasn't a good feeling. One of the students asked me if I was okay.

I replied that I wasn't.

Diana took me around to the police station and insisted that I report the matter, even though he was her son-in-law. I gave a statement, and the police suggested that I have an Apprehended Violence Order (AVO) put out on him so he couldn't come near me, Zak or my house. I was so shaken by it all. My heart was racing at 1000 miles an hour. I felt clammy. I started to develop pains in my tummy, and I kept it a secret for a few hours.

I mentioned to the lady sitting next to me that I thought I was having contractions. She then went and told Diana, who told M5 about what had happened. It was a Tuesday, I remember this because we had antenatal classes that night. I decided not to go to the doctor but to wait until class to talk to the midwife. She knew all about me because she was the midwife on duty when Zak was born.

We went into class, and I went straight up to the instructor, who was also the midwife, and told her what had happened. By that stage, my contractions were becoming more frequent. I was only 33 weeks pregnant. Antenatal classes were at the old nurse's home on the grounds of Glen Innes Hospital. The midwife suggested that we go to the maternity ward and get checked out, then put on a fetal heart monitor, which we did. I was put on the monitor and was given an internal examination in between contractions.

I had started to dilate, and I was in the early stages of labour. From that moment everything moved quite quickly. I was given a steroid via an internal suppository into the vagina to stop labour. It wasn't working. I was still having contractions. Glen Innes was two hours from a major hospital in Tamworth. There was no way to get me there in time to deliver a premmie baby, and they were afraid that I would have the baby in the ambulance on the way down.

I was then told that the flying doctors were coming to pick me up to fly me to Sydney. I was to remain very still in bed and not move around. I was terrified that I was about to lose my baby. I was so scared and angry. M5 contacted Diana to let her know what was happening, and she said that she would look after Zak for us, which was a huge relief.

I flew down to Sydney with the medical team and went into the women's hospital in Randwick, where I was put on complete bed rest. I had an ultrasound and decided to find out what sex I was having, as I didn't want to be the last one to know if I had to have an emergency caesarean again. I requested that if I were to have a caesarean, I wanted to be put entirely under and not go through another painful, horrific childbirth. Diana had arranged for Zak to stay with M5's parents, and she and M5 came down by train to be with me.

The longer I could keep the baby in me, the closer to home I could deliver. Depending on how many weeks she stayed in, I could either get back as far as Tamworth or Armadale Hospitals, or back to Glen Innes. Each hospital was graded differently for handling premmie babies.

My contractions finally stopped, and after two and a half weeks in a hospital in Sydney, I was allowed to go home. If I then went back into labour, Glen Innes Hospital had the capability to look after a 36-week-term baby. The only question was how we were going to get home. M5 and I ended up flying home, as there was no way that I could sit on the train for the eight-hour trip home without going back into labour. I had special approval to fly.

I had to go to court to have the AVO put on my abuser. I was so scared that I would run into him, that he would harm Zak or burn down my house. The AVO was granted by the court. I felt a bit safer.

I wasn't allowed to do too much, to try to keep the pregnancy to full-term. At 38 and a half weeks, on Friday, 11th April, I started to get contractions again. By Saturday morning, we were at an auction and my pains were increasing. So I took myself up to the hospital to check whether the baby was okay and that I wasn't dilating any further.

I spent the day with the fetal monitor on and being poked and prodded. I was then allowed to go home. I didn't sleep much for the next three days, having constant contractions. I went to my doctor on the Tuesday, and discovered I was only a centimetre dilated. He said that he would induce me the next day.

I arranged for Zak to go to my in-laws. I was ready. 8 am the next morning, I rocked up to the hospital, just wanting this pregnancy to end. They put the gel in to ripen my cervix, and now it was just a waiting game. My pains were increasing by the hour, something that I had never really experienced with Zak. By 3 pm, I was in full labour, lying on the beanbag and having my back rubbed.

Because of the steroids they had given me at 33 weeks, my fundal height had grown to an impressive 49 cm at 39 weeks pregnant. I was huge; my belly had a street map full of stretch marks, some as wide as 1 cm and 30+ cm long, dark purple tracks. The nurse suggested that I have a bath. I felt like a beached whale — I was so big that the water in the tub wouldn't even cover all of my belly. I was lying in the bath sucking on gas — it was going to be a long night.

As I was the only one delivering that night, I was taken into the labour suite at 9:30 pm after being in my room all day. My doctor did an internal examination, and I was only 2 cm dilated. I was gutted; I was so tired and exhausted from having contractions for five very long days. I just wanted it to end, I could've opted for a caesarean at that point, but knowing the pain of a caesarean, and keen to have a VBAC (a vaginal birth after caesarian), I said no.

I was heavily sucking on the gas. It took me all day to dilate a further one centimetre. I was in so much distress, thinking that it was going to take me another 40 hours to get to full dilation. My doctor suggested that I be given pethidine to help me sleep and get some rest. This was to be administered at the change of nursing shift.

M5 was annoying the crap out of me, more so than usual, I told him to piss off and leave me alone. Diana suggested to her husband Alan that he take M5 for a walk to get some food and then come back in a little while. I didn't want him anywhere near me. It was about 10:30 pm when I had the pethidine injection. By that time M5 had returned.

I just wanted to sleep. However, my body had other ideas. I thought I had to go to the toilet to do a poop, so I sat on the toilet and I rocked from side to side but nothing happened, so I hopped back up onto the labour bed.

I lay down on my side and tried to close my eyes. I let out a huge scream, saying I needed to push. I was told not to be silly, as I wasn't dilated enough to push. But to try and get some sleep. Again I thought I needed to poop, and no one thought anything different as I was only 2 cm dilated, so I went back to the toilet and rocked on it again, but still nothing came.

I climbed back into bed and lay on my left side for a few minutes, and then felt this almighty pain, it was about 11 pm and screamed that I wanted to push now! The midwife came running in to check why I was screaming. She said that she would check what was happening. I remember lying on my back, opening my legs and the look of horror on the midwife's face when she said, "Oh my god, you're crowning; don't push if you want your doctor to get here before the baby is born!"

She then rang my doctor to tell him to come back to the hospital as he had only just gone home, she then walked past the foot of my bed just as my waters broke and sprayed the other side of the room, and her, from the force.

I was trying not to push, and to wait for my doctor to get back, sucking hard on the gas. He returned and said that I'd be responsible for any speeding fines he got while coming along Church Street with his hazard lights flashing to get back to the hospital. At that point, I didn't care.

I had Diana holding one hand, M5 holding the other, one foot on the midwife's hip, the other foot on my doctor's hip, bearing down and pushing after I threw the gas away. At 11:28 pm on 16th April, Alexandra Victoria Martin-Bradshaw was born. I needed no stitches and had only a slight graze, and a body that was full of pethidine. Alexandra was born with a body weight of 8lb 1oz, a length of 51cm, and a head circumference of 35cm.

She was just perfect. I was in complete shock, as it happened so fast. I was told that if I ever had another child, the moment that I had contractions, I'd better be sitting on the hospital doorstep.

The following morning, I got a phone call, and life as I knew it changed forever.

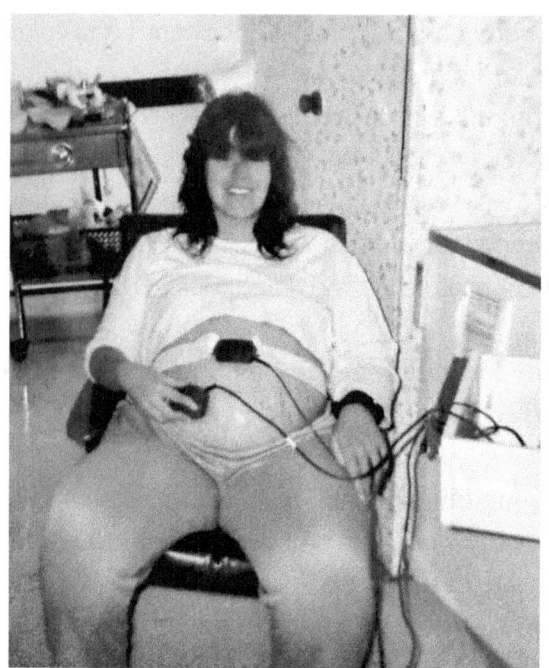
1997 Five days before Ally was born, Glen Innes Hospital

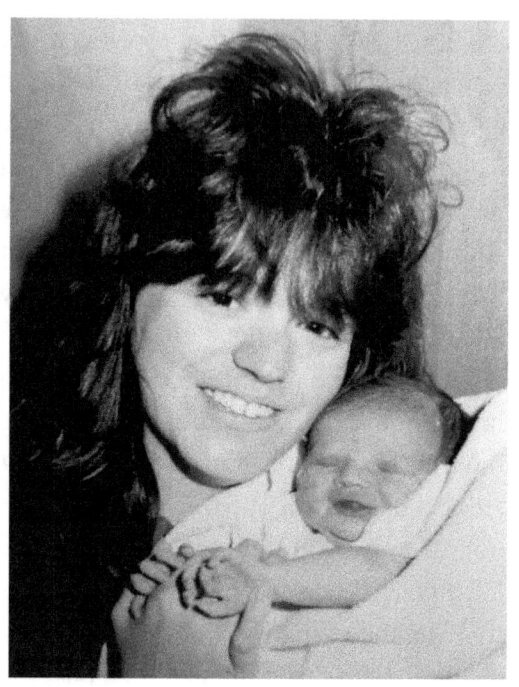
1997 Ally and me the day we went home from hospital

1997 Ally and myself at Wooli NSW

1997 Ally at 8 months old at Rangers Valley Dam NSW

1997 Zak and Ally

1997 Zak, Ally and myself

2002 Ally dressed as Barbie at Glen Innes parklands

CHAPTER 12

She Was Supposed to Live Forever

I couldn't believe I had given birth to a daughter. I was shell-shocked from her birth. I am one of the rare women who can describe what it's like to have a vaginal birth after a C-section. Both have their pros and cons. The next day, I was up and about. I showered myself and was receiving visitors, flowers and phone calls.

My Nanna Marie, who at the time had moved from Sydney to Victoria, received a phone call from Auburn Hospital. Mum had been taken to hospital a week earlier, with a urinary tract infection (UTI). Mum never drank enough water due to the fact that her throat muscles were affected by the MS, and she had trouble swallowing as well as talking. No one had told us she had been admitted. While she was in the hospital, they noticed that she was a little bit chesty, so they gave her a chest X-ray.

They found a spot on her lungs that then led to her having a lung biopsy. There was no family consent for this to happen. We were unaware that it had happened until the results came back. They told Mum that she had lung cancer, with no one there to support her when she was told. It was the third primary cancer she had. It was only then that they realised that she was no longer of sound mind to make any medical decisions about her health. Nanna called to break the sad news to Simon and me.

We had 24 hours to decide whether we would have half her right lung removed or leave it, as she would undoubtedly die.

Simon came up to the hospital a short time later, and we rang Nanna together. It was then that the three of us decided that we would consent to Mum having the operation; we had to do everything we possibly could so she could survive. Never in my wildest dreams did I think that something would happen to her.

Nanna had to go to Sydney to sign the consent forms, as I couldn't travel less than 48 hours after giving birth, and neither could Simon due to work commitments.

Ally was one week old when Mum had her lung operation. Mum was not very well at all. Ally was two weeks old when the four of us, M5, Zak, Ally and I, drove the regular eight hours south in our HZ Premier to Sydney, unsure of what we would find when we got there. It took us close to 12 hours to make the trip. As I was breastfeeding Ally, we had to keep stopping so I could feed her. It was a traumatic trip.

We stayed at M5's sister's place in Guildford — a little three-bedroom home. We slept on a mattress on the floor for the duration of our stay. Not an easy thing to do after giving birth.

The next day, we went to see Mum; it was a sight I'll never forget. She had so many tubes coming out of her — tubes in her nose, a tracheotomy, and three tubes out of her chest to drain the blood and the fluid. As Mum struggled to drink anything and eat due to her throat, she had a peg put surgically into her stomach, which enabled them to feed her a liquid diet; she was never able to eat normally again. Instead of only having 60 millilitres of fluid a day, she was having a couple of litres.

Nanna was as pleased to see us as we were to see her. Mum knew we were there and was able to meet her new granddaughter.

While staying in Sydney for two and a half weeks, I visited every single day. Each day, Mum was improving. She had had the majority of the tubes removed and was making significant progress, sitting up and talking to us as much as she could. The MS had affected her speech years earlier, so it was hard to understand her.

It was becoming more uncomfortable staying with M5's sister and her family. They smoked inside, her two children fought constantly, and having a newborn baby there, along with a four-year-old, just added fuel to the mix. I didn't want to go home, but I didn't really have a choice.

Mum was not allowed to go permanently back to the MS home unless I got her on a nursing home list somewhere. I had to try to find somewhere that could care for her with the tracheotomy and her decline in health and mobility. She was now fully wheelchair-bound.

Mum got to kiss Alexandra. She was very happy to meet her; she had always wanted a little girl called Alexandra, and that's what she had planned to call Simon if he'd been a girl. Alexandra's middle name, Victoria, came from her father's mother's middle name. She had two names from former Queens. This prompted us to give her the nickname 'Princess Pain' as she grew up. She was a difficult child.

It was tough to return to Glen Innes, leaving Mum there only five weeks after she had her operation. I cried most of the trip home. If I'd known what would happen only a few weeks later, I would never have left.

A few days later, she returned to the MS home, and I set about trying to get her on a nursing home list.

It was Friday, 6th June, when I got confirmation that Roseneath Nursing Home in Glen Innes would accept her on their list, and as soon as a bed became available, she would be transported back to Glen Innes. Roseneath was only a 10-minute drive from us and would make life a lot easier for us all, as Simon was now living back there too.

Monday, June 9, was a long weekend, and it was Zak's fourth birthday party when the phone rang. On the other end was an Asian woman whom I could barely understand. She said that she was a nurse from Auburn Hospital and she was caring for Mum. No one had even bothered to tell us that Mum had been readmitted to hospital on Friday. The nurse said to me that I had to come in straight away as my mother was dying. Not fully understanding her, my reply was "Do you realise how far away I am?" She repeated, "Your mother dying, come."

I couldn't believe what she was saying. It was surreal. I hung up the phone and rang Nanna straight away. She, too, had received a phone call. She asked me if I thought that maybe they were just panicking and that Mum wasn't dying. I knew in my gut that wasn't the case and that I had to get to Sydney.

I rang Simon, as he had also received a call. They had a 10-month-old son, my nephew Jesse. They decided to drive to Sydney, and Jesse would stay with his grandparents. M5 and I considered driving, but Diana wouldn't hear of it. It would take such a long time for us to drive there, and I was also in no physical or mental state to drive that distance. We had no money. Diana offered to pay for our flights so we could fly down that evening. Zak went out to my in-laws, and Diana drove us to the Glen Innes airport.

We caught the 7 pm flight. I knew that Mum was alive when we got on the flight, but I wasn't sure if she was alive when we got to Sydney. I was in such a state. Then we went to catch a taxi, and since it was Monday of the long weekend, there were hardly any cabs available. The line was huge. We finally got a cab and arrived at Auburn Hospital at 11 pm. Thankfully, Mum was still alive.

She knew who I was, and she told me that she loved me. I kissed her and looked into her eyes lovingly. I saw fear and confusion looking back at me. The look in her eyes still haunts me.

She also told me that my dad had been in to see her. He hadn't actually been there, and it had been 10 years since she had seen him. Mum kept saying that she loved him and that she also wanted to go home. She had the death rattle in her chest. You could hear her drowning in her own fluid. Her catheter bag was full of blood as her kidneys were no longer working. It was at that point that I knew for sure that she wasn't going to make it. I looked at her medical chart at the end of her bed, as I had become very good at reading them over the years with all of her hospital visits. She had been given only two paracetamol tablets all day.

I sat with her for a couple of hours and held her hand while trying to feed Alexandra at the same time, telling her to hold on, that Simon was on the way to see her and that we all loved her very much. She kept saying "Please take me home, please take me home." It was soul-destroying.

She was in the cardiac ward of Auburn Hospital, in a room with three other patients — all with varying degrees of ill health. The nurse's station was straight outside her door. Her bed was closest to the window with the privacy screens closed. At about 1:15 am, Simon and Marissa arrived. The nurse had shown us where the waiting room was and gave me a pillow and a blanket. I went and lay on the floor and fed Alexandra. I was so physically and emotionally drained. Simon and Marissa sat with Mum. I went down to check a few times. Mum had lost consciousness, and Simon was holding her hand. She was dying.

At five minutes to 4 am, the nurse came in and told me that Mum had gone. I bolted up off the floor, left Alexandra with M5 and ran down the hallway. I saw Marissa standing outside the door. I asked where Simon was and he was downstairs at the toilet. I walked into her ward and went behind the curtain. Mum was lying there, looking peaceful and finally out of pain.

I stood there for a long while, unable to comprehend what had just happened. She wasn't supposed to die. She was supposed to live forever. She was supposed to fight, like she had fought through everything else in her life.

What next? What were we supposed to do next? I had never had to deal with death first-hand before. Now I had no choice. Simon came back, and we held each other and cried.

As I was the oldest, I took the responsibility to call her parents and siblings to tell them of her death. The nurse directed me to a phone on the floor below us, and I went down there by myself to make the heartbreaking calls.

First, I called her parents, and Parpa answered the phone. It was 4.15 am. My words telling him that his daughter had passed and him crying on the end of the phone will stay with me forever. As parents, we think that we are going to die before our children, not the other way around. It was gut-wrenching, and the only time I've ever heard my grandfather cry. Next, I rang my Auntie Lyn and broke the news to her that her sister was gone, then two more phone calls to Mum's brothers, Jeff and Chris.

I told both that I would call back later that morning, as arrangements would need to be made. This was supposed to be a time in my life where I was celebrating the birth of my baby girl, not telling the family of my mother's death. I returned to Mum's ward on level 5 and went behind the curtain. The nurses gave us time to grieve with Mum, still in a room with the three strangers. We were conscious of trying to keep our noise down as we all cried in our sorrow. Mum looked so peaceful, finally out of pain, and oh, so beautiful.

Nanna had said to me on the phone before I left to fly down that if something happened to Mum, to make sure we got all of her jewellery, if she was wearing any. I was comfortable holding Mum's hand after she died, and took off her watch that she wore and gave it to Simon. I told him to keep it for Jesse. I then went to get the little signet ring that she wore on her wedding finger, which her parents had given her when she was 13. I couldn't get it off her finger. I started to panic.

Everything was racing through my mind. I couldn't leave it on her finger. I'd heard stories about how funeral homes take the jewellery off loved ones before they're buried, and I didn't want that to happen. Plus, I was trying to follow Nanna's instructions. The sun was coming up, and the nurse came in, and I asked about the ring. She explained that they had a ring cutter and went to get it. I held Mum's cold lifeless hand open while the nurse used the ring cutter to cut off the little ring. I've never had the ring repaired; it still has the cut in it and sits in my jewellery case.

It was about 5.30 am, and we all just stood there in shock wondering what we were supposed to do now. How could we just leave her there? It's not like when you go to visit someone in the hospital and say goodbye to them, and that you'll see them next time.

I went out to the nurse's station as the doctor was signing Mum's death certificate and asked them what we should do now. The nurse replied that it was our responsibility to call the funeral home and get Mum picked up. I explained that we weren't from Sydney and didn't know of any in the area. She then told me to look one up in the yellow pages. I was mortified.

The doctor handed me my mum's death certificate; her cause of death was complications from multiple sclerosis (MS). We had been told for years that you couldn't die from MS, yet here it was in black-and-white in front of me.

I walked back into the ward and explained to the others what the nurse said. We decided to go back to where we were staying, and I would make some phone calls after 9 am. We all needed some sleep. M5 and I stayed at his sister's house again — this time she was away — and Simon and Marissa stayed at her brother's house.

I got back to the house, M5 went to bed, and I sat on the lounge and howled in despair that I had let my mother down. That I couldn't save her. I felt so much guilt for putting her into that home and not being there for her, and not even being in the room when she took her final breaths.

I felt so alone and abandoned. I would carry this pain for many, many, many years to come. I'd had no contact with my father for 10 years and felt like I was an orphan. M5 had zero compassion for what I was going through.

By 9 am that morning, I had composed myself. I was worried that, from the shock of everything, I would lose my milk. There were lots of phone calls between my grandparents, my uncles and my aunt about where we were going to lay my mum to rest. Ultimately, it was up to Simon and me to decide. We chose Glen Innes. When Mum had repeatedly said that she wanted to go home, we took that to mean the place where we spent the longest, and she always considered 248 Meade Street her home. No one spoke up and said anything different. My Uncle Jeff and Uncle Gra were the executors of her will. I booked an appointment at 2 pm that afternoon for Simon, myself and my uncles Jeff and Chris who met us at the funeral home to make the arrangements. We were on a tight budget. Who knew every little change would cost so much?

She had been collected from the morgue by the funeral home, which was waiting for us to make a decision. Mum's final will never stated what she wanted done on her death, and she never spoke about it. We decided to have her buried, as she'd been through so much in life. I couldn't handle her having anything else done to her. We had to pick out her coffin. It had no handles on it as they cost more. It was a dark red gloss wood, with a cream satin inlay and a little pillow.

We decided to have a viewing so the family could say goodbye to Mum. She was always a very proud woman and dressed accordingly. However, it had been quite some time since she had been to the hairdresser or beautician. I made sure that the mortician had cut her hair and plucked the stray hairs on her face. She would've been mortified if people had seen her the way she was, and I'm sure she would come back to haunt me!

Mum had the most amazing long nails, like talon claws. I wanted them to be painted bright 'Hooker' red, but my uncles outvoted me. They said they were to be painted a neutral colour, beige and boring. I didn't have the energy to argue.

It was decided that I would pick out her outfit. Nanna and Parpa drove up that day from Woodend, Victoria, to Sydney. They stayed with friends out at Windsor. The rest of the family made their way up the following day. I went into the MS home to tell them of Mum's passing and to pick out her outfit. I chose an emerald green skirt and top, with a beaded necklace and her black slip-on shoes. I went out and purchased new underwear and pantyhose for her to wear. I made sure that she was buried with her bra on and her prosthetic breast in. All while trying to look after a newborn baby. It was beyond tough.

On Wednesday, Nanna and I went to the MS home and started packing up Mum's things to clear out her room, or they would charge us more. Things that I had left the day before were now missing. Someone had been in and stolen her expensive items. Who does that? It was like adding salt to the wounds. We never got those items back.

Mum was to have two funerals — one in Sydney and one in Glen Innes. Nanna asked me if I would do Mum's eulogy. I can't even begin to imagine how hard it was for my Nanna to bury her daughter. We sat down and wrote the three pages.

Mum's Eulogy

Marian, our Marian, our mum, one of a kind. Born at Darling Point in 1947.

Mum was educated at Woodend Primary, Kyneton High, Sydney Business College, and, in her later years, Glen Innes TAFE. Mum was an office manager and secretary, and a great mum and grandmother.

Mum won her battle against breast cancer at 28 years of age. She was the secretary and founder of the Victorian Mastectomy Association, and counselled women in hospital with the same condition.

At 33 years of age, she contracted Multiple Sclerosis, or MS. Despite Mum's disabilities, Mum worked hard and alone for her children — myself and my brother Simon. Mum had so much courage that she would address school children about MS and her disabilities.

My grandparents tell me of her indignation at 3 years of age, having to wear her baby sister's nappy home after falling in a creek, and as a teenager, the wolf whistles she received when modelling on a school speech night. Inevitably, Mum made the school choir, although as my brother and I know all too well, she was tone deaf. She was surreptitiously climbing in the kitchen window at 1 am, but her loving parent had lined up the empty milk bottles on the sink, so it was anything but a silent entry. They tell me Mum was grounded for 2 weeks.

Mum was a cub mistress for many years in Geelong; she loved music and could play the piano and guitar. Her favourite piece being Für Elise. Mum rode motor bikes and had her motorbike licence, she snow skied, raced speed boats and actually won a few races, and she used to run a petrol station.

Mum loved daffodils and helped sell them for 6d a bunch with Uncle Jeff and Aunty Lyn as children.

She belonged to the Youth Hostels Association and was a very good traveller.

Mum was the owner of a FJ Holden and it was painted flame red. It was outrageous but only Maz/mum could drive it. It was loud like she was.

Marian was shortened to May or Ming, then to Masher, from which originated the myth that Mum was a lady wrestler.

Mum was a member of the Glen Innes Quota club and was the first secretary for the Glen Innes High School parents' support group, and worked at the Garden Court Centre.

Mum had a great sense of humour, the strongest willpower and the biggest courage of anyone I've ever known.

Mum has been a brave and silent sufferer for so long and has earned this last and final rest. We, her family and friends, who love her dearly, will miss her.

God rest her soul, AMEN.

On Thursday, we had a viewing of Mum at the funeral home. I remember walking into the chapel and seeing Mum lying in the coffin with a large 'doily' over the top of her. Little beads all the way around, a smaller version of what would sit over a milk jug in olden days. I couldn't handle seeing Mum with that over her, so I asked the funeral director to remove it. We all wrote letters about everything that we could never say to her, but wanted to. Then we put them in the coffin with her. I put in some little fairies I had made with hobby ceramics, along with photos of Zak, Ally, and me. My letter told her I was sorry for all the pain and hurt we had caused each other, and how I had let her down.

Not all the family went in to see her. My Uncle Jeff, Auntie Dee and their three children, Kylie, Joshua and Julia, met us at the church. The viewing felt so rushed; everyone slowly made their way out, and I stayed behind. I told her that I was so sorry for not being good enough. For not being there for her to take care of her, and that I had failed her. Pretty much the same as I had written in her letter. I looked out the back window and saw the white van they would use to transport her. I've never been able to look at a white van the same way again.

We then went to the church.

There were about 50 people there, many of them in wheelchairs. I stood up and gave the eulogy without fault. I never cried through the service. I was numb. We had the reception at the MS home — a lovely afternoon tea. I had people coming up to me and commenting on how much fun Mum was. How she made everyone laugh. In my mind I was thinking 'What the actual fuck!' I asked them if they were sure it was my mum they were talking about. It was. Every time I visited or called her, she made me feel like it was hell on earth for her living there, like she hated it.

Friday saw M5, Ally, and me drive home with Simon and Marissa in his blue Commodore with the three of us sitting in the backseat. I had a large bag on my lap, containing various items, including nappies and clothes for Ally. It felt strange leaving Mum in Sydney, even for that short time. She was being transported later that day. The conversation was varied, and we were talking about how expensive it was to transport Mum from Sydney to Glen Innes. We joked that she wouldn't have minded if we had put her in a trailer on the back of us.

We'd been travelling for around 2 and a half hours when I began to smell nail polish, and I asked everyone else in the car if they smelled it too. They said I was nuts. Then, half an hour later, my sister-in-law remarked that she could now smell it too. Then it dawned on me that it was coming from the bag on my lap. I opened up the bag to discover that the bright hooker red nail polish that I wanted painted on mum's nails had leaked its contents throughout my bag — I took it as a sign that Mum had wanted to have that colour as well. We all had a chuckle as I tried to clean up the mess.

A couple of hours later, Simon's mobile phone rang. It was our father. That was the first time I'd heard his voice in 10 years. It was a very emotional time, and I was full of anger. He said that he couldn't come over for the funeral, but he would be over the following year. After the call there was a lot of discussion in the car about this subject. Simon had found him three years earlier when he got married, and invited him to his wedding. Our grandparents didn't go to Simon's wedding because my dad was invited, due to my grandfather's hatred of my father. My father never turned up to the wedding either — such a sad thing.

It was cold, wet and sleeting on Saturday, 14 June when we had mum's second funeral at the Anglican church in Glen Innes. None of my in-laws attended; they took care of Zak instead. I stood up again and read Mum's eulogy to all of her friends, and mine and Simon's who attended. I didn't cry. The funeral procession was led up Meade Street, within 30 m of where we used to live, and up the hill to the cemetery, where Mum was laid to rest.

It was so sad driving past our old home with Mum in the casket in front of us. I can't remember who the pallbearers were. We had no other family with us. The rest had gone back home and on with their own lives. We had to learn to harden the fuck up that day when we put her in the ground.

My mum's headstone was made from sandstone by my cousin Matty. My Aunty Lynn designed the plaque and had it made from stainless steel. A month later, Uncle Jeff helped me install it, after paying a permit fee to the Glen Innes council to put the headstone there. We didn't quite line it up with the rest of the row, and even today, she sticks out 20cm more than the others. She is in the lawn section, near the pine trees, in the row with the tap, and surrounded by people I know. When visiting the cemetery, Zak would want to play soccer where the dead people lived, promising he wouldn't kick the ball on their bodies. I said no with a smile on my face, as Mum would have laughed at that.

Six weeks after Mum died, I woke up in the middle of the night, and Mum was sitting next to me on the edge of the bed. She was in the clothes I had picked for her to be buried in. Her voice was different; the MS had affected her speech in the last few years and was very difficult to understand. But as she sat there, her voice sounded like it did when I was a child. Mum told me that I should not worry about her. She thanked me for everything I had done for her. She said that heaven was a place where we get all our body parts back, are healthy, and we go back to an age in our lives that we were most happiest at. She said she was going to live eternity at the age of 25, when Simon and I were little, Dad and she were in a good place, and before she was diagnosed with breast cancer.

I woke up the next morning and couldn't wait to share it with my nanna. My nanna remarked that she hoped that Mum would come and visit her too. What mum said to me about heaven has made it a little easier to deal with the idea of dying.

Three months later, I was not coping very well at all. I was angry with everyone. I hated the world. It was raining heavily one day, and I felt the need to go up to the cemetery and open an umbrella over Mum's grave to stop her from getting wet. We were going down to Coffs Harbour with Diana, Alan and Kat for a family weekend away. I broke down and didn't want to leave Mum. It was then that Diana suggested that I go and get some grief counselling.

I went to my doctor and was prescribed some antidepressants; not only did I have depression from my mum's death, but I also had postnatal depression from Ally's birth. I was not in a mentally good state at all. I had put on so much weight and was hating my body even more, as well as everyone around me. In July, I joined Weight Watchers for the second time, and weighed in at 117 kg. I was disgusted with myself. However, I didn't last very long at Weight Watchers and quit again for the second time. The pain that I was experiencing in my leg and my ankle from the break prevented me from exercising or going on any walks.

I took myself off antidepressants as I didn't like the zombie feeling they gave me and thought that they weren't working anyway; there had to be a better way to feel like my usual self. We spent a lot of time at Emmaville with my in-laws, sleeping in the old house, which was over 100 years old, next door. I had to duck to get in through the back door. It was a bitterly cold winter. I don't remember too much about the rest of that year. Both kids were growing, but as for their milestones, I can't recall many of them at all; it's all just a blur. I look back on photos from that time and don't even recognise my own daughter in them. It was a very sad time in my life.

Writing this chapter has been hard, recalling the memories and the emotions. You never get over the death of a loved one. You just learn to live with it. In spite of everything that Mum did to me, she was still my mum, and I miss her terribly. After a lot of counselling, I forgave her many, many years ago for the way she treated me.

1995 Mum's last Christmas

1996 Mum

1993 Four generations celebrating the Queen's Birthday with Mum, Parpa, Nanna and Zak. This photo was front page of the Glen Innes Examiner

1997 Mum after her lung surgery with Ally. Mum died 2 weeks later

1997 Mum's death certificate

1997 Mum's funeral service sheet

1997 Mum's funeral

CHAPTER 13

Waiting for God to Give Me a Sign

I met him, fell pregnant two weeks later, and fell in love with the idea of being part of a perfect family. I wasn't in love with him. I was in love with the idea of him. Wanting to be accepted.

We got engaged four months after meeting for the first time, and my belly was showing. My engagement ring was a piece of costume jewellery from the local junk shop, gold-plated and with a piece of glass as the stone. We had an engagement party in the backyard of the house I was living in, 40 Lewis St, Glen Innes. His family and my friends attended. I don't remember any of my family being there. He didn't have any friends outside of his family, as he had only lived in Glen Innes for about six months in total. My friends became his friends.

We had about 30 people attend the party. We had a cake and the fake ring. He wasn't working and was on the dole. It was so cold, colder than usual for that time of the year. I don't remember the date, but I think it was in October 1996. People wanted to know the wedding date, so I said it would be in two years' time. I can remember thinking that I had two years to get out of the mess I had put myself in. I just wasn't sure how I could do it at that point. I didn't want to be a single mum in a small country town with two children to two different fathers and not married. Known as THAT mum, and my children being teased about not having a dad.

We had zero money to do anything, no holidays, no new furniture, no new clothes. We were living on the poverty line. I was still living in a Department of Housing house. Zak and I moved out of Lawrence Street, where I had broken my leg, into one of the town's new 3-bedroom brick housing commission homes. As far as commission homes went, it was top-of-the-range.

M5 and I were fighting more and more. At one stage, the town had a plague of mice, and our home was no exception. I am terrified of mice. I have a phobia times 1000 about them. There was one particular night when I was ironing in the kitchen, and a mouse ran along the kitchen bench, having eaten through the flyscreen to get inside. He grabbed the mouse by the tail and chased me through the house with it. He had me trapped in the corner of the kitchen, dangling the mouse in front of my face and laughing about it. I was completely frozen with fear. By this time, I had begun to hate him, and I hated him even more from that day on. My world felt like it was closing in with hate and fear.

I lived with constant lies every day. It was draining. He was telling lies to the outside world about the fantasy jobs he had worked in the past, from a federal police officer to a private investigator. And I, too, was telling lies about how happy I was. My weight ballooned. I was cushioning myself from the outside world and hated myself more and more each day.

The date of our wedding was getting closer. I had planned everything on a tight budget. Our wedding cost less than $3000, and that included everything. We got a lot of help from family and friends:

- Aunty Lynny designed and made our wedding invitations and thank you notes.
- Diana made the wedding cake and the kids' christening cakes.
- A family friend was a DJ and did the music.
- I made my headpiece from old pearl necklaces I bought from garage sales and a roll of copper wire.
- My wedding dress was secondhand and cost $450, and it was a size 26!
- Ally's dress was secondhand and cost $30.
- The wedding cars cost a bottle of wine each.
- The bridesmaid's dresses were $30 from Rockmans. The dresses were black, and they wore their own black shoes.
- We had 60 people at the reception and paid $14.50 a head for a three-course meal cooked by the church ladies.
- My veil was $30 — it had a rip in it. I sewed it up.
- We hired the guys' suits, including Zak's and my nephew Jesse's.
- My bouquet of flowers and the girls' were Australian natives.

- I had gold sashes made from chiffon for all the girls.
- My sister-in-law took the video.
- We bought the basic photo package.

My grandparents both had gambling problems. So I chose not to have the reception at the RSL club where the pokies were; instead, I opted for the church hall. Because we were hiring the church women to cook our meals, we got the hall for free; this also included flowers for the tables.

I did everything the wrong way around, having my children first. Zak was five, and Ally was 18 months old. I thought it would be a great time for both kids to get christened. All we would need to do is pick their godparents and get another cake. So we did. The kids would be christened after we signed the marriage license. I was sad that Mum had passed 17 months earlier, and wouldn't be there to see me get married.

We had picked our bridal party. My matron of honour was my best friend Ali, with whom I went to school, and we had been friends since I was 13. Her husband, Mathew, was the best man. Remember how M5 didn't have any of his own friends? Then I had my cousin Myalie, and the groomsman was my brother Simon. My third bridesmaid was Kat, Diana's daughter, and the groomsman was Michael, who was M5's second cousin and is now deceased. Our flower girl was Ally, and the page boys were Zak and my nephew Jesse. All three of these kids are now married, and my children have their own children!

Everything was going to plan in the timeline, and the day was creeping up fast. The invitations had gone out, and everyone was excited to be coming. My family had to come all the way from Victoria. That was a two-day drive!

It was all becoming too much, and I started to panic. How was I going to get out of this? I didn't want the marriage; I just wanted a wedding. There was a HUGE difference between the two.

About two months from W Day, I rang my aunt and said I didn't want to get married. She laughed and said, "Don't you dare cancel this wedding, Justy! We have all booked our holidays in and have booked our accommodation!" They were booked into the caravan park in cabins, as there were a lot of them. I was trapped. I didn't even have the backing of my family to walk away. I thought God would give me a sign that it was not right. That I shouldn't be marrying him. Well, he did, and plenty of them, but I just didn't realise it at the time.

About 6 weeks out from the Wedding Day, I decided to get my underarms waxed. I'm the type of person who grows thick body hair from my Russian and Scottish genes, and also from having polycystic ovary syndrome (PCOS).

I wanted to be perfect for the big day, even when I knew deep down our relationship was toxic and wouldn't last. So, I booked in to have them waxed. I'd never had them done before and knew it would hurt like a bitch. And I was right. My armpits bled afterwards. It was so painful. I had been getting my eyebrows waxed by this beautician for several years. She ran a salon from her home. Her wax pot was a crockpot. Looking back now, I should have run. There was old dirty wax all around the sides of the pot. It was alarming.

Within a few days of being waxed, I had developed a lump in my left armpit. It was really sore, red and growing. Then it popped, and a vile, green liquid came out. I took myself to the doctor, and I couldn't see my usual doctor, so I saw the town's surgeon instead. He looked at it and said it was an abscess that would need to be drained. The next thing I knew, I was lying on the bed in his room, and he was injecting local anaesthetic into it. I explained that locals never really worked well for me. Before I knew it, he was performing a curette on my armpit, and boy did it hurt. He cleaned out all the gunk and pus and packed it tight with wadding. Each day for the next week, I had to go back to the doctor's surgery to change the dressings. It couldn't be stitched, as abscesses must heal from the inside out, so they packed it with gauze. It was disgusting.

It never occurred to me that it was from her dirty wax pot; I just thought it was because I'd never had my underarms waxed before. I was still waiting for a sign from above…

Tick tock, tick tock, tick tock… Time was passing quicker than ever.

We had to attend marriage counselling with the priest. We were to be married in the Glen Innes Anglican Church, and with it came some rules, including a requirement to have a few sessions of pastoral counselling with the priest. We went to his home, next to the church, for these sessions. I'm sure the priest was drunk on at least one of those occasions. The state of his home was terrible. There were empty wine bottles and beer cans on the floor, as well as dirty underwear lying about. Not something you'd expect to see from a priest. He was also going through a divorce, and he was to marry us! Again, I was waiting for a sign…

My dress I bought second-hand, and it was a size 26, but I was getting bigger and bigger every single day. My weight was out of control. My wedding dress wasn't one I had imagined I'd wear. I searched all over Northern NSW, from Coffs Harbour to Tamworth to Tenterfield. You name the bridal shop, and I went to it. I didn't want my dress to look like a maternity dress. We had had a bridal shop in Glen Innes, but it had closed down. I happened to be chatting with the owner, who was working in another dress shop, where I was still looking for my wedding dress. She commented that she had a dress she thought would be perfect, and if I didn't mind, it was second-hand and dramatically reduced in price. She had sold it to the first bride for over $2000, and she was now selling it for $450. I went to her house and tried it on. It was tight, but it did fit. She was also selling a corset to wear underneath. It was off-the-shoulder with little sleeves. Around the shoulders were satin fabric roses. It had some beading on it and was ivory in colour. I bought it. She also had a matching little flower dress, and it would fit Ally. I bought that too. It was so cute.

A week out from the wedding, I decided to do the right thing and tidy up my bikini line by not just shaving but getting it waxed, despite the fact that M5 and my sex life was pretty much non-existent by this point. I went back to the beautician to be waxed. That was a terrible mistake. It was on the 25th September at 10 am, I was lying there, watching her wax me as she reused the wooden stick, dipping it into the hot wax each time. How many other people had she used that stick on their vagina, and how many times had it been in that hot wax? She still hadn't cleaned her wax pot.

That evening was my hen's night. There were only three of us and we went to the pub. It was nothing exciting, no strippers, no party games, and by 9 pm, I felt terrible and wanted to go home. The next day was my kitchen tea, and I had a pain in my groin and felt nauseous. I was struggling to walk. I had about 12 women at my house, and everyone brought a plate to share. Again, we didn't do any bridal party games, and I just wanted everyone to go home. By Sunday afternoon, I was stuck lying on the lounge, running a temperature, and my sore on the right side of my groin had turned into two large lumps that had ruptured and were leaking pus down my leg. It was disgusting.

The first thing on Monday morning, I called and got an appointment with the doctor. Again, seeing the surgeon as I knew what I had and would again need them to be curetted. I was booked in at 11 am. I drove myself, and I hobbled into the surgery. I saw the surgeon, and he shook his head, saying they would both need to be lanced in surgery. I asked him if I should book in for that afternoon, and he said, "No, you'll have to go to the theatre tomorrow." I was in shock! I blurted out, "But I'm getting married on Saturday!" He replied,"Not unless you get this done, you're not." I suddenly thought about how I was going to walk down the aisle. Again, not seeing the signs.

I had five sleeps to get better. Somehow, I didn't think that was going to happen. I went to the hospital on Tuesday morning after fasting from the night before. As I had an infection, I would be last on the list, to avoid infecting all the other patients, a day of waiting and wondering with my anxiety about what was going to happen. I was put under a general anaesthetic at 3:30 pm. It was a very long day with no food or water. I was expecting to go home, even if I had to hobble, but the pain I was in was 10/10! They kept me in overnight. M5 was working at Roseneath Nursing Home as a nursing assistant. He was annoyed that I had to stay in overnight. Zak and Ally went to stay at Diana and Alan's for the night. Wednesday came, and I had to have my dressings changed.

I had two holes on the right side of my groin. One was the size of a walnut, and the other was large enough to fit an extra-large egg. The nurse pulled out a long piece of wadding about 2 feet long out of the smaller hole — the pain was excruciating — and repacked it with a fresh dressing. Then came the second one. I nearly passed out from the pain. This dressing was almost 4 feet long. I was amazed that so much fabric could fit inside the cuts on my leg. I had no idea how deep the holes in my leg were. I wanted to stay in hospital another night to control the pain, but M5 wouldn't take a night off work, and I had to go home at lunchtime to look after the kids.

Three sleeps and counting.

How was I going to cope? And yet I STILL couldn't see the signs!

My family arrived on Thursday, and I was so happy to see them all. My aunt embraced me, and I broke down with the pain I was in, hobbling everywhere when I walked, lying down, sitting and standing. I couldn't get comfortable.

Two more sleeps, and I knew I was trapped.

I had invited my dad to my special day. He was living in NZ. He couldn't come. I was very disappointed. He was invited to Simon's wedding 4 years earlier and didn't come to that either. The fact that he was invited was enough for my grandparents to say they weren't coming. They couldn't put their hatred away for one special day. It wasn't about them. It was about supporting their grandson. I had asked my Uncle Gra to walk me down the aisle months earlier. My uncle has always been there for me in my 54 years and never said a bad word to me.

That morning, two days before the wedding, Dad rang me out of the blue and asked for my banking details. I asked him why. In my 27 years, he had never given me money. He then asked how much the wedding cost, and I replied, $3000. He deposited that amount into my account. I was blown away. We had 18 months earlier lay-byed my engagement ring, a plain gold thin band with a very small, round, bezel-set diamond. I paid a deposit on it, and M5 was supposed to pay for the rest. He didn't. As everything for the wedding was paid, I used the money from my dad to pay for the rest, and we had enough left to put towards our honeymoon that we weren't going to take and couldn't afford.

One sleep to go, and I had been up to the hospital that morning to have my leg packed, but it wasn't getting any less painful. I sat up this time and watched them pull my leg open in the larger of the two cuts. It was disgusting. I saw the layers of skin and about 5cm deep into the fat in my leg. How was that ever going to heal? No wonder I was in so much pain. I sat and cried, and cried some more.

M5 stayed out at his parents' that night, and I had the kids with me. I woke up early — it was the 3rd October 1998 — and it should have been the happiest day of my life. It wasn't. I was so sad on the inside. I look back on the photos of the day, and you can see it in my eyes. I started the day at the hospital getting my leg packed, and then went downstairs to vote in the federal election. It was going to be a big day!

My bridesmaids turned up for hair and makeup. The boys went to play nine holes of golf, wash the cars and blow up the balloons for the reception. Simple tasks, one would think. However, not one of them took a watch, and instead of playing nine holes, someone thought it was a great idea to play 18 holes. It wasn't. They were running so late that they didn't have time to blow up all the gold balloons. The church ladies realised what had happened and took charge, making sure it was done. The reception looked amazing. Pansies in little vases on the table from someone's garden. My favourite flower.

Before I got dressed, I had to use the extra dressings I'd been given to replace the ones done that morning. My cousin, Myalie, sat on the bed with me and helped me. I had to remove the packing and open the cuts. The first one was 3 cm long and the second one was 6 cm long. I still carry the scars even today as a reminder of a time when things got out of hand, and I didn't stand up for myself when I knew I should have.

Our hair, makeup and my new dressings were all done, and our 'getting ready' photos were taken. I felt horrible. I was in pain, my dress was so tight and my bottom was so large that my dress sat 2 inches higher at the back than the front. I had had the seams let out on the sides of the dress, and that still didn't make enough room.

We got in the cars and drove to the church. We had dark green metallic Holden Commodores. It just happened that our friends all had the same colour cars, just different models. The bridal car was a Senator owned by my brother's boss at the time.

We all got out of the cars. The sun was shining. We lined up ready to walk into the church. I was christened in that church. Despite not being religious at all, I did feel a connection to this church. My brother was married there and my mum's funeral was held there.

We heard the music start. Orpheus Cannon in D. This was a song that I used to play on the piano. The kids looked adorable. I was shaking. I grabbed Uncle Gras' arm for stability. And we entered the church. Everyone stood up. I went to the altar and faced M5. He started to laugh, the priest conducted the service, and M5 laughed through the whole thing — an annoying little giggle. We went to sign our marriage licence, and Diana had made the most beautiful quill pen from a white ostrich feather for us to use.

The pen didn't work! How does that happen? AGAIN, I was waiting for a sign!

Someone from the congregation gave us a pen to sign the license. I became his wife. I sat while the kids were christened. Picking their godparents was easy. They had five between them. Ali, my best friend, Diana, Alan, M5's sister and his family's long-time friend, Rodney. Each child had their own cake at the reception.

We walked down the aisle as husband and wife — well, he walked and I hobbled.

Next, we went and had photos taken at the Craigieburn caravan park, where there were large granite boulders to pose in front of. M5 and I were having our pictures taken, and he pinched me at the top of my bottom. I had a pad of fat that looked like a lamb's tail, and he would tease me all the time about it. He pinched it hard just as the photo was being taken, and he laughed. It wasn't funny. Photos were done. We went back to the church hall for our reception.

Speeches were made, and each time I had to get up and sit back down, I was in agony and struggled like you wouldn't believe. M5 gave me no help moving my chair; the best man helped instead. That set a precedent, and I knew then that M5 wouldn't be there for me going forward in my life. I was right: he wasn't.

We had a family BBQ the next day at our home. Then the day after, we left for our honeymoon. We took the kids to the Gold Coast. We stayed in a cabin in a caravan park at Currumbin. I was struggling to walk and to change my dressings by myself each day. It was horrific. We went to SeaWorld, Dreamworld, and Movie World. It was exhausting, and I just wanted to come home. There was no love, and we constantly fought. He frustrated me in everything he did.

Aunty Lyn had taken 12 rolls of film, and I sent them off to be developed; only six came back. The developers lost the other six rolls. When going through the professional photos, there's one where I'm walking down the aisle, and a shadow is above my head. The shadow is in the form of a silhouette of my mum's portrait. God gave me so many signs; I just ignored every single one.

I got my wedding — not the princess one every girl dreams of — now I had to start living the marriage I didn't want.

1998 My honeymoon at Movie World with Zak and Ally

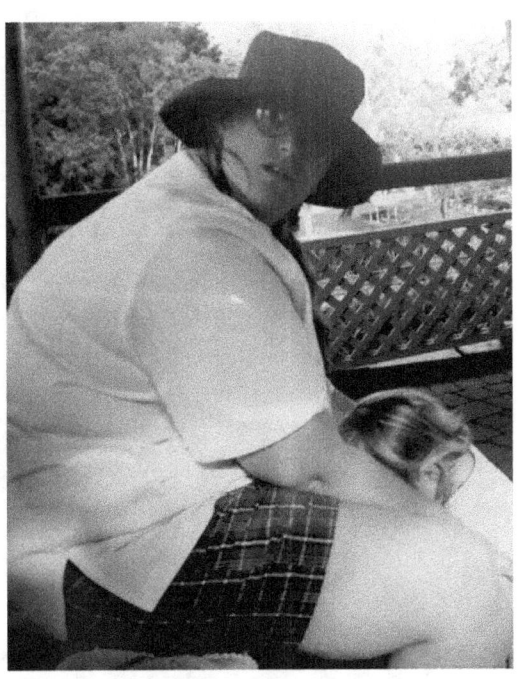
1998 Ally and me on my honeymoon at the Big Pineapple

1998 Ally, Zak and me on our honeymoon at Sea World.

1998 My wedding with Nanna and Parps

1998 My wedding

1998 Zak, Ally and me at our wedding

1999 Standing at my kitchen sink in the house I was building

CHAPTER 14

Choices I Made

For Christmas 1998, we drove the 14 hours from NSW to Victoria to Clifton Springs, about 20 minutes out of Geelong, to spend the festive season with Mum's family. My grandparents, aunts, uncles, cousins, my brother and all their young children were staying there. There were more than 20 of us, and we slept in the garage. It was entertaining trying to get all the kids to sleep in one big room.

I woke up one morning with a small bite mark on my leg, and a blister had formed. This worsened over the next few days, becoming red, inflamed and very sore. I went to the doctor and was told it was a white tail spider bite. He remarked that I was lucky my legs were so fat as the poison hadn't made it into the muscle of my leg and was still in the fat. I was mortified. I was put on antibiotics, and it took months to heal.

That same trip, my Aunty was ironing my dress for me, and told me that there was enough fabric in it to make a 12-seater tablecloth. I was mortified. I knew I had put on weight, but I loved that dress and thought I looked amazing in it. I never wore it again; I was too embarrassed to. That one sentence cut deeper than a knife ever could. Even today, when I think about it, I am reminded of the sorrow it caused.

Not long into the new year, my Aunt sent me in the post copies of the photos she had taken over our Christmas holiday. There was one photo where I didn't recognise myself. I thought my cousin sitting beside me was actually me. We both had the same colour tops on. I was horrified by what I saw. The sad-eyed, morbidly obese woman in the photo was me. I had to do something.

As the new year began, I found myself losing my mind. I hated the life I had chosen. The choices I made had put me in a position where I was losing everything I had worked so hard to achieve. All because I had given control of my life to someone else — someone who couldn't even manage their own life.

My husband kept me right where he wanted me. Mentally battered. I had given up on myself, believing his words that I wasn't good enough. I was morbidly obese. I believed I wasn't good enough. Looking back, I see that he was doing things behind my back; things that people only told me about after we split. I was later told he was having an affair with a woman in Inverell. I know now he was projecting his own guilt onto me. He would tell me I was so lucky to have him because no one else would ever want me. This fed my insecurities and fear that I wasn't good enough.

On the 8th February 1999, I joined Weight Watchers for the third time. I weighed in at 124.4kg! A size 26. I had gained another 24 kilograms in just over two years. How had I done that? I knew this time I would achieve my goal. I didn't realise how long it would take me to get there. For every kilogram I tried to take off, M5 would try to put those kilos back on. He was what is known as a feeder. After I joined Weight Watchers, despite knowing that I desperately wanted to lose weight, every afternoon he would bring home apple turnovers full of whipped cream. I now know this was control, part of keeping me where he wanted me to be. Undesirable to anyone else. His insecurities were controlling my life.

I had joined Weight Watchers the first time when I was about 15 years old; my mum had taken me as I was growing so fast and was larger than my peers. Weight Watchers was a room full of women singing a song about a pig pen. I was the only teenager there. I remember feeling so embarrassed and didn't want anyone at school to know. But because we lived in a small country town, the other women had gone home and mentioned it to their children, and in turn, the teasing escalated at school. I refused to go back the third week.

We never ate healthy meals at home. We ate a lot of deep-fried food. We drank zero water unless it had high sugar Tang or cordial in it, or we drank orange or soft drinks. I never exercised because it hurt if I ran anywhere. I saw my mum yo-yo diet for all of my childhood and into my teenage years. She would starve herself thin, eating off a bread and butter plate, yet had those Violet Crumbles hidden in the pantry.

At the beginning of 1999, M5 had a car crash with Zak in my little Holden Barina. He had hit a kangaroo on the way home from Emmaville, speeding. It was fortunate he didn't kill himself, but more importantly, that he didn't injure or kill Zak. The whole front end was damaged. I had the car repaired; then I gifted it to my cousin, who had two small children in Sydney and only had public transport to get around.

With my payout from my leg, I could no longer receive Centrelink benefits, so I needed to generate income fast. I bought myself a job, a women's fashion boutique in the main street of Glen Innes called Jangles Fashion Hut. My friends laughed; after all, I was the girl with the 'chook' bag in high school. I knew nothing about running a shop, though I was great with sales. I plunged headfirst into it. I also set M5 up in a car detailing business. To the outside world, we looked perfect, but on the inside, massive cracks were forming in every aspect of our lives.

I bought three quarters of an acre in an estate in Cramsey Crescent next to two doctors, ambulance officers, and police. I had the foresight to purchase the block of land in my name. I had $60,000 cash for the deposit on the home and needed to borrow $55,000 to finish the build. I wanted to keep up with the Joneses. Trying to show that I had a perfect life.

I wanted the security of owning my own home, something my parents never had. With moving and living in so many different homes, I wanted one to call my own.

It was only then, when I went to apply for a bank loan, that I discovered M5 had been bankrupt and hadn't told me. A minor detail in his mind. You'd think that would be something you would tell your wife. He was always full of lies and excuses, and nothing was ever his fault or responsibility. The lies keep coming throughout our marriage.

As a result, we couldn't use any of the income he was making from the car detailing business to help get the building loan. I applied for a loan through the Commonwealth Bank in Glen Innes, but they knocked me back — not because I had a bad credit rating, but because I hadn't owned the shop long enough to have sufficient financial records. We had signed the building contract and paid the deposit, and I was about to lose a large chunk of money, stuck with a block of land that would be useless unless I could get the rest of the money for the build. The amount of stress I was under was unbelievable. I had no parents to ask for help. I had to work it out on my own. And I did.

We were building a home through Hotondo Homes, and the builder had some connections and put me in contact with a mortgage broker. The broker then arranged for the Commonwealth Bank in Mildura City Plaza to finance my $55,000 loan. Construction got underway in August 1999. We were told the build would take 6 to 8 months.

I picked out the house plans. It was a large brick home. Light-coloured bricks, a dark tile roof with dark green trim gutters. It had four large bedrooms, a formal lounge and dining area, and a huge rumpus room off the kitchen and eating area.

The internal wall colours were pale yellow, and the carpet was dark beige. There were beige vertical blinds, cream tiles in the bathrooms, and light terracotta-coloured tiles throughout the rest of the home. They were very neutral colours, so very unlike me nowadays. Life is too short to be beige, and my house is nowadays a home, with walls full of bright colours. It didn't have a garage; we decided it could come later when we had more money. We had a massive retaining wall to build as it was cut too low to the block, a costly mistake I had to pay for.

The loan and the block were in my name alone. I was going to own my own home, something my mum had always wanted but had never been able to do. A home that I didn't have to move from anymore, a secure, loving home. A roof over my children's heads. A secure roof over my head. A home that would be a reason for my mum to be proud of me.

We had to erect the back paling fence. It was massive! M5 convinced me that he and his father could build it. I can't believe I was so gullible to say yes to letting them build it, but I did.

We bought the fence palings. My father-in-law and M5 put the posts and rails in, but they were mismatched and not appropriately joined. Next, the palings went on, one by one. The fence in total was about 120 metres in length, requiring 1,500 palings. Putting the palings on was a total nightmare. They had no idea what they were doing.

The block was not level; it had a slope up to the back fence, meaning the side fence was on an angle. He started in the back left corner and proceeded down the left side fence, about 80 metres. He kept the top of the palings level, which meant that by the time he got to the end of the fence near the house, the bottom of the fence paling was on the top rail with nothing under it! When I tried to explain what was happening to him, he got furious at me and started kicking off the fence panels towards me, narrowly missing Ally, who was only two years old.

The fence turned out to be an eyesore, and many people commented on how poorly it was constructed. This was one of the many lies I caught him in; I learned the hard and costly way.

I knew when I was building the house that I had picked the colours for resale. That I wasn't going to live in it for very long, unlike the house I live in now, which is bright and cheerful, and which I've no intention of selling, anytime soon. I just didn't realise how short the time would turn out to be in that beige house, and the heartache involved in selling it.

The shop got off to a good start, and I loved owning and working there. The job itself wasn't stressful. However, what made it stressful was having two young children to care for. Zak was in kindergarten, and Ally was in full-time daycare. On top of that, I had a husband who was constantly lying to me and everyone else and not turning up to work in his own business.

I would go on buying trips to Brisbane to look at clothing for the shop. It was my only freedom from what was happening at home. I'd spend a few days going to the clothing label warehouses and picking the next collection for Jangles Fashion Hut. I really had bought myself a job. I tried to find clothes I liked and would fit me because of my size. I couldn't. It was depressing. How did I get to this point? It wasn't the life I had mapped out for myself.

M5 had commitments to detail cars for clients, but he could often be found at Emmaville with his father, pretending to be a sheep farmer. This left me scrambling to find someone to cover for me at Jangles while I went to clean a car. At first, I didn't know much more than how to wash a car, but I quickly learned about cleaning vents and which polish to use. In addition, he had taken on a job as the eagle mascot at Eagle Boys Pizza, paid only in free pizzas. It was a cycle that only added to our weight gain. Both M5 and I had put on a lot of weight, as had Zak. I knew things needed to change, but I didn't know where to start.

One particular day, while he was off playing with sheep, he had cars booked in for cleaning and a party to attend at Eagle Boys. I ended up cleaning the car myself and then reluctantly dressed up as the eagle, despite my discomfort and suffering from claustrophobia.

The costume was suffocating and smelled like dead, dirty socks. I was hyperventilating. But I soldiered through it, worrying about my reputation in the business community. I was embarrassed that I was married to a man who never kept his word. Meanwhile, children were kicking, pushing and jumping on me as I tried to entertain at the party. When I finally got changed, I learned that he had been booked for two parties back-to-back, adding to my frustration and fueling doubts about our marriage. I was so angry! It was another nail going into the coffin of our marriage. How had I allowed my life to spiral so out of control?

The shop was losing so much money. I was constantly stressed. I was sinking down a deep, dark hole. I couldn't see my feet anymore because I had put on so much weight. I hated myself even more, and I hated what I had become. I was a slave to someone else. I had very little energy, and we survived on twelve takeaway meals a week. The other two main meals my mother-in-law cooked. Always a baked dinner cooked in lard for Sunday lunch, oh so delicious, she always let us get fresh white fluffy bread and dunk it in the hot drippings from the roast. We then ate a large meal of meat and vegetables, always followed by homemade hot creamed rice. For dinner, it was the leftovers. I have some fond memories of meals there.

I entered all the Glen Innes Chamber of Commerce window dressing competitions. It was the only form of art I was now doing. I didn't have much spare time or money for hobby ceramics. I won the Christmas window display, and the president of the chamber asked me if I would take on the chair of the marketing committee. Of course, I said yes. M5 didn't see it as a big thing, but to me it was huge. I felt honoured to have been selected. What I was doing had stood out, and I liked that. My prize for winning was a series of radio commercials on 2NZ. My catch phrase was *JINGLE JANGLE INTO JANGLES TO SEE JUSTINE*. It was sung to some elevator-style music. I thought I'd made it into the big time! But it didn't help sell any more clothes.

I was hiding behind the position of chairman because I was the captain of a sinking ship, and it was going down fast. I didn't have anyone in my corner. No one I could talk to. I was so embarrassed that I was failing and scared of what would come next. I didn't want to go bankrupt and lose my house before I got a chance to live in it. My days consisted of getting up early to get the kids ready for daycare and school. Off to work for nine hours, pick up the kids, feed them, bathe them and put them into bed. Shower me, then bed. Repeat. Too scared to count the money from the shop at the end of the day. It was like living in Groundhog Day. The only thing I had to look forward to was my new home that was being built. I had dreamt of owning my own home for many years.

I developed boils. I couldn't get rid of them, under my left armpit and on my bottom. They were disgusting. Green pus would leak from them all day. I was in so much pain. The combination of a poor diet, drinking two litres of orange juice per day and the stress all fed them. I was slowly killing myself. It took nearly two years and major changes for the infection to clear finally.

I had bought myself a white Commodore VN station wagon 12 months earlier with black tinted windows. Trying to keep up with the Joneses as most families who lived in 'town' had one of these vehicles. I wanted to be like everyone else. Something in my mind told me I had made it. Stupid, I know.

I loved that car. M5 had started a job at the Inverell Abattoirs and needed the vehicle to drive to work. It was a 130km round trip to work. Twelve months earlier, I had bought him a Toyota Land Cruiser tray-back ute. It was old, but it did the job for his car detailing business and also the makeshift sheep farm. I eventually discovered that their big sheep farm had only 60 mangy sheep that they kept on crown land — that should have been another huge warning sign. It was nothing but a nightmare and full of lies.

I had to drive this clunk of a vehicle to my dress shop, and he drove my Commodore to work. With the number of kilometres he was doing every day the Commodore soon needed new tyres. I didn't realise it at the time, and he didn't care.

He drove it into the ground and then finally lost control, ploughing into a tree. I got a phone call at Jangles from a guy saying that M5 had been in a car accident and had wrapped my car around a tree. The first thing to come out of my mouth was, "How was my car?"

I knew then the marriage was done. I asked if M5 needed an ambulance. He didn't. I jumped in the old ute and sped out the Gwydir highway to Matherson and beat the police there. One side of the car looked fine, but the other was completely totalled. It turned out that due to him neglecting the maintenance on the car, allowing all four tyres to become bald, it was a danger to drive. It was a costly mistake. It took weeks for the insurance payout to arrive, and then I had to buy another vehicle. This time, it was a red VP Commodore station wagon — complete with tinted windows, of course!

By November, we found ourselves in a situation where the shop wasn't doing well, and 'his' car detailing business had become the town joke. While I was trying to manage the dress shop, M5 would treat the cash register as his own personal ATM. He owed our friends and my brother money for bloody hay for the mangy sheep.

My brother Simon lived less than 1 km down the road with his family, and their two sons. I missed them terribly, as a rift grew between us, one I didn't cause.

One morning, when I was in Bi-Lo (the local supermarket) doing some grocery shopping, I bumped into Simon. He took one look at me, and I burst into tears. He told me to call in to his house that afternoon, and we would talk.

I felt some relief, but was extremely nervous about going there. He was the only one home. It was a sunny day, and we sat outside in his backyard. I told him how unhappy I was in life and how I wanted to end my life. I was in that dark, deep hole and couldn't see a way out of it, through all the bad choices I had made.

He told me he would help me and that everything would be ok. I wasn't alone.

Out of the blue, he told me to put on the headphones he had handed me, close my eyes, and just listen to the music — not to talk but to let the music take me to a place I needed to be.

I did what I was told for a change.

That piece of music changed everything!

As I closed my eyes and immersed myself in it, I saw my mum holding her hand out to help me. All these images and feelings played out in my mind. I felt like I had failed her; by putting her in the MS home in Sydney, I wasn't strong enough for her and I was the reason she had died so young. I now know that none of that was my fault, but at the time this guilt lay very heavy with me. I was still grieving her death.

Anyway, returning to the music: it was a piece by Douglas Spotted Eagle called 'Arrival'. I had tears running down my cheeks, and I felt like I wasn't in my body. It's such a powerful piece of music that it's recommended you don't drive while listening to it.

It goes for nearly eight minutes. At the end of it, Simon gave me a huge hug and said he would help me. I had no idea how he possibly could. But from that moment, my life changed forever.

1999 Clifton Springs at Christmas time

CHAPTER 15

Breaking The Arrow

My brother was part of a community of motivational entrepreneurs and coaches; he knew of an event coming up in Brisbane and thought it would be the perfect opportunity for me to immerse myself. To find the inner help I so desperately needed to find.

It cost $500 a ticket. I didn't have $500. I didn't even have $50 to spare. Simon got angry when I told him I couldn't afford to go and said he didn't care if I had to sell my TV to get the money, but I needed to be there.

He would cover the cost of my accommodation, and if I could come up with half of the $500, he would cover the rest. That's when I realised that finding the money wasn't the problem; telling M5 was the real problem.

How was I going to do that when I was so scared of him? I thought back to one of the arguments we had had, where he tore the pyjama top I was wearing as I was screaming for help. Someone in the neighbourhood called the police, and they turned up and knocked on the front door. Whoever that person was, I thank you; you may very well have saved my life.

I went home that afternoon and told M5 I had visited Simon, and that he was paying for me to go to Brisbane for two nights to attend a seminar. I didn't tell him I had to pay my share of $250, and I didn't sell the TV either! I took the money from the shop and bought fewer clothes for stock that month.

When I met M5 in 1996, he told me so many lies. There were so many red flags; my gut was telling me to run. But I chose to ignore them. I had big, blinding blinkers on. I chose to ignore everything. Not long after we started dating, he turned up with a box of meat, all cut up and packed. He told me he and his father had killed a steer on the family farm, and it was a gift from them. Let me put this into context. They didn't have a farm, and they didn't run steer — the meat he had bought from the local butchers and tried to pass off as something else. Talk about love bombing with a twist!

The next big lie he told me was that the reason he was late to my house was that he had just put his prized Commodore on a car carrier to Sydney for his sister, who desperately needed a car. Then he added that he had forgotten he had left $1,000 in the glove box but, oh well, she could keep it. Meanwhile, he was driving an old 'bomb' of a car. It didn't add up.

I was all packed to go, and M5 was still having a go at me as I walked out the door; he told Zak that Mummy didn't love him. Because if she did, she wouldn't be leaving him. Emotional and coercive control was a daily occurrence.

It was the hardest thing to do: walking out through that door with Zak crying, but oh boy, we needed to get out of the mess I had gotten us into. I knew that going would lead to a way out — I just didn't know how or how long it would take.

We arrived in Brisbane 5 hours later. We had a large family room with three queen-sized beds. Simon and Marissa took one bed, Marissa's brother, M6 and his girlfriend took another, and I shared the middle bed with Gail, my sister-in-law's mother.

It put the last nail in the coffin, having to share that room with M6. Why? Because M6 came into my life when I was 18. He had treated me terribly for the six years before I met M5. He had sex with me, yet would deny he ever did. Everyone knew, yet he made me out to be a liar for years. I just wanted someone to love me, as I had never felt that before. I allowed him to treat me this way for a very long time, too long, hoping it would get better. It never did.

So here I was, feeling more trapped than ever in this room. Trying to remain calm, but inside, I was screaming and crying in emotional pain, with feelings of never being good enough. I felt so embarrassed about how I had let my weight get out of control at 120kg, no longer being able even to see my toes.

It had taken me 12 months to lose 5kg. For every kilo I tried to take off, M5 would try to put 2kg back on me. He would often call me the town slut, and tell me I was so lucky to have him as no one else wanted me. I believed him. I believed I wasn't good enough. Some of you might wonder how that can happen. But when you're in a mentally bad place to begin with and then someone love bombs you, then bit by bit, they eat away at you through the language they use towards you. He isolates you from your friends and family. It changes you and your world — and not in a good way.

The time came to enter the seminar — a dark auditorium. A stage brightly lit at the front and 100+ chairs. The seminar was called Mind, Body & Spirit. I was excited and nervous as hell sitting there. It had a certain feel to it, similar to the hyped-up Amway seminars I used to attend. The room was buzzing with a positive vibe — lots of chatting and smiles.

I had attended personal development seminars when I was involved with Amway under IDA (International Dream Association), but that was many years before this. The facilitator's name was Adam. We were given a workbook to fill in for the day, and I still have it to this day. Recently, I got it out and looked at what I wrote and what I wanted to achieve. These were my goals.

One-Year Goals
- To be healthy, to be a size 16.
- To make my shop the best in Glen Innes.
- To have a gardener and housekeeper.
- To have a PW 50 motorcycle for Zak.
- Not to go to work every day.
- To have a dishwasher, a new bed, kids' beds, dining setting.
- To have the shop debt-free.
- To have a wardrobe full of beautiful clothes.
- To have all our bills paid off.
- To be a stress-free person and a better mother and wife.
- To do 100 sit-ups a day.
- To ride in a limo.
- To be in Weight Watchers magazine.
- Spend more time with my kids.
- To bring home $3000 per month.
- Lots of jewellery.

Three-Year Goals
- To take the kids to Disneyland for a week.
- To go on a month-long cruise.
- To pay cash for everything and anything.
- Weekly massage.
- To give the kids the best education money can buy.

- Go to the Barrier Reef.
- To have my hair done every 4 to 6 weeks.
- To have weekends away.
- Go to New Zealand.
- Travel Australia.
- Have my own photography shop.
- To become a Weight Watchers leader.
- To have a spa.

Seven-Year Goals
- Pay my house mortgage out.
- To own an SS Holden.
- To buy a home on the Gold Coast.
- To travel the world.
- Build a pool in the backyard.
- Own a big boat and caravan.
- Write a book: 'What to do when someone dies.'

Fifteen-Year Goals
- Write another book: 'Outstanding Sheds'.
- Want to do well in some awards. Win 'Weight Watchers Leader of the year'.
- Composing music.
- Retired and financially free.
- Living in luxury.

I felt like I was meant to be sitting in that room. There was nowhere else in the world I needed to be more than this place, right now.

One of the activities we had to do was a meditation. Which was weird, considering how many people were in the room. I've never been one to slow my mind enough for this actually to happen. To sit in the corner, 'umming', is one thing, but there are many other forms of meditation. We were told to sit comfortably on our seats and rest our hands on our legs. I looked around the room, and people sat in anticipation; I was no different. What would happen to each of us?

The music started. Wait… I knew that music!

Can you guess what they played? Yes, Arrival! What were the chances? I have recently been told by a very wise woman that there is no such thing in this world as a coincidence. Everything happens for a reason.

This time, the experience of listening to the music was far more intense, and I had a vague idea of what to expect. I went deeper into everything. Colours were brighter. Sounds were clearer. I saw myself as a thinner person. Something that I had never been able to see. I looked amazing. I had a lilac pair of size 16 pants for sale in my shop, and I saw myself wearing them with a killer arse. I was standing in front of my mum's grave, showing her and talking to her. As much as my mum and I had issues, I still loved her. I was still grieving her loss.

I could hear her voice, and she was telling me how proud she was of me. That everything would work out, and I would work out what to do.

I was sitting there crying with tears streaming down my cheeks, and yet I was not able to move my hands from my lap to wipe them away. I was outside of my body. But I was to sit in that moment. It was such a surreal experience to be a part of. One I still recall often.

In this meditation, I realised that my weight had controlled everything I had ever done in my life. The years of being called the family garbage disposal, then called 'tank' by the boys at school, had taken its toll on me. That feeling of never being good enough was slowly killing me, and very nearly did.

Every decision I had made was based on my negative body image, the men I had selected in my life and the overwhelming feelings of never being good enough. It was a relentless and toxic vicious cycle.

Hearing my mum's voice, telling me everything would be ok, was a shock. I hadn't heard her true voice in at least 15 years, as MS had affected her voice during a relapse that she never fully recovered from, when her MS changed to secondary progressive. Yet here she was, speaking to me as clear as day.

We were brought back to reality and the room was quiet with people looking around at each other. I felt very exposed, like everyone had seen my thoughts.

We broke for lunch. I didn't feel like eating as I was still numb with shock at what I had experienced. After lunch, we listened to a few more speakers and filled in the workbook. I occasionally look through that book at what I wrote that day, and what I wanted to achieve.

Next came the last activity of the day: real-life Indian (archery) arrows! We all lined up and waited to get on stage, and I was last. The instructions were clear: we had to stand with the sharp pointy end of the arrow against the nape of our neck, right where you would have a tracheotomy. Meanwhile, the feathered end was up on a board that Adam was holding. The idea was to walk into the arrow and break it into two. By doing so, we were meant to symbolically shatter everything that was stopping us, everything we had seen while meditating, and thereby affirm our ability to achieve our goals.

There was so much hype and energy in that room!

Each of the 100+ people in the room, one by one, walked onto the stage and broke their arrows. Some hesitated, and the arrow wouldn't break on their first attempts. But they were successful on the second attempt and screamed in joy, they had done it. Each person was cheered at their success.

I was last on stage. Lucky last. Letting others go in front of me. One by one. Not putting myself forward, and wondering how I could get out of the room. Fear engulfed me.

I remember what I was wearing — a dark red jersey maxi dress with a fine white stripe. I looked like a barber pole, now that I think about it.

I stepped onto the stage with fear and doubt. You see, going last didn't do me any favours. My mind went in and out of yes, I could do it, to no, what was I thinking? I would make a fool of myself. The fat woman. The last one, the one that wasn't good for anything or anyone. I wanted to run and hide. Anxiety was my constant companion. I was sweaty and wanted to vomit.

They positioned the arrow on my nape. I closed my eyes. Took a breath, leaned into it, and it didn't break!

Doubt overflowed my mind. I wasn't good enough. I couldn't do this. Tears started to flow. If I couldn't break it, I would be stuck like this forever. Nothing would ever change.

People started yelling at me that I could do this. The sound was deafening.

I was shaking. My safety goggles started to steam up from all the tears.

I tried again... it bowed only a little, and how it didn't pierce through my neck skin I'll never know.

In that moment, something in me clicked.

I tried for the third time. This time, I became angry, and told myself I could do anything and no one was ever going to stop me again! I leant into the pointy, metal end. It shattered into three large pieces. I burst into tears, and people rushed on stage and hugged me. I was overwhelmed with power.

I still have that arrow today as a reminder of where I was, what I did, and the person I've become. When I think of things I can't do, two things always come to mind. First, my mum always said that there was no such word as can't and second, what it felt like to break that arrow and all that can happen when you don't let fear or false beliefs tear you down.

When the arrow shattered, I realised three things from the meditation:

1. I had to finish building my house, and probably sell it.

2. I had to legally get rid of M5 and the mess and debt that came along with him. I didn't love him. In fact, I didn't even like him.

3. Finally, when I did all of the above, my weight would come off, as I had been using it as protection from the outside world.

It was one of the most emotional days of my life. A game changer. I owe this to my brother Simon. I don't think he ever realised the full impact it had and still has on my life today. Thank you, little bro x

After the seminar, I had the long car ride home and then the interrogation by M5, especially when he realised that M6 had also been there. In his mind, I was away for a dirty weekend. I didn't tell him all the details of what I needed to do to get myself and my kids out of the mess I had got us into. I kept that close to my heart. I didn't tell anyone.

I didn't have a plan for how these things were going to happen. But for the first time in a very long time, I had something he couldn't take away from me: I had hope.

1998 Modelling photo of myself

1999 Ally

1999 Ally and me with the Eagle Boy mascot

1999 I still have the books from the Mind Body and Spirit Seminar

1999 Lewis Street, Glen Innes

1999 The block I bought, and The Fence, Cramsie Crescent Glen Innes

1999 The dress I wore when I broke the arrow

CHAPTER 16

I Bought My Own Lawn Mower

It was 12.01am on 1st January, 2000, and we were all still alive. There was a lot of hype that the world would stop because of Y2K; computer programmers hadn't considered the equation of a new century on computers or something like that. I finished 1999 at a Bachelors and Spinsters ball, commonly known as a BnS ball. I had been the official ticket retailer and received a free ticket to the ball. It's usually a messy night, drinking as much alcohol as you can and lots of sex with a stranger, long before the advent of responsible service of alcohol laws. However, I remained sober as my husband at the time was doing security there. The world didn't end, time sure didn't stop, and I had a boring night.

It was the polar opposite of my first ever BnS in 1989 when I went to Tenterfield with two of my girlfriends. That was a messy night, with way too much alcohol. I drove my HQ to Tenterfield, an hour north of Glen Innes. It was my first BnS. I wasn't sure what to expect. We started with some decorum until they ran out of cups and soft drink mixers. How we didn't get alcohol poisoning still amazes me. They had rum in 20-litre containers and sheep-drenching guns as the dispenser. We were going up to the bar, and they were drenching shots of rum straight down our throats.

I picked up a guy and took him back to my car to do the deed, as you do at these events. I went to hop in the front seat, but one of my girlfriends was already there with a guy. I then went to the back seat, and my other girlfriend had a guy in there. So what does one do in such a situation? Well I grabbed my pillow and blanket, opened the boot, threw the spare tyre out and we hopped in there! Have you seen the size of those old Holden boots? They are massive. Things were going along great until some bugger walked past and closed the lid of the boot on us. Remember when I got stuck in a lift as a child? Well, me and confined spaces do not like each other and I hit panic mode, screaming for someone, anyone to let me out. I ended up sleeping on the cold ground. It was a night to remember, polar opposite to this NYE ball.

Welcome to the year 2000. I knew that I couldn't continue living like I was. I was sad, I was angry, and I hated my life. I was depressed and knew I needed a big change — one step at a time, one arrow at a time. I was still attending weekly Weight Watchers meetings and trying to slowly change the numbers on the damn scales!

On March 30, 2000, my home was ready for us to move in. It was stunning. I loved it. But I knew deep down that I wasn't going to live there for more than a few years. Not long after moving into our new home, M5 moved into the spare room. And there he remained until we split. We were constantly fighting about everything.

The goods and services tax (GST) was going to be introduced on 1st July that year, and that scared the shit out of me. My business was already failing, with more money going out than I was making. Two people were using the cash register as their own personal ATM, and neither of them was me! Little by little, bit by bit, cash went missing, taken by a crooked staff member who was a childhood friend, and by the man who was supposed to protect me and our children's livelihood. Together they were sending me broke.

I had to go to the police station and report my employee for stealing. She was also skimming the account of a youth club we were both part of. She was charged. I felt so sad and angry at the same time. How could she do that to me? To our friendship? She was dating a guy who had a drug addiction and she was supplying him with cash. Love really does make people do strange things.

When I was building the home we had just moved into, what should have been a happy time in my life was one of stress. Looking back, I was a mess. Morbidly overweight. Covered in boils — big, green, ugly, pus-filled boils! I worked out months later, after a lot of pain and scans, that the 2 litres of pure orange juice I drank daily wasn't helping, but was actually causing major reactions in my body. It was feeding the boils with the acid, and I eventually developed an intolerance to oranges from it. I now have migraines when I have any form of orange. Not to mention the calories in two litres of sugar!

M5 had a spending addiction. In a small country town, you were allowed to run accounts, and at the end of each month the bill had to be paid. Every time he walked out of the house he would buy something from shops like Home Hardware or Mitre 10. Thousands of dollars worth of crap. It was all piled up in the backyard.

We had no communication between us. I felt like I had to ask for permission to do anything. I was questioned all the time on who I was talking to on the phone, what I had done in my day, basically what hand I had used to wipe my arse with! I didn't realise any of this until after we had separated as it had become my way of life. My life had reached a point where I felt as though I was trapped in a cage.

At the time, I wasn't sure how I had even gotten to that point or allowed another human to do that to me. So here I was. Broke. In a house I'd just finished building, and in a loveless marriage to a controlling man, who had made me shrink as the woman I once was. I wished he'd have a car accident on the way home from work and wouldn't walk through the front door ever again. I had terrible, terrible thoughts about him, and how I could get myself out of the mess I had gotten and allowed myself to be in. I knew I was going to have a battle to get myself out of this huge mess. I just kept thinking of the broken arrow.

I finally made a decision to close Jangles. To take a loss. I had a huge closing down sale. I closed the doors on the 30th June 2000. Now what was I going to do?

My cousin Myalie was getting married and wanted me to be her bridesmaid. I so desperately wanted to be thin for it. But I just couldn't budge my weight. I couldn't find a dress to fit and it was all too hard. I couldn't even afford to pay for the dress. I had to say no to her. I was heartbroken.

We did drive to Geelong for Easter in 2001 and for her wedding. Our whole family would be there. We had her hen's night on the Wednesday. There were four of us. What trouble could we get into in midweek? A lot! We went on a pub crawl and ended up at a night club called Lambys. We were out on the dance floor headbanging to AC/DC when my forehead and the bride's nose collided. Thank goodness I didn't break her nose. We left there and went to a pub that was still open. I got chatting to a guy and we had one small kiss. In my mind, my marriage was well and truly over, I just hadn't plucked up enough courage to get him out of my house or life. I was scared of what he would do to me.

I said goodbye to the stranger. Outside the pub, my other cousin's wife started having a go at me about being a terrible mum because I'd kissed the guy. The other girls had to hold her back so she didn't hit me. I was shocked; we all were, at her reaction. We all took a taxi home. M5 and I were staying at the Moolap caravan park. He was waiting up for me. When I walked in the door, he was notably angry and aggressive in his tone. Then came all the questions: Where had we gone? What did we do? Who did we speak to? I saw this as my chance to end it. I was safe as it was a public place to tell. So I told him the truth. I had kissed another man. It didn't go down well at all.

Every time we had an argument since Ally's birth he would threaten that if he left, he was taking her with him. This was no exception. He went and scooped her out of her bed, and said he was flying back home. I was terrified of him taking her.

He didn't end up going to the airport. First, I had the car keys and second, he didn't have any money to book the tickets. We didn't speak, he climbed into Ally's bed and slept there the remainder of the evening. I lay awake shaking. I was one step closer to not being controlled by him.

We still had to get through the wedding in three days' time. My aunt knew something bad had happened at the hen's night, because my cousin's wife and I refused to be in the same room or talk to each other, and she was still giving me death stares. I explained to my aunt what had happened kissing the stranger. She could tell I wasn't happy in my marriage.

The wedding was a great night. All of our family were there celebrating my cousin's love and happiness. We drove home a few days later. It was a very long 2-day drive in virtual silence.

On our return home, M5 packed his clothes up, took his TV, doona, pillows, clothes and a few personal belongings and moved back in with his parents. He had owned very little in regard to home furnishings. I owned everything, except a new blue lounge. I was so relieved I could breathe. I had some freedom.

A month later, my brother rang. He told me not to get upset about what he was about to tell me. He explained that my cousin and his wife were expecting another child. I let that sink in. Then it hit me. My cousin had a vasectomy 12 months earlier. The baby wasn't his. His wife had been projecting her own guilt and shame about having an affair onto me. That split them up. It all made sense.

I was trying to do everything by myself. M5 was trying to get me back. He had stopped paying for anything. No maintenance for Ally. And I was getting zero from M4. I was paying for both mortgages. I felt so alone. I caved in and let him move back into the spare room. Things did not improve; they got worse.

It was Friday, 14th September 2001. My girlfriend Bertie rang me. We had been friends since we were 12, when she popped her head over the side fence and said hello. She explained that she had been invited out to another friend's birthday party, who belonged to the local female tug of war team. Bertie explained that she didn't want to go by herself, and would I like to go with her? Just as she asked me, M5 came into the kitchen with an angry look on his face because I was on the phone. I quickly blurted out that Bertie had rung me and she had asked me to go out with her that evening. Then I asked him if I could go. Bertie heard me ask and then said in my ear, "Why the fuck do you need to ask for permission to go out?" It was like someone had tipped a bucket of cold water over my head. I stumbled my words out and replied "I don't know." Just as I replied to Bertie, M5 said angrily to me, "I don't give a fuck what you do." I asked Bertie what time and where. She said her place at 7pm. I couldn't believe it. I was allowed to go out! Now what to wear? Nothing fit!

I went to call a taxi, but M5 insisted he drop me off. We pulled up at her place and there were half a dozen cars there. I said goodnight to my kids and thanked M5 for dropping me off. He replied he would wait up for me. I said, "Don't bother", and closed the car door. I had a few cans of alcohol with me, and I went inside. I knew nearly everyone there. We had a few drinks, then went to the local RSL club to meet everyone else who was invited.

I couldn't believe I was out. I hadn't been out since falling pregnant with Ally. It had been a long five years. It was so good just being out with friends. No one had any idea of what I was going through at home. I hadn't told anyone. I was too embarrassed.

The RSL had a good crowd that evening. Lots of people I knew. Over on the opposite table to us was a large table of men. Policemen. One caught my eye and smiled towards me. I turned around to see who he was smiling at and then realised it was me. I felt flattered. It had been a very long time since anyone had looked at me that way.

The party then decided to go on a pub crawl. Every pub in the main street, down to the Royal Hotel. Just like the 'old days', some 10 years earlier. After the pub we walked down to the Ampol, the same service station where I was a short order cook years earlier. After consuming our toasted sandwiches, a fight broke out in the car park. I was full of alcohol and courage, and I walked outside and told them to all grow some pubic hair and start acting like men, not like boys. The policeman that had smiled at me came over and asked me how I was. I replied good, now he was talking to me. One thing led to another and I walked around the corner and he picked me up. I didn't want to go home. Here was a man who was showing interest in me and saying all the right things.

We drove to a deserted dirt road in his small car, climbed into his back seat and had sex. I felt alive and wanted. How we fit in the back seat I'll never know, as neither of us was short and I weighed a lot! It was now about 3am and the cop dropped me off about 6 houses from my home. As I got out of the car there was a figure in the middle of the road yelling out, "You whore! You dirty slut! Where the fuck have you been? Who was that who dropped you home? You're nothing but a dirty fucking whore!" I was mortified, and scared that he would wake up the neighbours. I walked past him and inside the house. I was near my bedroom door; I'd never seen him so angry before. I was terrified. He told me there was a surprise waiting in the back lounge room. I walked down the hallway and saw my two babies on the lounge. Zak was 8 and Ally was 4 — he had dragged them around all night watching me from each pub I'd been in. Telling them how I didn't love them any more. How I had left them and didn't want them. I saw red!

As I walked back down the hall, M5 went to hit me. I ducked as his fist went past and he put a hole in my six month old bedroom door. I screamed at him to get the fuck out of my house. He grabbed his TV, pillows, doona and two bags of clothes and left in the car I had bought. I grabbed the kids and put them into my bed for the three of us to fall asleep. I tried to assure them that I did love them and that I would never leave them.

My marriage was over. I did the wrong thing by having sex with the cop. The only time I strayed in my marriage and I got caught. I knew two years, 11 months and two weeks earlier that I didn't want to do it, that we should never have married. Now we had to do the property settlement

I can clearly remember standing out front of the house having a tug of war with a garden hose. Yes, a simple garden hose. All my frustration and anger fighting to keep a $10 garden hose.

That was my tipping point. I was done. I stopped fighting. I let him take it. I just wanted my life back. I wanted to make my own decisions, without having to explain every action, every move, or every person I spoke to. I commented one day to him that I would keep a diary and write it in what hand I wiped my arse with, as I was questioned on every detail from the time I woke up to the time I went to sleep. It was exhausting. This was not the life I wanted or the future I wanted for my children.

The day that I let go of that garden hose, I bought my own lawnmower, a push mower, as there was no way I was calling him to come and mow the lawns. Of course he had taken the ride-on mower I paid for. He also took 26 ute-and-trailer loads of crap out of the backyard. That's where my money had gone! 26 loads, you might be thinking – how can that be? Well, let me tell you how he accumulated all that crap.

With all the crap he had 'booked' on credit around town, he had managed to run up $38,000 in debt. The even bigger problem was he had created these 30-day accounts in both our names.

I didn't realise until I booted him out that our new lounge, that he had bought from Sully's Furniture, was worth over thousand dollars. He actually convinced them to let him take it home with only a $100 deposit! They knocked on my door and told me what he had done, I was mortified and so embarrassed. He had sworn to me he had paid it off. They repossessed it. Just like you see in the movies, but it was real life.

I had paid for nearly everything. I was his meal ticket. When I booted him out of the house the first time, we had over $38,000 in debt, plus the house mortgage of $60,000. How was I going to pay for it? There was no way I was going to file for bankruptcy and lose everything. I went to the bank and got a second mortgage on the house. When we split I was left paying for it all as it was all in my name. I tried to get both loans combined into one to reduce the payments. The original home loan was over 25 years and the second mortgage was over 10 years. The bank refused to combine them. The stress from the financial pressure was suffocating me.

The stress of everything was causing my migraines to increase. There was one particular one that was so bad that I was paralysed in the lounge chair. Zak got the home phone and called 000 for an ambulance. He was 8 years old. I was so scared of what my body was doing and terrified of what both my children had to see of their mother.

Now back to the lawn mower. Calling him to come and mow the lawns would have given him a hook to come back in. That push lawn mower meant independence to me. It used to take me around 5 hours pushing it up and down the hill to mow the full block. It was a hard, long slog of time and hard on my body. But each step meant independence. It meant I didn't need a man to survive. I wasn't co-dependant. I could, and would, survive by myself. It meant I learnt to harden the fuck up.

He continued to stalk me for months after the marriage break-up. Telling me how much he wanted me back. I would organise a babysitter for my children and be out with my girlfriends at the local pub where he would come in and abuse me for being a bad mother. He would then start ringing the home phone and freaking out the babysitter so I would have to go home. He would then drive up and down the road outside my house, watching everything I did. This continued until he moved eight hours away, finally leaving us alone. He was to pay child support, but his $33 a month very rarely got paid. That did not even pay for Ally's monthly supply of yoghurt, let alone anything else she needed. We would get his tax return once a year, and then I'd wait for the abusive phone call about taking his money.

Not once in all of this time did I ever badmouth my children's fathers in front of them. Don't get me wrong, there were plenty of times I could have, but that was not fair to their innocent minds. I knew one day they would make up their own minds about their fathers, and whether they wanted to have a relationship with them.

When my marriage ended, I was still doing a few Mystery shopping visits and not much else. I applied for a job as Assistant Manager of Target Country and got the job. It was a good job managing two stores on the Main Street of Glen Innes. There wasn't a building at the time big enough to have apparel and manchester/kitchen items all in the same shop. So we would walk the Main Street with 10 shops in between. It was difficult going back to work for someone else, especially with having a chain of upper management.

There was one employee I had a feeling was up to no good. So I watched, waited and investigated. My suspicions were correct. She was making lay-by payments of very small amounts each day on her own lay-by, but not putting the money in the till. Amounts like $2.13 or 53 cents. The till was always out every single time she worked. I hated working out what she was doing because then I had to report it. It was stealing. Upper management fired her, and the police were involved. To make it worse, I knew her parents. Being a small town, everyone knew everyone. I started looking for another job, as it's always been easier to get another job when you already have a job. I resigned not long after. It was not the job for me.

Our Weight Watchers (WW) leader resigned, and they were looking for someone to take over as leader. I put my hand up as I was desperate to keep the program running. I was offered the job of one meeting a week in Glen Innes. I met all my KPIs of new members, regular members and weight loss per member. It turned out I was a natural at leading and speaking in front of a group. Numbers increased, and WW offered me a morning meeting to open in Glen Innes. Numbers kept increasing. The Armidale leader resigned, and I was offered a morning and evening meeting 100 km away. I saw this as a challenge to build up the numbers. To do back-to-back meetings like I was doing in Glen Innes. I was the only leader in the state who was offered a fuel allowance to get to work.

I managed to secure another job at the same time, with a company called Brands On Show, where I was responsible for merchandising brands like Pfizer and Procter & Gamble in supermarkets. I learnt how to do relays, what gondola ends were and how much money big-name brands paid to have placement of their goods on certain supermarket shelves. The supermarkets I had were IGA in Glen Innes, plus Guyra and Coles in Armidale. They paid me by the kilometre as well as by the hour. I could pick my own hours.

I managed to pick up another job in Armidale at Katies as their 1626 sales assistant. It was a 200 km round trip to work each time for a 4-hour shift, but I had other jobs to help, so I wasn't wasting fuel getting there. I was cheeky, getting paid double kilometres allowance for two of my jobs, fuel money for another, which then also paid me to get to the fourth. I made it work.

My day went something like this:

I would get my children ready for school and drop them off, then I would either do a survey, Mystery Shopping or a quick count of products in a Glen Innes supermarket, then on to Guyra to do the same. Then to Katies to work in Armidale, then finish the late afternoon with a Weight Watchers meeting either in Armidale or back in Glen Innes. I changed my name badge as I went, picking one of the four options. I had to be well-organised each day, or it just didn't work. I was fortunate to have Diana pick up the kids for me from school, or I would never have been able to do it all. I was on a sole parent's pension, and this all supplemented my income.

I managed to build the numbers at the Armidale meetings, and they both went to back-to-back meetings as well. It was about this time that I won an award for the largest amount of weight loss per meeting. My KPIs were through the roof, and I loved helping people.

I was working for Katies the day when Millers took it over. It was horrible. We had no prior warning, even as staff, that it was happening. We had women abusing us, because they wanted to buy clothes, but realised they could no longer use their charge cards. They got angry and threw them at us.

I was exhausted. I was working four different jobs at once and being a single mum. Survival mode. Something had to give. I resigned from Katies. But I missed that little bit of income and the discount I received on the clothes. Those 8 hours a week made a difference. I went to an Enjo party, and within a week, I had started as an Enjo consultant. I knew party plan only too well.

I had been selling Enjo for only 6 months when I made the decision to move to Perth. To start a new life.

I've never been out of work for very long. I had to apply to Enjo to take a leave of a few months to keep my 'membership' active and not rejoin. Unfortunately it took longer than that to move all our belongings across the country. Enjo tried making me pay more to sell their products. I declined, and never sold them again.

1999-2001 The house I built and owned at Cramsie Crescent, Glen Innes

2001 My 30th birthday at Cramsie Crescent, Glen Innes NSW

2002 One of my favourite photos from when my children and I were rebuilding our lives.

2002 The cabin in the caravan park my children and I lived in

The Main Street - Grey Street, Glen Innes

CHAPTER 17

I Love a Good Pull

I had not long ended my marriage and was excited to be starting my new life. I had so much more life in me. I had lost 11 kg and was walking every day. I joked with my friends that I had lost 95 kg of dead weight when my marriage ended. I felt back in control of my own life. Our town didn't have a gym, so I had to improvise. I started using cans of beetroot out of my pantry and lifted those to music. They worked fine until I went to eat a can of beetroot one day, and discovered I had shredded it with all the lifting and shaking. I swapped over to cans of spaghetti.

I had started looking around to date again. When you're single, they tell you to join sporting clubs to meet the opposite sex. We had touch football — I don't run, so that ruled that out. Indoor cricket? I close my eyes to catch a ball. So that was ruled out too. And besides, I went to school with most of the men playing those sports and I knew their ex partners and why their own marriages had broken down. I continued to walk the pavement and the road. I hated walking. It's boring and I would often fall over for no reason. But I was on a mission to improve my life and that meant getting healthy and becoming the vision I'd seen while meditating in Brisbane. I wanted that size 16 arse!

I would get my cans out twice a day and do arm exercises with them. I had an old walking video I would do when it was raining. Walking on the spot to music. Nothing was going to stop me. With each step I took, I regained my confidence. I had a smile on my face again. The kids and I quickly got into a routine. They often would come for walks with me or we would kick a ball around in the backyard. We started enjoying life again.

Being the local Weight Watchers leader meant I had to lead by example. My members would see me out and about walking, and would also see me at the grocery store and see what food was in my shopping trolley. I wanted to be a good role model for all, not just my members, but even more so my children.

On a Thursday afternoon, I bumped into a woman I'd met on that night out that changed everything. She asked how I was doing, as rumours had gone through the whole town of my separation. I explained I was in a much better place and rebuilding my life. She commented on my weight loss, and I explained I was trying to exercise and lose another 30 kg.

She then said, "Why don't you come and join the Jellybeans Tug of War Club?" I instantly had terror, horror and pain flash across my mind. I hated saying no to someone, so I looked for excuses to get out of it. I hated sports. High school had scared me.

I asked when the training was. She replied on Sunday, Tuesday and Thursday nights. I said that wouldn't work. I've got my kids and no one to look after them. She replied. That's okay. Bring them with you. She also said "We travel." I came back with, "I don't have the money for that, I'm a single mum." Her reply was, "We fundraise — oh, and there are men's teams." "Ok, what time is training?"

She explained that she would pick us up. I'm sure she thought I wouldn't turn up if I had to drive myself there. And to be honest, I think I would have chickened out. Sunday rolled around far too quickly. She was true to her word, and was there knocking on my front door to pick us up. She told me to wear old clothes and bring a pair of thick socks. I did what I was told, but declared that I was only coming to watch. She laughed at that.

Training was at the local showgrounds; if it rained or snowed they trained in one of the pavilions. In all weather, they trained. It was an intimidating sight when we got out of the car. I had forewarned my kids to behave. I thought I was going to vomit with nerves and anxiety. My heart was racing. She introduced me to the team of 10 girls and then the coach. He instantly asked me what size boot I wore. I stuttered, "A men's size 9", followed by "No, I'm just here to have a look!" He replied, "Well you're here now, and I see you have a pair of socks and old clothes — you might as well have a go!"

I didn't know what I was in for.

Two hours of training. Pulling on a rope with six girls of various shapes and sizes on each end. It was dirty work, lots of laughs and lots of screams. The two hours flew by. It was fun. The kids had fun playing in the dirt with the other kids who were there. I went to hand my boots back to the coach and he replied, "You'd better keep them, you will be back on Tuesday night!"

Guess I was coming back on the Tuesday evening. What they forgot to tell me was how sore I would be the next day. The minimal amount of weight training I was doing was nothing compared to the workout I had just had. I went back on Tuesday evening. There were a few things that were motivating me. Exercising would help the weight to come off, I was doing something positive for me and of course the fact that there were men's teams!

I had only been training for about 6 weeks when we had our first competition. The local Glen Innes Show. The only other teams that came to compete were men's teams. So we pulled against the men in front of the grandstand full of local people. I was so nervous. What if I stuffed up and forgot how to do it? What if I made a fool of myself. What if…? I couldn't have gotten out of it even if I tried.

It was raining, and we pulled in any weather condition. There were eight girls in a team, and the weight class determined which girls were selected to pull in our team. In the lighter weight classes I pulled anchor, and then in the middle and catch weight class I pulled 7. Tug of war is like rowing — you are only as strong as the weakest person in your team on the rope that day. And no one wanted to let their teammates down. This was my first time using a sticky resin called tacky that our coach would cook up by the batchful. You applied a small amount to the palms of your hand and clapped your hands together several times to spread it over the insides of both palms and all fingers. Once you had tacky on, you couldn't touch any clothing, so that meant no going to the toilet either. Tacky gave you grip on the rope, even in the rain. To get the tacky off we had to dissolve it with WD40.

My heart was racing as the referee commanded us to pick up the rope. We braced ourselves. Laying back on the rope with the tension tight, waiting for the command to pull. The funny thing is that you never really pull in tug of war — you actually push your legs into the ground. Your arms are just holding your body weight on the rope. You don't pull the rope with your arms. All move in your team in unison, backwards the 2 metres to get the white rag tied on the rope in our winning end. The crowd was yelling for us girls as we faced the first men's team. We won our first end, which surprised us as well as the men's team. The crowd cheered. However, the men's teams were not going to let the females beat them. We spent the next half hour being dragged through the mud. Sometimes like a flash of green.

I didn't realise how much fun I was actually having. We no longer heard the crowd cheering as we were consumed in trying to win. Well, actually just in staying upright and not getting dragged through the mud, time after time. By the time we walked off the middle of the oval, we could no longer see our green jumpers, as we were covered head to toe in mud. My perfectly groomed nails were splintered and covered in tacky.

When we went to change, I remarked to my girlfriend that all the men looked like Vikings! Bearded, scruffy men. Not one hot guy among any of them. She replied,

"Well I never said there were hot men's teams, just men's teams!" We both laughed and I was hooked on the sport. We were given one day off training. I thought I'd felt pain when I first started training — that was nothing compared to what I was about to face.

At my next training session, I was asked if I could play volleyball. I hadn't played since high school. Apparently, being on the Jellybeans Tug of War team meant that you automatically had a spot on the Jellybeans volleyball team on a Friday night.

Now picture this… I'm the person who, when the ball comes near me, closes my eyes. How was I going to play volleyball in competition? Where team mates depended on my so-called, non-existent skills? My high school sports teacher owned the indoor sports arena. He commented to one of my team mates one night that he couldn't believe I was actually, of my own free will, out on the court playing sport. I couldn't believe it either — me, Miss couch potato!

We were training hard for the NSW state championships. This would be the first time I had pulled against another female team. We drove the three hours to compete. The Jellybeans were a good team. No, actually we were a great team. We returned home from that competition winning all four weight divisions. I came home with four gold medals. I had just become a state sporting champion. Me, Miss couch potato. I was so bloody proud. I could have so easily not gone back after that first training session. But I did, I pushed through the physical and mental pain and showed up to train. Something inside me started to shift. I found grit I didn't know I had, determination I couldn't fake, and passion that kept me coming back. I wanted to exercise. I felt good after every training session and I started to lose a lot more weight. My moxie was rising.

We competed in lots more competitions throughout NSW and QLD. There wasn't just outdoor tug of war, but also an indoor competition that was pulled on a big rubber mat. We didn't wear boots, but instead Dunlop volleys. So the rubber would stick to the rubber mat. It involved leaning back on the rope, looking up at the ceiling and right hand over left on the rope. No tacky was allowed to be used in the indoor competition.

We would pull all day outside, then front up for evening pulls. It was so much fun. I loved it. My teammates would laugh at me because I always made sure I had make-up on and my nails done.

At the end of my first season of volleyball our team won! Ok, so it was the D grade, but that didn't matter. I participated in a sport where for most of the time my eyes were closed when the ball came towards me, and I won a little trophy. The next season we had to go up to the C grade. These girls soon became some of my closest friends at the time. We would all meet at the pub on the weekend and socialise. I had a life again. I had freedom and I was happy. I just didn't realise it at the time. I thought something was missing.

The team was training heavily for the National Championships to be held in Maitland. No one was game enough to miss a training session in the lead up to this competition. I was getting more nervous as we plowed through each training session, becoming fitter each week that went by. Before we knew it, we were piling up the cars with our uniforms and all wearing our team tracksuits. I was proud to be a Jellybean. I'd never belonged to a team before.

Going to competitions meant long drives, car pooling with teammates and lots of fun. We got there the night before and weighed in. This normally involved eight girls stripping off to just a crop top and bike shorts and all girls hopping on a set of cattle scales to weigh in as a team. Often we were over our team weight and would have to drop 1kg each to bring us under. This particular time we weighed under, so we were able to go out for a meal. We went to the Maitland city bowls club. It was busy, and there I saw him. The opposite end of the room. We locked eyes… I could say the rest was history, but where would the fun be in that?

He was tall, muscular and looked fit. His team walked past our table and a couple of them said hello to our coach. I asked him where they were from as their team name was the Canines. My coach responded that they were from Perth. I turned to my girlfriend and said "Great, I finally find a hot one and he lives on the opposite side of the country!"

The next two days went by in a blur. Ninety-six ends. In other words, we pulled 96 times on the rope in two days and one night. I had never experienced anything like it. We won a few of the weight classes, and I had just become a national sporting champion! It was a pinch-me moment. One still that defies belief. If I had first listened to myself, my own false belief, I would have never pushed myself. I thank my girlfriend who picked me up that Sunday afternoon. It started me on an adventure.

We had moved out of the house I built and my brother intended to buy it for his family. It was a relief to be selling it, I simply couldn't afford to keep it. I couldn't even put someone in to rent it and pay the mortgage as I was on a sole parents' pension. The rent would have been classed as income and I would have lost my pension and been in an even worse financial state that I was in now. It was a bitter-sweet moment. I was sad and angry that it had all come to this. Sad that I had lost my home, one I so desperately wanted to keep for the security of having a roof over my children's heads, and angry that I had put us into that predicament with a failed marriage that cost me everything.

We had to move out. It was mid-winter 2002 and there were no homes available in Glen Innes to rent. I had no choice but to move us into a cabin at the cheapest caravan park in town. All of our furniture had to go into storage, and we just brought our bedding and clothes in the cabin with us. I bought a small fan heater to keep us warm. Zak wasn't feeling well not long after the move and broke out in spots all over. He had chicken pox and even got them on his eyeballs. A few days later, Ally broke out in them too. Every day I had to take Zak to Armidale to have his cornea checked by the ophthalmologist. It was a nightmare. It pushed me to breaking point. To top it off it was snowing! It was freezing. Trying to bathe the kids in the bottom of the shower with a face washer covering the drain hole to get enough tar soup over them to stop the itching was impossible. I was so ashamed that we had become 'trailer trash', and I felt I had failed my children. I vowed to never be in this position ever again.

Not many people knew where we were living. To go from the most exclusive estate in town to living in a caravan was humiliating, but also humbling. I came crashing back to earth with a hard thud. After a very long three months, we finally got a home in Mossman Street. It was a quirky three-bedroom, one-bathroom home. Nearly every wall in the home was a different type and colour of brick. My landlord was a bricklayer. He had used the leftover random bricks from his job sites to build the house. I didn't care — we were out of the cabin, out of that caravan park, and we all had our own rooms again and a wood heater to keep warm. We weren't trailer trash any more. I vowed I would never put us in that position ever again. The next level down was living on the streets.

The back wire fence of our new home ran along a lane way, and I hadn't considered what that meant in regards to security. I withdrew all of my pension out of the bank to pay for our fortnightly food shop and rent. I had a trolley full of food and went to pay for it. I opened my wallet and there was no money inside it. I panicked. Where had all my money gone? I had to leave all the bagged up groceries on the counter and walk away. How was I going to feed my children? Things went from bad to worse. It turned out that the corner shop down the road from me had been robbed. They found the broken cash register at my back fence. The thieves had then come through my yard, and as the lock on the back sliding door was broken and we had been waiting since we moved in to have it fixed, we were easy prey to also be robbed. They entered the house, saw my purse, took the money out and left through the front door at about 3 am in the morning when the kids and I were asleep in the house.

I didn't sleep very well for months after this home invasion. I also went and purchased a cordless telephone to have beside my bed at night in the event of it happening again. The real estate gave us $100 to go towards food. The kids and I wrote letters to the local paper to the robbers telling them to get a job and to not take food out of children's mouths. Zak's letter told them to leave his pocket money alone. After it was published in the paper, I received an anonymous note in the letter box in lovely handwriting with a $20 note in it. I have no idea to this day who wrote that note. But I thank you. That kind gesture restored my faith in humanity.

I was manifesting someone to be my Prince Charming. I wanted a better life for the children and me. I knew staying in Glen Innes wasn't going to be that life. I had looked at renting a home in Armidale, 100km down the road. How would I move? What would I do without any support from friends? It scared the hell out of me.

M6 had been in and out of my life since I was 18. He was part of the muscle boy club, he also had the look of Thor about him. M6 had a very good body, and had girls and women across the town. For thirteen years I had zero boundaries with him. I would, and did, do anything for him. He knew it too, and used that to take advantage of me. He would come and knock on my bedroom window asking me to sneak him inside and have sex with me when mum was sleeping next door. We stopped when I was with M4 and then pregnant with Zak. Then stopped again when I met M5 until that relationship ended. Now he was back again, knocking on my door, wanting late night sex most weekends.

Everyone knew we were sleeping together — his family, my family — yet he always denied it. Always. He made me out to be the liar, and made me feel as though I wasn't good enough for him. I kept wishing and waiting for our families to know the truth. One day his sister rang trying to locate M6 and she thought she would try my place as there was a family emergency. He had been at mine most of the weekend. My kids were at their grandparents' house. I handed him the phone and said, "Your sister needs to talk to you." The look of horror on his face as he realised that finally his dirty 'me' secret was exposed. I dropped him to her place that afternoon. That was the last time I had sex with him. I finally felt validated. I didn't need him in my life anymore. That moment put a crack in his façade — it was a huge moment of truth for me. For the first time, I wasn't the one being made out to be the liar. I saw him for what he was: a man using me for his needs while denying my existence. I reclaimed my self worth that day and realised I no longer needed him.

The coach of the NSW tug of war team rang me and asked me if I would like to pull in Perth at the 2003 nationals. I jumped at the chance and said yes. I wanted to see the guy I had flirted with the previous year in Maitland and I wanted to travel.

This was my chance. I organised the kids to go to my in-laws, drove to Brisbane and flew to Perth by myself. I met up with the team at a hotel in the CBD. The next day we went to the grounds where the championships were to be held and the first person I saw when I got off the bus was him. We locked eyes and he gave me a cheeky grin. The team had t-shirts made with a slogan across our boobs that read "I love a good pull". It was the starter of many conversations.

We picked up where we left off 12 months earlier, however this time we spent a few nights with each other. He was 18 years my senior; he didn't look his age, nor did he act it. On the last morning when he dropped me back to the hotel, he remarked that I could always pop back over for a weekend! I replied, "Oh yes it's only one plane trip!" I don't know what I was thinking — yes, it was only one 5 hour plane trip and a 6 hour car drive to even get to the airport…

Well, that started it. We spoke daily on the phone. I flew back over a month later, then the next month he came over to me for a week. Every month for the following 6 months we saw each other. Before we realised it, we were in a serious relationship. The kids met him and adored him. Zak was in Year Four, and even took him to school for show and tell. The female teachers swooned over him. That fed his ego, and should have been a warning sign, but I ignored it and thought, wow, he wants to be with me. On one of his trips over, I remarked that the kids and I could pack up and move to Perth. He didn't even think twice and agreed. We decided to let the kids finish school that year before moving them across the country.

I continued to pull tug of war until 2005, changing teams to become a Canine in Perth. It was a lot harder to attend the competitions from Western Australia. We did a few local ones around Perth and flew a team of 12 over to South Australia for the National Championships at Berri. At a cost of $1000 per girl, it had become an expensive sport. I did become the Australian Tug of War secretary for three years. We only had one to two meetings a year and that was normally held the day before a major competition. I retired from the secretary position in 2006.

I learnt a lot from my tug of war days. Being in a team taught me patience, understanding, compassion and how to control my anger. It gave me confidence in my body image — Lycra isn't forgiving. It taught me that it didn't matter how strong you were, if someone wasn't having a good day then the whole team felt it on the rope. We all looked out for each other. The friendships I made in those days I still treasure today. We had become a family and I needed that more than ever at the time.

*2004 Australian Tug of War Championships Tenterfield, South Australian Team.
I pulled 2nd from the back.*

2004 Australian Tug of War Championships, Jellybeans Team

*2005 Australian Tug of War, Berri South Australia. Caines Team
— I'm pulling anchor.*

2005 Wyndham Lookout, Western Australia

Mossman Street, Glen Innes

CHAPTER 18

One Plane Trip

When I make up my mind to do something, I act on it straight away. Sometimes without thinking of the consequences. Moving to Perth was one of those decisions. I wanted to get out of the town where we were living. I had found my knight in shining armour to help me act on that plan. But moving across the country is no easy task; adding two young children makes it even harder. The most cost-effective way to relocate was to sell all of our furniture and keep only our personal belongings. That also meant moving my piano. M7 learnt that if you love me, you have to love my kids and my piano. We came as a package deal.

Once the decision was made, I quickly swung into action. Quotes on removalists. The cheapest I could come up with was $5000. M7 paid for us to move. I certainly didn't have the money. Things on the surface looked perfect, but I ignored the red flags; cracks had started to appear in our relationship.

I chose the date of January 26, 2004, to change our lives. To start afresh. We had organised farewells. Was I scared? Oh yes. Very scared! I asked myself whether I was doing the right thing, not only for me but for my children. But I was more terrified of what would happen if we stayed there. One outweighed the other. If I didn't do things because a sliver of a doubt crept in, then nothing would ever happen. I was also very excited about all the new possibilities. I wanted to own my own home again, to have the security of a roof over our heads. And M7 brought all of that.

In the middle of all of the hype of moving across the country, my body wasn't playing nice. I had a routine pap smear, and it came back with abnormal cells on the surface of my cervix. I had CIN 1 and 2. Cervical Intraepithelial Neoplasia. This meant I had to have a cone biopsy of my cervix. CIN is not cancer, but it can be a precursor to cervical cancer if left untreated for many years.

I travelled the one-hour trip for this procedure. They gave me an internal ultrasound and noticed a mass on my right ovary. It was measured and was the size of a large grape. I was told to go home and wait a few weeks before returning to have it scanned again. My mind raced to the dark side. Instantly thinking the worst. Two weeks later, I lay there in fear of what was happening. I did have pain on the right side. No one could tell me what the mass was. My mind went into overdrive, running through every bad scenario. Would they have to operate? Was it cancer? Was I going to die? Notice how I mentioned every bad scenario, not any good ones. Nowadays, I have trained my mind to focus on the positive side first, rather than the negative.

The lump had grown from the size of a large grape to bigger than a golf ball. It was decided to operate and remove it. I had to wait another couple of weeks for surgery through the public system. It was a very long two weeks. I didn't tell too many people what was happening. I didn't want to worry them, and I certainly didn't tell my children. I had sold all of our furniture, and we were sleeping on mattresses on the floor and eating our meals sitting in the middle of the lounge room floor. It was early December when I got a girlfriend to drive me the 100km to Armidale Hospital for laparoscopic surgery through my belly button on my right ovary. I hadn't even told my family what was happening. My kids went to their grandparents at Emmaville for the weekend, as it was a Friday. I thought I'd be sent home later that day or the next day and go and pick them up.

I signed the consent forms, and it was explained that they would try to remove it through my belly button; however, if they couldn't remove it that way, they would have to cut me from hip to hip. I didn't think too much about what could go wrong at that point; my only concern was making sure they would give me enough anaesthetic to knock me out and keep me asleep for the whole operation — waking up during surgery was a terrifying prospect.

I woke up in intensive care, in more pain than I imagined I would have. Vomiting from the general anaesthetic. I was all alone. I knew no one was coming, because only two people knew I was there, and one didn't even live in the same state as me! M7 had rung to see how I was. I was not in a good state and spent the next few days in intensive care before being transferred to a ward. My worst fears had come true. I had a very large incision, from one hip to the other. They had to open me to remove the dermoid cyst that, in a very short space of time, had grown bigger than a grapefruit. It was full of keratin, hair and brain cells. My aunt joked that I had been over the Nullabor one too many times when they found it, and I had some kind of alien inside of me. What had happened was that one of my eggs had decided to develop on its own without being fertilised. So that does prove that the female supplies the brain!

I spent a week in the hospital, and my brother came to pick me up after he got word from M7 of what had happened. I wasn't looking forward to going home, looking after the kids and having to sleep on the floor when I could barely stand upright. I had only been home a day when I received a knock on the door. Trying to get off the mattress on the floor was sheer agony. When I finally opened the door, I burst instantly into tears when I saw a man standing there. It was my father. He had flown from New Zealand after my brother's concerned call to him. He had come to help. It was the first time in my life that he had been there for me. Within minutes, I got a migraine from the shock of seeing him and had to lie back down on the mattress on the floor. My father stayed with us for a week. His support helped me heal — it's something I will never forget. He came to help.

It would be our last Christmas ever in Glen Innes. The kids went to visit their grandparents in Emmaville on Christmas Eve, and I didn't get them back until late that afternoon. I continued to improve daily, and the weeks passed quickly. I had two huge garage sales to sell off our junk and belongings that we no longer needed. I had kept a lot of things that were Mum's, and as hard as it was, it was time to let a lot of that go. The last few days before our move, I picked up M7 from Coffs Harbour airport, and he came over to help us fly back with a lot of our belongings. The removalists picked up 60+ boxes, one white cupboard, and of course my piano.

I had to sell my dark green Mitsubishi Laser. I still remember my number plates: JUZ71E. I loved that car, but I loved the idea of a new life even more. Somewhere I didn't feel I was being watched or judged with every move I made. I ran as far away from my hometown as I possibly could without leaving the country. To a place with no friends and only one other family member. Would I do it all over again today? Not in the headspace I'm in now. I have finally learned not to ignore red flags.

On 26th January 2004, it was Australia Day, the day to say goodbye to my family and friends. To start our new life. A new beginning. I picked that day to move purely because it was the cheapest day for flights, and we needed four one-way tickets.

I hugged my brother tightly. This was it; we were actually leaving. Four of my closest friends were at the bus station to give hugs and kisses. There were lots of tears as we climbed on the bus for the first leg of what would be a very, very long trip. I looked at both my kids and knew deep down I was doing the right thing. Moving to a place that would give them choices. Opportunities that they would never have gotten if we had stayed in that small country town. It also gave me a fresh slate. One where people didn't know my past. People had bets on how long we would last in Perth. Twelve months. Two years. They said, 'she'll be back with her tail between her legs when it doesn't work out.' Boy, were they wrong!

The bus trip was nearly 3 hours, and we then hopped on the XPT train at Tamworth. The next leg was a long train trip. The kids thought it was great. We pulled into Central Station in Sydney. We had so many bags and had to rush through the station to catch another train to Sydney airport. The kids had never ridden on an escalator, and Ally was terrified. I stood at the top and threw our bags on it, and then her, with M7 catching her at the bottom as she screamed all the way down. Even today, she will tell you about that trip — well, more to the point, the escalator. This was followed by a 4 hour plane flight to Perth and then a short taxi trip to our new home in Redcliffe. It was so much for the kids to take in. I was so anxious, nervous and excited all rolled in one.

On arriving in our new home, we were not prepared for a couple of things. It was hot. Really hot — 35 degrees at midnight and no air conditioning. M7 had bought the kids fans and new beds, but they were too wound up to go to sleep. Then we heard a loud noise above our house and went out at 1am in the morning to investigate. It was the police helicopter with its spotlight on, hovering over the neighbourhood, looking for someone who had broken the law in some way. I instantly felt sick to my stomach. What had I done? Had I actually made the best decision for my young family?

It was a hard January. We lived out of a suitcase until our belongings caught up with us. Somehow, they got sent to Redcliffe, Queensland, not Western Australia. I was not impressed. We lived next door to a park. The kids soon made friends with the neighbourhood kids. Ally was 6, and Zak was 10. I enrolled them at Redcliffe Primary School. M7 had a gym in the garage. We would watch him train for hours on end. Every night and most weekends. It wasn't long before the kids asked if they could train too. M7 was competing in a weightlifting code called All-round weightlifting and suggested we all compete too, as all ages and genders were welcome. We loved it and became 'the family that trains together, stays together'. Well, that was the theory anyway.

The summer holidays ended, and that meant the kids starting their new school, and me finding a job. I had to resign from Weight Watchers in NSW, as they were independently run in each state. I rang up to make an appointment for an interview, and the woman said to me, "Welcome to the team" as she confirmed my interview. That gave me good hope that I would soon have a job.

I had never received proper training in NSW to be a Weight Watchers leader. I was interviewed by the state manager, Karen. I was told I'd have to retrain, and they didn't have any permanent meetings to offer me, but she would call me if they needed someone to fill in.

Two days later, I got a phone call to fill in a meeting not far from my home. I was so excited. I hated not working and didn't expect M7 to support us. What Karen neglected to tell me was that she was going to be the weigher! Talk about an introduction to a new job — having the state manager in the room! I was so nervous, I hadn't even been retrained. After the meeting, Karen was stopped in the car park by the members who asked if I could be their permanent leader. The next day, I got a call and was offered the job! I wanted more. I needed more meetings for me to feel like an equal in my relationship with M7.

Over the course of the next few months, I took over more meetings, and I loved it. Helping more people, growing the KPIs. I was given the opportunity to do smaller meetings in the corporate world, where I was the recorder, weigher and leader. I would have my kit all together, which comprised the current week's program, some stock to sell, and of course the scales.

I helped get Weight Watchers into the Australian Liquor, Hospitality and Miscellaneous Workers' Union (LHMU), as we didn't belong to one. This then helped us get an award wage of just over $19 per hour for a leader, $17 per hour for a weigher, and not just a 9% commission on sales. I had great sales at all of my ten meetings. Thousands of dollars of stock each week. Zak, at the age of 15, became a weigher at one of my meetings. He also worked at IGA and as a ref at Laser Corps (laser tag). Taking after me with his work ethic.

We hired a campervan just before Easter in 2005 and the four of us set out to drive up to Kunnanura in far north Western Australia for a wedding. It was an amazing trip, full of adventures, and opened our eyes to how big Australia is. The kids loved it, finding giant green tree frogs in the toilet blocks. I went on later to own three of these frogs, and they feature a lot in my art works.

In 2007, two of my members achieved the WA state finals for Slimmer of the Year, and I finally reached my goal weight. One of my members won the state finals, and that meant she and I were off to the national titles for Slimmer of the Year. Although she didn't win, to be recognised as a leader with such achievements boosted my KPIs in all my meetings. I was now doing ten meetings a week. My weight continued to come off as I pretty much starved myself in order to get there.

I loved helping people reach their own goal weight. To see their lives change each week and their confidence boosted. I saw people join, fail, then rejoin 6 months or 12 months later. I saw people join once and get to their goal weight. I saw tears, and I saw happiness. I coached up to 500 people a week and impacted the lives of thousands of people. The pressure on me to get to my goal weight increased my obsession with losing weight to be perfect. Not a good combination.

We fitted into a nice routine. I decorated our tiny three-bedroom home, and we slowly got used to the heat. Saturday mornings, we woke at 6.30 am with M7 turning on Slim Dusty loud on the stereo, and that meant it was time for all of us to get up and clean the house, then do the grocery shopping. I am not a morning person! This killed me! Saturday afternoons were grocery shopping, and on Sundays, if we didn't have a weight lifting comp on, we would head down to the Swan River for a picnic and to throw a fishing line in or go for a push bike ride. The kids loved it. We saw live music concerts on the banks of the Swan River in South Perth.

I never did fit into the local school mums' groups. I felt so alone. I missed my friends. I never thought that I'd miss my old life, but I did.

Early 2005 saw me go under the knife again. I was having pain again in my ovaries and had been diagnosed with polycystic ovary syndrome — PCOS. I was seeing a new gynaecologist in Perth, and he suggested that I have my ovaries drilled — in other words, they were going to burn off all the cysts. He explained that it would just be laparoscopic surgery through my navel. I agreed to have the procedure done. What he didn't explain was the amount of pain I would be in following the operation from the carbon dioxide that they used to fill my abdomen, to give them space to work. I took myself to the hospital that morning via Taxi, had the procedure done and then took a taxi home. No one was there to greet me or help me, as M7 wouldn't miss a day of work to be there for me.

I had never experienced pain like it and thought I was going to pass out, then vomit, with 10 out of 10 pain. I had to wait for the gas to dissipate up through my shoulders, sleeping the night propped up over pillows, unable to lie down because the pain was horrendous. It took me a few days to get over it before I returned to work. My ovaries were all but fried, and I was left with a third of my right ovary and my left. I still felt pain every time I ovulated, and this went on until 2013, when I had the Mirena IUD inserted.

After living in the tiny house for 12 months, we decided to buy a larger home and put in a pool, on the other side of the airport in a suburb called South Guildford. This meant the kids were changing schools again. My work picked up, and I made friends through Weight Watchers. I was finally feeling at ease, and yet I also had blinkers on to what was really happening at home,

We lived within walking distance of the army base at South Guildford, where they held the army cadets. Every time we drove past it, Zak would express that he couldn't wait to join. When he turned 12 and a half, he enlisted. He worked hard in the four years he was there and got the rank of Warrant Officer 2. Ally also joined — well, not of her free will. We conscripted her to join for a year to teach her respect and discipline. It was a weekly struggle to get her there. They learnt so much in cadets, and it was the best $100 I spent on each of them every year.

My weight was slowly coming off, and by June 2007, after walking through the door of Weight Watchers for 445 weeks, I got down to 77.9kg. I had lost 46.3kg and finally became a life member of Weight Watchers. It took a lot of hard work and discipline — and in the end, some Duromine — to get there. I was proud that I had got there just in time to go to New Zealand and be on the lifting platform in Lycra. As the old saying goes: nothing tastes as good as goal weight feels. The problem with Weight Watchers was that their maintenance program sucked, and my weight crept back on. However, I never regained all of it.

I had much delight when I reached my goal weight, and rang my Aunty to tell her that I no longer wore a 12-seater tablecloth, but was now down to a four-seater! Her reply was that she had no idea what I was talking about and said that she had never said the first statement to me. She then apologised to me.

In 2007, I needed to make $5000 quickly! M7, Zak, Ally and I had qualified to compete at the All-round Weightlifting Championships in Christchurch, New Zealand. I had reached as high as I could go with WW, and my commission on sales really wouldn't stretch any further. I needed something else to do as well. So I signed up to sell plastic! I achieved my goal in only a few weeks and off we went to compete. I came in as a runner-up in the open female division, and both the kids won male and female junior world titles.

We all loved training together and had a purpose-built shed with commercial gym equipment in our backyard. We would train at least five days a week. Competing at any opportunity. I ended up the secretary of the Western Australian All-round Weightlifting. Both myself and the kids have world records still standing even today in that sport.

I joined Tupperware for the sole purpose of paying for our trip to New Zealand. Selling it came very easily to me. I had done so many other party plans that this felt like home. I paid off my super kit and, within 6 weeks, had paid for our holiday. We went away for two weeks, and I couldn't wait to get back home and get back into party plan mode. While I was away, I realised that I couldn't get any higher in my WW career and something was missing. I made the decision to step up to management. I wanted the Tupperware car.

In order to get the car, you had to become an associate manager by recruiting 5 people under you. Then the team had to sell $55,000 in 12 weeks to qualify for the car. My team was called Morpheus, not from the Matrix, but because Morpheus was the Greek god of dreams, and dreams become a reality when you set goals. I qualified for the car in 5 weeks. Weight Watchers saw this as a conflict of interest, as I was turning up in a Tupperware car to do a Weight Watchers meeting, even though I never mentioned it in the meetings. I was told I had to make a choice. Weight Watchers or Tupperware. I chose the latter.

I was so proud to achieve the car, but Zak hated it! It was a white Ford Territory with big pink Tupperware plastered up the sides. To top it off, of course, I bought hot pink car seat covers for it. I would drive around 1500 km a week doing parties, and helping my down line. I went to every sales meeting on a Monday night. Managers' meetings were once a month. Twice a year, we would launch a new catalogue and introduce new colours to update our kits. I still have all my Tupperware Diaries.

It was a lot of hard work. I would do a party. Come home and then do the paperwork. Either pick up the order at the next sales meeting or have it delivered. I mostly had mine delivered as I was making great sales and couldn't fit it the week's sales in my car. In what's known as record breaker week, I did 19 parties and sold close to $20,000 in sales. That is a lot of plastic to pack in one week, as it didn't come pre-packed. To give you a sense of the scale of how much plastic I was handling, I had 55 large cartons dropped off to sort through. My kids helped, and we were knee deep through the lounge, dining and kitchen in our home with small tracks to walk through. We gave a lot of the pieces nicknames, such as the serving centre, which was known to the kids as the UFO container.

I was a fantastic recruiter. Too good. I recruited at one stage nearly every hostess I had. I ended up with a team of over 60, but I had no party lines of my own left. I went from selling $150,000 a year in personal sales to less than $40,000 the next year. It was hard to find the balance.

I became one of the state's trainers of recruits nearly every Saturday morning at one stage, as it meant I got paid an extra $80 a week. Not much, considering what I was entrusted to do. Tupperware had a great incentive program for demonstrators and managers. Lots and lots of prizes. From trips to dishwashers and lots of plastic! I won pages of items, including a week's accommodation at what used to be known as Burswood Casino, which would have been amazing if I hadn't lived 10 minutes up the road from it.

Every six months, Tupperware would bring out a new catalogue in April for the Winter range and again in September for the Summer colours. These were launched at major functions called Sessions. Here, the two distributorships from Western Australia would meet for the day. We would find out not only what new pieces of plastic we were getting and the new colours for the season, but we would also find out who had won top sales in the state and country. All the awards were given out. It was at one of these sessions that I won number four in Australia for new manager sales for the year. Once a year, we would have a major conference for all the managers around Australia. It was a great excuse to be away from home and family life for the week. I loved getting dressed up for these functions. The glitz, glamour and the sequins!

One day, as I got out of my Tupperware car in a shopping centre car park, I was approached by a man named John. He saw the sign-written car and said he had a business proposition that I would be perfect for. I listened. I met with him and his wife to discuss the business venture. Sketchy I know! But I have always had an open mind when it comes to money.

Tupperware was hard work. Always trying to find new party lines, customers and demonstrators. I always said the first month I'd have to pay for the car, I would step down, and I did. In order to keep the car, your sales had to be a rolling three months and $55,000 in sales; otherwise, you had to pay the shortfall in a percentage. I had to pay $800 in that first month, and I handed the keys back in. Now what was I going to do? I took John up on his offer and joined a multi-level marketing business again, this time called Nuskin. Selling galvanic spas and anti-age creams for your face.

In my first week of selling Nuskin, I sold more than I had in months of plastic parties. So in 2009, I headed to Sydney for their major conference and started down that path. I was invited to speak on stage in front of 5,000 people about my experience with Nuskin. I remained a Tupperware demonstrator for the next two years, selling minimally to keep that status. Eventually I couldn't keep up the momentum of Nuskin with the price of each unit, so I stopped selling the product and was ultimately left with 6 spa systems that years later I threw in the bin.

I still keep in contact with my Tupperware family of managers, even today. When I visit Perth, I always arrange a catch-up. We talk about the memories we share of plastic parties, as well as what we are all up to now — I treasure those friendships. We had our own tribe.

I had an MRI in 2008 as I had tightening in my face and a lump I could feel on the right side of my neck. The results showed a large cyst in my brain behind my right eye. My ears, nose and throat (ENT) specialist said it was nothing to worry about, so I didn't. I did, however, get diagnosed with Myofascial pain syndrome in my face. The lump I could feel was a constricted neck muscle. I went to have dry needling done on my neck, under gas. It was the most horrific experience. I felt the fibres in my neck tearing and screamed even under happy gas. It did work, but only for three days. I was at home vacuuming the lounge room when all of a sudden, with a lot of pain, it constricted again. I was angry and disappointed. I never went back, but just put up with the constant pain and still do.

I was getting tonsillitis again; I hadn't had a bad run of it since 2004. Yet here it was, back again every couple of months. I was losing money, unable to work. I went back to my ENT, and it was decided that I would have to have them out again! It would be 32 years between operations. How did they grow back? Well, they didn't. When they were first removed in 1977, they ripped them out and left tiny bits. As I grew, so did those little bits. I got larger, so did they. Voilà — bits big enough for tonsillitis to breed on and thrive. I wasn't looking forward to the recovery after it, but I couldn't go on living like that. They also removed tonsil crypts that had formed due to a constant sinus drip that I had. I was in a bad way when I came out of surgery. How can something so tiny hurt so much? I spent the next two weeks lying on the lounge, drugged up to my eyeballs on Endone. I still get sore throats, but haven't had tonsillitis since.

M7 was drinking more and more every night. He would give me a kiss goodbye and leave for work at 5.20 am, delivering parcels all day. He would then return from work at 6 pm and go into our gym and train for the next couple of hours. The first thing that he would do when he finished training was come in and open some form of alcoholic beverage and consume it, every single night, until he passed out on the lounge. It reached the point where I didn't even try to wake him to come to bed and just left him there. I hated what our life was becoming.

He was never a violent drunk, except for one night when we had a gathering at our house for my Tupperware team. He had become paralytically drunk, consuming so much alcohol that he threw up in the garden bed in front of everyone. I was mortified. So embarrassed. I was supposed to be their leader, and here they were witnessing my dirty little secret of living with an alcoholic. Many times I wanted to return to the East Coast, to Glen Innes. But I was too ashamed and embarrassed to tell anyone what was happening. After everyone had left, it turned into a screaming match; he was a big, muscular man weighing close to 120 kg. He grabbed me in his arms and held onto me so tight and would not let me go. The kids were asleep in bed.

I screamed so loud that Zak came running in and screamed at M7 to let me go. I was so scared. I actually wet my pants from fear. He released his grip on me. I grabbed my handbag and car keys and told the kids to get in the car. We left. I wasn't sure where we would go, so we ended up in a McDonald's car park at 2 am in the morning, as it was the safest place under the lights that I could think of. We stayed there for a couple of hours, and then I had no choice but to drive us back home, hoping and praying that M7 had passed out and would be asleep. Zak had moved out of the main house and into what was my office, which was off the side of the garage. We parked the car up the street and walked back to our home and snuck into Zak's room, and the three of us slept in there that night with the doors locked. This went on for years.

What had I done? My decisions had put us in a terrible emotional position. I had to find a way out. His drinking continued to get worse, and I continued to work more so I wouldn't have to be at home. I knew that he wouldn't hurt the children. Even when he was home, there was no communication. And there certainly wasn't any sex. I wouldn't have sex with him when he was drunk, which left a small window of opportunity. Our relationship was dying. In all the years that we were together, he never paid me any compliments on how I looked, nothing at all. He said early in our relationship that that wasn't something that he ever did, as he had received plenty of compliments in his time and didn't see it important to give them, but oh boy, he liked receiving them! He would often say that many women he would see on a daily basis, dropping off parcels, would compliment and flirt with him. He would always make sure he told me what they said. I was made to feel that I was lucky to have him as my partner.

I could never understand how someone who trained as much as he did and carefully watched what he ate, would then poison his system with copious amounts of alcohol. It was nothing for him to drink a whole bottle of white port in one sitting. Writing himself off. Whenever I broached the subject, he would reply that he wasn't an alcoholic, as he didn't go to meetings! I was in a terrible place mentally and had no one I could talk to. After 7 years, we had reached a place where I couldn't handle him touching me or kissing me. We didn't even sit on the same lounge at night. It was sad. I didn't know how I could spend the rest of my life like this.

I couldn't tell my family, I felt so ashamed that I had put my children and myself into such a toxic environment. He was not a good role model for my children. They were growing resentful towards him and the damage it was causing to our little family. I didn't know how I was going to get us out of this mess I had yet again created in our lives.

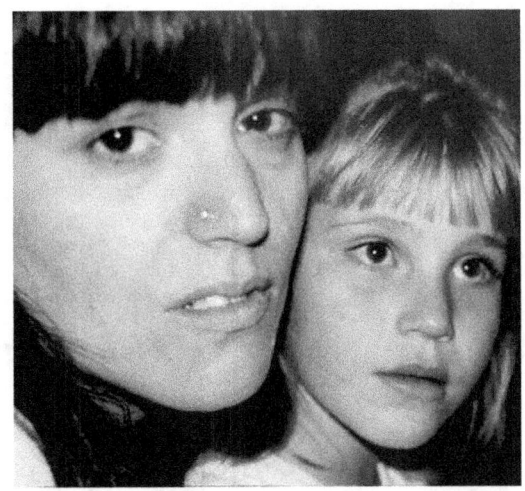

2004 Ally and me at Clifton Springs

2004-2005 McKeon Street, Redcliffe. The first house we lived in Western Australia

2005 -2010 Our house in South Guildford WA

2006 Pinch Grip 52.5kg, All-round Weightlifting, Belmont Sports and Rec Club, Western Australia

2006 Zercher 77.5kg, All-round Weightlifting, Belmont Sports and Rec Club, Western Australia

2007 Amanda and myself at the Australian Weight Watchers Slimmer of the Year Awards

2007 Christchurch New Zealand. Competing in the All-round Weightlifting World Championships

2007 Dad and myself. First time I'd seen him in 9 years.

 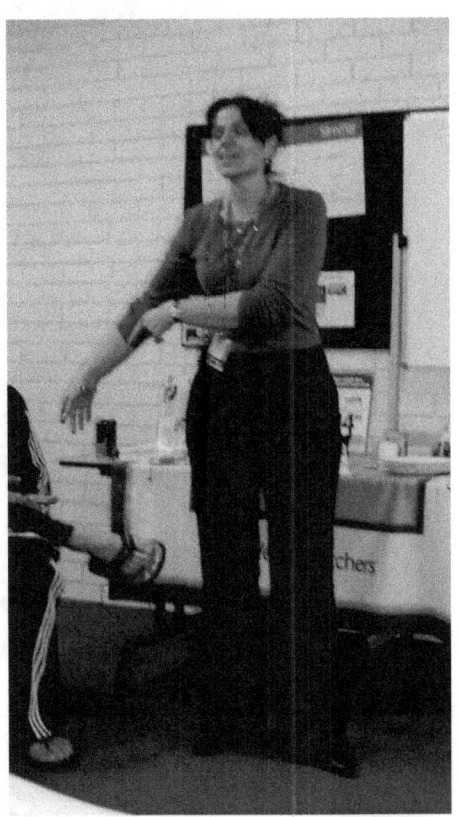

2007 Weight Watchers Leader *2007 Weight Watchers Leader*

2007 Zak, Ally and myself in Rotorua, New Zealand

2008 Tupperware sales meeting as a Manager, doing a demonstration

CHAPTER 19

Wake Up Call

It was the end of 2010; I am not proud to admit that I had an affair towards the end of M7's and my relationship. I craved affection; I yearned for attention. I met a guy on a 'sex' site for just a once-off 'date'. M8 was just supposed to be no-strings fun, a fling in every sense of the word, but it turned very serious after five days when he told me he loved me. I was speechless. That wasn't no-strings fun anymore, but one big fat ball and chain and my head was spinning. How could someone love me when I didn't even love myself? In the mindset I was in, I ran to it. He didn't love me. He loved the idea of me.

Nowadays, if a man tells me that he loves me in a short period of time — in under a year — or if he love bombs me, I run for the hills as fast as I can! It's a HUGE red flag. Well, actually, I just block them on every electronic device I can think of, then run. However, back then, I was drawn like a moth to the flame. I was attracted to it, but it drew me into danger that I didn't release. I felt I had a way out to leave M7; our relationship was over, and we were merely existing under one roof. No communication whatsoever. I craved what M8 had been giving me; however, I was blind to all of the red flags from the love bombing I received.

Relationships take time. And a good lot of time. I now know that a feel-good fuzzy feeling before love is called limerence, and some people are serial limerents. They long for that feeling. That feeling disappears after two to three years, and they are looking for their next hit, their next fix. M8 is one of those men.

It's like a drug, and they have never actually been in real love. Most will never know what real love actually is, and that is sad.

Limerence is a term coined by psychologist Dorothy Tennov to describe an intense and involuntary emotional state that is often characterised by romantic or obsessive feelings towards another person. People experiencing limerence may have intrusive thoughts about the object of their affection, feel a strong desire for the other person to reciprocate their feelings, and often exhibit behaviours such as checking for signs of interest from the other person, idealising them, and experiencing extreme highs and lows based on perceived reciprocation or rejection.

Limerence is distinct from genuine love, as it tends to be more focused on the idealised image of the person rather than a realistic and balanced view of their qualities. It can be an overwhelming and consuming experience, and individuals in a state of limerence may find it challenging to concentrate on other aspects of their lives.

It's important to note that limerence is a psychological concept and not a formally recognised mental health disorder in diagnostic manuals like the DSM-5. However, it shares some similarities with obsessive-compulsive disorder (OCD) and can have a significant impact on a person's wellbeing and relationships.

I left M7 and closed the door on that romantic relationship and moved straight in with M8 like a giddy teenager, head spinning from the whirlwind of it. It felt like the best of both worlds at the time; the kids and I had our time together, bonding for the nine days M8 was away working FIFO, and then M8 would come home for five days, and I had time with him. He said he never wanted children of his own, but was ok that I had teenagers. Hindsight is an amazing thing; in the five days he was home, our routine became disrupted. The kids became unsettled, and it wasn't fair to either of them. Zak and M8 often clashed over who was the alpha male, and this would often lead to lots of yelling. My heart was breaking for Zak. In recent years, I have apologised to Zak for the situation I had put us in at the time, not knowing any better.

I needed to make money, and I needed to make it fast. It was hot; 40+ degrees. We needed fresh meat for dinner, and I went into a warehouse butchers' shop to buy some. A woman was packing the fridges, and it was so cool in there. I commented to her that it would be a fantastic place to work, given the sweltering heat outside. She then asked me if I was looking for a job, as she had fired someone the day before. I said yes, I was. She told me to bring my resume in the next day. I did, and I walked out as a checkout chick and meat packer in a big fridge. This was fine when the weather was hot outside, but come winter, I would wear five layers of clothes to work just to keep warm.

It was not a nice place to work. We had security cameras in every direction in every room. It was my job to pack the freezers, which meant leaning into them and pulling out the old stock to put the new stock in first, then replacing the older stock on top. One day, my manager had taken a phone call, and it was the owner of the store. He instructed my manager to tell me to keep bending over as they were looking at my arse in the air on the video cameras. I was disgusted and so angry! He sat in his large office all day, looking at multiple screens that displayed everything we did. I should have quit right then and there. But I didn't. I needed the money. I felt cheap in the process. It was a job that was full of stress and sexism. It was vile, disgusting and degrading. I should have left long before I did.

However, I was constrained by our financial situation, so I felt I had no choice but to stay at the time. I did have choices; I just didn't have enough self-worth to stand up for myself with men. Never protecting my inner child. Boundaries!

There was one particular day I got a migraine, and I asked to go home and was told I couldn't. Now, those who have ever been near me when I get a migraine will tell you that it's not a pretty sight. How I didn't vomit that day beats me, but I did pass out in the middle of the store floor and woke up to them all panicking and the paramedics in attendance. I had an overnight stay in the hospital. That migraine scared me. It felt different to my normal ones. Stronger, more powerful and literally put me on my arse.

I had somehow managed to become the assistant manager of that store within 3 months. It was long hours but good money as we were paid under the meat workers' rate, not retail.

Upper management called me into the staff room and offered me my own store to run. I couldn't believe it! My own store. They never offered them to females to run. The store that they offered me was located in the opposite direction from where we lived and the kids' school. Ally refused to catch the bus to school, so I had to drop her off. I put my family first and declined the offer.

It was not long after this that I decided to run for federal office. I wanted to put my all into the election. I've never been one to do anything half-heartedly, so I resigned from my job. M8 supported us for a few months so I could devote my time to the campaign, and we topped up the cost of our living from the rest of my savings.

We moved in together way too soon — I now recognise it as another red flag. Our sex life left not much to the imagination.

Eight months after we moved in together, M8 was home from the mines, where he worked as a FIFO worker. This was 'fly-in and fly-out', to work in the remote Pilbara in Western Australia. His rotation was home for five days and working away for a nine-day turnaround. M8 insisted we try swinging.

I wanted ground rules. No playing with others separately, always in the same room with each other. No dating others outside of our relationship. He agreed. We met a few couples in the swinging scene, but we never had great experiences. M8 was always so jealous of the extra attention I would get, and he wasn't the centre of attention. I knew I would cop it afterwards, the cold shoulder or the abuse about how the evening went. I didn't want to swing anymore; I was hating it. Why couldn't he just love me? Wasn't I enough?

I had been selfish, thinking I needed a man to make me happy; I now know I don't. I was love-bombed, which then led me to set no boundaries for any of us. This is a common theme throughout the book that you will see.

It was Wednesday, 19th August 2010, and we had dropped both kids off at Army Cadets as we did every week. M8 seemed a bit edgy. I put it down to him being tired and having to fly back to work the following day. I was very careful about what I would say to him so as not to upset him; I hadn't even realised at the time that this was becoming a regular occurrence or that I was even doing it. I was being groomed.

He took me out for dinner at a nice little Italian place in Victoria Park in Perth. It was romantic; I wasn't hungry as we had eaten a large late lunch at Midland Gate shopping centre less than four hours ago. It didn't make any sense for us to be here.

I can remember thinking that this was a strange place for a quick meal, as we only had a few hours before we had to pick up the kids from cadets. Before I knew it, M8 had a little box in his hand, right in front of the whole restaurant. I remember thinking, 'Where did that come from? Where did he hide that?' He then asked me nervously to marry him, but did not get down on one knee, with a ring I had admired in passing one day at the jewellery shop. I, of course, said yes and slipped my new, bright, shiny ring onto my finger.

I was deliriously happy, over the moon. He had asked Zak and my dad in New Zealand if he could marry me. I thought that was strange as my father hadn't been regularly in my life for decades. But here was this handsome, muscular, sexy man — an ex-stripper — choosing me! To be his wife! Me! Someone he wanted to spend the rest of his life with. With all my faults. With my big fat legs and with everything else that was wrong with me. Yet he still wanted me. Me! I said yes. What I should have said was no and run! Hindsight…

I look back now and cringe at my lack of self-worth and how I thought I was so lucky to have a man like him, never thinking for a moment that he was lucky to have a woman like me. All because I didn't love myself first and didn't know how to protect my inner child from such red flags and, in the end: danger.

We were both working really hard. I had tried to get elected to the Western Australian Upper House in the Senate with the political party called The Australian Sex Party. Our engagement made it into the West Australian Newspaper on page 2 on polling day. This was unheard of in an election.

I always said that if I didn't get into Parliament on election day, I would start applying for new jobs on the Monday morning after, and that's what I did. One of the first jobs I applied for was a casual position at the largest bed furniture store in Midland, Perth. I had an instant connection with the manager during my interview; her mother also had MS. I walked out of that interview not with the casual position I had gone in for, but as assistant manager of that store. I was on cloud nine. Such a relief to be earning money again.

After being there a week, the manager had gone off on sick leave. That should have been my cue to run… and run as fast as I could in the opposite direction! I felt like I was drowning. I had staff who had been there for years who resented me coming in as a newbie to be their boss. I had to learn so much in such a short period of time, and I was struggling to remember everything, which was so unlike me. Upper management was in a mess, with very little communication or support for their staff. I felt like I was losing my mind. I was in a constant state of cognitive fog.

I went to my GP's with an infected belly button piercing and just happened to mention my eyesight was blurry. I had experienced something similar in 2001, but had put it down to an allergic reaction I had to the mascara I was wearing at the time. But this time I wasn't wearing mascara. He asked me if I had ever had the cyst behind my right eye removed. I hadn't taken that any further after my ENT had said it was all ok to live with it. But was it?

Within 24 hours of being at my GP's surgery, I was sitting across from a neurosurgeon shitting myself. I was petrified. Did he want to cut my brain open? Was history repeating itself? Had I ignored the cyst and now had cancer? Everything was going through my mind. The first thing I asked him was if he thought I had MS. I'm not even sure where that came from, since I was thinking about cancer. He replied he didn't think so, he thought my vision issues were probably from my migraines. He referred me to an ophthalmologist to check how well my vision worked. It turns out that when my vision works, it is 20/20, and when it doesn't, it's just crap. He suggested I was having cluster headaches, yet I wasn't having any pain. I now know that it was optic neuritis. None of it made any sense. There is very little I can do when my vision impairment flares. I can't read, watch television, or do any hobbies. I can get very frustrated, and just sleep a lot.

I had a repeat MRI in the tunnel of terror in 2010, and they found several white glowing bits that shouldn't have been there. A week after these results, I was referred to a neurologist. I again asked if it was MS, as my mum had MS and two cousins through my mum's side of the family — a strong genetic link. My neurologist dismissed this and diagnosed it all as having to do with my migraines, as I have suffered from them since I was 15. I asked why now, all of a sudden, my vision had changed, yet I wasn't having any headaches or pain. There was no answer; it fell on deaf ears.

I was put on Topamax for three months for the migraines and sent on my way. I was frustrated more than ever that I wasn't being heard and merely dismissed. No one knows our bodies better than we do, so why don't medical professionals listen to us more?

I was under so much stress from the new job I hated, my body was failing me, and I had no answers. The one thing I could control was where I was working, so I started looking for another job. That's when I spotted my dream job, the career I'd always wanted.

I lasted at the bed shop for six very long weeks before I was bullied so much that I quit. I had an interview all lined up the following week for a weight loss consultant position with Jenny Craig in Midland. The location was perfect, although it was upstairs in the retail sector. I waited nervously for the interview. I sailed through, impressing them with my experience in the weight loss industry, both with Weight Watchers, and my own personal weight loss success. Little did they actually know that harrowing journey.

I got the job and started the following Monday for a week's training. I really struggled with this and would burst into tears throughout the training. I hate role-playing exercises, and there were so many of them that week. I just couldn't remember what I was supposed to do and would burst into tears. I was baffled as to why I was so emotional. At first, I thought I was pregnant. I still to this day don't know how I passed that training, but the following week, I started as a weight loss consultant. We were assigned our own consulting room, and the location in the building was allocated according to how long you had worked there. As the newbie, my office was at the back of the building. It didn't take long before I moved my way up to the middle consulting room. I was proud of myself.

I had waited and worked hard to achieve my current position. They were very strict with our appearance. We had to be at goal weight, wear a navy business jacket and skirt. Black high heels and stockings. I always thought this was ridiculous, in Perth in the middle of summer. It could be 42 degrees outside and not much cooler inside on the second floor, and we would have to be dressed up to the nines.

The one thing that really gave me the shits every single day was that I had to remove my nose ring, as we were not allowed any body jewellery, only our ears, and even there we were limited to tiny earrings. I loved the rest of the job. Helping people achieve their weight loss goals, watching them bloom into new people every week. What I didn't like was the pressure of the KPIs for the retention rate. I thought Weight

Watchers was tough, but they were nothing compared to Jenny Craig. We had printed lists that we were expected to call every single day to get the members back through the door.

They were to be 'helping hand' phone calls, but they were solely to raise revenue, to get clients back through the door and spending money. I was abused, screamed and yelled at on many phone calls from voices of either guilt, anger or frustration that they couldn't lose weight and were no longer prepared to pay any more money to do so. I did convince a few to come back. I must have been doing a good job, as I was offered a promotion to Program Director.

I accepted the position and I moved into the front consulting room. I convinced myself that I was loving my job, but I was actually struggling to concentrate. I found I could no longer write notes on what the member was telling me, listen at the same time and work out their next week's order and instructions. Each day, the act of multitasking was becoming harder and harder.

I noticed something even more critical: I could no longer count. Not even to ten! It was all gone. I couldn't work out how to give the right change at work or balance the till at night. I couldn't even tell the time on a clock face. I couldn't use money. How was I going to ever function again in society? Luckily, we use EFTPOS in most transactions nowadays. I still can't work out if people give me the right change on the rare occasion I have to use cash.

I was on top of the world, but it didn't last long before I fell slowly down a dark tunnel, losing my grip and my mind, trying to hold on tighter to anything for what I thought was my dream. Nothing happens as fast in real life as what you see on the medical shows on TV. Though sometimes it can!

Over the next three months, I deteriorated even more. I couldn't lift my left arm, would cry for no reason, and would break into laughter, often at inappropriate times. I now know this is called the pseudobulbar affect. I was trying to hold it together in a new job and trying to learn. Remembering new things caused so much stress now that my short-term memory was gone. Then more things were failing in my body. I had pins and needles on my top lip, and even more concerning was that I couldn't count anymore, read the time, use money or multitask, and all I wanted to do was sleep. I felt like I was possessed. I was screaming on the inside, yet no one could hear my anguish on the outside.

Zak was 17 and had completed Year 12. He was accepted into the Australian Army at the age of 16, but I had refused to sign the paperwork until he finished Year 12. He picked up some work as a roof plumber, biding his time until his enlistment day. I had raised my son, he had lived under my roof for those 17 short years. On the

28th February 1999, I watched him swear his life to the people of Australia. I was full of mixed emotions. I was very proud of what he was doing; he became a man before my eyes. I was emotional that he would never live at home again and would be living over 3000 km away.

I was supposed to have a repeat MRI in early February 2011; instead, I waited 4 weeks until Zak enlisted. I didn't want my being diagnosed with anything to stop him from enlisting and fulfilling his childhood dreams. I hugged him dearly that day. Then I walked outside and bawled my eyes out.

I received some backlash from so-called friends for signing the papers to let Zak enlist. I had some horrible things said to me, such as, 'How could I let my son become a murderer? How could I sign his death papers?' I stood up for myself and said I was proud that he thought enough of Australia to put his life on the line and defend it and all the people in it, including them.

On the 2nd March 2011, I had my MRI, the third in a short period. This one showed even more white glowing spots. M8 and I had a combined 40th fancy dress birthday, trying to forget what was really happening in our lives

On 14 March at 8:30 am, I sat across from my neurologist with my girlfriend, Flik, when he mouthed the words, "*You have MS.*" The world as I knew it stopped in the blink of an eye. I went into shock, and felt relief, anger and fear all at the same time. Not once did that neurologist ever apologise to me for calling it wrong for over six months. This still makes me angry.

In the blink of my eye, the world I was living in changed forever, never to be the same again. I got the answers I was so desperately seeking. When you lose control of what your body and your mind are doing, it is terrifying, more so when you don't know why. I now had my why. MS. This disease has haunted me for many years up to this day. I've been living with it in my life since I was 9.

How was I going to tell my family when I was in shock myself?

I went out, sat in the car and made some tough phone calls. First, M8, my fiancé, was 1,400 km away working in the mines and couldn't be home for a week. He didn't take the news well, and I was so scared he would leave me.

Next were my grandparents, my mum's parents. My grandfather answered the phone, which brought back the memory of ringing them to tell them that their daughter had died. I was again ringing with bad news, and through my tears, I told him I was diagnosed with MS. He told me I had it wrong. I couldn't have it — the doctors had it all wrong. He put my nanna on the phone to explain to her. She was well aware of what I had been going through, and she had chosen to keep it from my grandfather at that stage. It was gut-wrenching to tell them I had the same incurable disease that their own daughter had, who died from complications. My nanna, over the years, carried a lot of guilt, blaming herself for me having MS. I would try to reassure her that I carried no hate or malice towards her; it was just something that happened. I had won the lottery, just the wrong type of lottery.

Next was my Aunty Lynny, who filled the void of my mum — another hard phone call to make. Lynny and Uncle Gra have been with me through thick and thin, and I'd be lost without their love and support.

The hardest phone call was to Zakariah, who had just enlisted in the Australian Army and was in basic training. I made contact with the Army Chaplain first, so Zak would have some support if he needed it. I didn't want him to find out and then feel he needed to quit the Army to come home to look after me. There were lots of tears, and I assured him I would be okay. History really was repeating itself.

I was to work from 1:00 pm to 9:00 pm that day, and was a mess, having flashbacks of Mum's journey with MS. How do you hold it together when your world has just crashed? When, in the blink of an eye, the future you thought you would live was now tarnished forever.

I called into work on the way home at about 11:00 am to tell my manager face-to-face rather than on the phone. Through sobs, I told her my diagnosis. Her reply was to go home and put my big girl panties on, get into my business suit and come back to work at 1:00 pm till close.

So I did!

How I did it, I'm really not sure. There was very little compassion. A week later, I was in the hospital, having a lumbar puncture, then my first round of steroids, for a relapse that had lasted for many months and was getting worse.

Work was getting harder by the day; from the bouts of fatigue and cognitive damage, I struggled to get through each shift. MS had given me an acquired brain injury. Steroids often take weeks to fully kick in. I discovered I became the bi*ch from hell when I had them. No sleep, suicidal, huge mood swings and weight gain! I hate them! I was not a nice person to be around, and unfortunately, Ally and M8 bore the brunt of all of it.

Four weeks later, my neurologist told me to stop working and take sick leave. The stress of work wasn't helping at all. Again, telling work didn't go very well. My manager told me that the big bosses in Melbourne wouldn't like me taking three months off on sick leave and that I was to quit. The next day, I received a phone call, and the head office approved my sick leave. My guess was that they were scared I would take it further if they made me quit or fired me.

I have been the child of someone who had MS, a carer of someone with MS, and was now someone who had MS.

I started my first disease-modifying therapy. A daily injectable called Copaxone, and a tablet called Tegretol. For both medications, I had allergic reactions and had to stop. I ended up with hives the size of bread-and-butter plates from the Copaxone. I clearly remember telling my neurologist what was happening. I couldn't wear jeans due to the pain and the itch. He told me I would have to put up with it! Like hell I was! The Tegretol gave me high fevers in the 40s.

The MS was taking hold of my body and my mind. I slept for the next three months, missing medical appointments, catch-ups with friends, and not picking up my daughter Ally from school.

I was slipping into the deep, dark hole of depression. I didn't want to leave the house; it was my sanctuary and becoming my jail at the same time.

My world had crumbled around me in such a short space of time. I was seeing a counsellor weekly from MS Western Australia. I desperately wanted to talk to someone. My mind was racing, my heart even faster. I had no one who could relate to what I was going through. I spent my waking hours at home, no longer working, looking at four walls, trying to do simple housework tasks. It would take me a full day to vacuum just one room. A week to vacuum the whole house. I would, without notice, burst into laughter without there being anything funny or then cry when I had no reason to. I could not control my emotions.

I would fall asleep mid-sentence or while eating dinner. I was so fatigued. I just wanted to sleep all the time. Nowadays, my life is on a pendulum. Hanging in the middle is my new normal, which is far from how my body once felt, and at any time the pendulum can be bumped, causing a wave of havoc through my body, changing my life again. Sometimes, settling back to my new normal often creates another new normal once again. Being able to adapt and modify has been my secret.

I was so scared of what my future was going to look like. I had been my mum's carer in my teenage years and early twenties. I had to make one of the toughest decisions in my life and put her into full-time nursing care. I felt like I had failed her by not being able to care for her needs anymore, as a single mother with a newborn baby.

I was scared that M8 would leave me when things got tough, just as dad left my mum. I knew what I was going to be in for, having seen what this disease did to my mum. I gave him a way out. I told him to leave, and that he could do better than the cripple I would become. He assured me he loved me and would be with me forever, no matter what. We would face an uncertain future together. He told me he loved me, wouldn't leave me and would walk beside me with whatever came along.

What was my purpose going to be for the rest of my life? What if I could no longer provide the basic needs of shelter, food, and clothing for my daughter? M8 earned too much money for me to get Centrelink. We had just lost $60k overnight and had more medical expenses than ever. Each MRI cost $800, specialist bills, pharmacy bills, and the list went on. I had become financially reliant solely on another human being. I felt humiliated and like a burden to him and to society. When M8 came home from work after each swing, it got to the point where he didn't like talking about my MS, and I had to pretend that it didn't exist. I had never felt more alone.

My neurologist also referred me to a psychologist, as he said a lot of it was in my mind. After three months of antidepressants and weekly psychologist visits, my psychologist said I wasn't the one with the problem. Clearly, my neurologist had the problem, as it was perfectly normal to feel the way I did, considering my family history of MS and what was happening to my body.

Zak had been in the army for three months in basic training in Koopooka. I missed him terribly. In the first four weeks, he was not allowed any communication with me.

My left leg was affected, with constant spasms in my hip flexor. I had a Lhermitte's sign, and every time I looked down, an electric shock would go from my neck to my feet and bounce back again.

Then my bladder decided it too needed to be in on the action, and I would go to the toilet to pee and think I was finished, stand up and then wet myself. I would have to psych myself into having a shower, as when the water runs down my legs, it feels like razor blades slicing into them.

The crunch came when I lost the ability to orgasm. I couldn't feel a thing. I think my neurologist nearly fell off his chair at the next appointment I went to as I demanded he fix me and give me my orgasm back. I went back to the hospital for another round of steroids. Too many of us experience a loss of sensation sexually and don't speak up because of embarrassment. Speak up to your medical team and be heard!

It was then decided that my MS was aggressive and Copaxone wouldn't cut it, as I had another relapse. So, I started monthly infusions of Tysabri. This was the big gun of disease-modifying therapies. I had to have a blood test to see if I had a virus in my brain called the John Cunningham virus (JC). If I had the JC virus, I would be at great risk of developing another incurable brain disease called progressive multifocal leukoencephalopathy (PML), which either leaves you in a vegetative state or kills you.

My results came back as JC positive, not something I wanted to hear. They considered the first two years of taking Tysabri to be safe, with 26 infusions. Then, going into the third year, the odds increase of developing PML. I stayed on that medication for 37 rounds, well into the danger zone. Every month thinking to myself, will I get PML? The stress was horrendous. All disease-modifying therapies come with a leaflet of fine print on the side effects and what could go wrong. Whoever reads what could happen? Certainly not me. It wasn't going to happen to me!

It was then that M8 suggested that we pack up and move across Australia to Geelong, where I was born and had family. He thought this would help with looking after Ally so she wouldn't have to go into foster care when I was in the hospital and M8 was at FIFO. In WA, I couldn't find any friends to look after her.

After months of waiting, the steroids started to work, and my leg, bladder, and orgasms all began to return to my new normal. It placed a high level of stress on our relationship. I felt like a massive burden on society and on M8, and I slipped a bit further down the dark hole.

I didn't want to live anymore. I couldn't find any hope in my life.

2010 - 2011 Jane Brook Drive, Jane Brook Western Australia

2010 Zak and Ally in cadets, picking them up from a week-long camp

2011 Zak in the army

2012 Zak, Ally and me

CHAPTER 20

The Sex Party

The year was 1982. I was in Year 6 attending Emmaville Central School, at eleven years of age. My brother Simon was in the same class as me; we were in a Year 5-6 composite class. It was a tiny school with about 110 children, from Kindergarten to Year 10. Everyone knew everyone.

We were classed as a disadvantaged school, so we had the opportunity to go on a school excursion to Canberra for just $30 per student. Two buses of students drove through the night, a long 10-hour trip to the Australian Capital Territory (ACT). We had three days to explore the major tourist attractions. We went to Telecom Tower, Lake Burley Griffin, the Bell Tower, a boat trip on the lake, the War Memorial, the Embassy, the Mint, a visit to Parliament House and to the movies to see Rocky 3.

Parliament House was fascinating to me. We got to sit in the House of Representatives' upper gallery and watch all the politicians conduct government business. I was mortified; they were rude, men picking their noses and talking over each other. They acted like young, spoiled children trying to get attention. I remember thinking there were not many women. We had a guided tour, and I was asked by the guide if I wanted to be the first female Prime Minister of Australia. The seed was planted!

I was never a leader at school unless it had something to do with music. There, I had a natural-born talent; for everything else, I tried really hard.

Mum used to say to my brother and I, "If there is something that you're not happy with or you don't believe is right, then don't just sit there and whine about it, do something about it." That has become one of my core beliefs, driving many of my actions, even today.

Fast forward to 2010, and an opportunity arose through friends. We had been out to dinner one evening with friends, who followed politics and were passionate about a particular political party. We spent the night talking about their policies and what they were hoping to achieve in the upcoming election. They were a new party and had never run before. I had never heard of The Australian Sex Party. I was taken aback at first by their name. It was so different from all the other parties. I could see it would be controversial — the black sheep of the political world.

But once I heard that the party stood for civil liberties, not the act of sex, everything our friends were saying struck a chord with me.

I had a flashback at the time, thinking about how Mum would drag us into the polling booth on voting day as kids and keep who she voted for a big secret. We were told it was rude to ask people who they voted for and how much money they earned.

A few weeks later, we were out for dinner with them again, and they suggested that I should run for the Senate, the Upper House. I thought they were joking. However, The Australian Sex Party (ASP) were looking for candidates. I didn't need much convincing to say yes. In the back of my head, I could hear my mum's voice saying, "Do something about it, stand up and be the change you want. Be that role model for your children. Start the change that's needed."

I had an interview with Fiona Pattern and Robbie Swan from the ASP. Filled in some paperwork, paid some money and the next thing I knew, I was the prime candidate for the Australian Sex Party, with Mark Coleman as my second.

I thought telling my family was going to be a challenge. I remember ringing my grandparents and telling my Nanna. I explained the policies to her and what we stood on. She told me she was proud of me once she got over the shock of the name.

We attended the double-blind ballot draw to see where we would be on the ballot paper. I was so nervous. I had no idea what to expect — sitting in a large room with all the candidates, mostly men, from across the state, a lot of stuffy, stuck-up people who didn't think their bi-products stunk! I thought most were full of hot air — 55 of us in total. I came out as number 7, or, as in the alphabet, the G spot; yes, we couldn't have planned it any better if we had tried. The Sex Party got the G spot. On the ballot paper was the only place every man could finally find the G spot!

The ASP wasn't about having sex but standing up for people's rights and civil liberties; some of the policies we stood for that year were same-sex marriage, legalising medicinal cannabis (CBD) oil and voluntary assisted dying (VAD).

It was an interesting experiment to be a part of. We had zero budget to run a full state campaign. Mark, who was second on the ballot, owned a Club X sex store and his partner was a voice-over actor for TV. He made some YouTube ads for us, which I acted in. One in particular was about the GST on tampons.

Scan QR Code below to watch the YouTube ad:

https://youtu.be/H60tj6zbMaw?si=ltJQ7dv8RAjL8v8S

Did you know they were classed as luxury items until 1 January 2019, when the GST on tampons was finally removed? Unbelievable! Don't even get me started on that.

How do you run a political campaign without money? You get very creative. My Aunty Lyn designed my campaign poster; I went to Officeworks and printed off various sizes and flyers. I popped them in the back side windows of my car. This led to people — mostly men — honking their horns at traffic lights and yelling 'did I swing both ways?' Not very original after the third time, let alone the 13th time!

Word got around because of the unique name. People just couldn't get their heads around it not being about the act of sex. My kids and I went to the local pet store, and by this stage, my face was everywhere in the newspapers, and I'd been on the TV news. The guy who ran the pet store recognised me and asked for my autograph! It was the first time I'd ever been asked for my autograph. Nowadays, it's a regular occurrence, but back then, it felt weird. The kids bolted to the back of the store, grumbling and moaning about how embarrassing I was.

When I do something, I'm never one to sit back and do it half-heartedly. Again, thinking outside the square, I purchased 6 metres of bright yellow fabric and some black fabric, got out my trusty old sewing machine that used to be my nanna's, and proceeded to cut and sew the giant words VOTE 1 SEX to create a big, yellow banner. The next day, the three of us went to an overpass on the Graham Farmer Freeway and hung it across the bridge.

We had so many positive reactions from motorists driving under it, honking their horns and giving us the thumbs up. We had been there for about an hour when the authorities turned up, gave us an official warning, told us we were breaking the law, and said they would fine us if they caught us doing it again. Apparently, you need to apply for a permit (of course you do) to put a sign beside a road — anything for the government to make some revenue.

The campaign head office sent us a large box of t-shirts for our volunteers to wear. We managed to recruit about 20 people, including the Order Of Perpetual Indulgence. They are men who dress up as nuns to protest about the wrongdoings of the Catholic Church. We would meet in Northbridge on the weekend and all walk around together, handing out my flyers, talking to people and answering questions. The t-shirts were bright yellow with the words 'Vote 1 Sex'. You could not miss us. I was never asked to kiss any babies, but I was asked to kiss plenty of men!

We decided to go where the crowds were. The football! We nearly got arrested when someone reported us outside Subiaco Oval, again because we had the word 'sex' on our tops and the police came to investigate. After having a chat with them, they told us they would vote for me and let us go. Not bad, huh!

I got invited to a lot of different events on the campaign trail. Many I didn't attend, including the one at a sex dungeon. I did get front-row tickets to Powderfinger's last concert in Perth. That was amazing.

The Glen Innes Examiner featured me on the front page of the paper where I grew up. This time, I had my black 'vote 1 sex' t-shirt on, with the headline 'Justine Speaks Sex: former local runs in Saturday's federal election'. It amazes me that people don't take the time to read, but just make assumptions about you. The town was rife with the rumour that I'd become a porn star. I mean, I'll be the first to admit I like sex and I did have a reputation – but not as a porn star!

It was an extremely stressful time in my life. It was far more stressful than I had anticipated, not just for me but for my family as well. Zak hid it from his friends at school — who wouldn't be embarrassed having a mum not only running for parliament, but for The Australian Sex Party!

It was during this time that I started to fall ill; my vision was significantly impaired, and my migraines increased. We were being interviewed for the NEWS on TV, and I had a migraine come on. I had to take my pain meds, but still did the interview. The world was spinning. To this day, I have no idea what I said or even if my speech was slurred, as I was off with the fairies. I was not in a good way.

Polling day came, and I opened the paper to find M8's and my engagement featured on page 2! This was unheard of; polling day is supposed to have a complete blanket of zero press about politics. Right there in black and white was a cartoon with M8 and me in bed with The Australian Sex Party!

M8 was away working, so I had a volunteer with me who was dressed up as the Mad Hatter from Alice in Wonderland. Fitting, really, as within six months, I felt like I was falling down a dark hole that I couldn't get out of. I made Zak and his girlfriend work at a polling booth, handing out flyers. No wonder he couldn't wait to leave and go into the army.

The results came in that evening, and I didn't get elected. I would have if they had just counted below the line, as there were six vacant seats for Western Australia. I did, however, come 6 out of 55 below the line and got 2.4% of the vote, which is higher than when the Greens polled for their first time running. I was very happy with this result. Imagine what we could have done with some money behind us! I thought that was the end of my political career.

Four years later, in 2013, The ASP contacted me again; this time, I was living in Geelong, and they asked me if I would run for the House of Representatives, the Lower House. The house I had sat and watched as a young girl. I wasn't sure I wanted to put myself through it all again. It was hard work. This time, they promised me more help and said I would have a campaign manager, Nigel.

I agreed to meet with Nigel and decide afterwards if I wanted to run. After meeting with Nige, we thought we would give it a shot. What were we thinking? Taking on one of the longest-held Labor seats in the state. Out came the yellow t-shirts — yes, I still had mine from 4 years earlier. A new campaign flyer and we were off. A photoshoot, new campaign posters and again no budget to do anything with. I was on a debate on the radio with all the other candidates and I ended up getting the most airtime as the hot discussion topic was same-sex marriage, and of course we were pushing for it.

I was single by then and was on a couple of dating sites; Nige and I decided to sign me up to all the dating sites. My dating profile picture was me wearing my bright yellow Vote 1 Sex t-shirt. We ran my campaign primarily through the dating sites. We didn't have to leave home and could contact people — well, mainly men — and give them our campaign speech about the policies we were running for.

I wore my t-shirt everywhere, again acting as a human billboard, including at Bellarine Secondary School, where Ally was in Year 10. One particular day, I had to go into the office and pick her up as she wasn't feeling well. I ran into the Principal and she took one look at my t-shirt and told me I wasn't to wear it in the school ever again. My reply was I bet she would never say that to a Labor or Liberal party member about their t-shirts.

Out of my mouth popped, "That's what's wrong with society nowadays, you all think of the 'act of sex' when you see the word 'sex', rather than gender-based equality." I grabbed Ally and we walked out. Nothing like telling the Principal what you think! Ally congratulated me. I think she was proud I had stood up to her Principal. I hopped into the car and it hit me. Ally still had two and a half years left at that school. What had I done? That was a face-palm moment.

There were ten candidates. I came in 5th out of 10 and in one area the Greens beat me by only one vote. I would have loved to know the percentage of male-to-female voters. Close again, but no cigar.

It's been over a decade since I last ran for Parliament. I am often asked if I would run again. Nope, no, nup, never! I feel I am much better able to help people with what I'm doing now than I ever could as a politician. People over the years have recognised me in Geelong as the candidate for the Australian Sex Party. But nowadays they recognise me more for all the other work I do to help people, and telling my story through my keynote speaking. There is still the odd guy on a dating site that will recognise me; yes, I'm back on them, as where else do you meet men nowadays? I think my history of running for The Australian Sex Party, as well as being disabled, scares a lot of men away.

Although many of the policies we were campaigning for didn't happen in WA or Victoria, or at a federal level in 2010 and 2013, these have occurred since, either at federal or state levels around Australia. In 2017, same-sex marriage became legal for all Australians and as well as equal rights for any sexual orientation. Prescription cannabis oil was made legal in Victoria in 2016 and in other states over the years.

In August 2017, I was having chemo for my cancer. I was very ill with an infection and was in bed for days at home, as the hospital didn't have any beds. I was living by myself. I was terrified each night when I went to sleep that I wasn't going to wake up. One day, while scrolling through Facebook, because there wasn't much else to do when you were stuck in bed, I saw MS Australia had put a post up calling for people's stories in support of VAD, or Voluntary Assisted Dying.

This was something I had always thought about after watching my mum's own health battles and watching my grandfather's horrendous passing. He had secondary bowel cancer and was in extreme pain for months. In the last week of life, he lost consciousness five days before he died. He was given no fluids or food and wasted away in front of us. We treat animals more humanely than we do our loved ones.

He was given small doses of morphine until I asked if they could end his suffering with a larger dose. Which ultimately they did. It still took another 10 hours of him moaning in pain to pass away. These memories are not something I choose for my children or grandchildren to ever have of me. When the time comes, and my quality of life is no longer what it should be, and I'm in extreme pain, I want the choice to end my life on my terms.

I didn't hesitate to put my hand up and sent off an email. Before I knew it, I was being interviewed for Andrew Denton's Go Gentle campaign and had all the TV crews interviewing me for various TV programs, including the ABC 7.30 Report, Seven News, Nine News, various newspapers and radios for interviews.

Scan the QR Code below to watch the TV interview:

I was invited to the Victorian Parliament for the launch of the VAD bill into the lower house, as someone who had three different cancers, two other blood conditions and multiple sclerosis. I wanted the right to choose over my body, not some medical professional sitting behind a desk who just saw me as another number coming through their door.

On the day the bill passed in the Lower House of Parliament, I was lying in Geelong University Hospital Emergency Department, unable to walk, live streaming it on my phone with a lot of the medical staff standing there watching it with me. It was ironic that here I was, someone who had pushed so hard for the choice, lying in an emergency ward, unable to walk due to extreme nerve pain. My legs and feet were on fire. It took three weeks of recovery in the hospital and about the same time for the VAD bill to go through the Senate, but it passed, and VAD became law in Victoria. It was the first state in Australia to give us a choice, with strict guidelines. Other states have also followed over the years.

Since 2018, I have been taking CBD oil by prescription for my MS and the nerve pain I experience. The motor laws haven't caught up yet. It is legal to drive with opioids in our systems, such as tramadol, but illegal for CBD oil. Hopefully, one day soon, things will change.

I would like to think I played a small part in making some of these things happen. I learned through all of those pivotal moments to stand up for what I believe in. Things may not change straight away, but you can make a difference, not only in your life but also in the lives of others around you. I stood up and played my part with grit, with determination and with a whole lot of moxie.

2010 Glen Innes Examiner newspaper interview

2010 Dressed and ready to go to the Perth Spank Ball

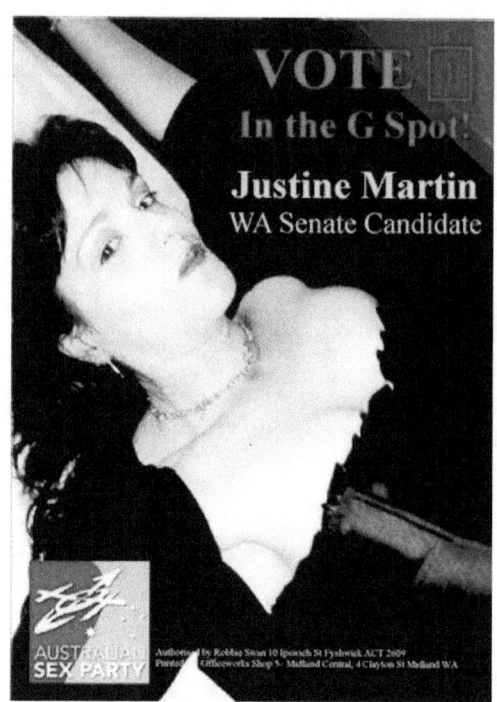

2010 Campaign poster *2013 Campaign flyer*

2013 Dating profile photo

PART TWO

CHAPTER 21

Returning Full Circle

When I was told to stop work by my neurologist, he advised me to find a hobby, as I was going to have a lot of time on my hands. I was shattered that I couldn't work. What is our purpose in life if we can't pay taxes and contribute to a working society? How will people see me when I tell them I don't work? Will they see me as a dole bludger? Will they see me as a no-hoper? Will they see me as lazy? Will they see me as entitled? Will they see me as not being good enough? Or was it, more to the point, how I saw myself? I think, looking back now, it was the latter. I know I felt shame and embarrassment telling people that at the age of forty I couldn't work anymore. The person who judged me the most was myself. The added stress I put on myself was huge. But it also became the driving force for me to earn my own money again.

I had always wanted to try painting and thought I would do it when I eventually retired at about the age of ninety! However, all I had now was time. I had a girlfriend who owned an art studio. I drove there every week for nearly four months and sat outside, struck with fear and crippling anxiety, too afraid to walk inside. I was so worried people would not see me as a whole person anymore, now that I was labelled 'disabled'. My deeply held belief that I was not good enough was going into overdrive. Every week I would drive home, angry at myself, crying, and screaming out of frustration.

Why couldn't I just walk inside the studio? Who was this person looking back at me in the mirror? I was becoming a shell of my former self, losing control of my life. That black hole was getting deeper by the day, and I was struggling to hold myself together. I cried a lot as I started moving through the process of grief.

One week, I got really angry with myself, and thought, *'What is the worst that can happen?'* I detected at the back of my mind a small hope that I hadn't given up. I just had to give myself a good talking to, and decide that I wasn't going to give in to this disease. Decide that my MS journey wasn't going to end the same way as my mum's, taking away her will to live. *'Just do it.'* So I walked in through the art studio doors, and my life and my future opened up in front of me. I took to painting like a duck to water. Apparently, I'm pretty good!

I'd lose myself in this new world where I felt whole, where nothing was missing from me, where I was not being judged. Where I was not feeling the pain and fear of what the future might hold, following the path that Mum took. I felt equal again to my able-bodied peers.

Life was hard. With M8 working away, Zak in the Army, and my health declining, I had no family to look after Ally when I was in hospital. If I couldn't find anyone to look after Ally when I was in the hospital, then she would have to go into foster care. This wasn't going to be an option, so M8 suggested we move back to my family in Geelong for when we needed help.

By the end of that year, I had packed up everything we owned. I had given notice to time in with Ally finishing school, however we received an eviction notice that was 4 weeks short of our moving date. Where would we live? I will be ever grateful to my good friend Gaily, who put us up in her home for 5 weeks. She looked after Ally and me, giving us the nurturing we so desperately needed.

We said our hard goodbyes to our friends, hopped on that iron bird in the sky and flew across the country to start our new life in one of the coldest states in the country. I left all my dreams on the western side of our big country. It was heartbreaking. M8 joined us a week later. Every piece of our furniture was damaged in the move. All of my furniture I had worked so hard to buy was either broken, scratched or dented. What had we done?

We knew no one but my small family in Geelong. It was tough to know where I fit in the extended family unit. I hadn't lived near any extended family for well over 20 years.

I felt like an outsider until I found my place. My days were like Groundhog Day. I would get Ally ready for school and drive the 10 minutes there, return home to four walls and do some painting or drawing. Cry. Paint. Draw. Eat. Cry. Eat. Talk to myself and wonder how I ended up here — what I had done so wrong to deserve all of this? Why me? Why not me? These are questions I still occasionally ask myself. I do believe I've been given all of this to show other people hope, through my story, that you can push through adversities and live a rewarding life.

My weight has always been an issue, and this time in my life was no exception. I put on 20kgs, I hated looking in the mirror, and I hated myself even more. I had hit triple figures, over 100kg; I felt disgusted, vile and angry at myself and the whole world. I had no compassion towards myself and what I was going through. I was not kind to myself at all.

The steroids my medical team had put me on for each MS relapse had kicked off my weight gain, which was exacerbated by no exercise, no movement and eating all day. It was a recipe for disaster. My world was spinning out of control, and I wanted to get off!

I had no idea at the time where that strong, fierce woman who had run for parliament was. Had she gone, or was she just lying dormant? Had I just shut her away? But that seemed like a lifetime ago. I didn't even recognise the person I was becoming.

I was falling further down that dark black hole.

Regardless of how I was feeling, I still had responsibilities. I had to drive my daughter. I was a mother. I dragged myself out of bed each day; Ally will never truly know how hard that was. I was imploding. I would then wait at home for six long hours, then go and pick her up and drive her to Olympic weight-lifting training five days a week. Home to cook dinner and wait for M8's 5-minute phone call each night. Then repeat. Groundhog. Black dog. Groundhog.

I had to do something. This was killing me. I had always been a social person; the isolation was the hardest thing to get my head around.

I made enquiries, and I enrolled in two art classes each week at a community centre. I was the youngest in the class by 25+ years, as other people my age were still working. Not medically retired as I was.

I longed for social interaction with anyone. To be at home in one's own thoughts for hours on end is dangerous.

The other class was the MS Social Support Day Program. This class was harder to get my head around. They were a lovely bunch of people to spend time with; however, a few of them reminded me so much of my mum and her MS in its later stages. This again sent my mind spiralling down the hole of what I thought my future looked like. It was a distorted reality, with my memories of Mum layering with my expectations for my own future.

It was confronting.

M8 and I were not in a good place. Our phone calls were getting shorter and shorter and were the same every night. There was no new conversation. Except for a woman's name that he occasionally let slip. I asked him a few times if she was an issue, and he assured me it was all in my head and everything was good between us. I now know that it was pure gaslighting.

During his five days at home, we would do very little. Not only did I not know anyone, but neither did he. We never anticipated how tough moving would be. I had moved across the country years earlier when the kids were younger, and although it was hard at first, we settled in more easily by making friends through work. However, when you're told you can't work anymore, you lose those connections. Due to my not working, we lost over $60,000 of income and our expenses went up, in addition to paying for M8's flights home, my medications, doctors, specialist appointments, and the list went on.

We fought a lot; he sometimes got physical with me. It was always about money. He would make me feel guilty for every cent I spent on food, fuel, rent and utilities, let alone buying clothes or going out anywhere. We dared not venture anywhere to explore our new area while he was still at work; the guilt trips and ear-bashing just were not worth it.

Parpa had been diagnosed with secondary bone cancer. He was dying. It was surreal to see him wasting away in front of our eyes. I would drive to Woodend to visit him and Nanna as much as I could. In the final weeks of his life he was admitted to the palliative care ward at Hospital. It was a long three hour drive to visit, but one I wanted to do. On one of my final visits I sat with him and we had a conversation. He told me he was sorry for all his wrongs towards me and my brother. Sorry that he had kept us from contacting our father. He knew that we had had very little contact with dad over the years and that life was short. He said I should make contact with him. I apologised to him for all my wrongdoing towards him. We made peace with each other.

A few days later he lost consciousness. I sat at the hospital from the Friday to the Monday, not going home. The hospital staff were amazing and let me shower there, and fed us as well. We were even allowed to sleep in the room next door in another ward. Parpa hadn't eaten or drank anything in five days. He would make groaning noises and was in pain. My aunty and I would alert the nurses and more pain meds were given. It was horrible watching him deteriorate before our eyes and not being able to do anything about it. It was the early hours of Monday the 12th when I went out to the nurses and asked if they could give him more morphine. They came in and gave him another dose.

My aunt and I were sitting on either side of the bed and the lights were off. I looked up to the end of his bed, and I saw a purple orb hovering over him. I think I saw a green orb leave my grandfather's chest and hover next to the purple one. Then a white orb appeared and it looked like the white one was stopping the green one from moving. The green orb then went back into my grandfather. I asked my aunty if she could see it. She told me I was nuts and to try and close my eyes, that I was just tired. I knew what I was seeing was real. This happened about four times before the morning light.

At 8.30am my uncle brought my nanna into the hospital as we knew it wouldn't be long. My nanna walked in with a bright green shirt on, the same colour as the orb! I nodded to my aunt and then across to my nanna. At around midday my aunt went outside to get some air and came in and looked like she had seen a ghost. She remarked that she now believed me. I asked her what had happened. She explained that she had been sitting in the rose garden when she saw two purple orbs dancing not far from her. I believed her.

My mum's favourite colour was purple, as was my great grandmother, NoNo's. I believe what I had seen was the purple orbs coming to take my grandfather during the night. My grandfather was ready to go, but the white orb knew it wasn't quite the right time; that he had to wait for everyone to come in to say their goodbyes. We had his favourite classical musical playing and we all sat with him; when he was taking his last breaths we all had our hands on him. My right hand was holding my nanna's hand and my left hand was on his heart when he passed. It was a privilege to be there to see him take his last breath, in a room with so much love.

I then had to go to call and tell all the other members of our family that weren't there, including one of my uncles, that his father had died. I will never forget seeing my nanna standing next to his bed and holding his hand. They had been together for over 70 years. It then hit me that I would never have what they did. A love that lasted a lifetime.

I was visited by a woman who worked for MS Australia, and she mentioned I may be entitled to a Total and Permanent Disability (TPD) claim through my superannuation. I might also have income protection through my super. I had no idea this even existed. When I started looking into it, I discovered I actually had three different super funds from the various jobs I'd had over the years.

I made enquiries through a no win, no pay solicitor, and the process began.

It was brutal.

To prove my claim, I had to jump through endless hoops. I had to attend medicals with specialists appointed by the super funds. I had neuropsychological assessments. More MRIs. More questions. More forms. More appointments. More pressure. It felt like I was being forced to defend my disability, as if I was on trial for being unwell. The whole process was exhausting and incredibly stressful. I was told not to hold my breath for the money.

M8 had gambling and steroid addictions, two very costly habits that often left us without money to pay the bills or buy food. On several occasions when M8 was home on R&R, we would argue, and he would twist things around to make it all out to be my fault. Then he would take off in our car and withdraw all the money from our joint account — leaving me without money or transport for Ally. He always held this over my head. In his eyes, everything that was wrong was always my fault. I could do nothing right. I was angry at myself because I knew this was not showing Ally how a man should treat a woman, especially one he is supposed to love.

Towards the last week of our relationship, we argued — we had both been drinking — when he pushed me, and I fell to the ground. He then proceeded to kick me in the stomach on the bathroom floor. Taking all of his anger and frustration out on me. He left to go back to work the next day.

Our phone conversations each night were getting shorter and shorter. One night after a 4-minute call, I texted him to say, don't worry about calling for the next few days, as Ally and I would be fine. He wrote back saying he had a lot on his mind.

The next night, he did call me, crying. He said he had done something very bad and needed to tell me. He had been texting a woman at work, and it had gotten serious with her. I asked if it was his boss, and he said yes. I was gutted. How could he do this to me and us? I asked him directly what he wanted to do. Was he leaving me or staying? He replied he didn't know. That was the longest conversation on the phone we had had in months. A whole 20 minutes.

The next day, the phone bill came in, I opened the email and looked through all the pages. There were thousands of text messages between the two of them. I looked at the phone calls. He had gotten off the phone with me the night before and called her. Their call lasted two hours. I picked up the phone and called her. Explained who I was. She said that M8 had told her I was in a wheelchair, we didn't have sex, and I had him trapped there. I asked her nicely to leave my family alone. She laughed and said she loved him and that she wasn't backing off. I hung up the phone and cried. I sent M8 a message saying I had just spoken to his girlfriend.

Within minutes, M8 rang me and abused me for calling his boss and that I had probably cost him his job. Me! All because I rang her. He was the one sleeping with her — it was more likely that he could have cost her her job. He was so angry with me. After lots of phone calls, he agreed to see a counsellor when he returned home 5 days later. I organised for a therapist to see M8, and then afterwards for me to see the same therapist. By the time I got home and walked in the door he blurted out it was over and he was choosing her.

His final words to me were that my having MS would affect his dreams and goals in life. But what about the dreams we had together? What about my dreams and goals?

A week later, he moved straight out of my bed into hers back in Perth. When he left, so did my financial support. How was I going to feed my child and put a roof over her head?

My whole world fell apart.

My self-esteem plummeted. It was a woman's worst nightmare. It was my worst nightmare. To be told you're not worthy, you're not good enough, when you already have been battling those fears for decades.

To have a disease that you have no control over used as the reason he doesn't love you and doesn't want to have a future with you, was the most pathetic excuse I had ever heard.

When he left, I thought he destroyed me in one fell swoop; in actual fact he had been killing me bit by bit for years beforehand, I just didn't realise it at the time. He had actually done me a huge favour by leaving. I wouldn't have achieved everything I have today if I was still with him. And that could not be more clear to me now.

However, at the time, I was a mess. I had stopped eating and sleeping. There was zero self-care. My family were worried about me, and my medical team had me on suicide watch.

I had to get us out of the contract to purchase our 'dream' home. There were the car repayments. Where would we live? How would we buy groceries? I didn't want to be all alone. All my friends lived 3,000 km away. I felt like I had no one.

The stress I was under was like nothing I'd ever experienced before. Not only was I in total shock at what had just happened, being tossed aside, but how was I going to survive? A disabled woman who could never work again, supporting a teenager whose father never paid her child support? Where was our next meal going to come from?

I felt like a complete failure in life, as a partner and as a mother! I didn't want to face it; I had hit the bottom of that hole and couldn't see a way back up. I wanted to end it all.

I had a distant cousin drop in one evening, and she brutally told me to get off my pity party. That she had never liked M8 from the start, blah, blah, blah. I was mortified. What gives people the right to rub more salt into your wounds? To tell you, after you have split up with someone who has hurt you, that your family never liked them? There is a time and a place for everything, and this wasn't it. She made me feel awful, that I was being selfish for the way I was feeling at the time.

The fear I was feeling was of not knowing how I could provide for us when I was deemed useless for society, let alone a fit mother. All kinds of things were running through my head: being an unfit mum and having Ally taken away by the authorities for a start. I was living in a nightmare, all because I ignored red flags. I take responsibility for that, but not in any way, shape or form for how he treated me or for his ongoing narcissistic abuse.

Then I did something stupid. I let him come back seven weeks after he left. He called me and said he was sorry and wanted to come back. Ally was competing at the 2013 Youth Olympics in Sydney and he wanted to see us. He wanted to be there for her. He missed us… blah, blah, blah. I agreed without even thinking about it. He still wanted me. Or so I thought. I turned a blind eye to everything bad he had done to me, and pushed away my own self-worth, to open the door and let him back in. He had thrown me a line and I grabbed onto it. The fear of being homeless and hungry was no longer on the table if he was coming back to us. I thought we would be ok.

I picked M8 up from the airport and it was like nothing had happened, except the conversation about his boss on the way home. They had had a huge fight, about me apparently. He raved on about how horrible she was and how sorry he was for the pain he had caused me.

He wanted to get straight back into the swinging scene, going to a party in Melbourne. I was like a love sick puppy and agreed to it. I was petrified he would leave again and he knew he could hold that over my head. The party was horrible. I had agreed to have BDSM performed on me. Whipped with a cat o' nine tails across my naked arse. The dominatrix drew blood and so she stopped. While I was being whipped my mind was racing at a thousand miles an hour. This wasn't the life I wanted. This wasn't a fairy tale. This was, in fact, a nightmare.

A few days later, we flew to Sydney to watch Ally compete. Things were good when we left Melbourne. We landed in Sydney and both turned our phones on. It all went downhill from there. M8 went to the bathroom and when he met me at the luggage carousel, he was in a mood. I knew better than to pry, and just kept quiet.

We got our bags and the hire car. We made our way to the CBD where I had booked us into a hotel not far from Chinatown. After settling into the hotel M8 stated that 'she' had sent him a text saying how sorry she was. He kept me in limbo land for 4 days, not knowing if he was staying with me or going back to her. I was beside myself. How could he do this again to me? I was going to be too much of a burden in his life.

We returned back to Geelong and he returned to Perth. We were done.

I went into survival mode, something that was, unfortunately, second nature to me. I sorted out a counsellor to start to set my mental health straight and went into

Centrelink to see how they could help. We were given Family Tax Benefit A & B, about $250 a fortnight. I also applied for the disability pension and was told it would take some time for it to be assessed. It took over four months for the pension to come through.

How would we survive? All I can say is that I swallowed my pride and walked through the doors of the local church in Drysdale that had a food bank and I 'shopped' for our groceries there for the next 12 months.

I had no self-worth because, yet again, I let him back into my life 10 months later, for one weekend. He had told 'her', the one he left me for, that he was away in a cabin south of Perth. Instead, he hopped on a plane back to me. I became the other woman! After that weekend, I realised that I never wanted to be in a relationship with him ever again and closed the door for good. I didn't like who he was, or who I was when I was with him.

Now, as I reflect on that time 12 years ago, I know now that I wasn't at a pity party but was, in fact, grieving. I was grieving for the loss of a lot of things at once.

The life I thought I was going to have of being happily married.

The relationship I thought I had with a man who I thought loved me.

And the life before I was diagnosed, because with him gone, I was finally allowed to grieve for all that I had lost in being able-bodied.

My life was never going to be the same.

After 15 long months, I was finally paid out for my TPD. Two out of the three superfunds.

The first thing I did was to go and do a full grocery shop to fill our cupboards, fridge and freezer. No more food bank. Next I paid off my defaulted credit card debt, the debt M8 had left me in. It felt like I was cleaning up yet another mess that never should have been mine to carry.

Then I bought myself a little car.

I had already sent the car back to M8, the one we had bought together. It was in both our names and he was demanding that I sell it. We had paid $55,000 for it, but the payout at the time was only $33,000 and I could only sell it for around $25,000. There was no way I was taking yet another loss. Not after everything he'd already taken from me.

So instead, I paid $1,450 to have it put on a car carrier and transported back to him. It was his problem not mine.

It could have rotted in my driveway, but the reality was, if the payments stopped, it wouldn't have been my credit rating that took the hit again. It would have been his. I needed him to give me his address, so it became his responsibility again, not something I was left managing. That took some effort, well, a lot of arguing on the phone, and when he realised I was standing up for myself and not letting him walk over me again he sent a text through with his details.

To be fair, I will give him credit for one thing: he did keep paying the repayments after he left on the car and also rent for 8 weeks, so his credit history wasn't damaged.

But mine already was.

And once again, I was left to rebuild — but this time on my own terms.

2009 Nanna and Parps, photo taken by Aunty Lynny

2010 Dad and Me

2011 Zak's army enlistment photo

2012 Zak, Ally and myself at Nanna's funeral, Kyneton Victoria

2013 Ally, Zak and me on one of Zak's leave trips home from the Army

CHAPTER 22

Not JUZT a Hobby

When I look back to 2011, I can see it clearly now. That was the year my world crumbled around me in such a short space of time.

At the time, I could not make sense of what was happening to me. I was seeing a counsellor weekly through MS Western Australia. I desperately wanted to talk to someone. My mind was racing, my heart even faster, and I had no one who could relate to what I was going through.

I spent my waking hours at home, no longer working, looking at four walls, just trying to do simple housework. It would take me a full day to vacuum just one room. A week to vacuum the whole house. I slept through doctors' appointments and school pick up. I would, without notice, burst into laughter without there being anything funny, or cry when I had no reason to. I could not control my emotions.

I would fall asleep mid sentence or while eating dinner. I was so fatigued. I just wanted to sleep all the time.

These days I feel like my life sits on a pendulum. Hanging in the middle is my new normal, which is far from how my body once felt. At any time the pendulum can be bumped, causing a wave of havoc through my body and changing my life. Sometimes I settle back to my new normal, but often it creates yet another new normal once again.

And when I think about it now, I can see that moxie showed up in my life.

Moxie is not loud. It is not bravado. It is not pretending you are fine. Moxie is adapting when your life has changed without your permission. It is learning how to keep living when your body is no longer the body you used to have. It is finding a way to survive, and then choosing to thrive.

Being able to adapt has been my secret to survive and thrive.

With every adversity I have faced, I have been forced to think outside the square, the box or even the cage. I have had to look at the problem I am facing and work out a solution to make life better. To not remain in a situation just because someone told me I could no longer do something, or some man was trying to control me.

Without the adversities, which I just call bad life moments, I would not have grown as a person. I have spent so many years in survival mode. If my children as teenagers had done the kinds of things I did, they would have been grounded for life. But I did not have anyone to guide me or look out for my welfare, or a mobile phone to put it all on social media. I was just trying to get through.

When I picked up that paint brush at the end of 2011, I had no idea where it would lead me. If I had known, I might have run away and hid, daunted by the knowledge of what lay ahead.

People often ask me how I do it all, but you have to understand I did not start everything all at once. Each business was birthed as I saw a need for a new service. Acting on an idea, rather than saying, oh, one day I would like to do that. Let me explain that little snowball that kept gathering size.

In 2012 I was struggling with everything. A new home, in a state that I had not lived in for thirty one years, and zero friends. A partner working away, home only five days out of every twenty one. The only thing I had that made me happy was painting and drawing. When I was creating art, I felt like I was a whole person again and forgot about all that was wrong.

I created every single day.

I had a sketch book and my art classes. It got me out of the house. Looking back now, I know that having a hobby is vital to build resilience. Look at how many people did not have hobbies when COVID hit, and how much harder it was for them.

There is only so much TV you can watch before it becomes boring, even with all the streaming services. Hobbies fill your time and keep your mind busy and productive. It is essential to focus on things other than the adversity you are facing.

I just have an uncanny knack for turning a hobby into a money-making venture.

Painting gave me back the sense of purpose that I lost when I had to stop work. If I could not make money and pay tax, what use was I going to be to society? I felt like a huge burden to everyone and that was not doing my head space any good at all.

The crunch came when it became a matter of survival. What could I still do in order to make money, to supplement my income?

I had a meeting with the MS employment agency and was told there was not enough time in the day or money in their budget to retrain me. I was devastated. What could I still do?

I knew working a normal job was never going to be possible again with my disabilities. After I sold my first painting for $300, I had a niggling feeling that I could make more money from it. That $300 felt like a million dollars to me. I could still contribute to society. I wasn't just a waste of space.

But then the voice in my head took control. Who did I think I was? I did not have a degree or even a certificate to help me sell my art. Who would buy it? Was I good enough? What would people think? Would they know that someone with a disability painted it, and buy it out of pity?

Any question you can ask, I played it over and over in my head.

Then I thought, they are not the one's paying my power bill or putting food on my table. If Ally and I wanted any quality of life other than the $24,000 a year we had to live on, I needed to swallow my pride and just try.

That was moxie in real life. Not confidence. Courage. Action while terrified.

I entered every exhibition I possibly could, in both able bodied and disability spaces, because I knew I needed credibility if I wanted to make a real name for myself. But if I am honest, it was not just about credibility. It was about proving something to myself. I had spent so many years feeling like I was behind everyone else, like I was the one who struggled, the one who did not quite fit the mould, the one who had to work twice as hard just to keep up. Art became the only place where none of that mattered. When I was creating, I felt capable. Strong. Able bodied in my spirit even if my body was falling apart. So I put myself out there. I held my own exhibitions, entered group shows, and entered competitions. And I started to win. A lot. And every time I won, it was like another crack in my old belief that I was not good enough. My confidence grew with every piece I created, my skills improved with every brushstroke, and for the first time in a long time, I started to feel like I belonged somewhere.

AWARDS

2025
Queenscliff Art Prize — Winner People's Choice 'Standing Alone' by Justine Martin

2021
Ausmumpreneur — Australian Creative Artist of the Year

2018
FEB Little Creatures Live Art Battle Geelong — runner-up
APRIL Paul Guest Drawing Prize Bendigo Gallery — entrant
MARCH Geelong Gallery Contemporary Art Prize — entrant

2017

APRIL Drysdale Rotary Easter Art Exhibition — entrant

2016

MARCH Bellarine Agricultural Show — Honourable Mention

MARCH ZONTA Conviction, Commitment and Courage Exhibition — First place for first-time exhibitor

OCT State Trustee Connected Art Exhibition — People's Choice Award for 'More Than Is Seen'

NOV IAN (Inclusive Arts Network) Exhibition Ballarat — entrant

OCT Royal Geelong Show Fine Arts — 1st & 3rd, Pair of Miniatures 2nd & 3rd

Disability Section — 1x 1st, 2 x 2nds, and Highly Commended

Other medium, DISABILITY — 1st, 2nd, 3rd, Highly Commended

AUG MS Art Show Blackburn Victoria — Packing Room Prize

SEPT Royal Melbourne Show Fine Arts — Commended for 'Conservation'

OCT State Trustee Connected Art Exhibition — Public Advocates Award for 'More Than Is Seen'

NOV ArtAbility — ADEC Award for 'Hidden Pieces'

NOV State Trustee Connected Art Exhibition — People's Choice Award for 'Out Of My Reach'

2015

JAN Bellarine Agricultural Show — Best Other Medium 1st 'Tranquil rainbow'

OCT Royal Geelong Show Fine Arts — 1st, 2 x 2nd, 3 x 3rd, Disability 1st, Best Exhibit

2014

OCT Royal Geelong Show Fine Arts Section — OPEN 4 x 3rd, 2 x Highly Commended

NOV State Trustee Connected Art Exhibition — Alan Merigan People's Choice Award Winner 'BASIL' second year in a row.

MARCH Bellarine Agricultural Show, OPEN Section — 2nd Other Medium 'Hollamby The Frog'

2013
Geelong Agriculture Show OPEN Section 2nd mixed media — 'A Bunch of Buttons'
3rd 10cm x 10cm — 'Two Little Frogs'
OCT State Trustee Connected Art Exhibition — Alan Merigan People's Choice Award Winner for 'I Can See You'

EXHIBITIONS

2023
Art of the Minds Exhibition

2022
Solo Exhibition at the Cafe Zoo

2021
Solo Exhibition at the Cafe Zoo
Art of The Minds Exhibition

2019
NOVEMBER Little Creatures Geelong — solo exhibition
Archibald NSW Art Gallery — entrant

2018
JAN Amped Geelong — exhibiting
FEB Little Creatures Live Art Battle Exhibition Geelong — exhibitor
MAY JUZT Art Gallery — solo exhibition
MAY 5"x 7" Exhibition Art IS… Little Mallop St Geelong — exhibitor
MAY Big Colours Exhibition 101 Ryrie Arts, 101 Ryrie St Geelong — exhibitor

2017
MAY Riot Art N Craft — window display
AUG AMPED Geelong — full-time exhibiting
AUG MS Australia Art Show — exhibitor
NOV Ocean Grove Rotary Art Exhibition — entrant
OCT The Old Auction House Kyneton — solo exhibition
NOV IAN (Inclusive Arts Network) Shearers Arms Geelong — exhibitor
NOV Bellarine Arts Trail — exhibitor

2016

JAN Spring Dale Artists Annual Exhibition — exhibiting

JAN Gallery Owner at JUZT Art Gallery 23 High St Drysdale — solo exhibitions

MARCH JUZT Art Karingallery James St Geelong — 2nd Solo Exhibition

MAY Riot Art N Craft — window display

SEPT State Trustee Connected Art Exhibition — 'More Than Is Seen' selected to exhibit at No Vacancy Gallery, Federation Square, Melbourne

2015

NOV Drysdale Fete — exhibitor

MAY Great Twilight Market — exhibitor

JAN Spring Dale Artists Annual Exhibition — exhibitor

JAN JUZT Art at Karringallery, 4 James St Geelong — solo exhibition

2014

OCT Spring Dale Artists Annual Exhibition — exhibiting

AUG MS Australia Art Show — exhibitor

OCT Connected Art Exhibition, Federation Square, Melbourne Victoria — 'Basil'

2013

OCT State Trustee Connected Art Exhibition — 'I can See You' selected to be exhibited

JAN Spring Dale Artists Annual Exhibition — exhibiting

I invested in a small, 3 metre square marquee, fold-out tables and tablecloths and got busy creating. I picked my better paintings and drawings and printed greeting cards with the help of my Aunty Lyn, who did the graphic design and organised a cheap printer for me. I bought in bulk and then had the tedious task of folding thousands of cards, and placing them with an envelope in a cellophane bag.

We had enough stock. I say 'we', because Ally helped me with every market. Sometimes we sold a lot, other times very little. If we sold a lot I would give Ally money and she would buy something special from the market we were working at.

I registered my business as JUZT Art. This business was special in every sense of the word. It meant a better future for us. One on my terms. MS was not going to rob me again. I would adapt and modify when things came up. And I did.

The name JUZT Art came about from the name I used to use selling hobby ceramics. Back then it was called JUZT Ceramics, from combining my first name, Justine, with one of my nicknames, JUZ.

I asked everywhere I went if I could sell my art there, all while battling the constant mindset war of not being good enough. Who would buy it? Blah, blah, blah.

To my surprise, sales did come in.

I increased my prices. I started Facebook and Instagram pages purely to sell my work and gain followers, so they could share it to their family and friends. Then all of a sudden, people were inboxing me to request commission pieces.

I was gobsmacked.

People were handing over their hard earned cash to hang my art on their walls. I had my purpose back, and it was not to make money. It was to make people smile when they looked at my big, bright, colourful artwork. Making money was a huge added bonus.

My art has saved me in more ways than one. Mentally, it takes me to my happy place. Where I can immerse myself in another world. I have used it for years as a form of meditation. To help slow my brain down and to clear all the negative thoughts around me. It gave me hope when I didn't have any.

I had a few people inbox me about doing graphite portraits of their loved ones. They are, without a doubt, the most complex drawings I have ever created. There was a young girl of 18, who had died two weeks earlier. A family friend reached out to ask for a commission piece of the young girl. She had died in a farm accident when the vehicle she was driving rolled — she didn't have a seat belt on and was flung from the vehicle. She was a stunning girl. I looked into her eyes in the photo the woman supplied. It took me two weeks and many, many hours to create that piece. I will never forget her face and her eyes.

After the third death portrait, I had to put a boundary up and say no to any more. They were affecting me too much emotionally.

I had my NDIS support coordinator suggest to me about 12 months earlier that I should teach art from my home studio for other NDIS clients and form a community. So that's exactly what I did. I put a call out through social media asking if anyone would like to attend a community group where they could make new friends, socialise with their peers and, as a bonus, create art. I got my first client and was blown away that I finally had some regular income. For the first time in 8 years,

I earned money every week. One client turned into two, then before I knew it, I had full groups. My clients loved it. I loved it.

It gave me the confidence that I could still work, maybe not at my capacity before 2011, but in a whole new way. I look back on my life before being diagnosed with MS, and I call it my former life. It's like a line had been drawn in the sand. Two parts to my story. Before and after. A reset. Born again but not through religion. I thought I was living my dream life back then, but boy, was I wrong!

In 2014, an opportunity fell into my lap. One of Ally's friends' fathers knew the owner of Cafe Zoo, a local cafe that had an art gallery inside it. After a meeting with the owner, I was offered a whole room at the cafe to exhibit my artwork.

I was so blown away by the offer.

Three years after picking up that paint brush I was now a professional artist. It was the perfect place to hang my paintings.

I would rotate my artwork every three weeks and started selling a lot of work. I loved creating more pieces and trying different techniques. I did not have a studio to create things in, only my kitchen table, and it was a pain in the bum packing it up after each session. I would have paintings drying all around the house on every flat surface I could find.

I am always working on more than one piece at a time. As I waited for paint to dry on one work, I was working on the next one. This meant I could build up collections a lot faster than waiting to complete a single work before starting the next.

I had been exhibiting there for about 12 months when the main artist, whose name was on the gallery, decided to leave. I was then offered the whole gallery to run.

To be a gallery owner was something I had never imagined would be possible.

I named it JUZT Art Gallery and offered space to new artists who had never exhibited before. They were given either 2 weeks or 4 weeks to hang their work, depending on the quality and the amount of pieces they had. To curate other people's work was extraordinary. It is still very much a 'pinch me' moment in my life.

I too was selling a lot of art. I added my range of greeting cards to a large card stand and sold thousands of these, individually and in packs. I still have these available on my website www.juztart.com.au for sale. Hint, hint…

A few times a year, I would pull out the visiting artists and do a solo show of just my own work. Around 40 pieces. It took a lot of work to get it all together.

When my work was not hanging in JUZT Art Gallery, I was looking for new opportunities to exhibit. I had solo shows around Victoria. I was hanging my art in doctors' surgeries, more cafes, more galleries and in a bar and restaurant. I was selling lots more. Commission pieces were flooding in.

I entered the Barwon Heads Arts Trail and became one of the committee members for the Barwon Heads Arts Council. Within 12 months I was the Vice President of the committee. We were working on getting Barwon Heads its own home, a hub for the community to use. I sat on the committee for 3 years. The hub opened up a few years after I left. It is nice to know I played a small part in it.

In 2018 I bought myself a new car and I had decals of my artwork all over it, branding myself. People would take photos of my car and tag me on Instagram wherever they saw me. Most artists do not market themselves properly. They paint amazing work, yet are too scared to show it to the world. Which is such a shame. Some of the best paintings in the world are sitting in the backs of wardrobes or in a garage or shed gathering dust.

I used all my previous business experience in the multilevel marketing businesses to self promote. I knew I needed to build a brand, not just an art name. Plastering my car with my artwork and JUZT Art sure helped.

I started an extension of JUZT Art called Van Go Decals. My artwork, printed on large decals for caravans and campervans to help people find and identify their own vans. All vans tend to look the same when they are in caravan parks, and people can find it hard to find their own vans. With the decals of my big, bright animals, people could identify their vans easily. Making life much simpler.

Painting became my escape before I ever called myself an artist. It was the place I went when my body hurt, when life felt too loud, when my mind needed somewhere softer to land. When I painted, I did not feel disabled. I did not feel broken. I felt able. Free. Calm. It took me to my happy place in a way nothing else could.

I started watching Colour In Your Life back in 2012. I never missed an episode. I would sit there studying how the artists worked, how they layered colour, how they created light, how they used their brushes. I did not realise it at the time, but I was learning. My art improved because of that show. Quietly, year after year, I grew. And I used to think, imagine if one day that was me.

In 2018, it was.

I was featured on Colour In Your Life, and during that half hour episode I painted Remmy. Remmy was my son's dachshund, a little dog I looked after in 2015 and 2016. He was not just a pet. He was family. Painting him on that show felt personal, full of love and memory. That episode was a turning point for me. Seeing myself there, being treated as a real artist, talking about my work and my story, was the moment something shifted inside. That was when I finally felt like a professional artist.

What I never could have imagined was where that painting would end up. Remmy became part of the Lunar Codex, a digital time capsule of human creativity. The collection was digitally miniaturised using high end archival technology and preserved on nanofiche and special ceramic systems designed to last thousands of years. It was loaded onto the Peregrine Lunar Lander and launched from Cape Canaveral. My artwork is now on the moon.

People often do not believe me when I say that. I can see it in their faces. But sometimes I look up at the moon myself and think, 'Oh wow… how the hell has all this happened?' Then I remind myself, it did not happen overnight. It came from years of painting through pain, years of dreaming, years of setting goals, years of not giving up even when life kept knocking me sideways.

In 2025, I was interviewed again on Colour In Your Life. This time I painted a watercolour illustration from a children's book called The Golden Duck, a book written by another author that I illustrated. To go back years later, not as someone hoping, but as someone established, was huge. Full circle. From the woman on the couch learning from artists, to being the artist others were watching.

That journey still blows my mind. From painting to cope, to having my work preserved beyond Earth. It sounds unbelievable, but it is built on something simple. Hard work. Big dreams. Clear goals. And that stubborn part of me that refuses to quit. That's my moxie on canvas.

JUZT Art wellness classes survived through COVID-19 when I pivoted and put them online. I came up with make-at-home art kits for my clients using items they could find in their homes — from strong coffee or tea to use as paint, scraps of paper (not loo paper, as that was far too precious!), cotton buds, make-up brushes, sponges, knives, forks and spoons to apply the tea and coffee on their paper or cardboard. Pens, pencils, lipstick pencils, textas, colouring pencils or even charcoal from wood fires. Whatever we could find in the home, we used. We had a weekly online show-and-tell, where we shared what we had created during the week.

I found some old music manuscript paper, and used it to make little paintings. I had so many of them, and I wondered what I could use them for. I have always been a giver, and wanted to help people who were mentally struggling during such a hard time.

I came up with the concept of care cards. I made hand-painted cards, then I put up a post on Facebook asking people if they knew anyone who needed a pick-me-up. Someone they knew who was lonely, someone that they wanted to send a message to, or maybe they wanted one for themselves. I created and sent out hundreds of these little cards in the post. I didn't charge for the card or the postage. They were free. I also wrote a little message in each one from the 'sender'. This simple act of kindness went a long way towards helping many people who were struggling during such a horrific time.

At the time, I had paid for a Source Bottle subscription. This is how I get into the media a lot. It's where journalists list a post when they are looking for a source for their article, when they're writing, or when they need someone to interview for TV or radio.

It was through this that a journalist reached out to me about my care cards, wanting to do an article on kindness. She wrote an article about my generosity in sending out the cards to complete strangers, for complete strangers. The article made the front page of the body+soul magazine in the Sunday papers around the country.

I've been in a lot more articles since 2021 and I've had hundreds of thousands of dollars worth of free publicity through Source Bottle. I have used it successfully to boost my profile in the media, giving my story more credibility, resulting in many people and organisations reaching out to buy my art or book me for speaking gigs.

I love painting with acrylics and watercolours. I have created a lot of work using inks, both water and alcohol. They both move differently and are fun to explore. My artwork is bright, bold and full of colour. I love seeing people's faces when they look at my work. I'm always drawing, whether it's in graphite, pastels or even Textas. It doesn't have to be exhibition quality, but I have found it's essential to have a hobby in your life. It actually helps build resilience.

I discovered a new medium: a cement modelling compound. It meant I could create sculptures without a kiln to fire them. I started small and created elephants, giraffes; in fact, lots of different types of animals. I started teaching one-day workshops on how to use it and became a wholesaler of the product. There are opportunities everywhere around us. I then challenged myself to make a large sculpture. After watching lots of YouTube videos on how to create the armature, or skeleton, to support the project, I got to work.

I had an idea. Now, when I get ideas, I follow through. I drew her on paper first, then set about ordering the supplies to make her. The armature looked great, hundreds of hot glue sticks, 100 metres of aluminium foil and lots of swear words. I forgot to account for the weight when it was wet. The bamboo supports in the legs were not strong enough to support her. After five hours of mixing the cement product and having her two-thirds of the way covered with a thick coating, she hit the art studio floor with a thud!

I was shattered. All that time, energy and money lying there in a huge mess. I couldn't give up. I had too much at stake. I grabbed a plastic tub, peeled the blob off the floor, put it in the tub, and covered it with wet towels. Then I found some garden stakes and proceeded to wire and glue her new legs on. Then I began to reapply the coating. There was only a certain number of hours left before the product would set and I wouldn't be able to mould it. My hands, arms, legs, shoulders, actually everything, ached and was spasming, but I finished her and had her propped up on more supports until she dried. I had finished her. Now, to let her cure.

She looked amazing. A five-foot-eight-inch coloured giraffe named Mavis. I went to move Mavis when she was finished, and I cracked two legs! What the actual fuck! I cried. I screamed, and I refused to give up! I got Selleys Knead It Multi Purpose Epoxy Putty and repaired the legs, and painted them again. I had her entered into the Birragurra art show for $990. She sold before the show opened. I was gobsmacked. I had just sold my artwork for nearly $1000! My own artwork!

What if I had never walked through that art studio door? What if I had let my anxiety win the day and stayed home, convincing myself that I was too tired, too overwhelmed, too broken to try something new? It is a question that still sits with me sometimes because I know how easy it would have been to say no. I had every reason to turn away. My body hurt, my confidence was shattered, and I was carrying the weight of a medical file that felt bigger than me.

If I had let my anxiety dictate my life, everything that followed would never have happened. I would never have rediscovered the part of me that found peace in colour and movement. I would never have felt my hands steady as they created something that was mine, not defined by illness or limitation. I would never have met the people who became part of my healing, my community, my future.

If I had not walked through that door, there would be no JUZT Art. No award-winning paintings. No exhibitions. No classrooms full of people learning to breathe again through creativity. There would be no colouring books, no commissions, no moments where I watched someone discover their own strength because I had the courage to share mine.

My whole life would have taken a different path. A smaller one. A quieter one. A life shaped more by fear than possibility.

But I did walk through the door. I walked in shaking, uncertain and overwhelmed, but I walked in. That single step changed everything. It reminded me that courage does not always roar. Sometimes it is just the act of showing up. Sometimes it is choosing to try. Sometimes it is refusing to let anxiety write the ending for you.

Art gave me back pieces of myself I thought were gone forever. It led me to new businesses, new friends, new purpose and a deeper understanding of who I truly am. And because I walked through that door, thousands of other people have walked through mine.

One moment. One choice. One step that changed my life.

That is the heart of moxie. It is not the loud victories. It is the quiet 'yes', whispered in the middle of fear.

I spoke to Mavis's buyer and explained that I would make her another one that would be bigger and stronger, because I didn't trust this one. Mavis came back home with me, and she proudly sits in my front yard. People stop all the time and take photos of her and all the other artworks I have created. I have an enormous frog that I cut out of marine plywood and painted on one of my side fences, and on the other side fence, I have a six-metre-long sausage dog. My house is also painted in my brand colours: turquoise, lime green, and mauve.

I often get asked to create commissioned pieces of my art. Nowadays, I have a sign out the front of my house that advertises all my businesses, but for 4 years, it just advertised solely JUZT Art. I have had many people knock on my front door asking if I can create something special for them or a loved one.

Mavis has done her job well. An old guy knocked on the front door while I was in the middle of teaching class. He sternly asked if I was the one responsible for creating the giraffe. My chest started to pound. The first thing that went through my mind was that I was in trouble for having her in my front yard, and I was going to get a hefty fine! I shyly said yes, and he yelled, "Awesome, I love her. How do I go about ordering one?" I nearly fell over from the shock! He then asked me how much. Now, don't get me wrong, I did love making the first two, but I soon realised they were worth a lot more than the $990 the first one sold for.

I blurted out $4,000, and he asked if I would accept cash! I took down all his details, got a cash deposit and walked back into class in shock. I went from selling my first piece in 2012 for $300 to now selling my artwork for $4,000! I felt invincible, like I could do anything. I started making 'Harry' the giraffe that evening. He now has a home in a garden under an orange tree in the middle of a house paddock on a farm. I have gone on to make two more. One is at an Airbnb, and the other I have lost track of. I increased the price again when I sold them.

Life was great. I felt like I was really getting somewhere.

But then.

Every time I started getting in front, my body had other ideas.

There were lots of doctors and hospital visits, and each time I took an art pad and black pens with me to scribble while I waited. Some of my best works have been created while waiting for an appointment. If I had a dollar for every minute I have spent waiting for medical appointments, I would probably never have to worry about money again.

All jokes aside, I have spent a lot of time in those waiting rooms and hospital wards.

I have tried to have the mindset of moving forward in life. There is a reason why the rearview mirror is smaller than the windscreen. Reflection is good, but staying in that mental state does no one any good. Learn from your past to create a better, more resilient future.

When I got through the heart surgeries, cancers and blood conditions and went into remission, people started asking what my secret was. How did I remain so positive?

I did not know. I just did me, every single day.

I got out of bed, made my bed, every single day, even if it meant I went and laid on the lounge for the rest of the day.

I had to work with my counsellor and a coach in order to work out what made me tick. How did I become so resilient, and how could I share my secrets to the world?

More and more people wanted to know how I overcame everything, and I registered my third business, Resilience Mindset, in 2019, to do keynote speaking.

And if I am honest, that is where moxie became more than just something I lived. It became something I could explain. It became something I could teach. It became the name I gave to the part of me that refused to stay down.

We all know what happened in 2020. The world stopped, and work for keynote speakers immediately dried up.

So I pivoted.

I offered webinars online, jumping on as many speaking platforms as I could, such as other people's podcasts and webinars, as well as my own live streams on Facebook, while I waited for the world to open up again.

Because that is what moxie does.

It adapts.

It finds a way.

It keeps moving.

I installed a professional gallery-hanging system in my home in 2017. 50 metres of track. It was not cheap. I am fortunate that my house has a very, very long hallway. I needed somewhere to store my paintings and hold exhibitions. I open the gallery to the public on certain weekends and by appointment. We have had amazing exhibitions there over the years. Including, recently, a project called Breaking the Barriers: Stories through the lens.

I had been coaching my neighbour, Simon, and his wife, Julie, about their photography business: changing their business name, and increasing the amount of work they were getting. They went from two weddings a season to being fully booked. They were the photographers and videographers for my daughter's wedding.

Simon popped over for a cuppa and said that he wanted to do his first photography exhibition. In the space of that 10 minute conversation, his little exhibition had grown legs. I had taken the idea and run with it. That is something I tend to do. Opportunities are everywhere.

It wouldn't just be any ordinary photography exhibition; it needed to convey meaning behind the image. I came up with the concept of having people who usually wouldn't have a professional photography shoot done, but who all had a story to tell beyond the lens. I wanted to break the barriers on what society sees as people with disabilities due to the international sign for disabilities being a person in a wheelchair.

This project quickly gained momentum.

We had decided to give people with disabilities an experience they would never forget. I asked one of my friends, Jo Jo, who is a hairdresser, if she would do their hair. Simon knew a make-up artist. We wanted to make each model feel special. To make them look like a superstar.

They each had their hair and makeup done, and their photos taken, and were then taken into another room and interviewed by me. Julie recorded each interview. I had the task of turning each interview into a chapter in the book; my team turned them into a podcast hosted on Resilience Mindset's Podcast and a vlogcast hosted on YouTube under my Channel @justinemartincorporation.

The two exhibitions we had were spectacular. A2-size portraits and the launch of the coffee table book. Every person involved in the project was bursting with pride. I entered the book in the 2025 ABLE Golden Book Awards, and we won Silver for best anthology. I am so proud of this project and the way it highlighted many people and their own stories.

When Chase arrived in 2019, something deep inside me shifted. There are moments in life that feel like a quiet unlocking, a gentle click of something finally settling after years spent slightly off balance. His birth was one of those moments.

When Ally told me she was pregnant, it took me straight back to the day I told my own mother I was expecting for the first time. I had hoped for excitement, reassurance and joy. Instead, I was met with rejection. She told me to get rid of it. No support. No warmth. No love. It was one of those moments that leaves a bruise on the heart.

So when Ally shared her news, I felt nothing but gratitude. Gratitude that I could respond differently. Gratitude that I could be the kind of mother and nanna I had once needed. Gratitude that I had laid down the baton, and I could break the cycle of hurt and replace it with love.

By the time Chase was born, I was already a hands-on nanna to Riley and Maycee. They had been staying with me every second Friday for years. They are Matt's children from before Ally stepped into their lives, and she embraced them as her own with full-hearted love. And I did too. I treated them no differently than Chase because love grows from presence and choice, not blood.

Then Chase arrived, and something inside me healed again. Becoming a biological nanna was a feeling beyond joy. Holding him for the first time felt like a soft mending of old wounds. His tiny heartbeat seemed to say that love still finds its way through everything.

My home quickly became their second home. I created a room just for them with two bunk beds, their own space filled with comfort, silliness and memories. Every second Friday, the three of them would burst through my door with bags, stories and wall-shaking noise and energy. I finished every sleepover absolutely exhausted, but it was the kind of tiredness that fills your soul rather than drains it.

In 2021, Cooper arrived, and he slipped into our family rhythm with ease. And I still have all of them over for sleepovers. I would not trade a single moment of the chaos, the cuddles or the crumbs.

Then, in 2020, Odin arrived in Queensland. His birth happened in the middle of lockdown while I was in Victoria. I could not visit. I could not hold him. I could not smell that newborn scent or kiss his little forehead. It broke my heart, the ache of loving a grandchild you cannot touch. But love finds its own path. As soon as borders opened, I travelled to see him, to make up for the moments we had lost.

In 2022, Maxwell was born, and in 2025, little Ripley arrived. All of them are in Queensland. My Queensland grandbabies. Distance changes the shape of love, but it does not diminish it. I visit them at least four times a year. Each visit is filled with cuddles, mess, giggles, and memories squeezed into the time we get together.

And now that they are getting older, FaceTime has become our lifeline. They call me to show me toys, drawings, missing teeth, scraped knees and school lunchboxes. They tell me stories. They talk over each other. They call me for no reason at all other than to say 'hello, Nanny'. And those calls mean everything.

I may not be able to have them for sleepovers as often as the Victorian grandkids, but they know I am present. They know I show up. They know I love them.

Being a nanna to all of them — to Riley, to Maycee, to Chase, to Cooper, to Odin, to Maxwell and to Ripley — has given me something precious. It has given me joy. It has given me purpose. It has given me healing. It has given me the kind of love I once longed for. And it has given seven little humans a nanna who will always show up with an open heart, no matter the distance.

2012 Graphite Turtle

2012 My first painting that I exhibited and sold

2013 MS Art Exhibition with Yellow Bird - SOLD!

2013 OCT State Trustee Connected Art Exhibition — Alan Merigan People's Choice Award Winner for I Can See You jpeg

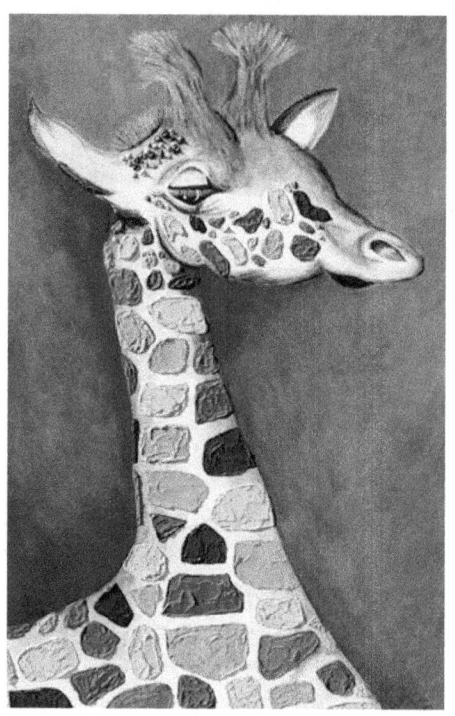

2014 Basil acrylic painting

2014 Giraffe ink painting

2014 NOV State Trustee Connected Art Exhibition — Alan Merigan People's Choice Award Winner 'BASIL' second year in a row

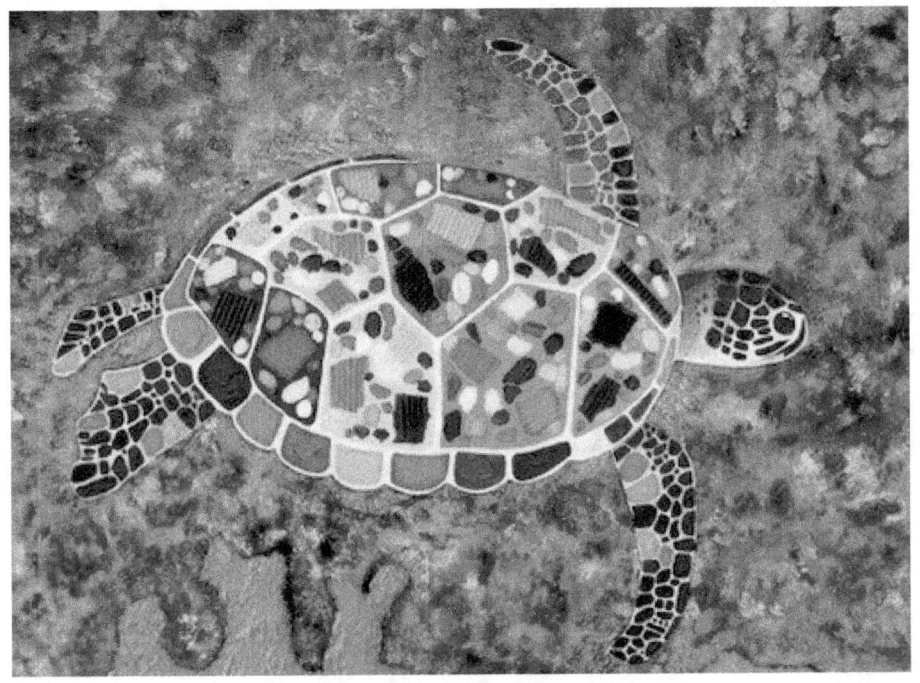

2014 One of my bright paintings

2014 Painting featured in MS Australia's In Touch Magazine

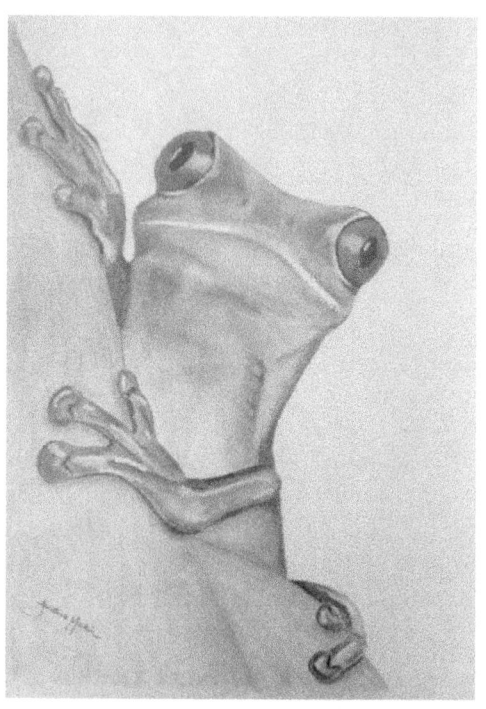

2015 Graphite drawing

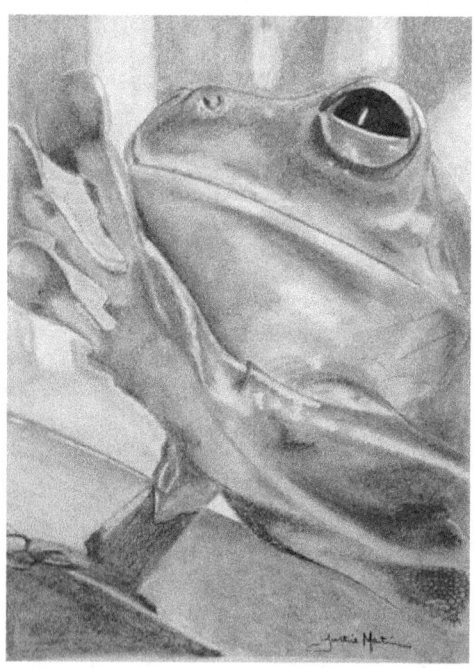

2015 Graphite drawing

2015 Graphite Fairy

2015 Ink fairy   *2015 JUZT art Gallery*

2015 Kiss goodbye to MS lips

2015 Maggie - ink stippling

2015 My market stall

2015 Self Portrait for Zonta International Conviction, Commitment and Courage Exhibition

2016 Disability Services Award

2017 Drawing in my art studio when I could use my hands again

2017 Exhibiting Ziggy Stardust in the middle of Chemotherapy treatment

2017 Amped Bar and Restaurant Opening Night in the middle of my chemotherapy treatment with my Hickman line

2018 Finger painting

2018 Finger painting

2018 Fingerpainting at Cafe Zoo, Drysdale Victoria

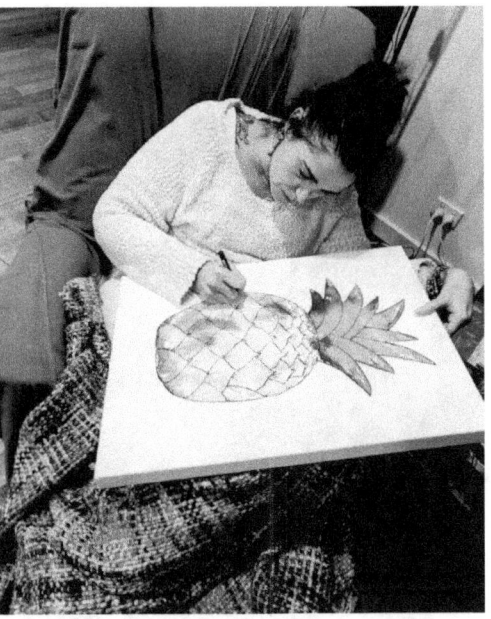
2018 Finishing off a painting in the lounge chair

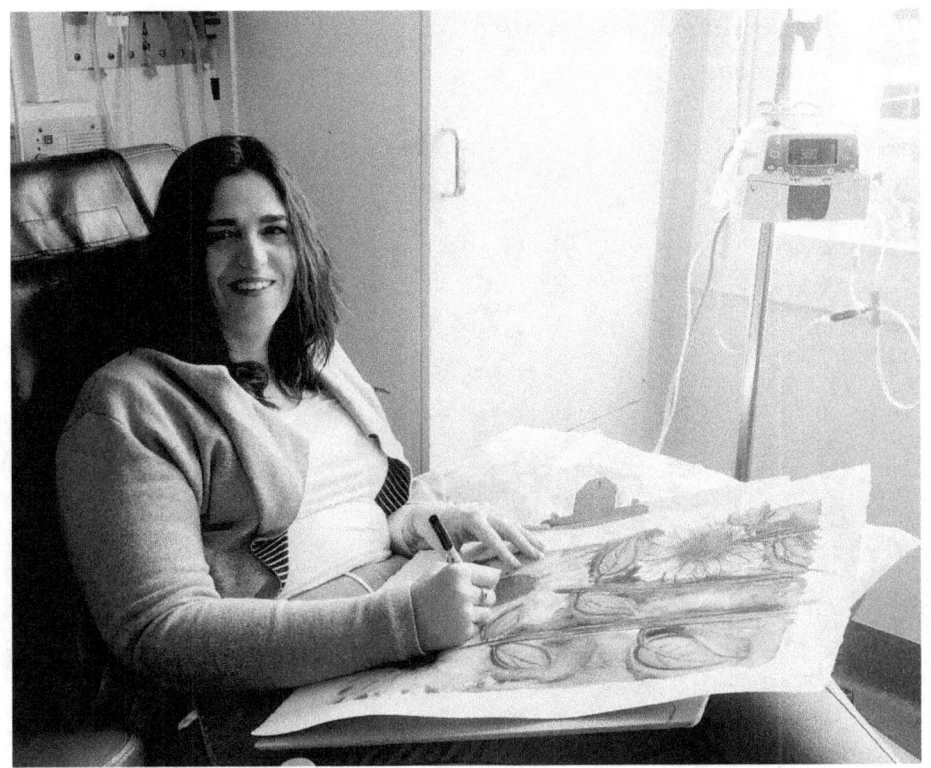
2018 Infusion at Geelong University Hospital and drawing to fill in the time

2018 Little Creatures speed painting second place

2018 Painting the You Yangs

2018 World MS Day window display

2019 Finger painting

2019 Finger painting workshop

2019 Mavis and me in my front yard photo shoot for Geelong Times Newspaper

2019 Mavis in my front yard

2019 My car with Van Go Decals

2019 Van Go Decals

2019 Watercolour painting sold overseas

2019 With Pansy in my art studio

2020 Frog on my front fence

2020 Harry with the orange tree

2020 My first large sculpture, Mavis

2020 My mini sculptures from Same Same But Different Book

2020 Van Go Decals

2021 Painting in my studio

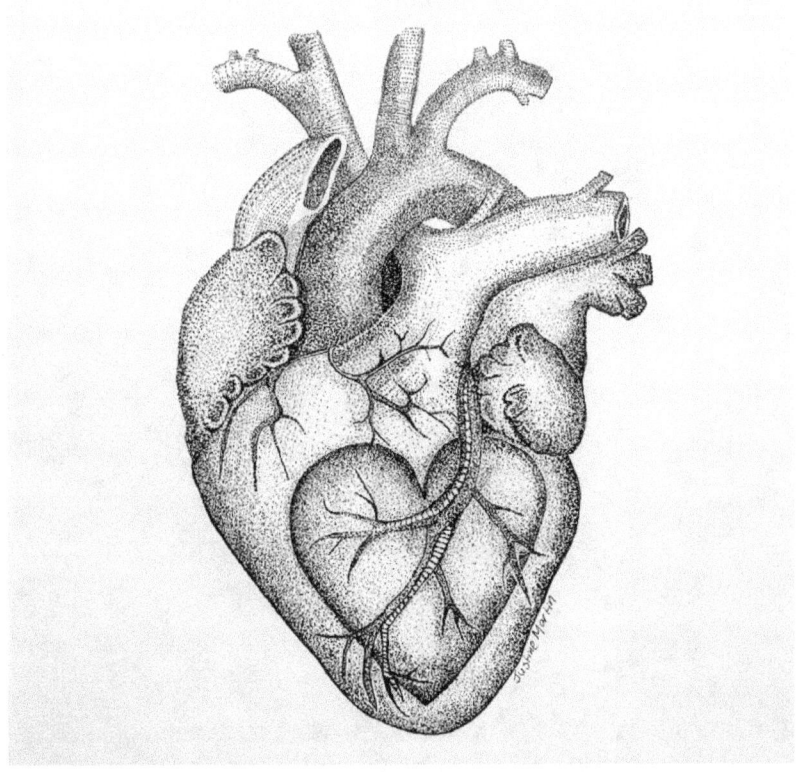

2021 Resilience of the Heart

2022 Painting in my studio

2022 Painting Same Same But Different

2023 6m Pansy on my side fence

2023 Digital art of Pansy

2023 Justine Martin Corporation and my home

2024 Digital painting of my neighbour's dogs

2024 Finding Hope book cover *2024 Painting Finding Hope Children's Book*

2025 Queenscliff People's Choice Award

The Golden Duck watercolour

CHAPTER 23

Broken Heart

I had been living for about 12 months with what felt like the wings of many butterflies fluttering in my chest. It would come and go 24 hours a day, 7 days a week, month after month. I had grown accustomed to the feeling. I self-diagnosed, putting it down to just a new MS symptom. I wasn't alarmed by it. So much was going wrong with my body, I could barely keep up. I was in a constant state of survival.

Mental note….one should never self-diagnose. And just as I was getting my life sorted!

The year was 2012, September: Father's Day. M8 had been argumentative all day as he hadn't got his own way in something trivial. Taking it all out on Ally. I stood up for her, which caused more stress.

That evening, I didn't feel very well, and the butterflies were jumping around more than normal. Then out of the blue, I developed a stabbing pain in the centre of my brain. It would last for about 20 to 30 seconds, then disappear for a couple of minutes, then return with force. The closest thing I can compare it to is someone stabbing a knife through my skull right into the centre of my brain, then back out again. It was horrific. I was scared. I thought my brain was going to explode.

Something was not right. I took some Panadol. It did nothing. I took some Tramadol, and that did nothing too. I normally hate going to the hospital and will do everything I can to stay at home for as long as possible. But as I screamed in pain, I begged M8 to drive me there.

M8 drove me to Geelong University Hospital's emergency department, where I was triaged straight through to the Doctors, avoiding the emergency waiting room. I was put on an Electric Cardiogram Machine to have an electrocardiograph, commonly known as an ECG. In between my screams from the pain, it felt like my brain was giving birth, with one contraction after another.

Alarm bells started ringing on the machine, and lots of people came running. They asked me questions about how my chest was feeling. I was irritable because it was my head hurting, not my chest!

I looked around at the machine in between the stabbing in my head and saw that my resting heart rate was 156 beats per minute. To put it into perspective, a normal resting heart rate is about 60 beats per minute.

The doctor asked me if my chest felt different, and I replied no. He asked me again if I was sure. I replied that it felt like it had for the past 12 months, full of butterflies. He looked at me strangely and then pointed out that they weren't butterflies, but rather that my heart was beating way too fast. He couldn't believe I had been walking around with this for so long and hadn't done anything to correct it. I just thought it was something I was going to have to get used to, another thing the MS had robbed me of.

The one major lesson I learned that day was that not everything that goes wrong in my body is MS-related. MS is just one thing. Everything else can and will go wrong.

I was now scared. Something was wrong with my heart, and it wasn't MS-related! Were my head 'contractions' and the feeling in my chest related? They didn't know. My blood pressure was abnormally high for me. I'm usually very low, and my core body temperature is also 35.5 on a good day. I have trouble keeping warm, and this adds to my fatigue levels.

After an hour, the emergency team got my head pain under control. They gave me pills for my heart to slow it down, wrote me a referral to see a cardiologist, and then they sent us home. To this day, I still don't know what caused my head pain; it's never come back like that. I can only guess that it was the amount of stress that I was under. Stress is a very dangerous thing.

I started on the pills and within a few weeks, I was at my first cardiologist visit. He was a professor, so he was more than just a specialist. He adjusted the medication as it wasn't working properly, and sent me to have a Holter monitor put on. It is a machine with leads that connect to your chest with electrodes, and it monitors the electrical activity of your heart to see how it's beating. Every time you feel something is wrong, you press a button which marks the recording, making it easier to see when things are going wrong.

It can also determine what parts of your heart aren't working properly by the signals it picks up. He then sent me on my way for six weeks. On my return, I explained I was getting giddy every time I stood up. The new pills were working, just too well. He told me I had atrial fibrillation. As I was going in and out of atrial fibrillation (AF) all day, when I wasn't in AF, my heart rate was dropping to 48 and was too slow to push the blood through my body. My medication was changed again. He also told me I had to stop taking the birth control pill as I was at high risk of having a stroke.

I then had to go back to my GP to discuss my contraception options. I chose to have a Mirena, which is an IUD, inserted into my cervix. It releases hormones that trick your body into thinking it's pregnant. My first implant happened in 2013, and I haven't had a period since. Having this device implanted was one of the most painful experiences I've ever had. It was done at the gynecologist's rooms, awake, with my legs up in stirrups. No dignity whatsoever. The gynecologist had trouble placing it into my cervix. My cervix is posterior, which makes it more difficult and more painful. I was screaming in pain and nearly passed out from the shock of it all. I then had to drive myself home after I vomited.

Once inserted, the Mirena stays in place for five years. He told me I would have to go under anaesthetic to have it removed and replaced. To date, I've had three. I haven't had a period since 2013. For me, it's been a great choice. A lot of other women have had complications from it. Because it tricks my body into thinking it's pregnant, I believe it's helping keep my MS in remission. You see, when you're pregnant and have MS, you go into full remission. Then when you have the baby, you are at higher risk of having a major relapse. I have not been on any MS drugs since starting chemotherapy in 2017. So the combination of chemotherapy and the implant is working. As I write this, I am in full remission from MS, and I have not had any new brain lesions since 2015.

With the birth control in place and the beta blockers not working properly, the only choice I had was to undergo heart surgery to correct the rhythm. That scared the shit out of me. I was referred to a cardio surgeon. He was very nice and had a great bedside manner. He explained that I would need a Pulmonary Vein Ablation. They would insert a catheter up through my groin, through to my heart. They would locate the pulmonary vein and burn every few millimetres around it. They then puncture a small hole in your heart and do the same to the inside of your heart. This vein is responsible for sending the electrical signal that stimulates the heart to make it beat. I had too many electrical signals going to my heart, causing the extra beats. In order to stop that, they burn parts of the vein; they can't burn all of it as that would cause the heart to stop beating altogether.

But before this operation could take place, I had to have a series of tests on my heart. This included two ultrasounds: one from the outside and one from the inside. The external one was a breeze. However, the internal one, known as a transoesophageal echocardiogram (TOE), is a procedure to look at your heart chambers and valves using a flexible telescope placed down your oesophagus. The telescope has an ultrasound scanner attached to it, allowing your heart specialist to obtain close-up views of your heart. It was terrible. I was to be put into a twilight sedation and then a long device would be inserted down my throat. I was so worried that I would remember it all. The specialist didn't listen when I expressed my concern that anaesthesia never works properly on me. It had yet again fallen on deaf ears! The amount of times I have had people from the medical profession gaslight me is unbelievable. It has to stop.

In recovery, the ultrasound doctor came around and said to me, "Now that wasn't so bad, was it?" I relayed word-for-word what he had said while I was 'under sedation'. He was shocked. I also told him that it felt like I was stuck in a chamber where no one could hear me screaming, and I couldn't move. And people wonder why I have medically-induced trauma.

A week later I was being prepped for my heart procedure.

This operation took seven long hours. I was in a real mess afterwards.

As I was wheeled back to the ward, I developed a migraine. Waiting for me was my daughter Ally, my girlfriend Gail, who had flown from Perth to look after me, and my cousin Mylie. I was lying flat on my back and had vomited a few times from the migraine.

I felt a rush of warm fluid in my groin and thought my bladder had let go. You see, having a general anaesthetic is dangerous for people with MS. It can lead to having a relapse. As I'd experienced some bladder issues in the previous years, I lay there in shock, thinking WOW that relapse happened fast. I said to the girls that I thought I'd just wet myself. They told me to stop being silly.

The nurse came in to check on me and asked if everything was ok. I explained I thought I'd wet myself. She said she would just check, and she pulled back the sheet. To everyone's shock, I was lying in a pool of my blood! What I thought was wee pulsing out of me was actually blood coming out of my artery in my groin. All hell broke loose. Ally screamed and nearly fainted. The nurse grabbed my hand and told me to press into my groin to stop the bleeding as she went and grabbed supplies to redress it. And clean sheets!

They then explained to me that even the slightest move I had to put pressure on the wound. This included getting up to go to the bathroom and rolling onto my side in bed. I complained to the nurse about how swollen my legs were, and they had to cut the hospital ID bracelet off my left leg as it was cutting in. No one questioned why.

I was discharged the next day and allowed to go home. My first question to my cardio surgeon was when I could go back to training for weightlifting. I was told to wait a week before I could go back. That made me happy as I had been training three days a week to compete as a Masters lifter in Olympic Weightlifting.

The following day, my belly was swollen and my legs even bigger. I drink a lot of water, and had not gone to the toilet to pass any of it. I had barely gone to the toilet since the operation. I felt terrible. After calling my specialist number, I was advised to go back into the emergency. Something was wrong.

Gail and I sat in the emergency waiting room and waited to be seen. My belly looked distended. I was extremely uncomfortable and had trouble taking a full breath. A little old lady in a wheelchair opposite me leaned over and said, "Don't worry love, you will soon have a lovely little bundle of joy to hold. It will all be worth it!" I turned to Gail and said, "What the actual fuck! She thinks I'm pregnant and am about to give birth!" Gail's reply was "Oh Justy, I'm sorry, girlfriend, but yes, you do look pregnant!"

Not what I needed to hear. I was soon taken to see a doctor. Apparently, they had pumped over 6 litres of fluid into me during the surgery, and then added in there all the water I'd been drinking, and I'd barely passed any of it. I had to have an ultrasound and an X-ray on my chest to see if there was any fluid built up around my heart. Thank goodness there wasn't. I was given fluid tablets and told to go home, where it would all pass in the next 48 hours or so. It did, and a week later, I returned to weightlifting at the gym.

My cardio surgeon told me that if the AF didn't come back in twelve weeks, it wouldn't be back.

Eleven weeks later, I was competing on a Sunday in January 2014 in Ocean Grove in an Olympic Weightlifting competition. I felt that familiar butterfly flutter in my chest, but with a lot more force than before. You could see and feel the main artery in my neck pulsating.

I took a video of it. I do that when things are happening on my body so I can show my medical team, while I'm trying to explain what's happening. It also helps with my memory — so while I'm writing this book, I conveniently have LOTS to jolt my memories.

It was really hot, and I told myself it was just because of the hot weather. I went to bed very nervous, thinking I might not wake up again. The next day, when I opened my eyes, I was relieved to still be earthside, and with no 'butterflies' in my chest. I carried on with my day, not thinking about it again. But my luck ran out, and when I woke on the Tuesday morning, it was back again. This time in full force.

We lived 100m from a doctor's surgery. I rang to get an appointment and explained that I had surgery on my heart 11 weeks earlier, and I thought maybe something was wrong. The receptionist booked me in for an hour later. I lay down on the lounge and waited, not feeling very well at all. As I lay there, I contemplated whether I should drive to the doctors or walk. If I drove and died while driving, I could kill somebody, but if I walked in the heat, someone might find me dead on the footpath. Ally wasn't home — she was staying at a girlfriend's for the night.

I decided the safer option for society would be me to walk there — on a 40-degree day! Not one of my smarter moves, but I didn't have any other way to get there without putting others in danger. It was by far the hardest 100m I have ever walked. I finally arrived at the doctor's, he put me on another ECG to check what my heart was doing. I looked at the monitor and sighed. He said everything was ok, and my heart was beating at a nice 65 beats a minute. I told him to take a closer look at that reading! He replied with "We'd better call an ambulance!" My heart rate was, in fact, 165 beats a minute. I convinced them not to call the ambulance, as I needed to go home first and pack an overnight bag and organise my daughter, and I promised I would call the ambulance when I got home.

They let me walk out of the clinic.

Remember that I said that it was the hardest 100m I had ever walked? It wasn't. The walk home was. I had to keep stopping as the world was spinning around me. I thought I was going to die. As soon as I walked in the door, I rang the ambulance. I explained that I had been to the doctors and what my resting heart rate was. The operator told me an ambulance was on the way. I left the front door unlocked and open.

I rang Ally next and told her the ambulance was on its way — she said she was coming straight home as she was only at a girlfriend's around the corner. I threw a nightie and toiletries into an overnight bag and then heard the sirens coming closer. Just as the Ambulance pulled up out front Ally ran inside with a terrified look on her face. The ambulance officer put another ECG on me, and my heart rate was now sitting at 175! They said they couldn't get the trolley into my house and asked me if I could walk while hooked up with all the ECG leads to the ambulance. They helped me up off the lounge, and everything was spinning. I managed to get out to the ambulance and onto the trolley bed. I told Ally to ring our cousin Myalie to tell her what was going on, and ask if she could stay with her.

I told Ally I was going to be ok and not to worry. I was petrified that was going to be the last time I'd ever see her. I told her I loved her as they closed the door. The ambulance drove the 20 minutes to Geelong Hospital with its lights flashing and sirens screaming. Alarms started going off when my heart rate hit 200. They were trying to put a cannula in my arm, and they had to pull over on the side of the Portarlington Rd to try and find one of my shitty veins. Once the line was in and I was hooked up, we tore up the road again into town.

I had lost the feeling in my right arm, and my hearing was going. I started to panic, thinking this was it. I was going to die. My chest was hurting. We reached the hospital, and the ambulance officers wheeled me in, all the while talking to each other, and then to the other ambulance officers in the emergency department. They were all looking at my monitor, talking about my resting heart rate. I was losing consciousness and they hit the panic buttons. My heart rate peaked at 217 beats a minute, which is nearly four times what it should be, or to put it into perspective, 150+ more beats a minute.

I had four doctors standing around me and some nurses. They gave me a pill under my tongue, which didn't work. Then a needle and then some more pills. It took a few hours to get my heart rate under 180 beats per minute. It returned to 165 beats about four hours later. I spent the night in the emergency room by myself. It was a very lonely night. I learnt to harden the fuck up that night.

The next day, I was allowed to go home. But how was I to get there? The ambulance had driven me there. Everyone else in my life, which wasn't a great deal of people, was at work, and I couldn't call them. The hospital wasn't going to let me go by myself. I convinced them that my lift was waiting for me outside. There was no one waiting. Ally and I were living on very little money, and I couldn't justify spending $70 on a taxi to travel the 25 minute journey home. So on a 40+ degree day, I walked to the bus stop, waited for the correct bus, then slowly made my way home. The bus didn't stop near our house, so again I had to walk. This time about 300m home in the heat. Not one of my smarter moves, but I really didn't have anyone to help. I felt so alone and upset. Why was this happening to me? I didn't have a clue.

Emergency discharged me, telling me I would have to have another ablation, because the previous one had failed. No shit, Sherlock! The only problem I now had was that my cardio surgeon was away on holiday, so I had to wait a month for my next surgery. I was back on beta blockers, which kept my heart at around 165 beats per minute. I was not allowed to return to training until everything was fixed. It was a very long four weeks. I became grumpy and moody and started to gain weight again.

I had only just recovered from all of the bruises on my left wrist where they inserted a device to monitor my heart rate last time!

My surgeon didn't think it would take as long this time, only four and a half hours or so under general anaesthesia. It was like deja vu with things going wrong again: a migraine after surgery and hemorrhaging again in the groin. However, this time they gave me fluid tablets before I left the hospital. I recovered quickly, but I wasn't allowed to go back to the gym for at least 4 weeks. I didn't want to go through another surgery, so I did what I was told and stayed at home to recover. Painting and drawing filled my days while I convalesced at home.

I had to have a six-week, post-operation check-up, and I was given the ok. Again, around the 12-week mark, I had to keep an eye on it, but the butterflies didn't come back! I was very, very relieved, and felt I was back to what had become my MS body's normal. At the six-month mark, I had to go back to my cardio surgeon for a check-up, and I expressed my concern that I felt something was still wrong with my heart. But this time it felt different. I wanted answers and booked an appointment to see my heart surgeon.

28th July 2014 was a very sad day. My Nanna was rushed to the hospital with a perforated bowel. I had tried to call her on the phone the day before, but it had gone to voicemail. We were all called into the hospital to say our last goodbyes. My cousin and I drove home about 11 pm from Melbourne. By the time we drove the hour home, she had died. I felt like I had lost my mum all over again. Nanna was only ever a phone call away. I used to call her weekly. I would always end the phone call saying "I love you…"; she would reply "Me too." On the rare occasion when she ended the call with "I love you", I would then call my cousin to squeal that Nanna had said it, as it didn't happen very often.

We had a viewing in the church and watched them secure the coffin lid. Zak was a pallbearer and wore his full army ceremonial uniform in her honour. Zak was the thirteenth family member to serve in the armed forces. Nanna was so proud that he joined the army. She was in the army in World War II. I miss her very much, even to this day. I would call her for advice to celebrate milestones in my life. She was, after all, there for my brother and me when no one else was. I sometimes forget she is gone and go to call, and then stop and remember she isn't there. Grief will come back in waves, without me even realising at times.

I was very fortunate to receive a family inheritance, which I put towards buying my home in 2016.

I had always wanted to visit a nudist beach. It was one of those quiet bucket list things that lived in the back of my mind for years, but I never thought I would have the courage to actually do it. The funny thing is, I discovered that the nearest one was only fifteen minutes from where I lived. It felt like the universe was having a laugh and saying, "Well go on then, what are you waiting for?"

So one day I did it. I packed a towel, took a deep breath, and drove there. I walked onto that beach and for the first time in my life, I stripped down to absolutely nothing — not for a doctor, not for a hospital, not for a partner, but for myself.

Becoming a nudist was one of the most empowering choices I have ever made. I did it to reclaim my body. To learn to like it again. To stop hating the lumps and scars and changes and diagnoses that had shaped it. To stand there in the sun and feel the air on my skin and realise that this body has carried me through cancer, MS, heart procedures, trauma, motherhood and grief, and it is still here. It is still mine. It is still worthy.

Not long after that, I took it a step further and started life drawing modelling. Never in my wildest dreams did I picture myself standing naked in a room full of strangers while they sketched me. But I wanted to keep pushing myself out of my comfort zone. I wanted to turn shame into power. And to be perfectly honest, the forty dollars was well worth taking my clothes off for an hour.

That little bit of extra money helped me get by during some very tight periods of my life. It paid for fuel when I needed to get to appointments. It paid for groceries when money was low. It paid for art supplies. It helped in more ways than I can count.

Those sessions did something even deeper. Every time someone drew me I saw my body through their eyes, not my own harsh ones. They drew strength, shape, softness, curves, lines and shadows. They drew a woman. Not a disease. Not disability. Not damage. A woman.

Standing there completely exposed taught me more about acceptance than any mirror ever has. That season of life was a turning point. It was the beginning of a new relationship with my body. A body I no longer try to punish, hide or change. A body I have finally learnt to respect.

2012 Australian Masters Games

2012 Winning Disabled Bench Press at the Australian Masters Games

2014 Clean and Jerk

2014 Zak home from the army with Ally and myself

2015 Geelong Advertiser article

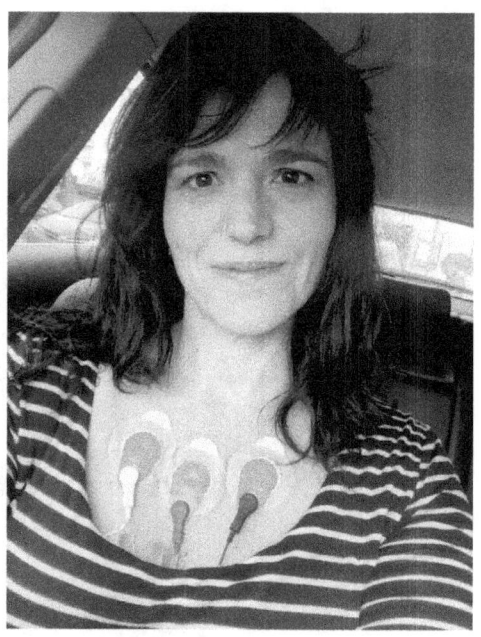
2015 Holter heart monitor

2019 Avalon Air show with Miss Molly, my wheelchair

Resilience Mindset Podcast

CHAPTER 24

Curve Ball

I wanted to live a normal life. I wanted someone to love me. But how was that possible when I didn't even love myself? In fact I didn't even like myself. I carried the burden of not being good enough, not being worthy enough, not being smart enough. When M8 told me that my MS would stop his dreams and goals in life, I figured that all men would feel the same way, and not see me as dateable. Not see me as a whole woman. I felt so flawed. So I shifted my mindset to just looking for a friend with benefits; hey, a girl's got needs! So I signed up for internet dating again.

I met some parents of Ally's school friends, and I would go out to the pub with them on a Friday or Saturday night. I began to regain some control over my life. I went on lots of dates with lots of strange men. I can't believe how many of them lied about their height or age, their photos, or all of the above. So much wasted time now I think back on it. I met a guy, M9, who was also a FIFO worker in the mines, off one of the sites. I was very wary because M8 also worked in the mines, hoping history wouldn't repeat itself. We made arrangements to meet next time he was back in Geelong. What I didn't realise at the time was that he was love bombing me, even from afar. Telling me everything I wanted to hear.

He assured me he wasn't like the average male. Well, he got that part right, he wasn't, in fact, he was pure evil. I was in such a dark mental place that I didn't see the red flags, and I put myself in his hands. I still shudder when I think about him and all that he did. We stopped sleeping together and remained friends when he got back with his ex-girlfriend. More about him later.

I wasn't well. My body was failing me yet again. I could feel a sudden jolt in my chest; this was happening about every 5 seconds all day and all through the night. My surgeon told me that it was quite normal, as they had been in my heart and messed around with it, that I would be a lot more sensitive, and to give it time to settle down.

I was pretty much told not to worry about it and to continue on with life. I felt like he had dismissed me and that he believed I was complaining about nothing at all.

I started living life again and ignored what my chest was doing. I had made some more friends by going out, and we would go out to various pubs in Geelong called The Max, The Sphinx, and The Elephant and Castle. The latter I still frequently visit. I have made many friends over the years from those places. One night in late October 2014, I was at the Elephant and Castle. It was packed with people and difficult to navigate through the crowd. A guy was trying to push past me, and I pushed harder against him to block him from going past. He looked at me and said "How you doin'?"; he also replied that I was too young for him. The funny thing was, I'm actually older than him. We still laugh about that today.

By the end of the night, I went home with M10, and we became a couple pretty much from that night. Then he came over for dinner the next night, and instead of flowers brought me a packet of licorice. I loved it! I hate receiving flowers as they remind me of sickness and death. I find them a waste of money. You have to watch them die before your eyes, then clean up the mess! So the fact that he had thought of something else made him a winner in my eyes. He had recently quit smoking. I hate dating smokers and told him so right from the start. I've put so much time and energy into trying to survive that I can't sit there and watch my partner slowly kill themselves. It's a strong boundary that I have always had. Both my parents were smokers, and both had lung cancer. M10 was different to 99% of the men I had dated. Kind and considerate. A gentleman. Opened up the car door for me. Cooked meals for me. Showed me at the beginning how a woman should be treated. My whole family fell in love with him. He taught Ally how to drive a kombi and how to surf. He was patient. He even let M9 rent a bungalow from him when he was home on R&R. Yes, strange, I know. Huge red flag!

We lived about 40 minutes from each other. His lease on his house had expired, and he was looking for somewhere to live, with M9 in tow. Ally and I had also received an eviction notice to vacate the house we were living in due to the owner selling it. It was actually Ally who suggested we all move in with each other and get a four-bedroom house and split the costs. So we did. We moved from Drysdale to Clifton Springs and rented a huge house so Ally could finish year 12.

It was when we were in the process of moving that Ally asked to spend a night at her girlfriend's. This was a girl I didn't like or trust. Ally assured me I could trust her at the age of 17, and she caught the bus to this girl's place. Ally then refused to come back home. I was gutted. I didn't know where she was for nearly 3 weeks. She was still going to school and thought she was a grown-up. It was at this time that she met a guy who was seven years older than her, who had three children. There were two boys aged five and three years, and a ten-month-old girl. I was not impressed. I had to bite my tongue if Ally was ever going to return to living at home. It was a parent's worst nightmare. The strange thing was, Ally and I hardly ever had arguments, which made her leaving even harder. With M10 moving in, she felt some freedom in not having to care for me and off she ran into the wrong crowd.

After being away for three weeks, she returned home. I walked on eggshells, worried I'd say something that would set her off and she would leave home again. She went back to school, but her boyfriend was picking her up when I thought she was at school. She had four months to go to finish high school, and she quit. She also walked away from weightlifting. A passion she had had for 10 years, and was extremely good at. The fighting between her and me increased, and we had a massive argument because she wanted to quit school, and also because I wouldn't let her boyfriend move in. She slapped me across the face, and after a lot of swearing at each other, she packed her clothes and moved out.

She moved into the garage of her boyfriend's house to become a step-mother to three young children. Not the life I thought she would live, and I became a nanna years before I thought I would, with the kids calling me Nar Nar. Life does throw us unexpected good curve balls, and I'm not sorry I caught it. I have the most amazing grandchildren. I don't treat my step-grandchildren any differently from my blood grandchildren. They all now call me Nanny.

M10 and I didn't spend much time together when he had time off from work, as he was restoring a car in Newcastle. He would work for four days, and then fly up to Newcastle, where he would be away for four days. It was beyond hard. I would often comment that there were three of us in the relationship. Him, the car and I. When the car was finally finished, we would take it on long drives. He made me laugh. M10 would often help me with my market stalls. He would help set it up and then come back and pack it all down. We had a Kombi called Lottie. I loved that car, but for some reason, every time I drove her, she would break down or something bad would happen. One day, I was turning the corner, and the back sliding door fell off!

M10 was a nice guy and didn't physically abuse me; however, our relationship was on a downward slope. He was drinking more and more each night. One bottle of white wine turned into two bottles, then into three. His mental state was slipping, and he started to smoke again, trying to hide it from me. He would go for days without showering, and he had depression. One time after the ninth day of not showering, I told him I would take him outside and use the garden hose on him, as there was no way he was hopping into our bed ever again unless he showered and brushed his teeth! The smell of jet fuel, stale white wine and cigarettes was enough to make anyone feel sick, then throw in the mix foul body odour. It wasn't long after this that he moved into the spare room, and our relationship was over. Not long after this, M9 moved in with his ex-girlfriend.

I was slowly adjusting to being an empty nester with Ally no longer at home. I would go and pick her up and take her out for lunch, and buy things she needed as she had very little money. My heart would break each time I dropped her back where she was living. I had to keep reminding myself that this was the life she chose. When she was in her last year of primary school in Perth, at her graduation, each student had to say where they saw themselves in ten years' time. When Zak had done it, he said he wanted to be a sergeant in the Australian Army. He got close and became a Corporal. Ally stood in the middle of the stage and announced she wanted to be married with two kids. Everyone laughed at her. It was horrible. I just wanted to give her a huge hug and say it's ok, they are your dreams, and you can do whatever you want. I remember turning to M7 and saying, "Well, at least she wants to be married first."

The funny thing was, a generation or two back, that's what most females aspired to do when they left school. Now here she was, a mum to three children, and she was happy. It didn't feel right for the children to call me Justine, so we came up with a name, Nar Nar. I became a grandmother overnight.

In mid-2015, I was going out of my mind with the constant thud every few seconds in my chest 24 hours a day, seven days a week! I went back to my GP and told her about it, and she suggested that I go back to my surgeon with a new referral. I had to wait months for an appointment. Nothing happens fast in the medical industry! And I meant to say 'industry', because that's what it is. There aren't many medical professionals with excellent bedside manner. I am lucky I have an amazing medical team on my side that does. I have learnt that if you don't like the doctors in your team, find new ones that you do. It's your life they have in their hands.

I went back to the surgeon and explained it was still happening and was driving me nuts in the process. I couldn't sit without background noise, as I could hear it and feel it in my chest. He suggested that I wear another Holster monitor, for a week this time. I remember thinking, 'A week! Why would I need it on for a whole week?' Two days later, I was back in there being hooked up to the device. I wasn't allowed to shower for the week, so I just sponge-bathed with it on.

I had to press the button again every time I felt I was having an episode. It was going to be a very long week! Not even 24 hours later, I rang my specialist's room and explained the device was flat. They explained over the phone that it couldn't be flat in that time period, as the battery had a week-long life. I explained that it was no longer working, and I was asked if I was only pressing it when I was having an episode. My reply was a stern "YES!" I was told to bring it back the next day and see if it had captured anything.

Three days later, I received a call asking me to come in and see my specialist. I wasn't surprised. There was something wrong, but what? I went in by myself as I always did, and still do with a lot of my medical appointments. It's become easier just to deal with the often bad news myself, rather than having to console whoever is with me.

My specialist apologised for not listening to me some 12 months earlier when I had expressed that something wasn't right. I was informed that the average person misses 25 beats in a 24-hour period, which is very normal. I, however, was missing one in every five beats, and the sixth beat was what I was feeling, as it was very forceful, as my heart started again. I had been putting up with this for 12 months' too long.

My only option was another surgery to fix it. I didn't cry, I just sat there in shock. Why was my body doing this to me? What had I done wrong? I asked these questions, and he couldn't answer. What he did say was that this surgery would be different. I would have to be awake this time. I said no way, I wanted to be fully put to sleep. I started to panic, and fear set in. AWAKE? NO WAY! It was explained that if I were under a general anesthetic, my heart would return to normal rhythm from the drugs and wouldn't be fixed.

I was petrified the morning of my operation. My surgeon explained they would give me a sedative to help, and I probably wouldn't remember much. Yeah, right, I thought, like that's going to work on me! I was on that operating table for another four and a half hours. The sedative didn't work, and it was horrific. I was lying there talking to my surgeon, looking at the big screen that showed a sonographic view of my heart with different colours on it, such as blue and red, all the while he was burning the front wall of my heart. It hurt A LOT! And I wasn't supposed to remember it. Yeah right!

There were people looking through a window in another room at us. I'm not sure if they were nurses, doctors or med students. I felt like I was in a frying pan and people were watching me being cooked from the inside out. I couldn't wait for that surgery to be over. Every part of my body hurt from lying perfectly still for so long.

As I was wheeled back to my room for an overnight stay, I commented that my chest felt different after this surgery than it had after the previous ones. It was very heavy, like an elephant was sitting on my chest — no migraine this time, which was a huge relief. I knew to push on the right side of my groin when getting up out of bed to go to the bathroom to prevent another haemorrhage.

I couldn't sleep because of the pain in my chest. I got up at 3 am, and it hurt to move. I went to the bathroom. On returning to my bed to lie down, I screamed in pain with what felt like knives in my back. I rang the buzzer for the nurse to tell her, and she brought me Panadol for the 'pain'. I knew she thought I was just whinging and being soft.

I have a high pain threshold. When you live with chronic pain day in and day out, your pain threshold increases. Many people do not take that into account. I was sitting on about a 7 out of 10 for me on the pain scale. I dozed on and off for a few hours.

At 5 am, I thought I had to go to the bathroom again and pulled myself out of bed with the aid of the triangle handle above the bed to pull myself up. The pain in my chest was intense; it didn't feel anything like this after the previous two surgeries.

After going to the bathroom, I climbed carefully back into bed, not wanting to cause the wound to haemorrhage. I was struggling to take a deep breath because of the pain in my chest. I went to lie back down and let out a huge scream from the pain. Out of 10, I was experiencing 10+. The nurse came in and asked me a series of questions:

Where was the pain?
In a score out of 10, with 10 being the worst, how bad is the pain?

My response was: in my chest, and right through to my back, and my pain was 1000!

She left the room after explaining she would get me pain relief and call the doctor. She soon turned with Panadol and stated the doctor wouldn't be very long. I couldn't lie down at all; the pain was too intense. The nurse brought in more pillows to put on my lap for me to hunch over, sitting up, to try to give me some relief. It didn't work.

Not long after, the doctor came in and examined me, and ordered morphine. They asked me if I wanted anyone to be called to let them know what was going on. At the time, I was living with M10 and I asked them to call him. He came into the hospital shortly afterwards and was quite shocked by what he saw.

The morphine hadn't hit the sides of the pain. It was getting worse. The doctor came in and said I had acute pericarditis. This is inflammation of the pericardium, the thin, double-layered membrane around my heart. I had developed a bacterial infection from the surgery.

M10 phoned my family and told them to come in. I was in a bad way. I was so scared I was dying. I didn't want to die! I was so scared for my family, particularly my kids. I was given three lots of morphine to control the pain, propped up on four pillows and started on IV antibiotics.

I will never forget the look of terror on my family's faces when they came to visit me. They, too, thought I was dying. I fought to stay above the earth. I hardened the fuck up… I wasn't going down without a good fight.

A week later, I was discharged from the hospital and switched to oral antibiotics with pain relief.

I had trouble breathing and also eating as the food went down my oesophagus past my heart. I learnt things about my body I had never known.

It took a very long seven weeks to recover from the pain and return to my normal. It's an experience that I'll never forget. Frightening doesn't even come close. I was terrified I was going to die. Life moments such as these change you forever. I came away knowing how precious our time on this planet is.

Nowadays, I occasionally get a little flutter in my heart that lasts no more than a few seconds. The fear stops me in my tracks. Then I resume what I was doing and don't dwell on what has happened. I harden the fuck up and get on with things.

2016 MS Ambassador

2017 Painting my new studio floor Barwarre Road Marshall Victoria

CHAPTER 25

The C Word

February 2016

I had been looking for about six months for a house to buy. I wanted a forever home. One where I would never have to worry about renting again. One where I could have my own art studio. Plenty of rooms for my children and their children to stay. I wanted what my parents never had; their own homes. I had owned homes in the past, but this one would be different. This one would be all mine. I took my time in purchasing it. I found it in Marshall. It was almost perfect. I say almost because it had tenants in it. I would have to wait until their lease expired. It was going to be a very long 6-month wait.

I had just gotten over my third heart surgery and was back in full swing, weight training five days a week. I was booked to compete in Hobart, Tasmania, for the Australian Masters Olympic Weightlifting Championships, as well as the Oceania Masters Championships and Pacific Rim Masters Championships. It was an exciting time.

May 2016

My hands started to turn purple, particularly my left hand. I didn't think too much about it, only that it was some strange new thing that my body was doing.

June 2016

I flew to Hobart by myself with the intention of staying for a few days after the competition to explore the island. I stayed in a hotel that was over 100 years old, and my room was in the attic. Not at all like the pictures in the pretty brochure. There was a tiny, narrow stair that led vertically up. I looked at it and wondered how I would ever get my overpacked suitcase up it! Those who know me will tell you I never pack light when I travel.

The room had a little oil bar heater, and no insulation in the roof. My breath caused clouds. I slept in my flannelette pyjamas with my socks, beanie and gloves on with my long puffer jacket over the top, and I was still freezing. I can't regulate my body temperature, and on a good day my temperature is 35.5 degrees!

My left hand was extremely cold and a darker purple during the night, and felt very painful while my normal colour came back into it when I got it warm. Lifting in a Lycra weightlifting suit in a huge hall was excruciatingly painful. My body ached everywhere.

Touching the cold metal bar didn't help with my hand strength at all. I managed to win Gold for my age and body weight in the Australian Masters Olympic weightlifting competition, and I secured second place in the Oceania Masters Olympic weightlifting championships and the Pacific Rim Masters Olympic weightlifting championships. It wasn't very hard to do as there were only two of us in the latter divisions and I was the only Australian Masters lifter there for my age and bodyweight. As my coach used to say, I was the best there on the day. I was the only one there on the day! Where was everyone else? Where were all the able-bodied competitors for my age? Definitely not competing in freezing Hobart in winter.

I stayed in Tasmania for the next three days, exploring Hobart, the Huon Valley, and Port Arthur. It was a struggle with my body failing me. I had trouble walking. My feet and hands were in agony. But I did it, and I was very proud of myself for being there and not letting the fact that I was alone stop me.

That trip wasn't just a holiday. It was proof to myself that I could still do hard things, even with a broken body and no one beside me. I had to dig deep and find my moxie, because there was no comfort zone to fall back into. It was just me and the island.

I forced myself to harden the fuck up, and I'm glad I did, because I had a great time exploring Tasmania. That was the first trip I ever did solo. I've since been on many trips by myself, but that one changed something in me. It showed me that fear, pain, and loneliness don't get the final say; I do.

One day, I will return there.

If I wait for people to join me on trips and holidays, I would never go anywhere. I've become very used to my own company. At least I can do what I want to do, when I want to do it.

I took photos of my hands and feet to show my doctor on my return to the mainland. I made an appointment with my GP, as I knew something wasn't right. I went to see her a week later and showed her what was happening, explaining the situation. Her reply to me was, "Don't worry about it. Come back and see me in four months if it is still happening." I was dumbfounded by this response. I wanted to know what was causing it. Was it the disease-modifying therapy (DMT) drugs I was on for the MS, or was it something else?

A week later, I was sitting in my counsellor's room telling her about my hands and showing her the photos. She asked me if I was happy with my doctor's response. I replied that I wasn't. She then suggested that I go and find a second opinion. It was funny. I'd never thought about that. You put your life in the hands of someone with a medical degree, hoping that they have all the answers when, in fact, a lot don't.

I rang around and found a new medical clinic to attend. There was a wait list of about 10 days. In the meantime, I had my six-monthly appointment with my neurologist. I showed him the photos and explained what was happening. I asked him if it was the new DMT that I've been on for about 12 months. Was it a side-effect? He was pretty certain it wasn't, and ordered a series of blood tests. He mentioned that he thought it was a condition called livedo reticularis.

So, of course, I went home and googled what that was. It is the clotting of the small blood vessels under the surface of the skin that can be caused by three things: rheumatoid arthritis, lupus or lymphoma. My mind started racing to the darkest places.

I felt so alone and scared. One really shouldn't use doctor Google.

July 2016

I received a phone call from my neurologist's office that he wanted to see me ASAP. Within a couple of days, I was walking through the doors to his clinic. My neurologist was away for three months on a research trip to the UK, and I had to see one of his colleagues. He explained to me that my bloods were not good and that I would need to be referred to a rheumatologist. He suggested I go back to my GP and get all the referrals done from there. You see, a referral from one specialist to another only lasts three months, but from a GP to a specialist lasts 12 months. I went back to my new GP and he wrote out referrals to a dermatologist and also a haematologist.

I walked out of those appointments numb. What was happening? I wanted answers, and I wanted them now!

August 2016

I finally got the keys to the new house I bought! I was over the moon. The same day, I took myself to the rheumatologist in Geelong. He examined me and looked at the photos I had taken of my hands and feet. He explained that he didn't think that it was anything connective tissue-related, so he ruled out rheumatoid arthritis and lupus and could no longer help me.

He suggested that I see a dermatologist to confirm that it was indeed livedo reticularis. I explained that I did have an appointment booked in a couple of weeks' time with a dermatologist after my new GP had written me the referral. There are three things that can cause livedo reticularis and he just ruled out two possible causes. Did he just suggest I had cancer? The day I should have been the happiest, with the keys to my new house, I was dealing with a potential cancer diagnosis. Did I mention the keys to my own new house?! My father had advised me to not buy a house but to rent forever. I chose to ignore that advice and went ahead and bought security over my head. Something I had never had before.

I felt like I was on autopilot, a ping-pong ball going from one specialist to the next without any answers, just more questions. I was trying not to let it affect me mentally. Easier said than done. I kept up my regular fortnightly counselling sessions, sometimes even going in weekly. I was a mess. It's the uncertainty of not knowing what's wrong with your body when you know there is definitely something wrong. Waiting for the answers is always the hard part. It always happens a lot faster on TV in those medical shows than it does in real life.

I am much better mentally when I know what's wrong. I can then formulate a plan of attack for the issue. When you have to wait for those answers, it is frustrating. I am not, nor have I ever been, a patient person.

13th September 2016

My dermatologist appointment came around. I went in to have the livedo reticularis confirmed by having a biopsy. I stripped down to my underwear and lay on the examination bed. The dermatologist took one look at my hands and my feet and said that she didn't need to do a biopsy; I definitely had livedo reticularis. She then asked how long it had been since I'd had a skin check done. I replied that my former GP had done one a couple of years earlier. She then said that as I was there with my gear off, I might as well have a mole map done. I figured it wasn't going to cost me any extra, so I agreed. My mind was racing and I wasn't really paying attention to what she was saying or doing.

There were two spots on my face that I had been concerned about. Just brown marks that appeared to be growing. She looked all over my body and kept coming back to a little mole no more than 3 mm in size on my leg. Taking lots of photos of it and then examining it on the computer. The next thing I knew, she told me to sit up, and she was standing there with a bottle of liquid nitrogen. She informed me that she was going to burn the two off my face right away. I was shocked. I blurted out, "What, right now?" I'd had in my mind that I would have to come in for a second appointment. You see, when she confirmed that it was livedo reticularis, I started to freak out that she just confirmed that I had cancer.

Now she wanted to burn things off my face. I had a 40th birthday party to go to the following weekend and was worried I'd be scabby for it. Yes, I'm a very vain person! My looks are the one last thing I can control with my body.

She put the dry ice on my face, and it stung. She said that she wasn't happy with the little mole on my leg and that she'd like to do a biopsy. I explained that local anaesthetic never works well on me. She didn't listen. She proceeded to cut a small hole in my leg. The dermatologist then explained that it could take up to 11 days for the results to come back, and not to worry about it, so I didn't. I was more worried that she had just confirmed that I had lymphoma. I went out to my car and did a live stream on Facebook, explaining to people to have skin checks done.

Less than 24 hours later, I was walking through a shopping centre when my phone rang. I didn't recognise the number. I answered it, and the woman on the other end of the phone explained that she was a nurse from the dermatologist's office. My heart sank. Why was she calling me? The results of my biopsy were in, and she told me I had melanoma. My reply was "No, I don't. I have lymphoma." She said, "No, sorry, you have melanoma. You're going to have to come in next week and have the rest cut out and contained." I was in shock. Was that why I was going purple? Had they mixed it up? I made an appointment for the following week to have the cancer removed.

I straightaway rang my GP and got an appointment that afternoon to see him. I wanted answers. I asked him if the melanoma was the reason why I was going purple. His reply was "No Justine, that's a separate issue." I blurted out, "What the actual fuck! What do you mean it's a separate issue?" He then explained that the melanoma was due to my weakened immune system from the MS. This disease just kept throwing me more curveballs. Talk about hardening the fuck up!

It was a very long week. I kept playing over in my head that I had cancer. How was this happening? Didn't I have enough to deal with? How much could one person go through? I didn't have the answers. No one had the answers.

A week later, I took myself to the dermatologist. The mole was on my right shin. Over the years, I've had lots of moles taken off my body, particularly my arms and my back, but I never really paid much attention to my legs. As a teenage girl, I would love covering my legs in baby oil to tan. Now looking back, I know it was not the smartest move. I lay in tanning beds, wanting that golden tan, and many times I was burnt to a crisp.

Now I was paying the price for all the damage I had chosen to inflict on myself. It was a long week's wait. Did I mention that nothing happens as fast as you see in those TV shows?

6th October 2016

My dermatologist was still away at a conference, and so I had her offsider. He had no bedside manner; he was a grumpy old man with a scalpel in his hand. I explained to him that anaesthetic doesn't work properly on me. He let out a huff and continued to cut my leg. Halfway through, I yelled. The pain was intense. I could feel him cutting my leg. He looked at me and asked if I could feel it. I remember thinking, 'No shit, Sherlock!' I did try to tell him before he started that he would need to give me a double dose. He paused the operation, topped up the local anaesthetic, waited five minutes, then proceeded to finish the procedure.

I remember looking at the specimen jar with a chunk of my flesh floating in it. Two things crossed my mind. 'Is that what cancer looks like?', and 'Fuck I hope they got it all.' I ended up with a scar that is 10cm long. He cut 2 cm deep into my leg to get clear margins, which in turn left a huge dint in my shin. I now had to wait to see if he had taken clear margins. It was a nervous wait. In the meantime, my purple hands and feet were now spreading. This is not what I needed, with still no answers and playing the waiting game for the haematologist appointment.

A few days later, the phone rang and I was told all the margins were clear. I cried with relief. A week later, I had to go in and have the seven stitches taken out. The scar has finally faded, but it's still a reminder to practice sun safety.

Ten days after the stitches were taken out, I walked into my first appointment at Andrew Love Cancer Centre. To say I was scared was an understatement. I had no idea what was ahead of me. I met with my haematologist. She was sent a referral with all my history in it. I commented that it wouldn't include that I had melanoma. She was shocked and asked, "When did you have that?" I replied with, "Last week!" I then showed her my leg. It was a different ice breaker to say the least. She then explained that they would need to do more blood tests to start with, and that I would need, at some stage, to do a bone marrow biopsy. That is a procedure where they drill a hole into the back of your pelvis with a device that is about as thick as your little finger. They then break 1cm of the bone off and also take samples of bone marrow. This was something I was not at all looking forward to.

My concern with all these tests was the timing. You see, I was booked for an overseas trip to Bali for my girlfriend's 50th birthday. I had so wanted to go on a holiday, to lie by a pool and drink cocktails. I'd never been on a holiday, ever. Strange,

I know, but any time I'd been away had always involved visiting family or competing in a sport. Now this trip was in jeopardy. She assured me that I would still be able to go.

I had the blood tests; they took 17 vials of blood out of me! I had to lie down for 10 minutes afterwards; they were worried I would pass out. This was followed by more blood tests the following week and a follow-up appointment with my haematologist. She was concerned by the results and said I would have to have the bone marrow biopsy when I got back from Bali. More blood tests followed that appointment. I was on weekly visits to the cancer centre. The results from the last test came back, and my blood levels were getting worse. My haematologist told me that they couldn't wait for me to get back from Bali to do the bone marrow biopsy, and that it would have to be done before I left. I expressed concern that I wasn't going to be able to go. She again assured me that I would be going on my trip.

It took what seemed like forever for the hospital to call to arrange the test; they also arranged for a PET scan and a CAT scan on the same day. I got a phone call to say it would be on Thursday, 3rd November at 9 am. That left less than 48 hours before take off. Again, I was assured I would be ok to fly. My Aunty Lynny came down to take me. The first one was the bone marrow biopsy, which was done downstairs at Andrew Love Cancer Centre. Shit just got real.

I was given the green whistle to suck on while they performed the procedure. Remember how I said that anaesthetic doesn't work properly on me? Well, you guessed it. The green whistle did very little to alleviate the pain of the procedure. I screamed repeatedly. The technician got what he needed with the broken bone sliver and the slides of bone marrow. I did take a photo afterwards of the slides and bone. Yes, I'm one of those people, oh and I also have a photo of the chunk they took from my leg!

Next was a positron emission tomography (PET) scan, which is an imaging test that uses radioactive material to diagnose, monitor and treat a variety of conditions and diseases, including cancers, tumours and other disorders. I don't remember too much about it, only having to lie still on a cold slab as they pumped radioactive crap into my veins, while the pain in my pelvis from the biopsy was excruciating. Last was the CT scan, which is a computed tomography scan. It uses a series of X-rays and a computer to create detailed images of your bones and soft tissues. The procedure itself didn't hurt; it was just painful again lying flat on my back for the duration of it.

The tests consumed the whole morning and into the afternoon. My aunt took me home. I struggled to sit in the car and felt like I needed to vomit from the pain. I took strong painkillers when I got home and lay on my left side in bed, unable to roll over. The next day, my girlfriend, who I was going to Bali with, came to visit and see how I was. I was struggling to move, and sitting was painful. More than I thought it would be. I sat crying at the kitchen table, wondering how the hell I would be able to sit on the plane the next day. Realising at the moment just how unwell I actually was. My Aunty Lynny laid down the law and said I wasn't to go to a third-world country with an open hole straight to my bones and that I would end up dead if I did. She was, of course, right. I had the hard conversation with my girlfriend that I wouldn't be going to Bali the next day after all. I was gutted. I was angry with the world. Why me? Why not me? What makes me so different as to think I would be invincible, and immune to getting a life-threatening, incurable disease?

My friend went to Bali and found someone, within hours of me saying I couldn't go, to replace me. She then posted photos of her holiday on socials and tagged me in every single one of them! Every time I opened up Facebook, I would see another post of the fantastic time they had. To add even more salt into my wounds, my travel insurance company wouldn't give me my money back for my flights or accommodation as they saw it as a pre-existing condition, which was ironic because the doctors hadn't officially diagnosed me yet.

Then things went from bad to worse in the following weeks.

I needed something else to concentrate on. I decided to renovate my house. I had a four-car garage and thought I could split it in half and build a professional art studio. That would mean putting up a wall, knocking one out and putting in a huge window and French doors. At least it gave me something to think about besides my health. I set about finding tradies to come in and do the hard work.

My breathing became worse and so did moving my fingers and toes. I could barely bend them and it hurt when I did. I couldn't hold a paintbrush or a pen. What was going on?

2016 Australian Olympic Weightlifting Masters Championships at Hobart Tasmania - doing a Clean and Jerk

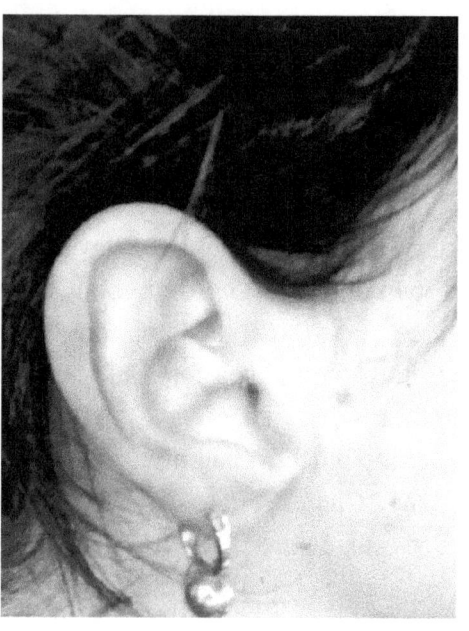

2016 Livedo reticularis in my ears

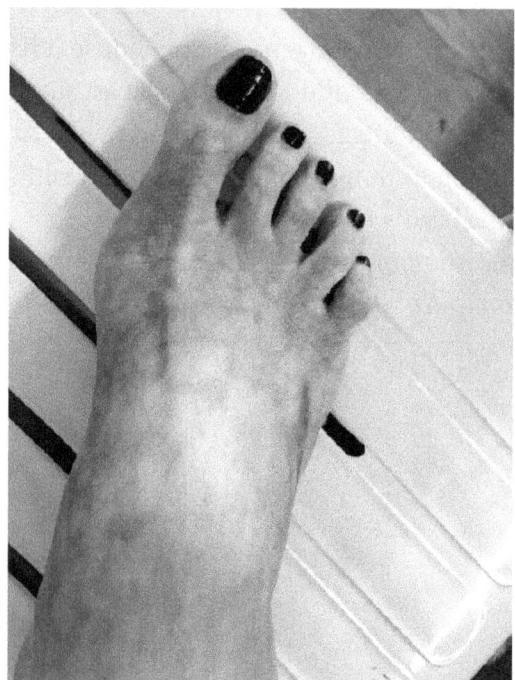

2016 Livedo reticularis in my feet

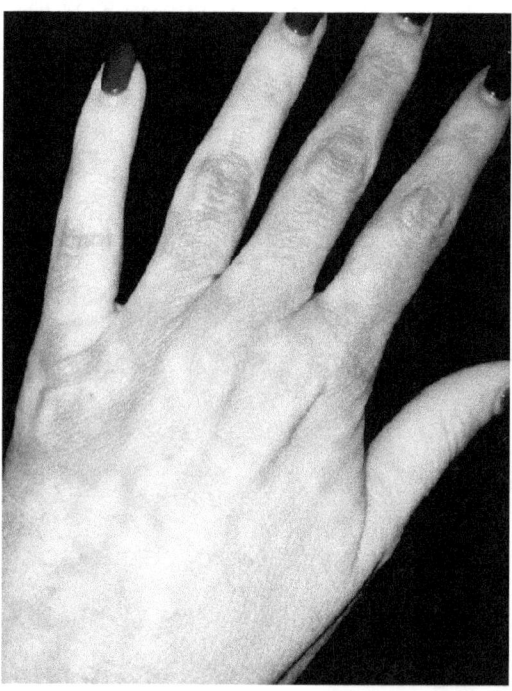

2016 Livedo reticularis in my hands

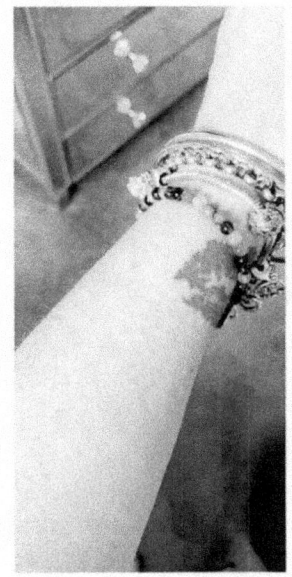
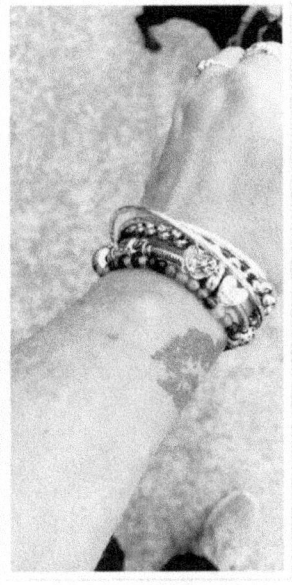

2016 Livedo reticularis in the right picture, left side is normal jpg

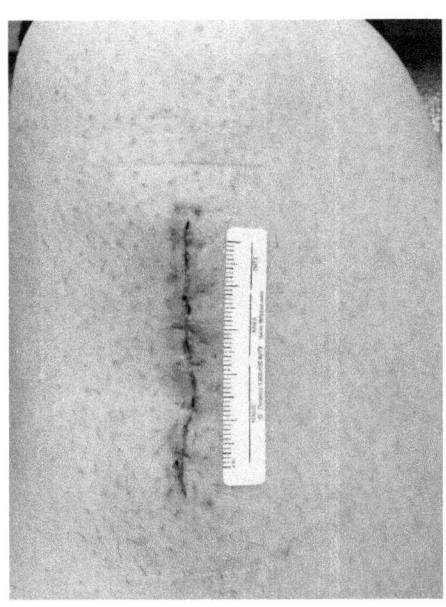

2016 Melanoma removed on right shin

2016 September spots burnt off my face

2017 Standing in the middle of my new art studio with Remmy

CHAPTER 26

Happy New Fucking Year

December 2016

I had developed decreased lung capacity. I couldn't get a full lungful of air. It felt like someone had their hands around my lungs, squeezing them, and I lost the ability to move my fingers and toes properly. Hard lumps were forming in my joints, and I was in a lot of pain. It hurt to breathe, and it hurt to hold a pen and a paintbrush.

How was I going to return to my happy place of painting and drawing if I couldn't hold either implement? I was frustrated and scared. My body wasn't behaving as it should. I never stopped counselling and was going in weekly for debriefing appointments. It really helped. I strongly believe that it's not my children's, family's or friends' responsibility to hear me vent about what's happening with my body and my life. I don't want that kind of relationship with them. They don't know my deep, dark secrets, but my shrink does. I pay her to listen; I pay for a non-biased, non-judgmental conversation. I go in there and have verbal diarrhoea. I let it all out to her in a session, and I walk out feeling much lighter, and emotionally ready to tackle my week ahead.

I've been seeing the same counsellor (shrink) for 12 years. I'm not sure how my mental health would be without paying for those hundreds of sessions. Asking for help is never a sign of weakness but always a sign of strength. And you can't build resilience in your own life without asking for help. It builds moxie.

Asking for help had never come easy to me. I have had to learn this strength over the years as my body has failed me.

It was the week of Christmas 2016 when I was diagnosed with another blood condition called mixed cryoglobulinaemia, also known as IgM. A big word I shouldn't know how to pronounce, let alone spell. Mixed cryoglobulinaemia is a rare disorder caused by abnormal proteins in the blood that precipitate in cold temperatures, leading to systemic vasculitis and symptoms such as skin lesions, joint pain, kidney damage, and neuropathy, often associated with infections, autoimmune diseases, or certain cancers. In other words, my bone marrow was making too many cryoglobulins and was causing inflammation around all my internal organs and joints. It was also what was causing the livedo reticularis. But what was causing the IgM?

Why was this happening to me? What had I done in a past life to deserve such pain and sickness? Not a goddamn thing! That answer made it even harder to deal with. I was angry and wanted to scream at the world one minute, then to crawl into the fetal position and cry the next. I wanted someone to hug me and say it would all be ok and not let go. But I didn't have a partner to stand beside me. I knew I was in this for the most part alone. I would have to harden the fuck up again.

That Christmas was one of the hardest I have ever had to get through. I had similar emotions in 1995, knowing it would be one of the last with mum, and here I was repeating them. The hard reality of death, and wondering how much longer I was going to live for. Was this going to be my last Christmas? What would my children do without me? On New Year's Eve, I was a blubbering mess when the clock struck midnight. I was trying to hold it all together, but emotions and fear crossed with alcohol are never a good mix, and I broke down, thinking I was going to die.

Happy new fucking year to me. When I woke up on New Year's Day, I knew I had to change my mindset, or that it was going to kill me. I had to look at things that made me happy. Spending time with my family and close friends was crucial. I made sure my will was up to date. I wanted everything in order so I didn't have to worry about the mess I would leave my affairs in when the time came. Most people don't get around to having a will because they think they will live forever. I can tell you 100% that none of us will be here forever! As much as I wish that were the case.

Having blood work done every week was draining and painful. I have shitty veins, and the years of MS DMTs have left my veins very damaged and scarred.

January 2017

The waiting game was killing me! They knew I had cancer from the bone marrow biopsy, but they weren't sure what kind. Why does real life not happen like in the movies? Within a few hours, you get sick, then they diagnose your disease, then you have treatment, and then, if it's a happy movie, you go on to live a dream life. Simple! But real life is not like that. There is a lot more waiting.

I had no scheduled face-to-face appointments, but I did have a telehealth one on Thursday 12th January — a phone call from my haematologist. I was so worried about what this call would bring. I was home alone when she called. It was not the news I wanted. Her words still ring in my ears. "I'm sorry, Justine, but I have your results. You have chronic lymphocytic leukaemia (CLL) and small lymphocytic lymphoma (SLL)."

Wait — what? What did she say? Two cancers? Where the fuck did the leukemia come from? She went on to explain that both cancers were in the same cells. How did this happen? How did I end up with three primary cancers, two different blood disorders and MS all at the same time? I stood in front of the bathroom mirror and just looked into my eyes. I looked deep into them and saw my reflection staring back. I thought this is what cancer looks like. Cancer looks like normal people.

I had to wait until Monday to go in and see what would now happen. It was a long 5-day wait. My emotions were all over the place. My haematologist explained that I would have to come off the DMT for my MS as I couldn't be on both at the same time. That would kill me. That's easy to type, but it was not at all easy to just stop the meds and start chemotherapy the next day. Aubagio, a daily pill I was taking, takes two years to come out of your system naturally. I didn't have two years. Every day, my symptoms were getting worse.

My hands, arms, feet, legs, ears, chin and nose all had livedo. It was now happening at a high room temperature of 19 degrees, which meant I spent a lot of the time purple and in pain. I was warned I had to warm up each area as fast as possible so it didn't cause necrosis, and parts of my body to drop off.

I was given a chemical flush, a solution I had to drink three times a day for the next three weeks before chemotherapy could start. It was a vile, salty, thick liquid. I had a housemate, who had been homeless, and I had offered my spare room for her to rent until she got on her feet again. I enjoyed the company. She commented on what she thought the solution looked like. My reply was that it tasted like it, too. I dreaded having to swallow that fluid three times a day and nearly gagged on every glass. I had no choice but to harden the fuck up and do it.

Its purpose was to bind with the DMT and prevent my system from reabsorbing it. Then I had to wait a few more weeks just to be sure it was all out of my system. During this time I kept getting tagged in posts of an artist overseas who was creating the most amazing work by finger painting. As I couldn't hold a paintbrush or pencil, I wondered if I'd be able to do it.

I tried, and created a frog. I sold it a few months later for $400. That made me very happy. I could still go to my happy place and create art. I wanted to feel normal and not sick and dying.

March 2017

On the 22nd, I woke up from a restless night's sleep. I felt drained for the day even before it began. My mind was running at a million miles an hour. Would I lose my hair? When I was told I would be on chemo, my thoughts instantly went to being thin. Chemo patients become skinny. I was thinking that finally, I would be thin — choosing to ignore that I was about to start on one of the world's most dangerous drugs and could possibly die.

My cousin Myalie and my daughter Ally met me at my house, and we drove to the cancer centre together at 8.30 am. I had very little sleep the previous night. So many thoughts were running through my head. The fear of the unknown. Was this going to work? Was I going to die? How much time did I have left? What if this didn't work? How would my family cope with all of this? Why me? Why not me?

We were very quiet for the 15-minute car trip to the Andrew Love Cancer Centre. Parking is a bitch at the hospital, or the lack thereof. We made sure we got there in plenty of time. We were directed to wait in the wellness lounge. What a name to call a waiting room at a cancer centre! We entered to find the smell of cookies baking in the community kitchen. There were separate waiting room pods, or you could choose to wait on lounges and play games or jigsaw puzzles. Not your typical waiting room. Plenty of chatter, and volunteers asking if we wanted a cup of tea. I was far too nervous to drink or eat anything. The place was busy but also had a strange, calming, homely atmosphere.

After about an hour's wait, we were taken through to the day ward where the chemotherapy is administered. There was a lot of paperwork to fill in, and then the process started. As per usual, it was hard to find my vein. I was put on a combination: a chemotherapy drug called Bendamustine, which is derived from the mustard gas of World War 1, and an immunosuppressant called Rituximab. I was to have it over a couple of days every four weeks. The Bendamustine I had to be on for six months, and the Rituximab for 18 months. My first dose didn't go as planned. There are a lot of side effects that come with these drugs. The first dose took over 8 hours to administer. They start the drip at a slow flow rate and then increase the speed each hour. There were two of us on the ward who started the same treatment within 10 minutes of each other. The elderly gentleman sitting next to me had an allergic reaction to our treatment; alarm bells went off, and the doctor and nurses rushed to his aid.

They increased the speed of my drip, and I started to get itchy ears, and my hearing went funny, and so did my vision. I didn't feel very good. My blood pressure dropped. The nurse came to check on me and asked me how I was feeling, and I explained my concerns. The next thing we knew, panic buttons were hit. I, too, then had a team of medical practitioners around me. The look of fear on Ally and Myalie's faces was evident.

It occurred to me at that moment that my cancer journey was very hard on them both. It was hard for me, but in my mind, I was being proactive by going to my appointments, starting treatment and trying to stay alive! For my family that had to sit helplessly on the sidelines, it must have been heartbreaking and frustrating to not be able to do anything.

They stopped my infusion, and I had to wait for an hour before it could be started again. It was a very long wait as I watched the minutes on the clock. We made idle chat amongst the three of us as we all watched this new world in front of our eyes. The time came to restart it, and they increased the dosage at a much slower speed this time around. At 6 pm that evening, we could go home, only to repeat it all the next day.

Day two, and I felt like it was déjà vu. Repeating the nightmare that had become my life. Into the wellness lounge, the smell of baked goods, the long wait time and into the ward for the nurses to try to find my elusive veins. It was a traumatic experience. Ally couldn't stand to watch me being jabbed with a needle. After the first day, I went by myself. The day ward was one big room that had 12 day chairs in it. Every chair always had a body in it. Men and women, all adults and all different ages. There was no privacy. The ward was busy. Many patients had lost their hair, they had dark circles under their eyes. Their skin was very pale, and some were shades of yellow. The nurses were chatty and friendly, and there were the volunteer tea ladies who came around and asked if you wanted a cup of tea or something to eat. Ironic considering that most people lose their appetite on chemo.

Day three, repeat. It was going to be a long day. I was tired and emotional. The treatment's side effects had started, and they gave me strong anti-nausea medication. Bloods were taken every day. Each day, they had to put a new cannula in my arm. It was black and blue with bruises, and traumatic for both the nurses and for me, trying to locate the veins.

My haematologist popped into the ward to discuss putting a Hickman line in my chest. It was a line that goes directly into the heart to administer the chemotherapy, and stays there for up to 12 months. I agreed. I was booked in two days later, on the 24th at 9 am. It was a day-stay surgery. I was awake. I lay on my left side. They administered a local anaesthetic. I started to panic, knowing it wouldn't fully work. The nurse laid a blue sheet over my head and neck with a square hole cut into it for an opening to access the incision site. The doctor made two incisions, one at the base of my neck above my collarbone and the other just above my right breast. They fed a long tube through the holes into my heart. I screamed and cried simultaneously. It was an extremely painful procedure. I felt even more nauseous. I wanted them to stop. I wanted everything to stop. Let me off this whirlwind ride that I didn't ask to be on.

I had a long 25 cm tube sticking out of my chest and stitches holding it in place. I was in shock. Shit just got real. I couldn't hide it, it was very prominent with two leads coming off the one into my chest. I knew it would make the following months of treatment a lot easier. I had to have it flushed with special medication to stop clots from forming in it, and I had to be so careful not to get an infection in it. A week later, the stitches were removed. Every week I had to go into Andrew Love and have the line flushed so it wouldn't get a clot. Every week I had to get blood drawn. If I went to pathology to have them done, they couldn't use my Hickman line.

It was a long month spent lying on the lounge watching TV, vomiting and endless blood tests. Nausea became my constant companion.

Before I knew it, it was time for month two, starting on 3rd April. Repeated but a little easier. Through my Hickline line, they could take my blood, which was a lot easier, and then start my treatment. The two days that month were much faster, shorter days, and passed without incident. However, I woke up on the 6th covered in an itchy rash. My face was hot and flushed. I also had another bubbly rash on my whole body that was red and purple. On top of the livedo reticularis rash that I still had. I presented to the emergency department, very worried. I was transferred back to Andrew Love, and it was determined after a biopsy that the extra rashes were a combination of the treatment having raised my cryoglobulins, causing the IGM to increase and also an allergic reaction to the Bendamustine. The only solution was to put me on steroids to reduce the inflammation and control both. If something were to go wrong, it always would with me.

Month three meant another bone marrow biopsy. This time, on the left side of my pelvis. They decided not to use the green whistle but to instead give me a sedative through my Hickman line in a room off the day ward. I was hoping it would be pain-free and a quick procedure. I was so wrong on both accounts.

The medication they used had little effect, and on the third attempt to break off the 1cm of bone and after two vials of medication being administered, they called it a failure. I was traumatised. They did get enough bone marrow to determine that the combined treatment I was being given was working. That was a huge relief. In Australia, they did cancer treatment differently to other parts of the world. In a lot of countries, they test all the treatment options first in a laboratory to find the one that works best; here they put you on a treatment plan they hope will work, and then you wait three months. They repeat with a bone marrow biopsy and then see if it's working. The nurse apologised to me the next time I went back to the ward for what had happened. It turns out she too was traumatised from it. I apologised for screaming so loud and nearly breaking her hand when I was holding it.

I was having trouble with my housemate. She was still going out to the pub on weekends and was bringing random men home. Besides hearing her having sex with them, having strangers in my home was a serious health risk for me in my condition. My immune system was severely compromised. The chemotherapy was doing its job in wiping out my bad cells, but also my good cells. I had no immune system to fight any infections. I had to be so careful. I had to ask her to move out.

Now I was totally alone in the house, with just me and my thoughts. Oh, and my bucket! For a few days in the third week of the cycle, my Aunty Lynny would drive from Woodend and pick me up to spend a few days with her and my Uncle Gra. We would go on a day trip to a new town. We started off trying to do the alphabet, but skipped a few letters. We visited Alexandria, Bendigo, Castlemaine, Daylesford, Eildon, Heathcote, Inglewood, Kyneton, then skipped to Nagambi, Trentham and Yea.

They felt helpless, as did most of my family. This was one way they could do something for me. It took my mind off things, I got home cooked meals and a lot of love. Most of my friends stopped visiting, and that hurt. I was allowed out one night a month with my friends, as long as my bloods were ok. It was normally the last Saturday night before I was due back at the cancer centre on the Monday for the next round.

I started gaining weight, even with the nausea. Steroids are evil, but it came down to the lesser of two evils. Each month, a bit more. Kilo after kilo. My mental health was suffering. By the time I went into remission, I had put on 20 kgs. The only time I thought I would be thin, I ended up huge! But not dying was the priority. I would deal with losing the weight when I knew I wasn't going to die. My hair started to fall out and I lost about a third of it. I had it cut off to my shoulders. It grew back differently.

I had to have blood tests done twice a week, then they were cut back to once a week. It was during one of these routine tests that they discovered my neutrophil levels were 0.01%. My hematologist decided to repeat the bloods to just make sure. She told me to isolate myself from everyone, just in case it was correct. Having low levels of white blood cells is extremely dangerous. It means you have zero protection from any infections.

The following day, Ally called me. She sounded terrible and asked me to organise a doctor's appointment for her. I did, and I went and picked her up without thinking twice, and we drove the 20 minutes to her doctor's. Not really thinking about myself, only about how sick she was. As us mums do.

It turned out that she had pneumonia and tonsillitis. On our way back to her house, my phone rang, and it was my doctor who said that my levels were correct and that I had no protection at all from any infections. She told me I needed to go straight to the hospital. I hung up the phone and looked at Ally and calmly said, "Open your window, Bub." I opened all the other windows in the car as we drove. I dropped Ally off at her house and headed straight to Andrew Love Cancer Centre.

I was taken straight through to the day ward. I was given a Filgrastim injection straight into my stomach. It was then explained to me that my bone marrow over the course of the next week would make millions and millions of white blood cells. I was to remain isolated from everyone, and oh, by the way, it's going to be painful.

I drove home with all kinds of terrible thoughts in my head. How much more could my body handle? Over the course of the next week, I could barely get out of bed. Despite their warnings, I was wholly unprepared for the pain that followed. Every bone in my body was on fire; the pain was excruciating. But I knew that this pain meant that my bones were producing white blood cells. It sucked living alone. No one came to see if I was ok, and I didn't ask for help because I really didn't know what I needed. I was a mess physically and mentally.

Repeat bloods a week later, and my levels had risen. I've never been back to that low level. It took another four years to return to near-normal levels. I am still leukopenic, which is a type of white blood cell deficiency. I receive other people's antibodies — called Hygenga, it's a weekly infusion that I have learnt to do myself since March 2020, when COVID-19 started, and I could no longer go into the hospital for IVIG infusions. These are the same blood products that the Olympian Michael Klim is on. It gives me some protection so I can be around people and germs. I still need to be careful if anyone is sick, as my immune system is now compromised from the MS, cancers and all the treatments I have been given to keep me alive.

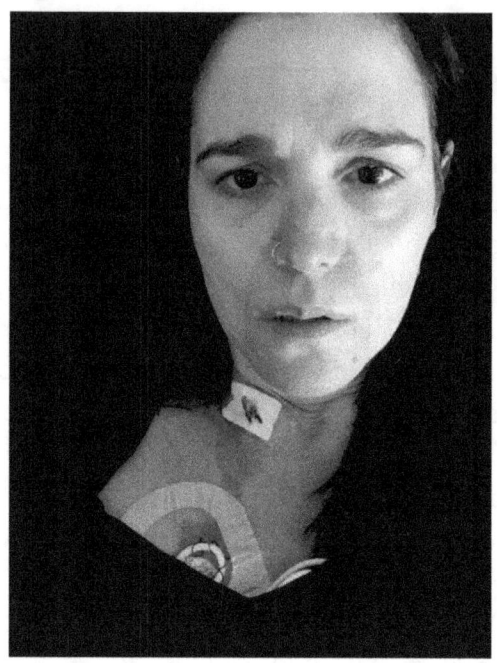

2016 Straight after having the Hickman line put in

2017 Article in Barwon Health's Magazine

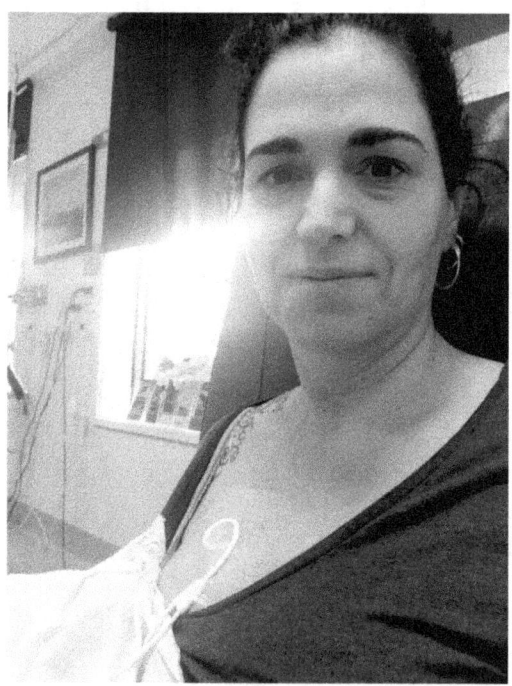

2017 Feeling sick at Andrew Love Cancer Centre

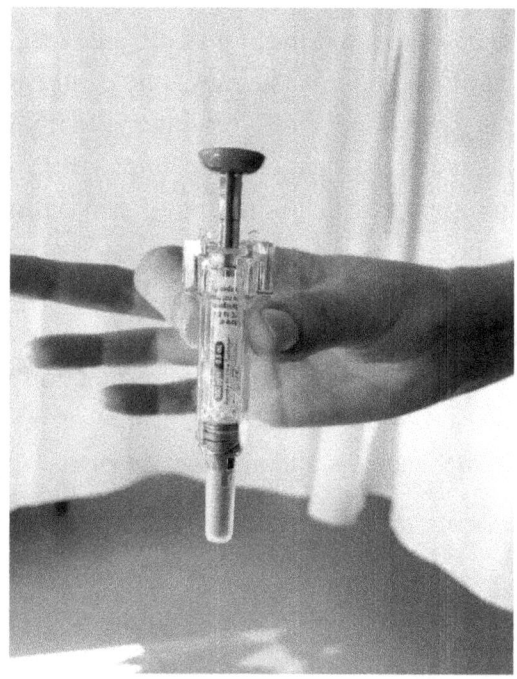

2017 Filgrastim injection straight into my stomach to make white blood cells

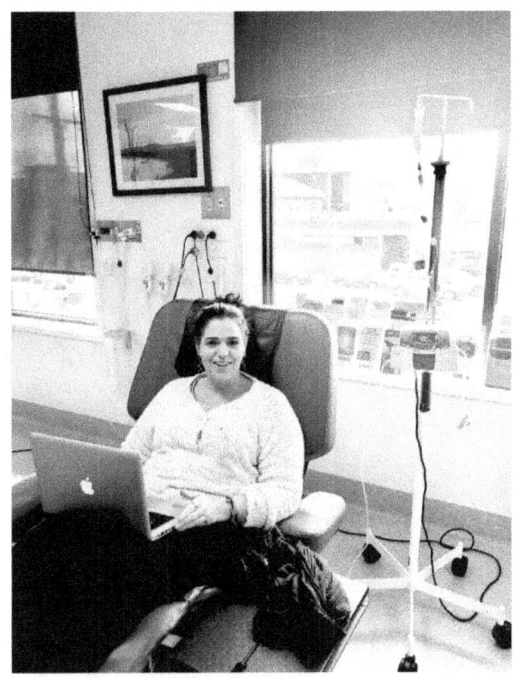
2017 Having chemotherapy and working

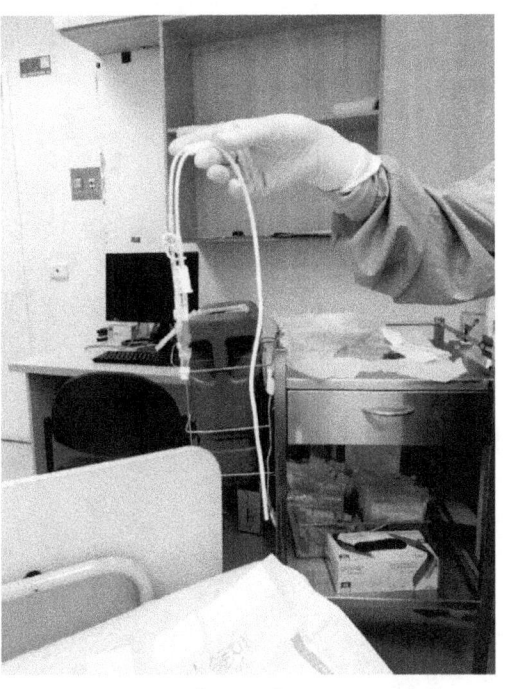
2017 Hickman line removed

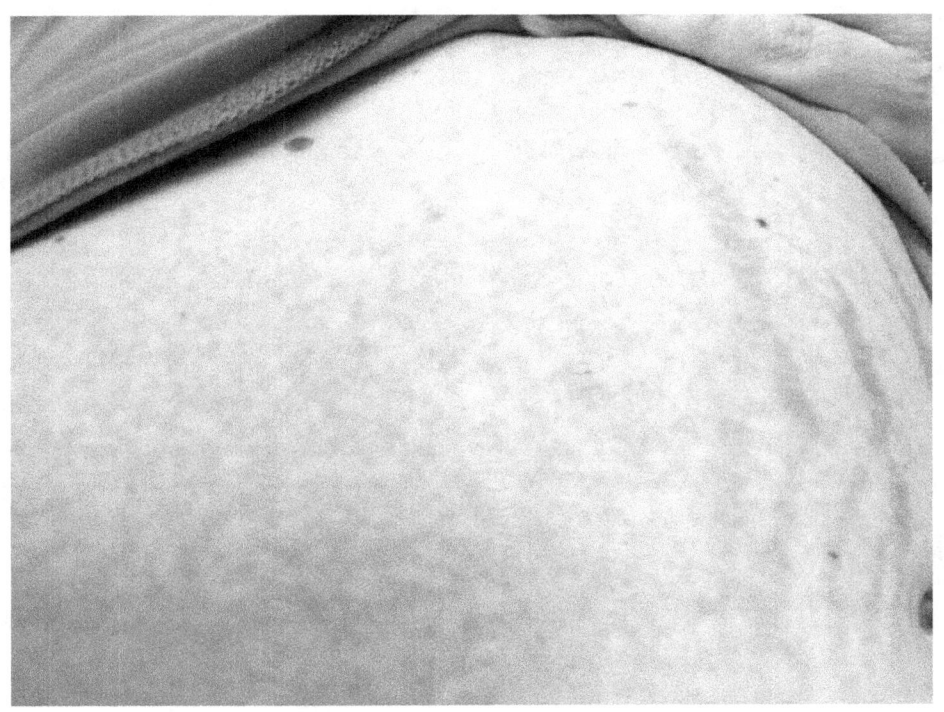
2017 Livedo reticularis and mixed cryoglobulinemia

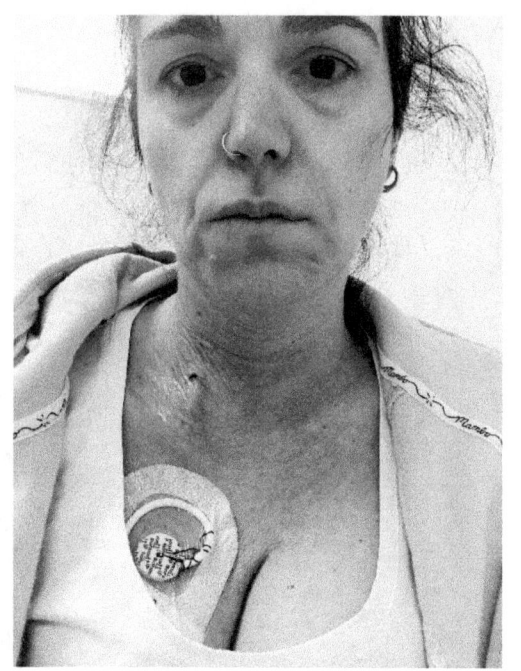

2017 Reaction to first round of chemotherapy

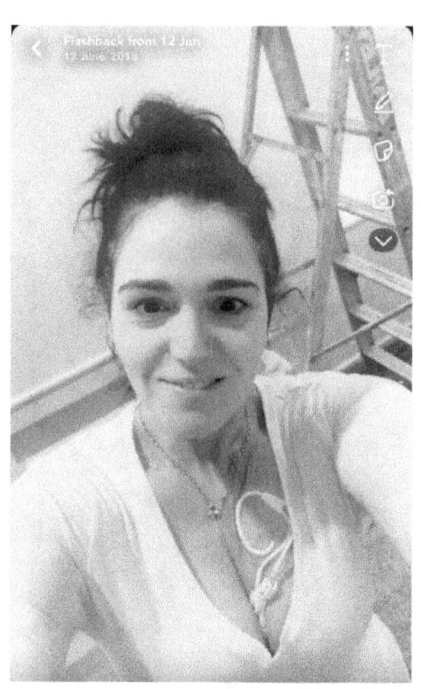

2017 Renovating during chemotherapy

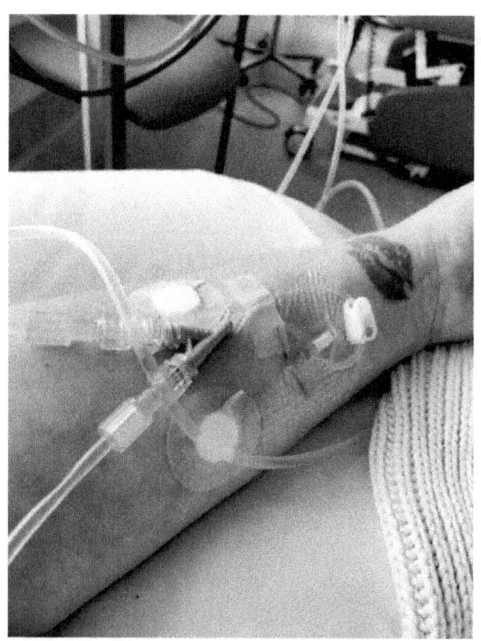

2018 IVIG infusion

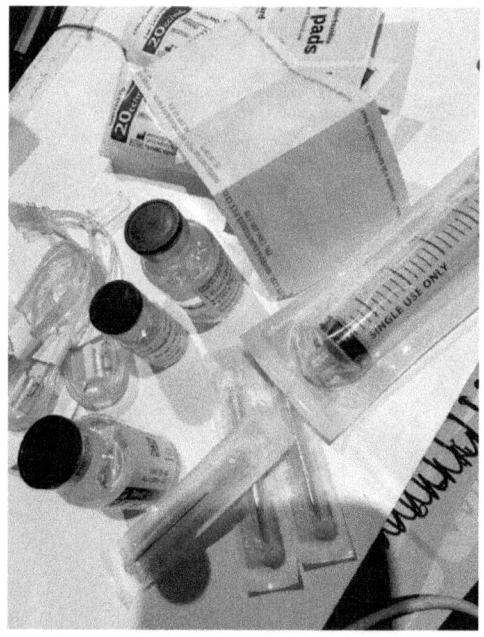

2020 Weekly SCIG therapy

CHAPTER 27

VAD

In early August 2017, I picked up a bug — a chest infection that knocked the shit out of me. I was told that if my temperature were to rise above 38, I was to present to the cancer day ward or, after hours, to the emergency department. My temperature was 40! I did the right thing and caught a taxi to the day ward. It was the same day that M10 moved to Tasmania. I remember it vividly as I had to say goodbye to him as I got in the taxi. Not the farewell we had planned. He was crying, as was I.

The hospital was at capacity, and they had no beds. I was given some antibiotics and sent home. I climbed into bed feeling very sorry for myself, so alone and so scared. I went to sleep that night, not knowing if I would wake up the next morning, or how many days it would be before someone found me. I was like that for five days. Alone and scared. I didn't eat and couldn't get any further than my bathroom. This was not how I wanted to live my life. At that point, I had no quality of life at all.

While lying in bed, I was scrolling through Facebook, and on the MS Australia Facebook page, I saw a post about voluntary assisted dying (VAD); they were looking for people with MS who were in favour of it. I sent them a message.

I had lost so much strength lying in bed for a week. I'd had my last round of chemotherapy, but I had another 12 months of Rituximab ahead of me. My haematologist decided to take out the Hickman line. The risk of getting an infection directly to the heart outweighed the risk of trying to find a vein.

I presented myself at the cancer day ward, and I was taken into a treatment room. I lay down on the examination bed, and with no pain relief, the nurse wrapped the end of the Hickman line around her hand, told me to take a deep breath, and she reefed the line out of my chest in one movement. I screamed in pain as my blood showered up the curtain and wall behind me.

It was brutal and barbaric. So much medical trauma in my life.

Unfortunately, in the process of doing this, a plastic cuff broke off inside my chest. This can sometimes happen, and of course, it happened to me. I was given the choice to leave it there or to have it removed. I chose the latter; however, I waited for 12 months, until after Zak's wedding, as I didn't want a big scar on my chest for the photos. Yes, I'm vain.

Andrew Denton's Go Gentle Office reached out to me to be interviewed for their website. The interview transcript is still there today. I wanted to tell my story to help others.

Justine Martin's story

It was six years ago when Justine Martin was diagnosed with Multiple Sclerosis, a degenerative illness that left her with crippling pain through her legs and feet. The news turned her life upside down and forced her to confront her own mortality, knowing that her mother had died of complications from the same illness.

"I saw how much she had struggled, and I didn't want to be like that. I didn't want my children to sit there and wait for it to happen."

This year Justine suffered further blows with a diagnosis of small lymphocytic lymphoma and chronic lymphocytic leukaemia. She is currently undergoing chemotherapy.

"I've had some horrific days. Days where I've gone to sleep and thought I wouldn't wake up."

"Until you've experienced acute terminal pain, I don't think you have the right to say someone can't have access to assisted dying."

Diagnosis

When Justine was diagnosed with MS she was forced to quit her job in retail and program management and instead turned to painting. "I couldn't work anymore because of my symptoms. When you can't count money, there's a bit of an issue."

"I joined the art classes more for the company. I was sitting at my home by myself in isolation and that's never a good thing."

Living with pain

Justine says being diagnosed with MS has meant learning to live with pain.

"When I have a shower and water runs down my legs, it's like razor blades slicing through my skin. It's like electricity is going through my whole body, it just shoots out wherever it likes.

"I get to the point that pain is so bad in my feet that I can't put them on the ground. I hold off going to the toilet and then as a result get urinary tract infections.

"There's always pain there, it's just whether it's 1 or 20 on the scale. Nothing really works for the pain. It feels like my body just doesn't like me."

Loss of her mother

Not only has Justine been forced to confront her own death, but she lives with the memory of her mother's death. She was 26 years old with a seven-week old baby when her mother passed away.

"It was a cruel death, and happened over a 24 hour period. She had fluid in her lungs, and my brother and I had to sit there with her. It was traumatic for both of us.

"She had a peg [feeding tube] in her stomach, and a breathing tube. She had no quality of life. She had lost the will to live a long time prior to that because of the MS.

"She often spoke of ending her own life. She just didn't have the means to do it. Her biggest fear was becoming incontinent."

Justine says living with chronic illness has changed the way she thinks about her life.

"When you get a diagnosis of MS, of cancer, of heart disease, it instantly changes who you are overnight. All of a sudden you're confronted with your own mortality.

"Before you're diagnosed with these illnesses you think you're going to live forever. You think you've got all this time.

"But life isn't limitless. Time is the most precious commodity on the planet. We can't buy it, we can only use it once. How you spend that time should be up to you.

"What healthy people don't understand is that, in the blink of the eye, your whole world can change, and it will never be the same as what it was 30 seconds ago.

"I've had that happen several times in the last six years, where the life I knew was no longer. It's gone, instantly gone.

Having a choice

Justine says the way someone's life ends should be up to them.

"Since my mum died I've believed there should be assisted dying. It's extremely important that we have a choice.

"If you want to live your last moments in pain, that's ok. But it should also be that if I want assisted dying, that's ok too, that's my choice.

"It comes down to choice and about wanting to be in control.

"When you have an illness like I do, you lose control. You lose control of what your body wants to do every day.

"To be able to be in control and say – OK, on this day, I've got to a certain point, this is enough, I want to go – it will feel like I have a choice."

Thinking about the future

For now, Justine is confident her cancer will go into remission, but her MS will still need managing.

"There's no guarantee I will stay in remission, or how long my quality of life with MS will last.

"This year has been horrific in terms of facing my own mortality, and potentially heading down the same path as my mum. I've had a lot of time to think about it.

"I want to be able to say goodbye to them, if the time comes, and they can say goodbye to me.

"It would be such a relief to know that if it ever got to that point, that I had the choice to end my life in the way that I wanted to end it, at a time that I chose."

As told by Justine Martin, www.gogentleaustralia.org.au

It was not long after this I had all the major TV stations wanting to interview me. I was on the ABC 7.30 report and across all the news stations and paper media for various interviews. I was interviewed for national and international radio programs. This time about dying and not about a sex party.

October 2017

I was asked to referee the world championships for All-round Weightlifting in Perth. Thinking I was superwoman, I jumped at a chance and I booked a flight. I really wanted to compete; however with no training in 18 months and with a body so full of toxins I was glowing green, I settled for refereeing. I had a great week over there and caught up with 30 friends. It was my first trip back in six years. It made me sad, realising how much my life had changed, and how little control I had over it. If I'd never got MS, oh, how my life would be different. Then I thought, if my mum had never got MS, how mine and Simon's lives would be different.

I can't dwell on what-if and what might have been, but rather deal with the hand that I have been dealt, and make the best out of that situation. Adapting or modifying as I go.

I returned from that trip as an invited guest to witness the VAD bill being presented to the Victorian Parliament.

November 2017

I missed seeing Zak and Amelia. I hadn't seen him in a year. I had a lot of Zak's childhood toys that I felt he should now have at his own place and he had been stationed in the Army at Newcastle. Not really thinking too much about it, and in between treatment days, I drove myself the 11 hour trip to Newcastle. I spent a week there and I drove myself home. The trip home I spent singing to my heart's content. I was happy. I was alive and back 'living'.

I had to get home as I had won a major art award through Actions On Disabilty Within Ethnic Communities (ADEC) and my artwork was being used on the front cover of their publication. I was also the guest speaker. I woke up that morning with a really sore throat and had trouble talking. I drove to Melbourne not feeling very well at all. Over the course of the next three days my throat became worse and I began to sound like Minnie Mouse. Then I woke up and I was back to normal. This happened a few times over the next couple of months

As soon as I overdid anything, my throat would become inflamed again. My trip away to Newcastle put me back on the lounge for a week. I was struggling to walk. My feet were so painful. I cried while walking to bed one night; with each step, my feet felt like electricity was shooting out of them.

I climbed into bed and struggled to take painkillers as my throat was so sore that I couldn't swallow. I barely slept all night. My bed is about 4 metres from the toilet. I woke up and went to walk to the bathroom and realised I couldn't put my feet on the ground without intense pain. I needed to go to the toilet. I screamed when I placed my feet on the ground and held onto the wall for support to get to my bathroom. I looked at my feet and they were spasming. The closest thing I can compare them to would be to imagine both feet cramping at the same time, and your toes sticking out in odd positions, both above and under your feet.

I had to try and get back to my bed. In excruciating pain and again holding onto the wall for support, I managed to flop onto my bed.

I had never felt pain like it. Even the sheets laying on my feet hurt. I was in trouble. I rang 000.

I had been sleeping with the front door unlocked in case something would go wrong, so people could get to me. Nowadays I have a key lock box so I can give emergency personnel the code to get in. I explained to the Ambulance officers what my feet had been doing and that I was unable to walk. They saw my open bedside draw which at the time was full of every pain medication known to man. I however had not been able to take any of it because my throat was so sore.

I knew what they were thinking from the questions they were asking me. She is a prescription junkie! She is faking this to just get more meds. They told me they couldn't get a stretcher in my house, which was complete bullshit! When I bought this house I made sure there was easy access for wheelchairs and stretchers. They just didn't believe I was in pain, as you could only see my twisted toes. They brought a wheelchair in and I had to stand on my feet to get on it. I screamed. This despite my high pain threshold, from living in constant pain for years.

Once they got onto my front path they told me I had to transfer onto a stretcher. My front path is made from 10mm river gravel into the cement. I remember looking at it and looking at them thinking you have to be fucking kidding me! They helped me out of the wheelchair, and as I placed my full weight on my poor feet on the gravel I screamed so loud they heard me across the road and up the street. It was at this point that I think they realised that I wasn't bullshitting. They offered me the green whistle. Yes, the same green whistle that provides very little pain relief for me.

I sucked on it hard. Nothing.

I was taken to the hospital emergency department. I explained I was neutropenic, so could not be around other patients. I'm 179cm tall. I take up the whole bed. My feet were hanging at the very end of the bed with no protection. A nurse walked past the end of the bed and bumped into my right foot. I screamed a shrilling scream, this time causing everyone to stop and look at me. Two doctors came over and asked a lot more questions and did a neurological exam on my legs and feet.

As I was waiting for my results, laying flat on my bed trying not to panic, wondering if I was ever going to be able to walk again. It was 29th November. It's a date I'll never forget as I was live streaming the VAD bill as it was going through the Victorian Parliament. Counting the votes for and against it. As the final votes came in I had a crowd of medical professionals standing around my bed. It passed. I cried.

I have a friend whose mum, who had MND, recently used VAD. I sat and listened to her talk about her mum's journey. How hard it was for her mum and their whole family. To hear how her final days were, and how grateful they were that their mum could access VAD. I would like to think I played my little part in helping so many people now and in the future who need to access VAD.

My mum would have been proud of me. I stood up for something that needed to change and followed it through. Because of that, many people will now have the chance to make their own choice and find peace on their own terms. It brings me comfort knowing that what I fought for will spare others from unnecessary pain and suffering.

Recently I learned that another mother of a dear friend chose to use VAD. It deeply moved me as this is now the second family I know personally who has made that choice. I feel truly humbled to know that in some small way my words and advocacy may have brought comfort or clarity during such an incredibly difficult time. Knowing that my efforts helped ease the suffering of those who might have otherwise endured a cruel and painful end fills me with both sorrow and gratitude.

I spent nearly two weeks in the hospital. So many things were going wrong. One department not talking to another. Tests going missing, tests not being done. No one listening to me. I had a cancer appointment but it was against protocol for an inpatient to go to an outpatient appointment. So they cancelled it. My haematologist didn't even know I was in hospital because no one had bothered to tell her. I couldn't afford private health, so I was in the public system. I didn't have a choice of who my roommates were. The first lady I was put with had MS and Parkinson's. Up until that point in time I didn't realise that you could have both at once. The second patient was a man who had pneumonia. I expressed my concern about being in a room with him, as I was neutrapenic. The doctor said I wasn't neutrapenic, according to my blood test that morning. My reply to her was, you haven't done my bloods in three days. Those are someone else's results. They moved him out that afternoon.

I had to learn how to walk again. It took days before I could handle putting my feet back on the ground. I had Physiotherapy for 10 minutes each day. I had to regain strength. I managed to waddle out to the corridor and sit near the nurses station on a comfy lounge chair. Ally was with me. It was nice to be out of my room. We were sitting there chatting when a lady in her sixties came up to me and started belting me with her toiletry bag. I couldn't get up to get out of the way. Ally stood there screaming for someone to help me. Alarms got pushed. People came running. I was battered and bruised. I put in a formal complaint.

The next person they brought into my ward was a woman during the middle of the night. By lunchtime, the next day they moved her out and brought in a team in biohazard PPE gear and wiped down her side of the room. I complained that they were doing that with me still in the room, with no airflow or protection for me.

I had NDIS Funding and I rang my Support Coordinator to find out how much I had there and for them to organise support for me when I went home. She told me I should access it through the portal. I explained I was flat on my back in the hospital and was unable to do so. And that it was her job, not mine.

I was waiting for a bed to become available at the Rehabilitation Centre. It was going to take another few weeks.

After the biohazard team had been in, I asked the nurse to get me discharge papers. I was going home. She told me I couldn't do that. I told her, just watch me. Give me the papers. I'm out of here. I rang Ally to come and get me. I hired a walking frame from the hospital and I went home. I thought if I stayed in there any longer, they were going to kill me.

I reported everything to the complaints department at the hospital. I went on to become a consumer advisor, improving patient care so no one would have to go through what I went through. If you want change, then you have to play your part. Stand up and act, don't just sit there and whinge that the system is wrong.

I volunteered my time for Barwon Health at Geelong University Hospital for many years, serving on seven different committees. Several at the same time. I was the only consumer advisor on the refurbishment committee for the new day ward at Andrew Love Cancer centre. I've been on the meals committee, the Consumer Advisory Committee which answered to the Board of the hospital, plus many more.

I stepped down from all committees in 2021, for a few reasons. I was frustrated with government policies, we were in the middle of lockdowns from COVID-19 and also I could see my time would be better used elsewhere.

I am still a current patient of Barwon Health, and will be to the day I die. I often joke there are only a few places at the hospital that I haven't used, the renal unit and the morgue — and I'm trying hard to stay out of both!

2017 Andrew Denton from Go Gentle and myself at Parliament of Victoria

2017 Bald spots from the chemotherapy

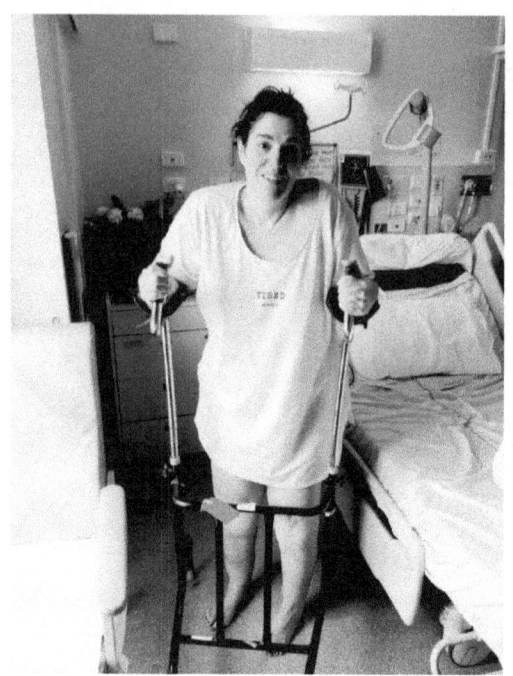

2017 Learning to walk again at Geelong University Hospital

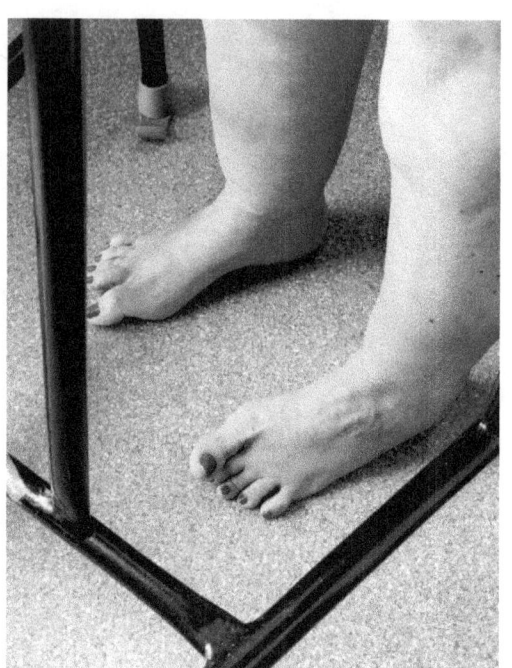

2017 My feet spasming when learning to walk again

2017 Royal Melbourne Show with Ally and Maycee

CHAPTER 28

Their Voices

This was first published in a book I co-authored called Release The Shackles in 2021. It was a strong piece I wrote. The first piece that made me a published author.

> *I'm here.*
> *I sit — silent, waiting, watching.*
> *I can feel the life in you. Every breath you take. Your happiness, your drive and your goals in life. The love you share for those around you, your total being. I can feel the innocence in your mind: naive, carefree, full of hope, full of life.*
> *I so want to start the process of drawing each and every breath from your body, to take what is mine. Taking over each cell of your red, salty, flowing liquid of life, to gain strength and feed my ravenous hunger.*
> *Others would say I'm lying dormant; however, I see you, I'm stalking you, waiting for my perfect time to start the kill.*
> *I'm fully focused on where I am and what I'm about to do. This game of waiting and watching is over.*
> *Attack! Attack! Attack!*
> *I make it fast, multiplying at a rapid rate. Consumed within a sponge encased in its hard-shell that holds your body up.*
> *It tastes wonderful. I'm longing for more. You barely notice I'm here. You're a little more tired than usual, aching all over. I'm having an effect!*
> *This is only subtle; this is not good enough. I must work harder and faster.*

> *Yet months pass by… your life is full of accomplishments, celebrations, an abundance of love; but finally, you begin to struggle. This drives me to work a lot harder.*
>
> *I shall not let you win; I'll not let you win. It's time to take ownership and destroy.*
>
> *Attack! Attack! Attack!*

I'm moving forward in my life.

My long-term relationship has just ended, though we remain good friends. I'm sad but I know I've made the right decision for me. We were too different; it was never going to work, no matter how many times we tried.

Time to move on with the next chapter of my journey in life. What's next for me? I'm not one who can live without goals and ambitions. Even in my darkest days, I strive for the next dream.

Buying a house! I think so. I feel the need to have the security of a roof over my head, which means I don't have to move anymore. I'm done moving. I've come back to the state where I was born, to have the support of family – something that I'm still trying to get used to after living away from family for 30 years.

After looking through many different homes, I've found one that feels like my own. I'm going to buy it – a huge commitment, but one I want to make. It's not the first home I've owned, but this one will be all mine. I can make my own mark on it. Bright, bold and colourful. Life is too short to be beige.

A place to call my own – somewhere for my children, Zakariah and Alexandra, and my grandchildren to come back to if they ever need a roof over their heads. Something I didn't have when I was their age, some long-term security for us all. It's perfect. I will have an art studio of my own. Somewhere I can create my masterpieces of bright colours and start teaching art to other disabled people.

Contract signed, money exchanged. Yay! It's mine! However, the purchase of my new home comes as a package deal, with tenants. I can't get them out until August. The next five months are going to take forever.

I feel so tired. Am I doing too much? Trying to get things packed so I can move, but this feels different. This doesn't feel like my normal multiple-sclerosis-fatigue tiredness. I tell myself I need to push harder. I need to get this done. If I don't do it now, I'll have no one to do it for me.

I notice a painful purple rash on my left hand. Should I be worried? I think I'll go to the doctor to check it out. She doesn't seem worried, but something just doesn't feel right. I think I'll go for a second opinion; it surely can't hurt.

One doctor sends me to two doctors, and I end up at three more doctors. Will someone please tell me what's going on? I just need a diagnosis so we can fix it. Why do they all look and sound so worried? I'm over all the tests. I'm over being a pincushion with needles. Please! Just give me some answers. I'm just so tired, so weak. I'm having trouble breathing. I'm having trouble eating. What's going on? Waiting for the results… it's frustrating. What can it be?

Today, I'll get the keys to my house. Yay!

But first to check in with the doctors on my latest tests. Wait… What? Are you sure? No! It can't be! How? Today was supposed to be the start of my new life. Tissues! Where are the tissues? I have to tell my children. But *how* can I tell my children? I don't know how much longer a life I'm going to have. Why me? Why not me?

Wow, what a ride!

I have empowered this red salty liquid to produce higher levels of proteins called cryoglobulin – mass production in full force. Oh, we are gonna have some fun causing the shell more damage.

We're gonna make a great team, biochemistry and I.

I refuse to just wait and watch, to lie idle. The time to take over and destroy is now!

Our first target is the left hand and arm. We'll start by clotting the small blood vessels. Hopefully, she won't notice. The longer she doesn't realise, the more damage we can do.

One hand isn't enough!

The enemy has noticed something isn't right. We need to increase our speed and strength; time is of the essence.

One hand has become two. Still not enough.

Feet! Yes, let's move to her feet.

Not enough.

More. More. More. I lust for more! What next?

Her neck. Her ears. Oh, yes. Her nose, lips and chin.

That's it. My partner is increasing their strength, as I, too, increase my intensity. What's the next strategic move in this war with the shell?

Bones – tick. Joints – tick. Skin – tick.

The best is saved to last… the soft playground of life itself.

With the help of my love, the biochemical, I'm going to instruct my queen to take everything and not to look back – all the internal life mechanisms.

Oh, it's such a joy to watch my plan working. We grow stronger day by day. I can feel her struggle with every breath – the bitch has to force herself. We grow that little bit stronger with every breath she takes.

Enemy incoming! Look out! No! No.

How can this be happening? I've never smoked, I've watched what I ate, and my diet is clean. I was once morbidly obese, but that was in my twenties. I only drink water. Okay, the odd social drink of vodka and soda, or a nice red wine. I exercise three times a week, lifting heavy objects. I've represented Australia as an athlete. I keep my body and mind fit.

I feel like I'm in a movie, watching someone else's journey. Yet, I know it's my own nightmare, one that I'll need to fight for a happy ending.

I need an excellent medical team, one I fully trust and who will support me with my wishes, and who will do right by me. A team who will fight as hard as me to keep me above ground. I refuse to be made to feel like a number.

Who reads the small print? Who pays attention to medication inserts? Certainly not me. It's never going to happen to me. Yeah, right. Because now it has. You'd think that by taking medication for one disease, it would help give you a healthier, better quality of life – not give you another incurable disease times three. Now, I have to fight for my life, and trust other people with my health and survival.

I've what? *Three?* Three primary bad cells?

That's all they are to me. I refuse to say that word. I won't say the C word; they're just bad cells that need to be attacked. I'm going to war! I'm going to war for me and my family.

Attack! Attack! Attack! With whatever it takes.

I sit in the Wellness Lounge of the Andrew Love Cancer Centre at University Hospital Geelong, waiting and watching other people who also have bad cells in their bodies. Some people are engulfed with sadness and fear; some have no hair, and some have tubes coming out of their chests. I see their loved ones, and they see me, so I'm trying to keep a brave face. Inside, I'm in sobs of tears and fear. Consumers of the service, we have no choice but to be here.

The staff are lovely, calm and friendly. The Wellness Lounge Manager is a delight to talk to, especially when I'm traumatised. My mind is always racing. How will my body react to this poison? Will I survive? They're going to give me a chemotherapy drug called Bendamustine – a derivative of mustard gas from World War I – straight into my shitty veins. My dose at this precise time of the month is 2-to-3 days of poison, administered every 28 days.

How can *that* be good for me?

What choice do I have? I can't be operated on as the cancer is in my bones. I'm very grateful it's contained there and hasn't spread to my lymphatic system, unlike my great-grandmother and uncle.

I smell baking! Is it cookies or a cake? So comforting. Like hugs from a nanna, wrapping her arms around the scared little girl that I am. It smells divine. But I'm too nervous to even think about eating. Maybe some food will settle my nerves? Nope. I'll probably just throw it straight back up.

I don't know who's more confronted by my illness – me or my support team of my daughter and my cousin. Actually, I think they are, since I'm being proactive in this fight for my life. They're just the innocent bystanders, full of worry, unable to help. My heart goes out to them.

The biochemical and I have merged as one. Oh, the power we have. The thrill of the chase. To consume is power. We own each other, in every cell in the hard case. Craving, growing stronger and richer daily. The bitch is struggling, no longer able to do simple daily chores.

We are awesome.

Oh, we're so powerful. Her breaths are shallow, and her toes are unable to bend. She's not the master anymore. We are! We're winning. Time is ticking. We are king and queen of the bitch.

Wait. What's this?

A probe into the inner casing, drawing some of us out. This can't be good. Time to regroup, time to think of a Plan B.

We taste different. They've changed the formula! 'Detoxing her system,' they call it. What does that so-called medical team know? A taste, a chemical taste, is encasing us — noooooooooo!

This is not good. How many days must we endure this? I'm feeling weak. She's going to knock me off my throne.

I must check that my queen hasn't had a similar reaction. Oh! My queen has had the opposite reaction – she's gaining strength and more power. The chemical is making the biochemical morph.

Here's to power. The war is far from over. Bring it on bitch!

Why can't things be simple and run-of-the-mill for me? If it's going to go wrong, it certainly will for me. One hour into this, and my first reaction hits. Nurses and doctors surround me. Stop the infusion! More drugs, to stop the allergic reaction. Why me? Why *not* me?

An hour passes, and my vitals are back to normal.

Start again. Slowly.

Day one done – tick.

Back tomorrow for more. I'm scared. I'm terrified. But it will not win. I can't let it win. It will not win.

My veins are shit. I'm awake while they insert a plastic line into my chest, delivering the toxin straight to my heart and blood stream — the first line of defence.

> ***I'm taking what is mine – every cell and breath from your body. Thank you for feeding my queen. The toxic liquid you've given us has made her quadruple in strength.***
>
> ***Blister rash. Purple rash. Cryoglobulinemia rash. We are winning, my love.***
>
> ***Attack! Attack! Attack!***

I can't hold a paintbrush or pen; my hands hurt. I have lumps where there shouldn't be. Why isn't it working? I was never a patient person. I'm just so tired. How can this be happening? My art takes me to a happy place, but how can I create when my body hurts so much?

Yes! I can still move my fingers… rubber gloves… paint… canvas… finger painting like a child… *Yes! I can paint!* Oh, this changes my world, my recovery, my future.

You prick! You've caused my hair to fall out! I thought people were supposed to lose weight when they have chemo? But no, of course not *me*. I've gained weight with all the steroids to keep the allergic reactions at bay. What? Another needle stuck into my pelvis to break off some bone and test it's still alive. Please put me under! I can't do a third one wide awake. If only pain meds worked on me.

With each round of juice, I WILL the devil to dissipate, to leave my body and let me live. To see my children marry. I want to meet my future grandchildren. I want to meet the man of my dreams and to live a long, happy life.

> ***We're losing power. Each day, I feel you grow stronger. Determination is an understatement. You have such a positive will to live. Who has such strength?***
>
> ***You're killing me! You're killing us!***

I spend my days in forced lockdown, in my home, keeping other people's germs out. My family and friends know they can't visit or come near me with even the slightest sniffle. I'm now permanently immune compromised. Life as I knew it will never be the same. But I have a life. I'm not six feet under.

Chemo is done and dusted! I long to hear the word 'remission'. One day. One day, I'll hear it. Treatment, however, is far from over — ongoing treatment for my weak immune system. I have to do weekly infusions myself from home.

Time to start living again.

Back to the gym. Rear ended on the way home from my second session. Sigh. Not happy. A trip to Perth! Two weeks of 'normal' life. Wow, what a trip. Catching up with thirty-three friends over two weeks.

Another trip. This time, driving to New South Wales. Who says I can't? I have a lot of living to make up for. I head off, driving myself twelve hours north to Newcastle for a break with my son and his wife. The return trip takes me fourteen hours, and it's a huge effort. I'm not well; in fact, I'm very sick.

Is it back? I can't put my feet on the ground. I can't walk. I'm scared — phone triple zero.

You thought I was dormant. Well, guess what girlfriend? I'm back! I've been lurking here, watching what they did to your immune system and how you fought so hard to stay alive. I thank you for that. You've made it even easier for me to play within the tree, branching throughout your whole body, stopping the messages from reaching your extremities. I'm taking control of you. You, my dear, are walking a thin line of good health by overdoing things and giving me back control. I'm not going anywhere! I'm with you forever. This is a massive reminder for you.

Don't you ever forget it.

To lose one's independence, to be a burden, is something I'll never take lightly. I'll fight. I fight to walk again. The happiest of days for me is to walk back into a gym and pick up heavy things. It's the simple things that make me happy.

How can I plan for the future when I don't know if I'll be here tomorrow, let alone in five years' time? I'll live each day like it's my last. With no regrets. Fully jammed packed. One with dreams, goals, love and happiness.

REMISSION! I'm in full remission! I did it! I won!

You do realise there's no cure, bitch? Be happy you've won this round. We're all lying dormant here… we sit and watch… until the next round!

My life has changed. For the better.

Some would say that I've gone mad to think this when so many bad things have gone wrong.

In the past ten years, I've been diagnosed with multiple sclerosis (MS), had three heart surgeries, pericarditis, livedo reticularis, mixed cryoglobulinemia, three primary cancers at the same time (melanoma, chronic lymphocytic leukaemia and small lymphocytic lymphoma stage 4), pitting on the eyeballs, a broken big toe and a cracked rib. More recently, a broken arm and torn cartilage from domestic violence. To say I've been to hell and back is an understatement. But I'm still alive and fighting to remain so.

All of this has taught me that time is the most precious commodity. You can't reuse time. You can't borrow or even steal it. And you sure can't buy it. Choose wisely what and who you spend it on. There's no rewind button. Live in the moment. Enjoy every moment.

I'm releasing the shackles of negative things and looking at the positive things that have come from my journey, from my survival. I strongly believe that my purpose, after having gone through all this, is to *help others*. My story is someone else's survival guide.

2021 Release the Shackles front cover

2019 The Colour of Pain. My story of cancer, MS and my life

CHAPTER 29

It Didn't Just Come Off

About the age of 8, Mum and Dad took us to a Chinese restaurant in Moorabbin for a meal.

When we went for weekends away motorbike riding, we would stop into Baccus Marsh on the way home and have Chinese.

Mum would take Simon and I to the South Melbourne markets, and would always buy us steamed Dim Sims.

When we were living in Glen Innes, Mum would buy frozen bags of Dim Sims, and we ate hundreds of them. That would take our memories back to when we lived in Melbourne.

The last meal my parents and Simon ate together, when Dad came to visit after not seeing him in nearly 4 years, was at the Gum Wah Chinese Restaurant.

I have a strong emotional connection to Chinese food. When I moved to Perth, all I wanted to eat was Chinese. In 2005, I read a Weight Watchers book called 'Don't Eat Your Feelings', and everything suddenly made sense.

Most of the time, I don't actually want to eat Chinese. I just need a hug. When I moved to Perth, I was homesick. Eating Chinese, particularly Dim Sims, for a short period of time gave me comfort, when what I really needed was a huge, tight hug from someone close to me, someone who loves me.

The same thing was happening with doughnuts — in particular, hot jam-filled ball doughnuts. Why? Because my Nanna in Geelong used to buy them for me and heat them up in the oven as a treat. Yummmm... I couldn't walk through a shopping centre without eating a doughnut. After reading that profound book, I decided not to eat them at all. Instead, I would buy them for the kids. Making them eat the doughnuts gave me a similar feeling as eating them myself. It hit me like a ton of bricks what I was actually doing one day when they both refused to eat them, and I got cranky. I stopped buying them altogether that day, and that meant walking the long way around at the shops, so I wouldn't walk past any doughnut shops.

Certain foods trigger many feelings in me. I can't buy little packets of chips. I love crisps. I would buy the kids the multi-packs for school lunches. They never got to eat many of them. I would eat one of every flavour and then fold up all the packets and put them into one of the empty packets, so it only looked like I'd eaten one packet, then place that into the bin. Then blame the kids for eating them all.

On my third Weight Watchers (WW) journey, my mindset was different from the two previous times I had joined. I walked in through the door for me. Not for anyone else. The first 12 months only saw me drop 5kg. I worked so hard at it. But it just wouldn't budge. It didn't help that I was living with a man who was a feeder. He wanted to keep me fat so no one else would want me, and so I wouldn't leave him. When I had lost 13kg, I did get rid of him, and lost 95kg in an instant! Legally, I might add. I didn't bury him — though at times I wanted to!

I started in February 1999 and reached my goal weight over 7 years later.

That's 445 weeks of hopping on the scales every week at WW to get to the top of my healthy weight range, at 79kg. With the last 10kgs, I starved myself and went on Duramine. Exercised seven times a week, weightlifting and walking every single damn day. My weekly weight loss was 100g a week. I became obsessed. I felt like a huge failure. AGAIN, not being good enough.

It was heartbreaking. And when I did reach my goal weight, I didn't have the body that I had dreamed of having all those years, with amazing-looking legs. Why didn't I have toned, shapely, long legs? I exercised so much. I did everything right. No one could explain it. I lost a total of 46 kilograms and I still had the same shape, same legs, with fat pads on my shins, no visible calf muscles, a banding of fat above the ankle where the leg starts, knees that would bend further back than what is supposed to be possible. My legs hurt to touch, and would bruise easily. I couldn't run, because it felt like shards of glass slicing under the skin. No one could explain why.

My weight has yo-yoed for years since getting to my goal weight of 79kg. When I got to goal I vowed I would never get back over the 'ton' mark. To me that is 100kgs. I once read that most rugby league players are over 100kgs, and that thought has never left me. I never wanted my weight to be compared to a rugby player's. I have had such an unhealthy relationship with food and my weight for as long as I can remember.

When I went through chemotherapy, my entire focus was on survival. I put on 20 kilograms and eventually hit 101.9 kilograms. I was fighting for my life, and my mindset was very clear. Live first. Everything else, including losing the weight, could come later. Once I finally went into remission from CLL and SLL, I remember sitting on my couch, exhausted but grateful, and scrolling through Instagram to try and feel normal again.

That was the moment I came across the profile @eatthatcaketoo. There she was, this gorgeous young woman confidently posing in her bathing suit. She was, in every sense, morbidly obese, and yet she had the exact same legs as mine. The same shape. The same look. I remember thinking, wow, you are so brave sharing photos like that openly on social media. Now, I am no stranger to vulnerability. I have done nude modelling before, but what she was doing felt like a whole new level of courage. She was not hiding a single thing about her body. She stood there boldly, and something inside me cracked open.

I started reading through the comments. Some were supportive and full of love. Others were cruel and dripping with hate. Those hateful comments made me angry and sad. Then I began reading her replies, and I noticed she kept mentioning a condition called lipoedema. I had never heard of it in my life.

Like anyone trying to understand their own body, I did what any of us would do. I opened Google. What I found shocked me to my core. Every symptom. Every image. Every description. It was like someone had written a medical explanation of my entire life. I ticked every single box. For the first time ever, something actually made sense.

The very next day I called my GP and booked an appointment. I wanted answers. I needed answers. When I sat down in his office I had a piece of paper with the word LIPOEDEMA written across it as if I were presenting a case in court. I handed it to him and said I thought I had it. He laughed at me. He told me there was no such thing, that it was a made up American word. He insisted that I had lymphoedema and needed lymphatic drainage massage. He handed me the details of a physiotherapist who specialised in it and sent me on my way.

Weeks later, I arrived for the appointment. I explained that I suspected I had lipoedema. She asked me to take off my pants so she could examine my legs. I stood up, pulled down my leggings, and before I could prepare myself emotionally, she blurted out, "Oh yes, you do have fat legs." I was mortified. Hearing someone say it out loud crushed something deep inside me. I knew I had big legs. I have lived in this body for decades. But hearing those words spoken so bluntly was like being punched in the chest. I swallowed hard, forcing back the tears and the humiliation. My instinct was to run out of the room and never come back. Fight or flight was screaming inside me.

I gathered every bit of strength I had and continued with the appointment. I told her my doctor had said lipoedema was a made up word. She laughed and called him a fool, then handed me a brochure for Lipoedema Australia. I opened the pamphlet and it felt like someone had finally switched on a light. All the reasons my body behaved the way it did were suddenly right there in front of me. Why I could never lose weight like other people. Why I bruised so easily. Why running caused so much pain. Why my hips were always at least two sizes bigger than my waist. Every oddity, every frustration, every insecurity I had stuffed down for years finally had a name. Lipoedema is inflammation of the fat, not just normal obesity fat but a different type of fat. It's fibrous and contains nodules. Lymphoedema is when your body carries extra fluid in the lymphatic system. I also had mild lymphoedema, but my main issues were from lipoedema.

She recommended I join Lipoedema Australia, read up on it, and receive regular lymphatic drainage massages. My head was spinning, my mind racing faster than I could process. I got into my car and immediately called my Aunty Lynny. I told her everything. The diagnosis. The symptoms. The shock. The relief. The pain. And then the biggest bombshell of all. Lipoedema affects eleven per cent of all women.

Eleven per cent! All those years of confusion and shame, thinking something was wrong with my willpower or discipline, and the truth had been sitting quietly out there waiting for me to find it.

Finding out I had lipoedema did not just explain my body. It validated my entire lived experience. It gave me back my dignity and helped me understand myself in a way I never had before.

Lipoedema is a condition most people have never heard of, yet it affects so many women and often goes undiagnosed for years. It is a chronic and painful fat disorder that causes an abnormal build-up of fat cells, usually in the legs, hips, buttocks and sometimes the arms. It is not caused by overeating or lack of exercise. You can be doing everything right and still notice your legs getting bigger, heavier and more painful. Many people live with tenderness, swelling and a constant feeling of heaviness, and it can take a huge toll physically and emotionally.

What surprises most people is how common it actually is. Lipoedema affects up to eleven per cent of women worldwide, and yet so many are dismissed or misdiagnosed. It often runs in families and becomes worse during times of hormonal change such as puberty, pregnancy and menopause. This leaves many women feeling confused, ashamed or frustrated, because they know something is wrong but struggle to get anyone to listen.

There is no cure at the moment, but there are treatments that can make a real difference to daily life. Conservative management includes compression garments, manual lymphatic drainage, low impact exercise, hydrotherapy and an anti inflammatory lifestyle. These can help reduce pain, swelling and mobility issues. Some people benefit from specialised surgery such as lymph sparing liposuction which removes the diseased fat and can significantly improve symptoms. It is a long process and not always accessible, but it has helped many people regain comfort and movement. Early diagnosis and supportive care are essential because the condition is progressive, and the sooner people understand what they are dealing with, the better their outcomes.

Lipoedema is real, valid and deserving of much greater awareness. Many women live with pain, shame and confusion simply because they do not have the right information or support. Talking about it helps empower others to seek answers, advocate for themselves and receive the care they need. I am hoping that if you're reading this and this resonates with you, your own body and weight loss struggles, that you too look into what it might be.

I had always known there was something different about my legs. They never looked like my girlfriends' legs. They never moved like theirs or felt like theirs. But they did look exactly like my mum's. And my Aunty Lynny's. And my dad's mother's. And my mum's grandmother's. It ran through the women in my family like a thread, and yet no one had ever been given a real answer. I knew something was going on, but I had no idea what. I just carried that confusion quietly through my life.

The truth is, I have always hated my legs. I still dislike them. I envy women who can slip on a pair of shorts or wear a cute little skirt without a second thought. I watch them move so freely and I feel this deep ache inside me, wishing I knew what that felt like. I have body dysmorphia, and it colours everything. I do not see myself the way I truly am. When I look in the mirror, I still see the obese woman from my chemotherapy days. That version of me is long gone, but in my mind she lingers, loud and unforgiving.

Living with a body that has never made sense, and never matched how hard I have worked, has shaped me. It chipped away at my confidence. It made me question my worth. And until I discovered lipoedema, I carried that shame like a secret I could never shake.

Now, looking back, I understand there was never anything wrong with my effort or my discipline or my character. There was a medical condition sitting beneath the surface the entire time. For the first time in my life, the pieces fit. And even though I am still learning to love my legs, I finally know they were never the enemy.

Finding out I had lipoedema did not just explain my body, it changed the way I live inside it. Once I finally had answers, I began learning how to support myself properly, both physically and mentally. These days I manage my lipoedema very differently. I understand what my body needs, so I treat it with far more care, patience and respect.

One of the biggest changes has been using a Lympha Press. It is a compression system that helps move fluid through my legs, easing the heaviness and reducing pain. The first time I used it I could not believe how much lighter my legs felt. It is now a non-negotiable part of my routine and it truly helps me stay mobile and comfortable.

In 2022, after years of my body reacting to everything like it was under attack, I was finally diagnosed with Mast Cell Activation Syndrome, better known as MCAS. It was one of those diagnoses that didn't fix anything overnight, but it gave me something I had been desperate for: an explanation.

Mast cells are part of the immune system. They are meant to protect you. They release chemicals like histamine to help fight infection and respond to threats. But with MCAS, those mast cells misfire. They overreact. They release histamine and inflammatory chemicals at the wrong time, for the wrong reasons, and often for no obvious trigger at all.

For me, it explained why I could react to things most people never even think twice about: foods, medications, heat, stress, smells, infections, even hormones. It explained the random flare ups, the rashes, the swelling, the gut symptoms, the itching, the feeling of being inflamed from the inside out. My body wasn't being dramatic. It was being chemically hijacked.

The scary part was that my symptoms and blood results were serious enough that doctors needed to rule out something far worse. So I had a bone marrow biopsy. They were looking for cancers and other blood disorders that can mimic MCAS. It was terrifying, sitting in that space of not knowing whether it was 'just another diagnosis' or something life changing again.

When cancer was ruled out, the MCAS diagnosis finally made sense of the chaos. It gave my symptoms a name, and more importantly, it proved I wasn't imagining it. My body had been fighting battles I couldn't even see.

My diet changed as well. Both lipoedema and MS are inflammatory conditions, so everything comes back to the level of internal stress your body is carrying. I cannot afford to eat foods that send my system into a flare. Sugar is out and anything that increases inflammation is gone. I eat a mainly carnivore diet because it works beautifully for my body. Meat, eggs, simple whole foods. No guesswork. No guilt.

Just what helps me function. I follow an eighty/twenty lifestyle. At home I stay strict because it keeps me stable, but when I am out socially I enjoy other food, as long as it does not trigger my MCAS. I know my intolerances and I do not push those boundaries.

Alongside diet and compression I lift weights three days a week. Strength training has become one of the most powerful tools I have. It keeps my joints supported, my body mobile and my MS symptoms more manageable. It does wonders for my lipoedema too. But it has also become something deeper than exercise. Lifting makes me feel capable and grounded. It gives me a sense of ownership over my body again after years of feeling betrayed by it. It is not just physical strength; it is emotional strength.

The biggest change of all has been how I treat myself. I look after my mind now. I do not stand in front of the mirror and call myself dreadful names any more. I do not punish myself for the shape of my legs or the history of my body. I have stopped the constant war I fought for so many years. Instead of tearing myself down, I speak to myself kindly. I remind myself of everything my body has survived. Cancer, MS, trauma, treatment and years of confusion. This body has carried me through all of it.

As I finish writing this book I am sitting at around 80 kilograms. I am still outside that so-called 'healthy' weight range, but I no longer measure my worth by a number on a scale. I have lost most of my normal/obesity fat, and what remains is the lipoedema fat. I can see the lumps and I can feel them under my skin. They are a constant reminder of what my body carries and what it has endured. I am learning to love this body, or at the very least to respect it, because it is the only vessel I am ever going to have. It has battled cancer, chronic illness, trauma and years of misunderstanding, and it is still here, holding me up.

These days I can look in the mirror without feeling completely disgusted by what I see. I see a woman who has fought for her life. A woman who keeps getting back up. A woman who is slowly learning that her body is not an enemy. It is her companion on this journey, lumps and all. And for the first time in my life, I stand beside myself rather than against myself.

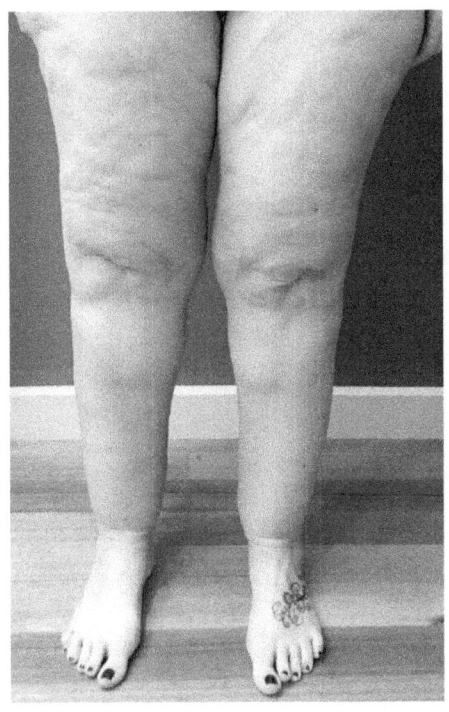
2017 My lipoedema legs

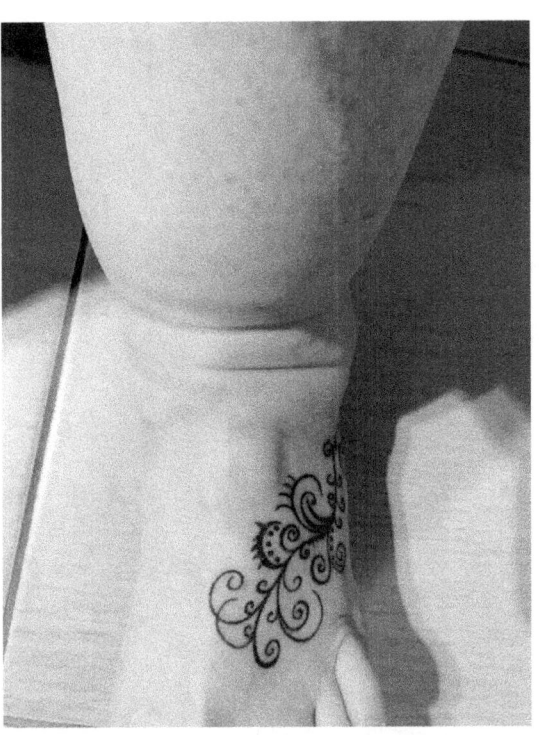
2024 Lipoedema cuffs at my ankle

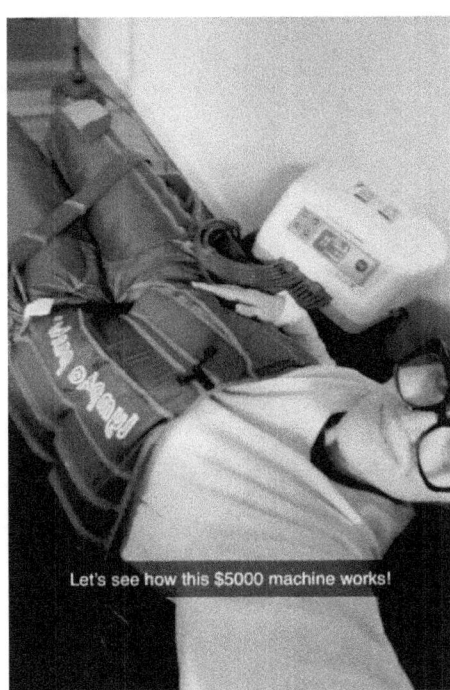
2025 Me in my Lympha Press

2025 Modelling at the Australian Lipoedema Conference

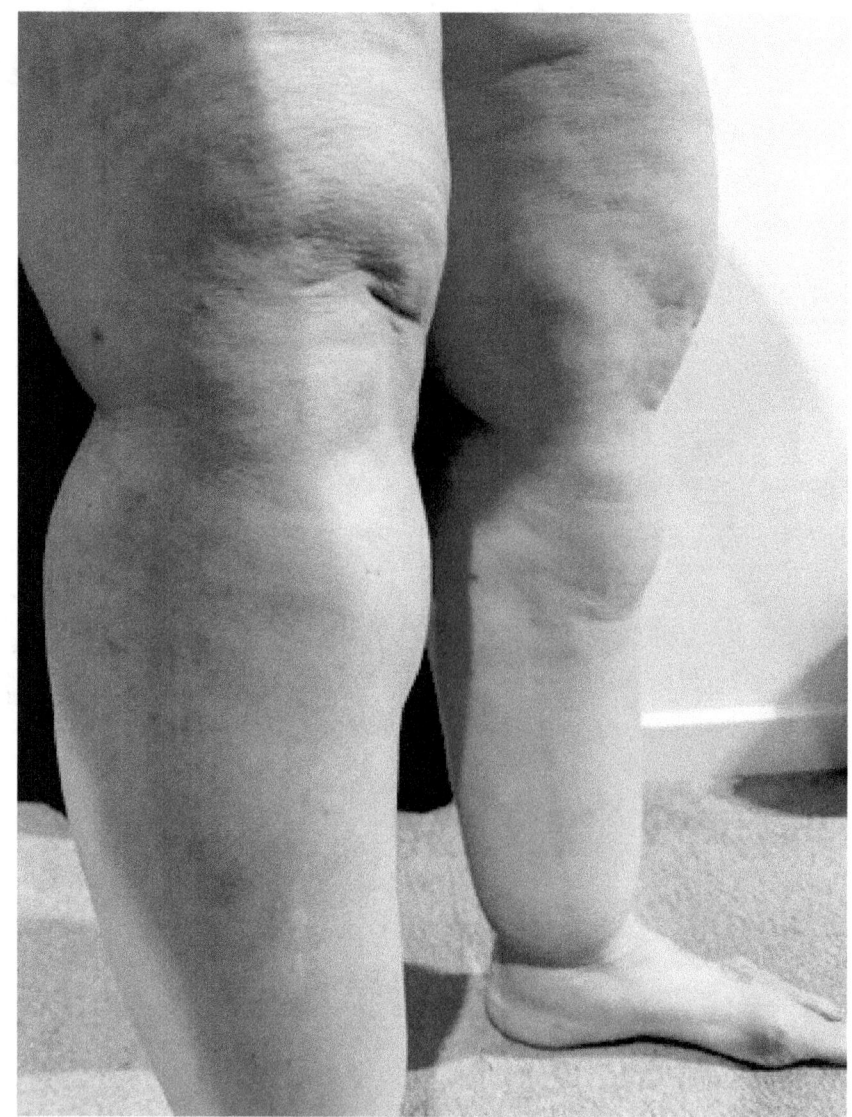

2023 My legs with lipoedema

CHAPTER 30

Spock

A lot of what I learnt about painting and drawing I got from the 'University of YouTube' and the TV show, 'Colour in Your Life'. I started watching the show in 2012 and dreamt that one day I would be on it. I watched every episode and studied how people used all the different mediums. I put in an expression of interest to be on the show in 2016. Graham Stevenson personally rang me, and I said 'yes' straight away. However, being diagnosed with all the cancers put a spanner in the works — at least in the timing of filming the show.

He put my application on hold until I recovered. It was $5,500 to be on the show and I paid my deposit. I was so sure I was going to live that I made future plans. I didn't stop dreaming. In 2018 I felt I was well enough to record the show. The Colour in Your Life team came to my home studio. Sophia and Graham spent the day interviewing me and recording my episode while I painted 'Remmy', who was Zak's dachshund.

I remember thinking, how on earth did a girl who failed English and nearly lost everything end up here?

The episode aired. People watched. People connected. People wrote to me from around the world. My art was suddenly in living rooms in countries I had never visited. That alone would have been enough to bowl me over.

But then came the wildest part.

My episode was included on a memory card that was placed inside the lunar lander and sent to the moon. Yes, the actual moon. Out of all the places my art could have travelled, it ended up on the surface of the moon.

When I heard the news, I sat there stunned. My mind went blank for a moment, as if my brain needed a second to download the absurdity and the magic of it. A girl from Glen Innes whose first art award was a blue rosette in 1981, who spent years thinking she was never good enough, now had her artwork sitting in a tiny craft on the actual moon.

I laughed. I cried. I swore. I told Pansy. I rang a friend just to ask, 'am I hallucinating?'

Because here is the truth. I never made art thinking it would lead anywhere. I did it because it saved me. Because creating helped me breathe through grief and illness. Because it reminded me that my hands could still make beauty when my life felt broken.

And somehow that same art, that same creativity born from pain and stubbornness and hope, left the earth.

It was one of the defining moments of my life. Not because it made me famous. Not because it gave me a new title. But because it was proof that when you follow your purpose, even through fear and doubt, life opens doors you never imagined. Sometimes those doors even open straight out into the galaxy.

The fact that my art is on the moon still makes me grin like a kid. I tell people with pride, not ego. It is not about bragging. It is about the sheer wonder of what can happen when you refuse to give up.

If you had told that little girl in Glen Innes, the one sitting on her bed drawing while the world around her felt too loud, that one day her art would touch the moon, she would never have believed it.

But here I am.

Here she is.

We did it.

Back when my first episode of Colour in Your Life aired, I thought that was my once-in-a-lifetime moment. I mean honestly, how do you top your artwork being sent to the actual moon? I had mentally stamped that experience as one of those wild, never-to-be-repeated things that you tuck into your heart forever.

Well, life clearly had other plans.

Because this year, I was filmed again.

When the invitation came through for a second episode I had a little moment. A proper sit-down, hand on my chest, holy hell moment. It felt like a full circle nod from the universe. Not only had I survived everything since the first filming, I had grown, healed, rebuilt and risen in ways I never expected. To be filmed again in this chapter of my life felt powerful. Affirming. Like the world was saying, 'we see you'.

The second shoot was different. The first time I was nervous, excited, a bit shocked to even be there. This time I walked in knowing who I am. Knowing my worth. Knowing what my art represents. Knowing the impact I have now compared to back then. I felt grounded. Present. Proud. There was no pretending. No playing small. Just me, my story, my resilience and my creativity laid out honestly.

The crew even commented on how much stronger I seemed. More sure of myself. More alive in my purpose. And they were right. That first episode was filmed in a chapter where I was rebuilding. This second one was filmed in a chapter where I am thriving.

Standing there with cameras on me again, I thought about how far I had come. From almost losing my life. From cancer. From MS flare-ups. From domestic violence. From grief that almost crushed me. From feeling like I had no future, to standing here, being celebrated again for the art that saved my life.

It is wild to think that my work has lived in two worlds now. One episode on earth. One episode on the moon. And another, filmed this year, ready to go out into the world again. Ready to reach new people. Ready to help someone else discover their own resilience and creativity.

Being filmed again reminded me of something important. Life is never done surprising you when you keep saying yes. When you keep showing up. When you refuse to quit, even when your world feels like it is falling apart. Doors open again. Opportunities return. The universe circles back and says, 'you are not finished yet'.

And I am not.

This second episode is not just a film shoot. It is a marker of my growth. It is proof that my story is still unfolding. That my art still has more to say. That I am still creating a legacy bigger than anything the little girl in Glen Innes could have dreamed of.

Mid-2018 saw me swiping right again on Tinder. Life felt like it was starting to move forward and I thought I might dip my toe back into the dating pool. I was sitting in Melbourne waiting for a date who was running late and annoying me to the point where I pulled out my phone and started swiping left and right. Then I stopped. There on my screen was this guy with evil eyes and the most dramatic Spock eyebrows you could imagine, paired with a completely bald head. I swiped left for a very firm no.

My date eventually turned up. He was a genuinely nice guy, but that was the problem. Back then I did not know what to do with a nice man. I drove back home to Geelong afterwards feeling restless, and decided I needed a night with my girlfriends. So we hit our local pub for dancing and a few drinks.

I was standing at the bar and looked down to the far end. My stomach dropped. I was one hundred percent certain the man standing there was the same Spock eyebrow guy I had swiped left on earlier that day. He caught me staring and made his way over. He said "Hi", and the first thing that fell out of my mouth was, "You are on Tinder!" He smiled and said, "Yes I am." I replied, "I know, I swiped left on you today." He laughed, but I could see it in his eyes. He saw me as prey.

He bought me drinks all night and we went home together. There were red flags everywhere. I chose to ignore every single one. He love-bombed me from the start. Dinners, day drives, constant affection and attention.Telling me he had never met anyone like me. I had just survived cancer and treatment. I was carrying a lot of extra weight. I was relieved to still be alive. Having a man show interest in me felt foreign after the previous two years. I was vulnerable and he knew it.

He kept telling me about some big overseas deal he had done and how he had huge amounts of money coming in. According to him there were only five people on the planet who could do what he did. To this day I still have no idea what this mystery career was supposed to be. But he wove the story well. He took me house shopping in Melbourne, telling me we needed a city home as well as my house in Geelong. He even booked a private inspection of a $7.5 million property in Port Melbourne and told me we could renovate the bottom lounge into my art studio.

Then we went to test drive a $350,000 Land Rover and sat with the salesman picking colours, as if we were about to sign our lives away. He wanted us to have matching cars. So buy not just one car, but two. Part of me knew it was ridiculous, but another part of me started to believe it. That is how good scammers are. They slip under your skin. They bend your reality. They sell you a dream and make you feel foolish for questioning it.

The nice car he had been driving was not even his. It was a hire car. He had no money coming in — he was doing handyman jobs on Airtasker. Yet he continued to tell me the millions were arriving any day. He drifted off to Melbourne again, saying he needed to see a solicitor about a court case with his former employer. He returned with $7,000, which he said was from winning the case. Meanwhile the hire car was gone because he had not paid for it and he was now using my second car. I had just bought myself a brand new one and he slid right into my life like it was his.

His mental state deteriorated fast. Then one night he simply did not come home. I called and called him. Nothing. By midnight I was terrified and rang the police because I honestly thought he had taken his own life, and I was worried he had crashed my car in the process. The police stayed in contact with me every hour, updating me. They put out an alert on my car. They tried calling him too. Just after five in the morning they rang to say they had spoken to him. He was alive and on his way home.

I felt indescribable relief, but also intense anger. When he finally walked through the door I was sitting up in bed, exhausted, furious and scared. I asked him where he had been and he refused to tell me. What he did not realise was that the police had already told me he had been at the casino gambling. He climbed into bed, ice cold, curled into the fetal position beside me and sobbed and begged for forgiveness. I felt sick.

A few days later I travelled to Woodend to see my aunty. I had planned to stay the night, but at eight that evening I changed my mind and rang him to say I was coming home. My call woke him. When I got home he was suddenly all over me and we ended up having sex. Straight afterwards, he jumped into the shower, got dressed and told me he was driving to Sydney. He had work up there and needed to collect more things from his storage shed. Then he walked out the door without even giving me a goodbye kiss. I was stunned.

I tried calling him the next day and received a text saying he had arrived safely. After that every call went straight to voicemail. Eventually I sent him a message saying I knew he was with his ex because there was no other explanation for ignoring me completely.

Within an hour he rang. I asked if he was with her and he said 'yes', and that she was sitting right next to him. Then he told me he had never loved me and that everything had been a lie.

The idiot had forgotten that most of his belongings were still at my house. Designer clothes, his computer, all of it. Two days later he turned up wanting his things. I wanted answers. He would not let go of his phone and tried packing everything with one hand which I thought was strange. He said we would talk once the car was packed.

As he headed for the door I noticed his phone was on a live call with his ex. I saw red. I grabbed for the phone and screamed at him, "How dare you bring her into my home!" He dropped the bags and stormed outside saying he would call the police for abuse. My rage took over. I dragged the bags of his belongings outside and threw them onto the wet road. The bags split open on impact. Then I slammed the door.

Ten minutes later he knocked again. He wanted his computer. I think he was scared I would throw that on the road too. I had forgotten it was even there. I wish I had thrown it. He still had her on the phone. I told him he could have it only if I spoke to her first. He was trapped. He had no choice. She could hear everything and he could not risk her thinking he was hiding anything.

He stood in the doorway while she and I spoke for twenty-five minutes. I could not believe she was taking him back after all he had done to her and her daughter. I learned he had been texting her the entire time he was with me. Even when he was next to me on the couch, sitting with me at dinner, or lying in my bed.

I handed the phone back, told him to take his computer and get out of my house.

A few days later, he sent a text apologising. I replied that I did not accept apologies through text messages and that he had treated me like a business transaction. If he wanted to apologise, it had to be face-to-face. We never met again, and I never accepted his apology.

He is still with her. They now have a lawsuit against them for money he swindled from another woman after me, when he broke up with the ex again. They deserve each other completely.

Looking back now, it is crystal clear that he was a narcissist through and through. Narcissists do not fall into your life by accident. They hunt. They study. They choose people who are kind, empathetic and open-hearted. People who have been through trauma or illness. People who know what it feels like to be alone. They know exactly who will give them the attention and validation they crave. I had just survived cancer. My self esteem was fragile. My body was changing. I was trying to rebuild my life. I was the perfect target.

A narcissist starts by love bombing. They shower you with affection, compliments and attention until your nervous system becomes addicted to the high of being wanted. Then they begin to pull it back, inch by inch, and you start trying harder to get back to the version of them you first met. They condition you without you even realising it. You begin second guessing your own instincts. You start believing their lies. You start ignoring your own needs. Before you know it, your world shrinks until everything revolves around them.

They take and take until there is nothing left in you. Emotionally, mentally, spiritually. They feed off your insecurities and twist every weakness into a weapon. They convince you that the chaos they create is your fault. They make you doubt your memory, your judgement and even your sanity. The constant push and pull becomes a cycle that feels impossible to escape.

That is exactly what he did to me. I ignored red flags because I was exhausted and starving for affection. I accepted poor behaviour because I was grateful someone was looking at me at all. He played with my emotions, soaked up my empathy and left me questioning everything I had ever known about myself.

The damage a narcissist does to your mental health is slow and silent. You do not even see it happening until you are knee-deep in confusion, self-doubt and heartbreak. It was only once he was gone that I realised how much of myself I had handed over without even noticing.

He was the biggest con man I have ever met. I ignored every red flag because I was vulnerable. I wanted love. I wanted to be wanted.

I still remember sitting in my shrink's office and hearing her tell me that he would not be the worst man I would meet. She said there would be someone even more evil. At the time, I could not imagine how anything could be worse than M11.

But she was right.

Dating as someone who has disabilities is hard — throw in there herpes as well — it's tough finding the right time to have those conversations. Some men think I will be a burden on them, a cripple, that I'll ruin their dreams and goals in life. Because I have gone on to achieve so much in my life, with all the awards and successfully running five businesses at the same time, men now remark that I'm intimidating. My reply is always 'no, you're intimidated; that's your issue, not mine'.

In 2018, Zak and Amelia were married in Townsville, the place where their story first began. They met back in 2013 when Zak was stationed there with the army. What started as a simple meeting quickly turned into something steady and real, the kind of love that grows quietly until one day you realise it has become part of the foundation of your life.

Watching them marry felt like gaining a daughter rather than losing a son. Amelia fitted into our world with such ease that it felt as if she had been part of us all along. She is warm, thoughtful and strong in her own right, and she loves Zak in a way that is both gentle and fierce. As a mother, you hope your children find someone who will see them clearly and love them deeply. Zak found that.

Becoming a mother-in-law twice over, first with Amelia and then with Ally's husband Matt, changed me in ways I did not expect. It is a different kind of parenting. You are still there, but you step back a little. You guide without holding too tight. And you love them as if they have always been yours.

I have always told the two of them that they can call me for advice whenever they need it. Life throws curveballs, and sometimes you just need someone to talk things through with, someone who will not judge, someone who understands family love in all its messy, honest forms. I want them to know that I am only ever a phone call away, no matter how busy I am or where I am in the world.

Seeing Zak and Amelia build their life together reminded me that families grow in the most beautiful ways, not just through children, but through the people our children choose to love. And in that moment in Townsville, watching them promise their futures to each other, I felt my heart stretch wide enough to make room for all of it.

2018 Colour In Your Life filming in my studio

2018 Remmy who is on the moon

2018 Remmy, Pansy and myself

2019 Pansy

CHAPTER 31

Laying Down The Baton

Having so little self-worth and boundaries over the years has put me at risk, especially with men. I have been in relationships and friendships that I should not have started, let alone continued. I attracted these toxic relationships like bees to honey. M9 had been in trouble with the law. His was such a far-fetched story that I'm ashamed to say I believed it. He had convinced both me and his girlfriend that he was innocent of the crime of stalking for which he had been imprisoned. I am a loyal friend. If I let someone into my life, I welcome them with open arms. In the past, many people have taken advantage of my kindness, and M9 was one of those.

I visited him while he was incarcerated every Saturday. It was a four-hour round trip. I made sure he had money in his account to spend. This went on for three months. When he was finally released on parole, he had nowhere to live. I foolishly offered him my spare room to move into until he got himself sorted with a job and somewhere else to live. He didn't have any family in Australia and wasn't a permanent resident.

His girlfriend dropped him off, and I also foolishly let him use my other car that I hadn't sold yet. He became very comfortable living at my home. I started to resent him moving in. If I went on a date, he would act very strangely about it. He was screwing around behind his girlfriend's back. He had a violent temper. Several times during the course of our so-called friendship, he tried to commit suicide and was committed to the psychiatric ward.

He would insist on picking me up from the pub when I had been on a night out with the girls, rather than allowing me to catch a taxi home. There was one night when I had too much to drink, and he picked me up. He forced himself on me. I kept saying no. He finished violating me and got off me, said goodnight and went to his room. I went and locked myself in my bathroom. My home was no longer my safe space. I wanted him out of my home and out of my life. But how was I ever going to do that? It was his word against mine, and I felt like all my power had been stripped away.

I made a decision that while he was under my roof, I would never put myself in a drunken, vulnerable position again. And I never did.

I had been holding on to the baton, repeating the pattern of bad relationships learnt from my parents before me. Passing the baton to myself through each bad relationship. From one bad relationship to the next. How would I ever let go of it and break this pattern of behaviour? How was I ever going to stop attracting abuse into my life?

At the beginning of the COVID-19 pandemic, I met M11 online. We had spoken a few years earlier. He lived three hours from me, but we were both in rural Victoria, so we could travel to see each other. I would spend three days with him, and then he would come to me on his days off. He love-bombed me. Flowers. Bottles of vodka and champagne. Dinners out. We were limited in what we could do and where we could go due to the lockdowns. Things moved along way too fast. He was very fit, and into bodybuilding.

He only worked in a casual position, and was free to move with no other ties. Within a few weeks of dating, we became Facebook-official. My Facebook profile clearly stated I was in a relationship with him. His Facebook profile, however, said nothing. He claimed he couldn't post about our relationship because of his job. Very few of our photos together were ever on his Facebook page, as he never allowed them to be on his profile. Claiming, again, it was because of his job. It wasn't. It was so he could still live his second life.

He insisted I download an app on my phone called Life360 so we could track where each other was on the road, and he explained to me that if I broke down, he would know where to find me. I did have full roadside assistance and knew I could call them for help. That fell on deaf ears. At the time, it seemed like he was being caring; I know now that it wasn't caring at all.

With the lockdown 'ring of steel' coming into effect, it was getting harder to visit each other and to go through all the checkpoints on the three hour drive. Before I knew it, M11 surprised me by resigning from his job and moving in with me. Like I said, way too fast and soooo many red flags, and I ignored every single damn one. I was in shock that someone who looked as good as he did wanted me — an overweight, disabled woman who had little self-worth.

I offered to come and help him pack, but he became agitated and told me 'no', he didn't want me there, and he would do it all himself. The day before he was to move in, I noticed on his Life360 pin that he wasn't where he had said he was. He told me he was at work, yet his pin told me otherwise. I questioned where he was and why he didn't answer my calls all day. He replied that he had been busy packing all day. He didn't have much gear to pack! I had a sinking feeling in my stomach that he was up to something. I then ignored it.

I was over the moon, blissfully unaware. I had felt so alone for so long, and COVID-19 lockdowns didn't help. I did create a storm in a teacup by having two alpha, narcissistic men (M9 and M11) under one roof.

M11 got a job at a jail in Melbourne and would commute there every day. Tension started building between us. When we first got together, there were no secrets, or so I thought. We both shared our phone passwords. He was bi and had a fetish for younger men. But he told me he loved me and he would only be with me. I naively believed him. He wanted to swing, and I said no. I hadn't ruled it out entirely, but I wanted us to build trust and a solid relationship before I even considered doing something like that again. My previous experience had been a nightmare with M8. I also didn't want to fail him or not be good enough, and would do anything to please him.

It was becoming more uncomfortable with M9 living there. I finally plucked up enough courage to ask him to move out. M9 didn't thank me for helping him out, giving him a roof over his head, giving him food to eat and a car to drive. Or even saving his life when he attempted suicide. I was in the lounge room when M9 and his girlfriend moved his belongings out of my spare room. He never came in to say goodbye; just left his key on the bookcase, and to this day still owes me $2,500. He is currently in jail for the rape of his ex, and then he will be deported back to the country where he was born.

One night I was woken up at about 3 am by the light of M11's mobile phone. I lay very still, and he couldn't see I was awake. I watched him text naked photos of himself and BDSM pictures to a woman. I recognised her name. She was the woman he was seeing before me. I rolled over, got out of bed and went to the loo. I asked him who he was texting, and he said no one; he had been on Facebook, just scrolling. I asked him for his phone to look at, and he wouldn't hand it over. He got out of bed and told me I was imagining everything and to go back to sleep. I knew what I had seen. I knew he was trying to gaslight me. Always telling me I was imagining things or had it all wrong. I had started questioning my sanity.

The next day, I tried to open his phone, and he had changed the password. He had two phones. One was in his ex-wife's name, but he was still paying the bill; he had convinced the telephone company that she had lost the SIM card and that she needed a new one. He then bought a cheap phone and activated it with that new SIM. He wasn't divorced from her. Yes, I know — red flags!

He desperately wanted to find out who she was seeing. Months earlier, she sent me a message through Instagram, telling me how evil a man he was, and that he had given her a concussion, and the woman before her two black eyes! He talked his way out of that, saying she had a mental issue and couldn't let him go. That it was all made up — I naively believed him, I trusted him, and I desperately wanted someone to love me.

She put an IVO on him. At the time I thought it was very strange, as she had moved on with someone else, while M11 kept telling me she wanted him back — another red flag.

What he didn't realise was that I could still access the second phone; he forgot to change the password on that one. I saw all the photos of every person he had been with — sexually explicit photos and videos with the dates on each and every one of them. I saw that the night before he moved in with me he was with the woman he was texting from my bed. She was dressed as a baby, drinking from a baby's bottle and holding a teddy bear while he held her like an infant. I felt sick and vomited. I couldn't believe what I had just seen. The man I trusted and loved had lied straight to my face.

Through his Life360 location, I caught him out again. He was meeting up with the guy he was sleeping with before I came into his life; M11 was supposed to be on the opposite side of the city, when in fact he was at this guy's house. I confronted him about it, and yet again, he talked his way out of it. Gaslighting me at every turn.

He moved out of my house early in December 2020, into a flat in Melbourne, supposedly closer to work, to make it easier for him. That wasn't true. It was so he could go back to sleeping with other people — women, as well as young men. I turned a blind eye. I had convinced myself that I loved him, and he kept telling me he loved me.

In my world, love was always linked with trauma because of how my own mother had treated me as a child. Where had my self-worth gone? Who was this person I had become? My work was affected; everything was falling apart. I was a nervous wreck. I just wanted to be loved. He showed me no respect.

Our relationship became even more volatile. He told me that in order to make him happy, I would have to sleep with men in front of him. He didn't want to swing with women and nor did he want any bisexual men there. He would sometimes just watch, and other times he would join in. Then he finally convinced me to go to a swingers club with him. I had totally lost control of my life.

He was a dominant, alpha man, used to getting everything he wanted, including BDSM. I hated being submissive. I tried, and I couldn't obey. He put a belt around my neck and choked me until I passed out one night. Breath play, he called it. He repeatedly fingered me so violently that he caused internal damage, which I've recently had to have surgically repaired, requiring seven stitches. I'll never look the same down there again.

He saw something in me I never knew was there. He said I was a perfect domina. He would want me to tie him up and do things to him I never knew possible. So, although I was supposed to be in charge, he was actually calling the shots by filling my mind with what he wanted me to do with him. There were some very sick things he made me do to him, and I will never repeat that for anyone or on anyone.

I'm not a domina. I hate pain. What I did find out was that I had no boundaries and would do anything for the love I thought he would give me. It all originated from my not feeling good enough for him. Scared he wouldn't find me good enough and leave me.

On New Year's Eve, it all literally came crashing down. We had an argument outside of the pub because I had put my hand on his throat as he had instructed me to do as a domina, yet he did not like it because I had kissed him at midnight at the pub that way. He wasn't the alpha he had wanted everyone to think he was. I left and came home, leaving him there.

He finally came home at 1 am. We had another argument, and he violently threw me into my hallway wall at home. It was with such force that my feet left the ground, and I went backward through the air nearly two metres. I screamed when I hit the hallway wall and floor. Everything hurt. I lay on my belly and couldn't get up.

He yelled at me to stop crying and to get up off the floor.

My iWatch had detected a fall and had gone through all my emergency numbers, and no one answered, so it then called 000. By this time, I had crawled to my bedroom, and he helped me sit on the edge of my bed.

I looked at my right wrist and knew it was broken. I could hear my watch talking and then realised it was the emergency 000 operator. He grabbed my phone off the bed and spoke to the emergency operator, and said we needed an ambulance. We were told it would be a three-hour wait. Everything was hurting. We called a taxi to take me to the emergency department at the hospital.

He was so worried I would tell them what he had done. I didn't. I was too scared to. I told them I fell over drunk when I got home. The nurse looked at me strangely, then looked at him. She knew something more had happened from my injuries. While we waited for me to be seen by a doctor, I turned to him and said, "You just broke my arm!"

After I said that, he got up, looked at me in disgust and left me sitting there. I was crushed. After four hours, he came back, just as I was being examined. Again, I told them I had fallen over, while he stared at me from across the room, behind the doctor and nurse. They knew that wasn't what had happened. The number of injuries I had, and where I had them, didn't add up to just a fall.

He had broken my right arm, with the radius bone broken right through, and had cracked the ulna bone, and torn the cartilage in my right wrist. He also caused a hematoma on the back of my head the size of an egg, and broke my tailbone.

I hit the ground with so much force, I now realise I am lucky to be alive.

They plastered my arm, and he drove me home. He stayed with me for a few days until we had another argument. This time, about another woman. He left and went back to Melbourne. Saying it was all my fault.

My world had just crumbled; not only had he left (which was a good thing), but I couldn't use my right arm in any way, shape or form. How was I going to be able to do anything? How was I ever going to be able to paint again? I was terrified. My family and friends all helped. I couldn't cook a meal for myself, open a bottle or even do up my bra.

He had deleted me from Facebook, which had changed my Facebook status from in a relationship to single. I had put on Facebook that I had a broken arm. Then people started asking questions, inboxing me, and putting two and two together. My family knew what had happened and how my body was broken.

I was rushed back into the hospital a few days later, as my arm had swelled and was compressed in the plaster. I had the plaster cut open to release the pain, and then had to visit the plaster clinic the following week. They asked me again what had happened; this time, I told them the truth. I was the victim of domestic violence. I sobbed when I said it out loud.

He had convinced me that it was all my fault. He gaslit me for the whole relationship, little by little; I just didn't notice it. I didn't press charges. Who was going to believe me?

I continued to see him for the next seven weeks. During that time, he started dating other women. One in particular he liked. I realised I had become the other woman. He was love bombing her just like he did to me. Not only had he broken my body, but my mind as well.

I stopped all communication with him. He would text and email me. I wouldn't reply. One message came through my Facebook business page six months later, as I had him blocked everywhere else, at 7.30 am, just as I was pulling up to the hospital for hand therapy. Perfect timing to remind me of what he had destroyed in my life and the pain I was still in. I blocked him again on that page.

Two years later, I got an email from him, baiting me to reply. Stating he had deleted all of our photos and videos. I sent it to junk mail, where it belonged. He should have deleted them when we broke up!

At the end of 2022, 23 months after he broke my body and arm, I finally had surgery to repair the damaged cartilage in my right wrist. I had to wear an arm brace for two and a half years from the damage another human did to me. It wasn't my fault. He should never have touched me, let alone violently pushed me.

He was a narcissistic sociopath. He knew the system and how to weave his way out of everything.

Have I seen him since breaking up with him? Yes: in 2023, my son Zak was celebrating his 30th birthday with a party in Townsville. I flew my daughter and her family up there for the celebration. We had a couple of days to ourselves, and we decided a day trip to Magnetic Island would be a nice way to spend time with my grandchildren. We caught the ferry over and then hopped on the bus to Horseshoe Bay on the other side of the island. The two older kids were with my son-in-law Matt in the water, while Ally and I sat with the two younger boys under the trees. I was facing the water, and she was facing the street and the local shops.

Out of the blue she said, "Mum, I think that's M11!" "WHAT?!" I replied. I spun around and saw him holding hands with a short, black-haired woman I had never seen before. I started to shake. Ally called Matt back and explained to him what had just happened. He decided to take Maycee to the toilet so that he could walk past him. I started to freak out. Of all the places in the world, here he was over 3,000 km from home and only metres from me. Matt returned and said it was him. He had seen Matt, looked directly at him, then nervously lowered his eyes.

I could see him through the trees. They had gone to one of the local cafes and were sitting out the front. He had taken his T-shirt off, showing his large back tattoo. It was him. I couldn't sit there. I couldn't bear to be near him. We packed up our things, caught the bus to the other side of the island, and then took one of the last ferries home. For the rest of that trip to Townsville, I kept looking over my shoulder.

I am reminded every time I walk down my hallway of what he did to me. I am reminded every time I look at my arm. I am reminded of him every time I move my arm, by the pain I'm still suffering. I am reminded every time I go to paint and draw of the time he stole from me, and that I will never be able to draw like I did before he broke me. I am reminded every New Year's Eve of what someone who said they loved me did to me.

The words of my counsellor kept ringing in my head: 'There will be one worse…'

I found him.

I knew I needed help mentally. The common denominator in all of these relationships was me. Me, who had zero boundaries. Who was never taught boundaries, who never protected her inner child.

If things in my life were going to be different, then I needed to be different. I needed to find out how to stop attracting the same narcissistic men into my life.

Someone told me to do some research on protecting your inner child. I read as much as I could online. I didn't even know what it meant to protect one's inner child.

I read about boundaries. The things my mum failed to provide for me. There are five basic things a parent provides for their child:

- Survival: physical needs for food, water, shelter, sleep, and safety/security
- Belonging: relationships and friendships, and feeling accepted, cared for, and loved by others
- Power: feeling capable, worthy, and having pride in accomplishments
- Freedom: the need for independence and the ability to make choices, create, and explore
- Fun: laughter, pleasure, enjoyment, and humour.

My mum failed on three of these — belonging, power and freedom. I had to learn these as an adult. If only I had known about this as a child, my life would have been very different, and much easier.

I discussed this with my counsellor, and I have learnt how to parent myself in the last four years. It's been challenging. I have to say to myself, if I don't want my own children doing it, then I shouldn't be doing it. To not put myself in danger ever again.

When I met Deany, I was still healing from all the damage that had happened to me, and the grief I still carried. He was an extraordinary man. You can read about him in the next chapter.

I've come a long way with men, especially in the past five years. I have started dating again, but there is no one special in my life who I would consider a long-term partner as I write this. Time will tell if I ever enter another long-term relationship again.

I have recently watched on Netflix, and also read, Stephanie Woods' story, FAKE. It hit so many nerves, and I can see so many similarities. These men deliberately seek out women who are powerful and successful, but emotionally vulnerable at that particular moment in their lives. That vulnerability is what makes them a target. It is not a lack of strength or intelligence, but a temporary openness they know how to exploit. To them, this creates what they believe is easy prey. These men are gutless and will never change. They treat women as possessions and pieces of meat.

I have risen above it all and have become powerful in myself, realising that I am finally happy in my life and that I don't need a man to make me so. I had always thought that in order to be complete or to be happy, I needed a man. I know now that it couldn't be further from the truth. If you're not happy with yourself before you enter into a relationship, then a relationship will never fix that, but in fact will probably make it a whole lot worse.

Yes, it would be nice to be in a relationship and have someone to share life with, but I am enjoying this chapter of singlehood while it lasts. I now take myself out for dinner, and travel on my own. I'm not waiting for someone else to take me.

The men I date now, I go in with my blinkers off, eyes wide open and with a clear set of boundaries. I can't say I've stopped attracting narcissistic men, because they still see me as a target. But I am no longer easy prey. I'm now well aware of what to look for and who to avoid.

I have finally laid down the baton I held onto for so long. I am no longer the person I was. I have boundaries, and I protect my inner child above everything else.

2021 April - With the arm brace I had to wear for over 2 years

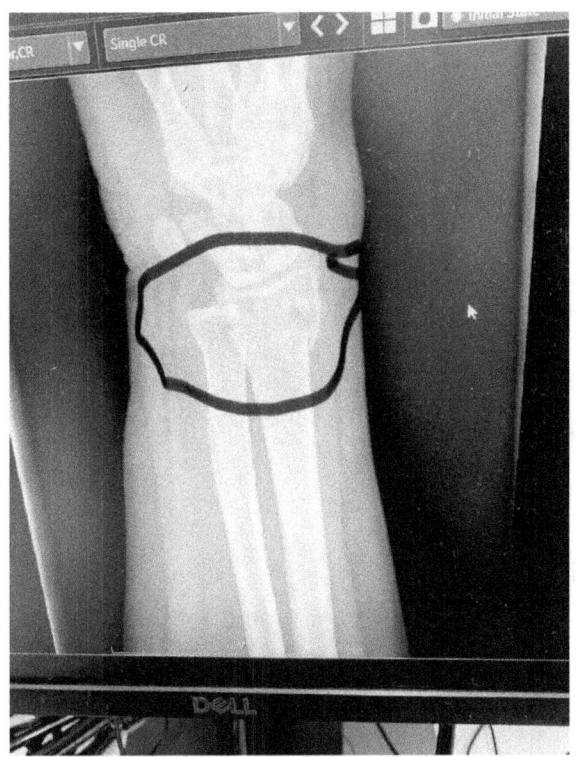

2021 Broken arm

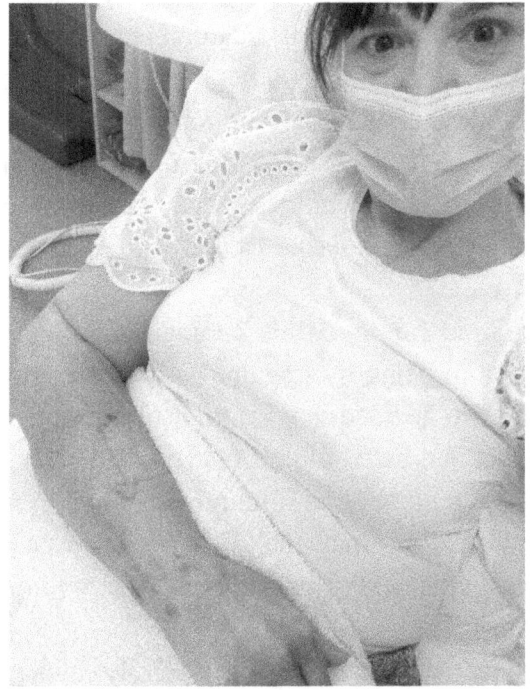

2021 Plaster change day

CHAPTER 32

You Were Not Supposed to Go First

2021 was a horrific year. I started the year being thrown into a wall by someone who said they loved me. I was determined not to let them define the rest of my life. I refused to believe that all men are tarred with the same brush. I ventured back into the world of internet dating. Well — what I should have written was, I dipped my toe back into the shark-infested waters of the internet dating paddle pool. I didn't hold much hope of finding someone that: a) I was attracted to too, b) wasn't scared off by my disabilities, c) wasn't a narcissist, and d) who lived locally.

Internet dating can be scary. So many scammers are on there. But nowadays it's almost impossible to meet someone any other way. No one introduces you to single friends, no blind dates, and men just don't approach you when you are out. I refused to pay for the dating sites, so it was back to looking on a free site.

I started chatting to a guy who didn't tick all the boxes to start with. He didn't live locally, but in fact, in the north-eastern suburbs of Melbourne, and his name was Dean.

We started dating, and I enjoyed his company and affection. But I had trust issues and was so scared of being hurt again, both mentally and physically. Deany was so patient with me. He decided that in order to spend more time with me, and because his lease had run out, he would move from Melbourne to Geelong. Now in previous relationships, I would have let him move in straight away, but I was keenly aware of the need to protect my inner child, so I said no to moving in with me. I helped him find a house in the next suburb to mine — a five-minute drive, just down the road.

We started dating. He became part of my family, and Ally, Matt, and all my grandbabies loved him. And he loved them too. He helped look after them, which was a brave thing to do with the four kids aged from just 1 to 10 years old. He bought them toys and played games with them. Just like any grandfather would. He made me laugh. We spent a lot of time getting to know each other. Deany would tell me all the time that he loved me, and my reply was, "Well, don't hold your breath for me to tell you that back."

We would look after the kids every second weekend on a Friday night, and I would tell them goodnight and that I loved them. Dean would always comment that he couldn't wait for the day I would tell him that, too. I'd have a chuckle and comment, "Yeah, right, don't hold your breath."

We did what most couples do when dating. Out for dinner, exploring new restaurants each time — although we did have our favourites that we would fall back on, such as Korean BBQ. We loved going to the movies, especially Gold Class. We would go there just for the dessert! Dean loved the deconstructed chocolate brownie. We watched Maverick Top Gun there twice because we loved it so much! It makes me smile when I think about it, and I cry every time I watch it again.

He dressed up for Ally's fancy dress birthday party as a pimp, and he had a great time, despite only knowing me at the party.

Don't get me wrong, he came with some red flags, and I did see them, and was very wary. But this time I raised my concerns with him instead of pretending they didn't exist. I had just returned from a week away to Townsville to visit Zak and his family. We were at the local play gym with Ally, my girlfriend Jo and all the kids. Jo commented that she would love to go away for a weekend, and I replied that I would love to go with her. Dean spoke up and said I wasn't allowed to go anywhere ever again! The conversation went quiet, and he knew he had done something wrong. I waited until we got home and addressed his remark. I explained that no man would ever tell me again what I could or couldn't do. That if I wanted to go away for a weekend with a girlfriend, I would. He apologised.

Jo and I started brainstorming where we would go for our warm weekend away, as it was the middle of winter and both of us hate the cold. We thought about going far north to Cairns, and then I said, "Let's go to Bali for a few extra days!" The next thing I knew, we were booking flights for a 4-night trip away. Dean commented that he had a bad feeling about the trip and that something would go wrong. I laughed it off and just put it down to him not wanting me to go away.

Dean was off work on workers' compensation from an injury to his left arm. He had to have surgery on his elbow in July. I made him go up to his parents' place for a week to spend time with them before his upcoming surgery. I looked after his South

African boerboel, Nyla. She weighed 57 kg, and my dog Pansy, who only weighed 5 kg, was alpha and ruled over her! They were yin and yang.

On Deany's return, he complained of shortness of breath and chest pain while walking along the beach, and I made him go to the doctors. A week later, he had surgery on his elbow and spent over a week living at my place while I cared for him. He had a massive bruise on his arm and was in a lot of pain. We had spent the weekend together and at a family day down at the Otways for the football team that my son-in-law played with. I was shocked at the colour of Deany's face compared to the rest of him and took a photo, making him put his hand up to his face to show the colour difference. It wasn't normal. I told him he needed to go back to the doctors that week to get checked out. That was on the Sunday.

Deany was helping Matt get into construction and find a job. He had organised for Matt to get his white card and also an interview with a construction employment agency for future work on Tuesday morning, 2nd August 2022, at 9.30 am. Deany was always early, and he and Matt joked about Matt not being late when Deany picked him up at 7.15 am — leaving plenty of time to get into Melbourne in peak hour.

The night before, Deany came to dinner at my place and decided not to stay so that I could sleep in. I felt something in me, and when he hugged me, I held on tighter than normal. I nearly told him I loved him, but something held me back and I didn't voice it. Deany gave me a hug, told me he loved me and left at 9.30 pm. I still have the Ring doorbell footage of him leaving.

I got a text from him at 10.06 pm saying goodnight.

My phone started ringing at 7.22 am, and it was Matt asking if Deany was at mine because he hadn't turned up. I said I'd try to call. I rang a few times and it rang out. I jumped out of bed and threw on a tracksuit, and called Matt back, saying I was going to Deany's to check if everything was ok. I called all the way there, and there was no answer. That was really strange.

I got to Deany's, and I could see Nyla through the front door, barking at me, and Deany's bedroom light was on. His blind was up about an inch, but I couldn't see in there very well. Something just didn't feel right. I rang Matt and said I was coming to pick him up, as he had dropped his car off for a service for the day. I picked up Matt and said we needed to go back to Deany's. We kept trying to call him.

When we got to Deany's, Matt could see Deany lying beside the bed and the window. I called 000 straight away for an ambulance and animal control, as I didn't know if Nyla would let us inside, even though she knew me. At that point, Matt jumped the side gate, which was locked, and ran around the back to find the back door unlocked. He then ran to a woman over the road and borrowed a screwdriver to get the gate open so I could go inside. My head was spinning, and deep down I was fearing the worst.

Once the gate was open, I ran around the back and called for Nyla. She came pounding up to me, and I put her on her lead that was hanging there, and Matt held onto her. I entered the house yelling out Deany's name and walked towards his bedroom where the light was on. The house was really warm, with the heater set to 24 degrees.

I ran into his room and found him lying on the floor. Dead. I screamed and fell to my knees beside him, touching his chest and hoping to feel it move, trying to find his pulse. I re-live this moment every single day. The image in my head. The look on Deany's face. Matt came running in after hearing my screams and pulled me off Deany and dragged me outside. For a very long time, every time I closed my eyes, I saw him lying there. Mouth wide open, eyes staring into nothing. Fear across his face with no life in him.

He had been dead for a while. I didn't do CPR, as rigor mortis had already set in, he was changing colour to dark shades of purple and his limbs were stiff. From the look of it, he had gotten up and had a shower, as he wanted to be up at 5.30 am to take Nyla for her walk, and then he would have his breakfast. Well, he did shower and was wearing clean jeans and socks. I found him without his top on, lying on his back with his hands on his chest, wedged between his bed and the wall. He had been trying to get to his phone to call for help.

He had two scratches on his face, and it took me a while to work out how he got them. It then dawned on me that Nyla had done it. She had tried to wake him up and, in the process, had scratched him.

Matt rang Ally and my girlfriend Jo to tell them as I sat in my car in shock. The ambulance finally turned up, and also animal control. But we had already calmed Nyla down, and they weren't needed. Next, the police turned up and took my statement. I was down as Deany's next of kin from his surgery. Someone had to tell his family. The police asked me if I wanted them to do it. I said no; as a final gesture to Deany, I would do it. It wasn't my first time having to ring loved ones about someone's death.

The coroner turned up to take Deany's body. I got to sit and spend a lot of time with him, and when I was ready to say my goodbyes, they would take him. I sat beside him for a very long time and said goodbye. Told him that I loved him and that I was so sorry I hadn't told him when he was alive. I told him I was angry at him for leaving me all alone and that I was sad that we weren't going to have the happy life he talked about all the time.

I felt it was also important for Nyla to say goodbye to him. They wheeled him out on the gurney in a black body bag with a fabric cloth over it. I let Nyla sniff the trolley and the bag, and we said our final goodbyes. The coroner couldn't tell me how long the autopsy would take. There were longer-than-normal wait times with COVID-19. Dean was triple-vaxxed.

I grabbed Deany's keys, Nyla and her food, and drove home, crying all the way. I had to compose myself enough to call his family. Deany was right that something would go wrong, just the day before I was to leave for Bali.

I made the hard calls to his family. Not something I would ever want to do again. Deany died without a will, which complicated everything. His family took Nyla two weeks after he died and rehomed her. It felt like I was losing him all over again and letting him down by not keeping her. The home she was sent to in Townsville didn't want her. It was and still is heartbreaking.

It took four very long weeks for the coroner to release his body. Four very long weeks until we could have his funeral. His funeral was in Sydney, and it just happened to be on the same day as the first day of a conference that I had paid over $3,000 to be at. I paid for Ally, Matt and myself to fly to Sydney for Deany's funeral. Deany was cremated. I wasn't allowed to speak at the funeral, and there wasn't one photo of him and me together in the photo tribute. It hurt. I don't know where his remains are. I often drive past his house where he died and just sit out the front for a few moments and talk to him. Many times, Deany would say I had to take care of myself as he was worried I would die, and he wanted me around for a long time. He wasn't supposed to go first. I have grieved for a long time. I have been angry for a long time, I have been sad for a long time, and just when I think I am ok, it all comes flooding back. The police organised counselling for me. And I went to my regular counsellor for help too.

Deany was a fit, 57-year-old man. He weight-trained five days a week, watched what he ate, drank one glass of red wine a night — yet in the blink of an eye, he was gone.

I had found a man who accepted me for who I was. And now he is gone. It's been a very tough few years. It has taught me to harden the fuck up. I've learnt again that time is precious and that you need to make the most of each and every single day. To tell your loved ones that you love them to their faces when they are alive. To appreciate your tribe and all the love that they bring.

This has changed me forever, in ways I couldn't have imagined. It cemented in me that time is precious. I didn't realise for the next three years what I was doing to cope with the grief of losing Deany. I became ultra-focused on work.

2022 Ausmumpreneur, two days after Deany's funeral. It was all a blur.

2022 Deany on Facetime to me

Deany and myself at Ally's fancy dress birthday party

Deany and myself at the wine bar

Deany and myself having a movie night

Deany supporting me when I competed in 2022 Strongman at Strong Geelong

Dinner and movies with Deany

CHAPTER 33

Finding My Voice

2019 was a big year for learning. In August, the Geelong Small Business Festival was on. I attended a few workshops to learn as much as I could about small businesses, as it had been 19 years since I owned a conventional small business. I did a workshop on how to start a podcast… tick, did that, my podcast is called Resilience Mindset and is available on all major podcast streaming platforms. It's been quite successful, and I have won awards for it.

I went to another workshop called Business In Heels. Listening to women telling their success stories of their own businesses. I am now one of the mentors for their business, giving back to other women who are just starting. I went and saw a successful artist who works for Pixar. Wow, what a dream job to have: illustrating. I am now an illustrator of children's books.

I saw an advertisement for a workshop on how to create more time, with Les Watson. The 1-hour workshop was $20, and, not having much money, I thought that was a bargain and I could afford to attend. Off I went with very little expectation, despite his claim that he could show me how I could get an hour back every day! I entered the room at the NAB business centre known as The Village. Something about the name resonated with me — The Village. I didn't belong to a village or a community and hadn't done so in a few decades since leaving Glen Innes.

The first person I met was a woman named Liz. She had an amazing smile, long curly hair, and was so friendly and welcoming. She was the manager of The Village. Unfortunately it has since closed due to COVID-19, but Liz is one of my closest friends nowadays.

We were in the 'boardroom', which had a huge table that seated 20 people. I was so nervous. My anxiety was going through the roof, but I knew deep down I needed to be there. I sat next to a woman named Deb and across from another one named Helen. The facilitator, Les, had his lovely wife, Merry, in the room as well. Every seat was taken. There were bright fidget toys all along the centre of the table, along with Post-it notes. I had a notebook with me as instructed, and right on time, Les started. It would have been poor form for him to arrive late to this workshop or to start late. I was very keen to see how I could find more time to do things in my world. Oh, and Deb and Helen have also become very close friends.

The one hour went by so fast. We did a data dump. This is getting everything out of our heads and onto paper, everything that needs to be done in our businesses and in our personal lives. Everything that needed doing in our personal environment. Room by room, we went through our homes, and all the tasks in our businesses. I filled up over 12 pages that day with tasks that needed to be done. It was overwhelming. Les gave us the strategies to complete that list.

I knew I needed help. My home was cluttered; I had boxes that I had not unpacked since moving in. You see, when I moved into my house, I was immediately diagnosed with cancer and blood conditions. I didn't have the energy to unpack everything, and boxes were piled up on top of each other.

I couldn't get my car into my garage because of all the boxes in there. Zak came home and offered to help, and we ended up having a huge fight. He was ruthless, wanting to throw everything away. I wanted to keep everything. Panic and fear went through me as we started, and it all became overwhelming. We couldn't continue. I began to attend counselling, knowing that my reaction wasn't normal, and I wanted to get to the bottom of it.

I have a strong attachment to 'things' and to people; while the people are explained through the book, the things haven't been. It's a trauma response in a few different ways. Let me explain. I didn't have security when growing up, as those that I loved and wanted love from, were not there for me, such as my father being absent and the way my mother treated me. Then throw in the mix that I've had to live on handouts and food banks, I've become attached to items as they bring back happy memories, and at times that's all I've had. Getting rid of 'stuff' is bloody hard, and I still battle with it every single day. I buy way too much 'stuff', in particular clothing.

I have so many clothes, and it's not often you will see me wearing the same items in the same month. Everything is now in order in my wardrobes, and yes, that's plural. I have a full-size walk-in robe that is spilling over at the sides and also the wardrobe in my spare room that houses all my coats and formal dresses. I am at a space limit there and really need to try and sell some items or give them away.

All my clothes are organised by category, for example, jeans together, tops and T-shirts, skirts, long coloured pants, leather jackets, other jackets, short dresses, long dresses, exercise gear and jumpers. Then, within each category, they are colour-coded. It does make it so much easier for a few reasons. I can find things easily, it's quicker to get dressed, and because I have support workers who put my clothes away, it's easier for them to know where they go, and then for me to find them again. BUT I really need to stop buying so much 'stuff'.

My office was in the most enormous mess. I had things in large bookcases and boxes everywhere, with a small track to my desk that had a foot high pile of paperwork sitting on it. Paperwork that needed to be filed away in a system I didn't even have. Every time I walked into that room, my heart would race, and I would become so overwhelmed by it that I would just dump more things in there, turn around and walk out, closing the door. Something needed to be done. I asked around and found a woman who creates a place of calm. Someone who is a professional organiser. That is what I needed. Someone to come and help with the huge task that lay ahead.

My garage is where we started, and we went through everything. I bought garage shelving, plastic tubs and a Dymo labeller. We sorted it into keep, sell and rubbish. Yes, it took hours — ok, more like days — to complete, and after 5 years, it still is in order. It does get untidy at times, but it is very easy to pull it all back into order. It looks amazing.

Next, we started my office; just the thought of it was crippling. I had to keep moving out of the room to stop the panic attacks. I would have to set the organiser one box at a time to do. It was a long task that required tenacity, but we got through it. Because the room didn't have a wardrobe, I always found it overwhelming to work from. I was going to install a cupboard storage system, when I decided instead to put two sets of bunk beds in that room for my grandchildren and turn bedroom number 4 into my office, which already had a wardrobe with sliding doors. I just needed to put shelves inside of it. That meant more culling and more sorting, with some going into the garage with the purchase of more shelves and labels. I'm so glad I stuck with it. Room by room is organised. The laundry, the bathrooms, the kitchen, and all the bedrooms. Everything now has its own place. Because of my memory issues, it makes things so much easier and less frustrating to find, and everyone who works in the house knows where things are meant to be. I have OCD; my things have to go back in the exact place and exact order they were in before, like when someone unpacks the dishwasher, and the coffee mugs or glasses are not lined up in order in the drawers.

At the end of the time lord's workshop, his wife, Merry announced another workshop she and Les conducted. A writing group. Helping people write a book.

I had attended a seminar a few months earlier on how to write a book in 48 hours, the whole day sitting there listening to the woman upsell the program and not actually tell us how to write the book. My ticket to this event cost nearly $70, and I discovered that the woman who was sitting next to me had paid only $8 to be there. I was in an extremely unhappy mood when I found out about the price difference. Then, after sitting there all day, I found out that the actual workshop to write a book in 48 hours costs $25,000. It was tempting, and I did have the money sitting there in savings, but that was my nest egg, and to blow it all in one fell swoop was outrageous, even for me.

Now here I was, sitting in a room, with someone promising to give me back an hour a day, and who could teach me how to write a book! You see, I wanted to continue my dream of speaking on stages around the world as a keynote speaker, but to do that, you have to have written a book. Why? Well, a book gives you authority, and you become known as an author. Sign me up! I wanted to start there and then. I waited a few weeks, and then enrolled and paid $245 for the 6 weeks.

My mind was racing. How would I start? What would I include? I knew it had to be a story of my life. Just what parts of my life? I went in with eyes wide open, and I discovered a world I never would have thought I could be a part of.

When I had my neuropsychologist assessment after being diagnosed, the results said that before the MS, I had had a higher than average intelligence. I was blown away. I'd been told for most of my childhood I was dumb! I thought I was never good enough. Words are so damaging. Be careful of the words you give to children, and never impose your false beliefs on someone else, or even on yourself.

Sitting in that writing group, I really did wonder if I would be good enough, and if I could actually write a decent paragraph, let alone a whole book. We did various activities each week. Out of all the 12 paid clients in the group, I am the only one who has written and published one book, let alone the 14 that to date I have either written, illustrated or anthologies I have contributed to. I feel very proud of myself, and I do pat myself on my back. Did you know that 80% of people want to write books, yet only 5% actually do. An even smaller percentage actually publish their work. That is such a shame, with so many untold stories just sitting there waiting to be written and read. To leave their own mark on history and a legacy for future generations to read about their lives. I wish I knew more about my family's history. There is no one left alive to ask about such things, and that saddens me. So much history is lost.

In early 2020, I saw an ad on Facebook and LinkedIn about writing your own book and speaking on stage. Right where I wanted to be! It was a free webinar, and

I knew there would be a hook at the end of it to purchase something. I thought I'd watch it and see what the two guys had to say. The first guy was saying that in order to be taken seriously as a keynote speaker, you needed to have authored a book. The second guy, Andrew Jobling, an ex-AFL St Kilda footballer and author of multiple books, explained how he had written his first book when he was $100k in debt and had never thought of himself as a writer, yet here he was with eight books under his belt. More to the point, he believed we could be writers too. I was hooked! I wanted to know more from both.

I sent emails to each of them, and Andrew was the only one who bothered to reply to my request. Within a week, I had signed up for his writing and mentoring program. Fast forward four years, and Andrew and I have recently conducted a workshop together on writing and publishing. I am amazed at what I have achieved in that time!

In 2020, I joined yet another writing group; by now, I think you know I never do anything by half. Why did I join three? Well, I believe in learning as much as I can, from different perspectives. The group was run by the Barwon Heads Arts Council. We went on to learn how to write short stories. It was a group of about 12 people, and we would meet every Sunday afternoon at the Barwon Heads library at the local primary school for a few months. The facilitator set us tasks to write about, and it was through these sessions that I created a chapter about my cancer. I have republished it in a book called Their Voices, as I still feel it's one of the most powerful pieces I have written.

I submitted that chapter for the first anthology book I participated in, called 'Release the Shackles', which I had stumbled across via an advertisement on my Facebook feed. It cost me $1,200 to be part of this project. The profit was to go to a charity, but the book never sold enough to make any profit, as far as I know.

However, it did become an Amazon best-selling book, and more importantly, I became a published author. I'll never forget the day the box of books landed on my front porch. Me, a published author! I, who couldn't spell to save myself. I remember ripping that box open and getting the book out and smelling the pages as I quickly flicked through to find my name in print! Oh, that smell of freshly printed ink. Then I burst into tears over what I had achieved. I couldn't believe I was a published author and my words were out there for the world to read.

Every book that is published in Australia, under the copyright law, either a paperback copy or an ebook, has to be sent to the National Library of Australia to be entered into their catalogue. It just blows my mind that I now have work sitting in the national archives of Australia to become a history book in the future.

2021 saw the publication of the second book I contributed to, which was the Ausmumpreneur book called 'Courage and Confidence'. This book cost me $5,000! Yes, you read that right. It was a lot of money to publish 3,000 words. I received 50 books in that contract and still have a lot left. It too was an anthology I contributed to with other business mums from around Australia. My chapter was called Reinvention: Resilience, Overcoming Adversity and Thriving in Business. The profit from this book goes to fund scholarships for the Women's Business School. I happened to have won that scholarship in that same year. I have been very fortunate to have won scholarships over the past three years. At the same time as I won that one, I applied for another one through Women's Biz Global — it was three months of business mentoring. I learnt a lot.

The same year, I penned a chapter for the Business In Heels book called 'ROAR, Finding Your Strength Within', which again cost me $1,300 to be a part of. There were twelve of us in this book, each talking about a different aspect of our businesses and our lives. I also illustrated the book's front cover. My writing had been published in three books in under 12 months, and I felt like I was on fire. During all of this, I was also writing this book that you are currently reading. It has taken forever, with many different attempts to start it. Looking back, I can now see that I was avoiding writing it by creating new projects to work on.

Writing this book has been hard. Bloody hard, actually. It has brought up painful memories as well as happier times. It put me back into counselling, asking hard questions. Things that I thought I had worked through, but in reality, I had just buried deep under lots of layers. It's been very cathartic writing it. If for no other person than me, to help me get it all out and clear in my own head, and also to take you, the reader, on a journey through the years.

In 2021, I had a Facebook friend who was putting another anthology together to go with her podcast called 'Victim to Victory', and I thought, 'What's another anthology book?' Yes, again avoiding writing this book. I wanted to take control and show people that I wasn't a victim in my own life, that I had come through everything and felt the victory in doing so. My writing coach, however, wasn't happy that I was actively avoiding finishing this book, and tried to ban me from doing any more anthologies. I didn't listen.

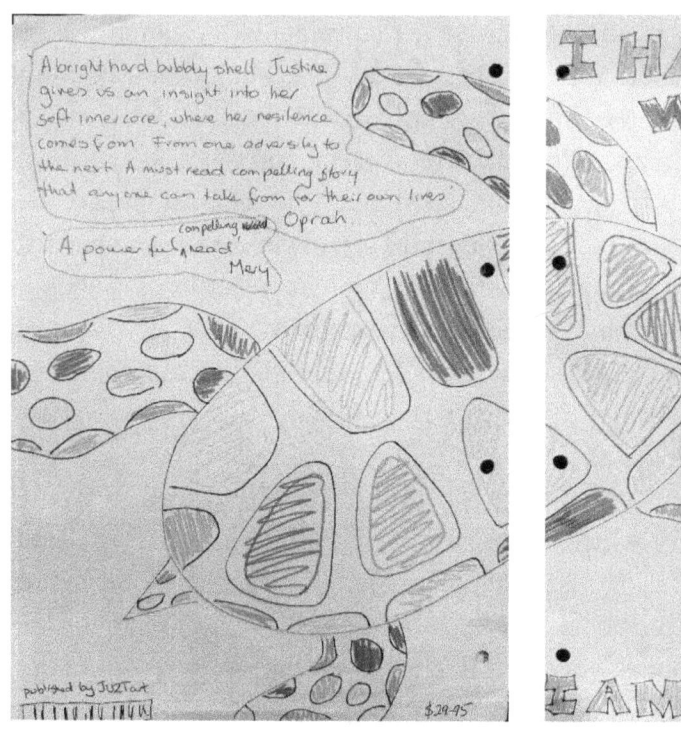 

2019 The mock up cover of this book before it was called Moxie

2021 Courage and confidence *2021 ROAR Finding Your Strength Within front cover, with my artwork*

2021 Victim to Victory front cover

2022 Les and Merry Watson and myself

2024 Co-authored book I'm so glad you left me

2024 Hear Us Roar co-authored book

2024 My writing coach, Andrew Jobling. Thanks for all the help and support getting Moxie done.

I never thought I'd be good enough to write a book

CHAPTER 34

Same Same But Different

In 2021, I decided I wanted to leave something meaningful for my grandchildren, so I wrote my first children's book, which I called *Same Same But Different*. The idea came from my little miniature sausage dog, Pansy.

I got Pansy in 2018, after the bulk of my cancer treatment was completed, when I went into remission. She filled a huge void in my life. For as long as I could remember, I had always been caring for someone: my brother, my mum, my partners, my children. Suddenly, the house was quiet. I was experiencing empty nest syndrome, and Pansy became my companion.

Sausage dogs had always been part of my life. My nanna had one when I was little, and in 2015 Zakariah had one named Remmy. When Zak had to return to the army base for three months, he asked me to look after Remmy. Of course, I said yes. Soon afterwards he got a second dog, a little girl named Lacey.

The three months turned into twelve. Remmy was twelve months old and Lacey only five months old when I picked them up from the airport. When it came time for them to go home, Zak asked if I wanted to keep Lacey, as I had become her mumma. I seriously considered it, but I was about to start chemotherapy, and knew I wasn't capable of caring for another life at that time, let alone my own. Saying goodbye broke our hearts.

Twelve months later, the dogs escaped from Zak and Amelia's yard just a week before their wedding. Remmy was found, but Lacey was never seen again. That loss stayed with me.

In 2018, when I finally felt ready for a dog of my own, I went to look without any intention of buying. The breeder had two puppies whose mother had died when they were only a week old. The boy wouldn't come near me, but the little girl climbed all over me. I left, then returned armed with everything I needed and picked her up. I named her Pansy.

Pansy is Little Miss Anxiety. She wees when she gets nervous, excited, or overwhelmed. She doesn't discriminate. That got me thinking. Wouldn't it be wonderful if the world treated people the same way, without judgement, hate or hierarchy. We are all the same, yet all different. That became the foundation of *Same Same But Different*.

Years earlier, in 2015, I had enrolled in a Certificate I in Creative Industries, believing I needed qualifications to be taken seriously as an artist. I breezed through it, but the doubt remained. I later enrolled in a Certificate IV in Visual Arts. My health deteriorated, and despite being ahead academically, the pressure of attendance requirements forced me to withdraw. I hated quitting, but I realised something important.

None of the great masters ever held certificates. Being an artist comes from practice, skill and instinct, not paperwork or debt. That was the last time I chased qualifications.

Instead, I entered exhibitions, put my work in front of people, and won awards. Winning awards built credibility, and credibility created opportunity.

My NDIS support coordinator suggested I teach art to other people with disabilities. I didn't think I was good enough, but after a few conversations and a single social media post, I had my first client. Then another. Before long, I had enough work for a full day.

Teaching is exhausting for me. I need support workers to help with physical tasks, and my fatigue is relentless, but the work gives me purpose. I expanded to a second day, which also meant more structure, more costs and more responsibility.

Around this time, I joined Les and Merry's Creating Success Program. It was a twelve week course focused on business fundamentals, habits and systems. It changed everything. I began using a paper planner, keeping all my notes, appointments and medical information in one place. My brain finally had a system that worked.

I committed to doing the work. Not just attending sessions, but implementing what I learned. Structure, boundaries, planning, conflict management. My businesses grew because I grew.

Then COVID hit.

With exhibitions closed, I had to rethink how and where my art could exist. Drawing on my own memory issues, I created Van Go Decals, artwork designed for caravans and campervans to help people easily recognise their vehicles. The name came from my uncle, combining Van Gogh and vans.

The business never fully launched due to logistical challenges, but it still exists under JUZT Art, waiting for the right time.

Through JUZT Art, my live finger painting gained traction. I began teaching finger painting workshops for adults, including corporate events. One even took place at a nudist camp in winter, which was certainly memorable.

I later combined live finger painting with speaking, using art as a way to tell my story. From that, Team Fingerprint was born, blending resilience education with creative expression for workplaces.

2021 saw me enter my first business awards, something I had never thought I'd do. I had been introduced to the Ausmumpreneur awards and thought I would enter. Now, I'm never one who does anything by half. I figured if I was entering one award, I might as well enter a lot more. I had trouble with all the paperwork and understanding everything. So I outsourced the writing of my award entries. I entered 11 different categories that year, made it to the finals for 9, and won 5!

- GOLD Coach Of The Year
- SILVER Disabled Business Excellence
- SILVER Creative Entrepreneur
- BRONZE Business Pivot
- BRONZE Overcoming The Odds

Not bad for a newbie. Unfortunately, that year there wasn't a face-to-face conference, and it was all done via Zoom. I sat there nervously in front of the computer screen waiting… watching… and then my name was called out. That was a turning point for me. The impact on me of being recognised for the work I have been doing by my peers and the community cannot be overstated. I was contributing to society. It was a real 'pinch me' moment.

It drove me to work even harder and enter even more awards. And then to win more.

As my workload increased, I realised I needed more support. I met a woman through networking, and she helped me manage the systems my brain struggled with due to my ABI. Asking for help was a turning point.

By late 2021, there was a clear shift. My businesses had outgrown what I could manage alone. I no longer saw support as weakness, but as growth.

JUZT Art classes returned to face-to-face and have continued to grow, helping many members of the community find creativity in their own world. Art and creativity is something that I have always wanted to share. Having my arm broken saw me reach out to seek even more support. There are even more things I can no longer do with my right arm since it was broken; unfortunately, the damage is permanent.

I was missing creating in my own world when I had my arm broken. Not knowing if I could ever use my wrist again was terrifying. I wasn't sure if I'd be able to illustrate my work. I adapted and modified my painting techniques, and all of a sudden I had a completed manuscript of Same Same But Different. Now what to do with it? My writing coach encouraged me to submit my manuscript to publishers, and I did, to thirty-one of them. Publishers take their time assessing a manuscript, months if not years. I sat and waited. A few months went by, then within the space of a week or two, I had received not one but five contracts! I was blown away! Me, who failed English all the way through high school, had written a children's book, and five publishers considered it worthy to publish for children to read. I knew I was onto something.

I read through each and every contract before saying yes to any of them, including all the fine print. I'm so glad I did — you see, hidden in the small print in each of them was that I wouldn't be allowed to use my artwork or anything similar in anything else! No, that was not going to work. That would mean I would be unable to create anymore in my style, thereby preventing me from creating income-generating pieces. What that meant to me as an artist was that anything else that I created that looked remotely the same, including my sculptures, I couldn't sell without breaching that contract. I was in a pickle. I could have resubmitted it without the illustrations, or let one of the publishers take it on and not produce anything like it, and no longer make money on my sculptures and paintings. I chose neither.

I would have really liked to have illustrated it differently, but I wrote it when I had a broken right arm, and there was no sign of it healing in the immediate future. So I adapted my painting techniques, learned to paint with my left hand, and did lots of dots with a special piece of plastic in different sizes, and I managed to fill the book with bright-coloured animals, with Pansy as the key character on each page.

Myself, my children and my grandchildren are all in the book. Although since that book was written, I have a few more grandbabies. I was in a meeting with my staff brainstorming what we should do. Then excused myself and went to the bathroom. Now I don't know about you, but I tend to have my most amazing ideas either in the shower or on the loo! I returned to what we called the boardroom and announced that we were going to start our own publishing business, and 'Same Same but Different' would be our first title. The look of shock and disbelief on my staff's faces was priceless. Their reply was, "You were only gone for a minute!" and I replied "Yes! That's all it takes! Now, how are we going to action it?"

We did a mud map, more commonly known as a mind map. I like to call them mud maps as they tend to help you get out of the shit that you're in. Anyway, I digress. The conclusion was that I needed to do a publishing course to make that a reality. That night, I signed up to do a course, and within 24 hours, I had picked and registered another business called Morpheus Publishing. So why Morpheus? Well, if you remember, my Tupperware team was called Morpheus. It just felt like a little of the old me was still there, plus Morpheus is the Greek god of dreams, and I want to help other people achieve their dreams of being published authors.

Publishing that first book tested my team and me. Learning everything about the publishing world and putting it into practice. But on 14th September, after hours of hard work illustrating and working with my Aunty Lynny on the layout of the book, we launched Same Same But Different at my home, with over 50 family, friends and business acquaintances who came to celebrate. It truly was a night to remember. Not only did we launch the book, but also Morpheus Publishing to the world!

I wanted to create a publishing business that helped other disabled people tell their stories. The people that society needs to hear from, yet who rarely get the opportunity to speak. I wasn't sure how that was going to happen. But I did know it would. When you have a dream and start moving towards it by taking small steps, then all of a sudden, bigger things happen.

2022 saw me launch my podcast, Resilience Mindset, interviewing with other people who had their own stories of resilience, whether in their personal lives or through business. The first season was 26 episodes long, and the second season was 28 episodes. After the first season, I published a book of all the edited transcripts called Resilience Mindset Wordcast Season #1. This podcast has won awards and made it into top 10 lists for national podcast awards. When I record the podcast, I also videotape it. From that I make a VLOG, and you can watch all the videos of the interviews on my YouTube channel:
https://www.youtube.com/@justinemartincorporation

This was a difficult year for me with the loss of my partner Dean. It made me question everything. My values, my time left on the planet and who and what I wanted to spend it with. The business was growing, yet my brain was struggling. The more I was doing, the more overwhelmed I was becoming, yet to the outside world, things looked normal. There's so much I used to be able to do, but I just can't anymore. Multi-tasking is one of them.

I looked into hiring a Virtual Assistant. I had met a businesswoman through Ausmumpreneurs. Her name is Yona, and she runs a VA agency. I had a meeting with Yona and signed up to work with her agency for 40 hours a month to help with the bookwork. My VA's name is Mylen — what are the chances of having someone working for me that has the same name as what MS attacks: the myelin sheath. Freaky!

Every task was taking me ten times as long to complete as it should have. It was so frustrating; the constant mistakes I was making because of my brain capacity were costing me money! Our first month, we only managed to use my VA for 25 out of the contracted 40 hours. I was cranky; I had wasted 15 hours. Three years later, Mylen now does well over 160 hours a month. It has been a game-changer for me. She does all the things I used to be able to do and understood how to do, but no longer can, as well as new things that I can't do. I asked for help and showed strength in doing so. Asking for help is never a sign of weakness, but always a sign of strength and growth.

In October 2022, my team and I went to the Geelong Business Excellence Awards as guests to see what it was all about. I hadn't entered these awards as the process is time-consuming. At the end of the evening, I turned to Suzie and said, "We are going to enter this next year, and I know we can win!" Arrogant, maybe, but I sometimes get this feeling that I know I can achieve something. When this happens, I don't shirk from it, but embrace it fully and go for it. This was one of those moments

I found a website called Sauce Bottle. This is a website reporters use to look for sources for their stories. When you subscribe to emailed sources, you receive two emails a day with all the sources to apply for. I have picked up so much free media, and I always ask for a backlink to one of my businesses. I have been featured on the front page of the national body+soul magazine in all major newspapers, That's Life and Take 5 magazines, plus loads more.

From this media attention, I have sold paintings and coaching sessions, and it has helped build my public profile, enhancing my brand, which has then built my credibility as a keynote speaker. It has been an effective way to market myself without paying hundreds of thousands of dollars for advertising.

I have also had the opportunity to write articles for major magazines and websites. One in particular being https://www.mamamia.com.au/ms-disease/.

They wanted someone to talk about the dangers of celebrities talking about their own health battles, such as MS. This came about when Christina Applegate announced that she was diagnosed with MS and Selma Blair documented her journey with the medical procedure HSCT (Hematopoietic Stem Cell Transplantation). They wanted me to acknowledge that the average Australian can't afford what the rich and famous can in their own health care. I wrote the article, and it went viral. This caught the attention of MS Australia, as did the work I've been doing educating people about having MS. The next thing I knew, I was sitting in my boardroom across from their CEO, having a meeting over lunch.

He was keen to organise more things for me to do with MS Australia. I said I'd have a think and see what we could come up with. It didn't take long for me to come up with the perfect project, using my experience of taking part in anthologies. Morpheus Publishing would publish an anthology from people with MS from all around Australia. Each would tell their own story, in a 3000-word chapter, of what it's really like to live with this incurable disease.

Most people know of MS due to the fantastic marketing campaign, the MS Readathon; but most people don't know what it's like to actually live with this disease and what it does to our bodies and minds. We got started straight away, and within weeks, we had 25 people ready to start writing their chapters.

None of them knew how to write a chapter, so we formed a community group, and met over 30 times in the 6 weeks. Each author could attend the online Zoom meetings as many times as they wanted. By the time the book was published, everyone knew each other's stories. We invited MS Australia to contribute their own chapter to the book, and also the CEO to write the foreword, and they accepted, right up until the eleventh hour. Then, after reading the chapters from the other authors, they said that they wanted to 'edit' the book. I found this very strange as I had just spent over $2,000 having it professionally edited.

After much discussion with MS Australia, we realised that they didn't want to edit the book but instead to censor it. They explained that they are a conservative organisation and that the stories didn't fit within their rules. I was blown away and so angry. This book was written by the people they are supposed to represent. The people who live with this horrible disease each and every day. We all told the truth. It wasn't made-up lies. Some of us are no longer on disease-modifying therapy drugs (DMT), some are controlling our MS with diet, some have had HSCT, and some are on a mixture of all of it.

All are just living their own lives and wanted to show the world what it's like to live with MS. It wasn't positivity porn nor doom and gloom. I interviewed everyone in the book for their own podcast episode on my Resilience Mindset Podcast and VLOG on my YouTube channel, and we brought out a sub-season of the 25 authors. Something very few of them had been a part of.

We called the book Whispers of Resilience: Our Stories of Multiple Sclerosis (MS). It sat at number 1 on Amazon for three months and, as I write this, hovers between the top 10 and 20 in Neurological Diseases. I'm so proud of this book. I've been asked who I wanted it written for. My reply was, for everyone! One in five people is affected by someone who has MS. It costs the Australian government over 1 billion dollars a year. That's a lot of money. Most people know of MS, but not what it does. Whispers of Resilience is for you, whether you are newly diagnosed or have had it for years, whether you are a carer of someone who has MS or if your mother, father or best friend has it. Or if your work colleague has it. I know of neurologists who are now handing it out to newly diagnosed people to read, to give them some insight into the full and rewarding life that they will still be able to live.

You can purchase your own copy of Whispers through Morpheus Publishing and all major online bookstores.

3D prints of Pansy made by Zak and myself

2021 My first Christmas with Dad in 39 years.

2022 Article in the Geelong Advertiser

2022 Geelong Times article

2022 SSBD book launch

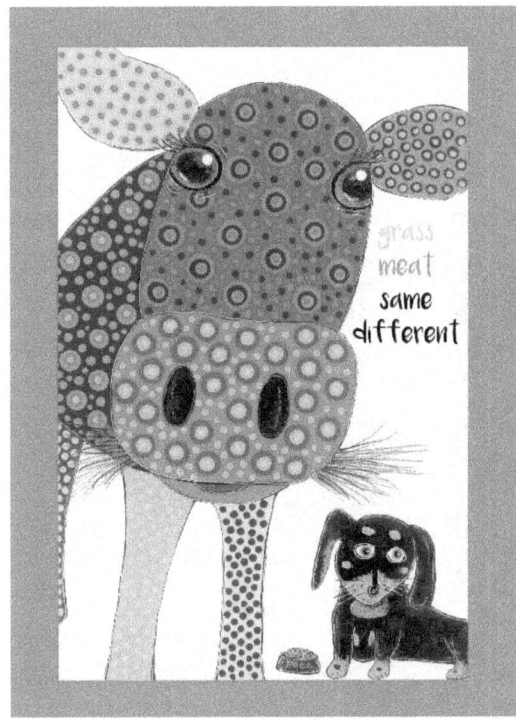

A page about eating from SSBD

A page about family in SSBD

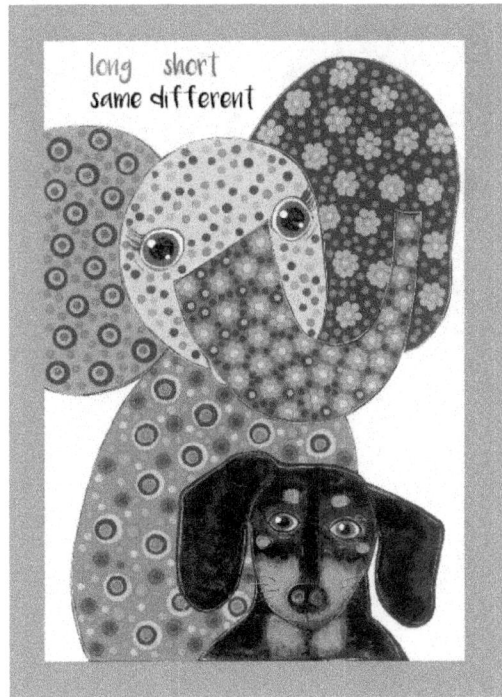

A page about noses in SSBD

Front cover of Same Same But Different

Pansy and herself at a market stall. 3D print by Zak

CHAPTER 35

Adapt and Modify

Adapt and modify. These two words have shaped the woman I am today. They are simple words, ordinary even, but together they became the backbone of my survival, my healing and my growth. They are the reason I am still standing, still smiling, still creating and still living a full life, even after everything my body has thrown at me.

For a long time, I did not know that adapting was a strength. I thought it was something you only did when life pushed you into a corner. I thought modifying meant admitting defeat. I could not see then what I know now. Adapting is not weakness. It is resilience in motion. Modifying is not giving up. It is choosing a different path when the old one disappears beneath your feet. It took me years to learn that lesson. Years of fighting myself. Years of grief and exhaustion and frustration. Years of breaking down and building myself back up again.

In 2023, I realised, maybe for the first time in my adult life, that I was genuinely happy. Deeply happy. Not just functioning. Not just getting through each day. Not just putting on a brave face because people expected me to. I mean the sort of happiness that sits warm in your chest, that feels like you are finally living inside your own skin instead of fighting your way out of it. It was the year everything clicked. The year I saw the woman I had become with clarity instead of criticism. The year I realised I had done it. I had rebuilt my life.

And the wildest part of that realisation was knowing that my happiness had come from me. Not from a partner. Not from a job title. Not from outside validation or a single moment of luck. It came from the choices I made, the boundaries I set, the healing I committed to and the courage it took to walk through hell more than once. I learnt to soften, to listen, to forgive, to step back and to step forward. I learnt to take up space. I learnt to say 'no'. I learnt to choose myself. And that one choice, repeated again and again, changed everything.

Goal setting has always played a huge part in my life. It is how I stay grounded when everything else feels unstable. Goals give me direction. They give me something to aim for when my health feels unpredictable or my mind feels foggy or my body feels weak. Without goals, I feel like I am drifting in the wind with nothing to hold onto. I need structure. I need purpose. I need something ahead of me. Goals do that for me. They always have.

But setting goals when your life is full of medical appointments, unknowns, flare-ups and exhaustion takes courage. It takes a willingness to fail. To try again. To set new goals when old ones collapse. To adapt them when reality gets in the way. I learnt that the hard way, but I learnt it well. My goals have carried me through every rough patch. They have been the stepping stones on a path I once thought I had lost entirely.

Before I reached this point, though, there was a long stretch of life where everything felt impossible. Everything felt out of reach. Everything felt like a battle I could not win. When I think back to 2011, to the start of my cognitive challenges, I see a woman who was trying desperately to hold her life together through sheer force of will. My memory slipped like water through my fingers. Numbers stopped making sense. I could read a sentence ten times and retain nothing. Conversations evaporated as soon as they ended. Learning felt beyond me. Remembering felt beyond me. Living felt beyond me.

Brain damage is the blunt term for it, and some days it truly felt like parts of my mind had been knocked out like windows in a storm. I did not recognise myself. I did not know how to function in the world anymore. I did not know how to rebuild a life around cognitive loss. And I definitely did not know how to be patient with myself. Patience was a lesson I learnt slowly and painfully.

But the moment everything shifted was the moment I stopped asking 'why me?' It is such a dangerous question. It keeps you stuck in the past, drowning in the unfairness of it all. I had to choose between being swallowed by self-pity or finding a new way to live. So I chose to adapt. And then I chose to modify. And those two choices have carried me through every challenge since.

I began learning differently. Watching instead of reading. Asking instead of pretending. Recording instead of relying on memory. Repeating tasks until they become muscle memory. Repeating them again when my brain let go. I had to become my own teacher, my own advocate and my own support system. I had to fight for myself in ways I never expected. And every time I adapted, I rebuilt another part of myself.

One of the biggest changes in my life came in 2018 when CBD oil finally became legal by prescription in Victoria. I will never forget the relief I felt. I had lived with chronic pain, spasms, neurological issues and insomnia for so long that the idea of genuine relief felt like a miracle. When I was finally able to legally access CBD oil under medical supervision, it was life-changing. My pain eased. My body softened. My sleep improved. My mobility stabilised. I became functional again in a way I had not been for years.

CBD oil became a vital tool in my life. If I go a single night without it, my body reminds me immediately. It is not a luxury. It is a necessity. And when I ran for the elections years earlier, cannabis law reform was one of our policies. I stood up publicly and advocated for the legalisation of medical cannabis, not for recreational use but for controlled, ethical, medical access. Thousands of people like me were living in pain, fear and silence. So to see it finally legalised felt like a personal victory. I would like to think that in some small way I contributed to that change. It is something I am genuinely proud of.

October 2023 was one of the most emotional months of my life. My daughter Ally married her partner Matthew. I flew home with Amelia and my grandsons, my heart full from the moment I stepped on the plane. The whole family was coming together. After everything Ally had been through, she deserved joy. She deserved stability. She deserved a day full of love.

But her story had deep wounds beneath it. Years ago, she had cut ties with her biological father after a painful argument where he told her she was ruining her life by being a step-parent. It devastated her. When her boys were born, she asked me not to tell him. And she never heard from him again. Eight years of silence. Then one day she saw on Instagram that he had remarried, and his two stepdaughters were the bridesmaids. It shattered her heart all over again.

So when she told me she wanted to invite him to her own wedding, I was surprised but supportive. We posted the invitations and waited. We received nothing. Not a reply. Not a text. Not even a returned envelope.

I poured myself into her wedding. I spent more money than I should have, made every decision I could to make the day perfect, and held her hand through every moment leading up to it. She looked breathtaking. She wore a stunning dress in off-white, her bouquet was made up of flowers from my own wedding dress and new ones. And the day was as perfect as we could have hoped. Nothing major went wrong. Laughter filled the air. Family gathered. Love radiated. My girl deserved that day, and seeing her so happy made every moment worth it. Even though her father never came. Even though he has still never met his grandsons. That part still breaks my heart. But she moved forward with grace, and I admired her deeply for it.

Days later came the Geelong Business Excellence Awards. I had entered JUZT Art, Resilience Mindset and myself as Business Leader of the Year. I did not expect to become a finalist in all three. When the email came through, I sat in disbelief. I bought a table at the ceremony and filled it with people who had lifted me, supported me and shaped my journey. I wanted Ally and Matt there because I wanted them to see the world I had built through resilience, grit and growth.

When they announced my name as the winner of Business Leader of the Year, my breath left my body. I am the first disabled person to ever win that award. The symbolism of that moment is something I still hold close. Twelve years earlier, I was at rock bottom, convinced my life was over. And there I was, standing on a stage, recognised for leadership, strength and impact.

A judge later told me I was an influencer of life, not in the social media sense. He meant that I change how people see possibilities. I carry that compliment with me everywhere. It reminds me why I do what I do.

October was already a big month with Ally's wedding, but it became even bigger when Zak won Townsville's Business of the Year. My boy. My firstborn. The kid who grew up pulling everything apart to see how it worked, who was always tinkering, building, imagining. The kid who became a man in the army and then had his whole life flip upside down when both his knees blew out during a trench exercise in 2018. He went from serving his country to being medically discharged, injured, and starting again with nothing but $900 in his account and the grit he inherited from me.

Instead of crumbling, he did what I have spent years teaching him without even realising it. He adapted. He modified. He refused to let life stop him. With that $900 he bought drone parts, built a tiny online store and started what would become Rising Sun FPV. At first, it lived in his garage. I remember teasing him, saying it looked like NASA had opened a discount branch in Townsville. Bit by bit, that little garage business grew legs. Then wings. Then a complete engine.

His community grew. His skills grew. His reputation grew. That garage became too small, so he moved into his first premises. Then that space filled. Then another. And now they are moving into a warehouse. A proper warehouse. A testament to every hour he spent fixing, tuning, teaching, racing and building something he believed in. What started as a hobby became a thriving company with another growing beside it, Rising Sun 3D, his 3D printing business. Two businesses, both built from the ground up by a man who once stood on a parade ground thinking his life had fallen apart.

So when he walked on stage in October and accepted Townsville's Business of the Year, I cried. Proud tears. Deep mother tears. The kind that hit your heart before your eyes. He built that life. He carved that path. He earned every moment of that recognition. And knowing his story, knowing where he started, makes it even more powerful. I still smile every time I think about it. I am so proud of everything he has achieved, and everything I know is still coming. His business, Rising Sun FPV, is now one of the biggest drone racing suppliers in Australia, and he did it all off the back of nine hundred dollars and a refusal to give up.

Watching both my children build strong, stable, loving lives has shown me that I must have done something right along the way. They both have good partners, good hearts and good heads on their shoulders. They are resilient. They are kind. They are steady. People sometimes ask me, half joking and half serious, "Is there anything you cannot do?" And I always laugh and say, "Yeah, relationships!" Maybe one day that part of my life will change too. But my children and their partners know one thing for certain. They can call me any time for advice, support or grounding. I am only ever a phone call or flight away.

Two of my biggest mistakes in life are also the two things I love the most on this planet. My children. And I would not change that for the world.

People always look shocked when I say that, but it is the honest truth. I was young, I was naive, I was not ready, and life was chaotic. I did not plan a single part of becoming a mother. I stumbled through it, learning as I went, hoping I was doing it right, praying they would turn out all right in spite of me rather than because of me.

And somehow, they did. They grew into good humans. Strong humans. Humans with heart.

My so-called 'mistakes' became my greatest teachers. They gave me purpose when I had none. They taught me responsibility, sacrifice, unconditional love, and resilience long before I understood the meaning of any of those words. They forced me to grow, to mature, to soften, to fight, to keep going when life was an absolute mess.

Zak and Ally are two of the greatest loves of my life. They made me a mum, even when I had no idea what I was doing. They made me show up. They made me try harder. They made me better.

They were never really mistakes.

Just unexpected blessings disguised as chaos.

And I would not trade a moment of it. Not one.

Not long after this, I travelled to London. It was the furthest I had ever travelled and the first time I had done anything like that alone. For someone with cognitive impairment, airports and train stations are minefields. But I had a plan. I wore my Hidden Disabilities sunflower lanyard, which quietly signalled to staff that I needed help without having to announce anything publicly. Some airports understood it well. Others did not. But I managed. I asked questions. I trusted myself. I breathed through the anxiety. I did it.

That trip gave me something I did not expect. Friendship. Deep, soul-nourishing friendship. Bianca, whom I had met through Ausmumpreneurs, became one of my people. We explored London together, laughed in the rain, got lost, found our way again, talked endlessly and connected in a way I didn't see coming. She feels like family now.

I also met Robyn through Ausmumpreneurs, and she became a quiet, grounding presence in my life. There is a calmness to her that makes people feel safe. She is the sort of friend you do not have to perform for, the kind who understands without explanation. Those friendships were the unexpected treasures of that journey.

From London, we all travelled to Ireland for a writing retreat at Crom Castle. And that is where I met Dr Tererai Trent. A woman whose story, mission and spirit changes lives everywhere she goes. Sitting beside her at dinner felt like sitting beside wisdom itself. She carries a presence that is hard to describe. She sees people. Truly sees them.

One afternoon on a bus, she turned to me and said, "We are going to do remarkable things together." I felt those words deep in my heart. They felt like the truth I had been waiting to hear.

And with all the courage I had, I asked her if she would write the foreword for this book. When she said yes, I felt deeply humbled. To have someone of her calibre and influence believe in my story is something I will never forget.

Around this time, my father returned to Australia after many years overseas. Up until 2021 I had only seen him seven times since I was nine years old. Seven times in more than four decades. When you grow up with that kind of distance, you learn not to expect much, and to protect your heart. So when he moved back, it was strange for both of us. Awkward. Uncertain. We were practically strangers trying to step back into something that had never really existed.

He came for Christmas that year and met his great-grandchildren for the first time. Part of me hoped that maybe we could start again, that time might soften things. But too much time had passed. Too many years lost. It was not from lack of trying, but the connection never arrived. As he now battles cancer, I have had to grieve the relationship I once imagined we would have. It is a quiet grief, a private one, but it sits beside the other truths of my life and has shaped how I show up for my own children and grandchildren.

Adapt and modify have been the foundation of so many parts of my life, including business. Geelong Residential Cleaning and Garden Maintenance began because Ally and Matt struggled to find work. Both are on the spectrum, and both live with anxiety. Traditional work environments were overwhelming for them. But Ally is an exceptional cleaner, and Matt is a brilliant gardener. So I told them I would start a business, and they could work for me. Two years later, the business is thriving. They have independence, confidence and pride in their work. One day soon, the business will be theirs entirely. Watching them grow has been one of the greatest joys of my life.

Adapt and modify. These words have guided me through illness, motherhood, leadership, heartbreak, reinvention, travel, advocacy and growth. They have taught me that nothing is truly impossible. Everything can be rebuilt in a new way. Everything can be learnt differently. Everything can be shaped, and reshaped, and reshaped again.

I rebuilt myself piece by piece. And in 2023, I saw clearly, maybe for the first time, just how far those two simple words had carried me.

2023 Ally's Wedding Reception with My family

2023 Crom Castle where I attended a writing retreat

2023 Dr Tererai and myself discussing the law of coincidence. She told me there was no such thing. I've lived by this motto ever since.

ADAPT AND MODIFY

2023 Harry Potter's Platform 9 3/4 at Kings Cross Station, London England

2023 My Aunty Lynny who designed the front cover of Whispers of Resilience

2023 On a bus tour around England

2023 Stonehenge, England

2023 Whispers of Resilience book launch

Dr Tererai Trent and myself talking about my life story and my tattoos

CHAPTER 36

Fair Weather Friends

My Nanna always told me that there are people who come into your life when things are going great and disappear when they go bad. She called them fair weather friends.

At the time, I nodded along, the way you do when you are young and assume you understand what an older person means. I did not. Not really. Understanding words and understanding life are two very different things.

She was so right.

When I was younger, friendships felt permanent. People felt fixed. You assumed that if someone had been in your life for years, they would always be there. Loyalty felt automatic. History felt like a guarantee. No one tells you early on that some people are only capable of walking beside you when the road is smooth.

It took years of living, losing, surviving, falling apart and rebuilding for my Nanna's words to sink in.

As I have grown older, I have become deeply aware of how much the people around you shape your inner world. The old saying that we are the sum of the five people we associate with most is not motivational fluff. It is lived truth. I have felt it in my body. Spend time with someone who is negative and constantly criticises everything and everyone around them and you carry that energy home with you. It clings. You walk through your front door into what should be your safe haven and collapse on the lounge emotionally exhausted. Not because the day was hard, but because the negativity was relentless. I have lain there asking myself why I kept putting myself through that, knowing deep down that this heaviness was not who I was anymore.

For a long time, I did not have boundaries. I did not even know what boundaries were meant to look like. I wanted to be liked. I wanted to belong. I wanted to be chosen. I wanted to be loved.

I was raised by a mum who was doing the best she could with what she had. Dad leaving fractured our family, and Mum's health meant much of life became about survival rather than nurturing. Parenting felt heavy. Somewhere in that space, I learned to smooth things over, to keep the peace, to put other people first. I never learned how to protect my inner child, and that put me in danger more than once. I kept trying to earn love from the wrong people.

Friends are the family I choose.

That sentence came from experience, not theory.

For many years, I confused tolerance with loyalty. I believed that staying, enduring, and forgiving endlessly made me a good friend. I did not yet understand that loyalty without boundaries slowly erodes your sense of self. I kept people close long after my body had started signalling that something was wrong. Tightness in my chest. Exhaustion that sleep did not fix. A quiet dread before catching up with certain people. I ignored those signals because I thought walking away made me selfish.

Looking back, I can see how much energy I spent managing other people's moods. I adjusted my words, softened my opinions, and swallowed my discomfort to keep the peace. I told myself this was kindness. It was not. It was fear. Fear of being disliked. Fear of being abandoned. Fear of being alone.

Learning boundaries was not a single moment. It was a series of small, uncomfortable decisions. Saying no when I wanted to say yes. Ending conversations when they became cruel or draining. Allowing silence where I once would have filled the space. Each boundary felt terrifying at first. But each one brought a little more peace.

What I eventually learned is that the right people do not punish you for having boundaries. They respect them. The wrong people react badly because the boundary removes their access to you. That realisation changed everything.

I have friends from every decade of my life and from every chapter. Kindergarten. Family friends. Cousins. Primary school. High school. College. Work. Illness. Sport. Hobbies. Motherhood. Travel. Socialising. Internet dating. Business. Networking. So many different circles that once existed separately and now overlap. Because I have lived in three different states in Australia, my friendships stretch across the country. Distance has never defined closeness for me. Intention has. When I travel, I try to catch up with as many of them as I can. Social media helps us stay connected, but nothing compares to sitting across from someone, sharing time face to face.

Throughout my life, I have made many friends and even more acquaintances. Social media likes to remind me how many so-called 'friends' I have. But adversity has a way of sorting them out very quickly. When life became truly hard, only a handful of people reached out. Often, they were not the ones I expected.

When Ally and I were evicted, fear wrapped itself around everything. Home is meant to be safety. When that disappears, it shakes something deep inside you. It was my friend Gaily who opened her home to us. No judgement. No hesitation. Just come and stay. You are safe here. Years later, after my first heart surgery, she flew across the country to look after me. She did not ask if I needed help. She simply arrived. That is not fair weather friendship. That is family.

I have friends who know my patterns well enough to notice when I disappear from social media for a few days. They inbox me. They call. 'Are you okay?' That simple question has anchored me more times than they will ever know.

One day, an acquaintance who lived down the road knocked on my door because she had a feeling something was wrong. She trusted her instinct and acted on it. She was right. That knock may well have saved my life. Sometimes the people who change everything are not the ones you have known the longest, but the ones who listen to their gut and show up.

And then there are the people who disappear.

When I was diagnosed with MS, some friends vanished. They did not know how to talk to me anymore. They were uncomfortable. I was still the same person, but my diagnosis made them uneasy. Later, when cancer entered my life, more people quietly faded away. Some who had stayed through MS could not endure that. Messages slowed. Invitations stopped. Silence crept in. That was when my Nanna's words finally made sense. Fair weather friends love the sunshine. They vanish when the storm arrives.

Illness strips your life down to its essentials. It removes the distractions, the small talk, the performative friendships. When your body is fighting for you, you no longer have the capacity to carry relationships that require constant effort from only one side.

When I was diagnosed with MS, I was still trying to make things comfortable for others. I reassured people. I minimised my own fear so they would not feel awkward. I learned quickly who could sit with discomfort and who could not. Some people simply vanished. Others stayed physically present but emotionally distant. They spoke carefully, as though I had become as fragile as glass.

Cancer took that lesson further. It revealed not just who could stay, but who could truly stand beside me without needing to be reassured themselves. Losing people during that time hurt deeply. It felt like abandonment layered on top of fear. But it also brought clarity.

I stopped chasing people who could not meet me where I was. I stopped explaining myself. I stopped shrinking my reality to protect other people from discomfort. Illness taught me that presence matters more than words, and consistency matters more than promises.

The friends who stayed did not always know what to say. They stayed anyway. They showed up imperfectly. That mattered more than anything else.

I have always held friendship in high regard. I am the person who organises our high school reunions. The connector. The keeper of history.

I have learned to recognise red flags too. I once had a girlfriend I met through the local pub. She went through friendships quickly, which should have been a warning. At the time, I was new to the area and lonely. We went to the same pub every Saturday night. I chatted with the regulars, including men I had spoken to on dating sites and some I had been on dates with. The conversations were brief and harmless. What I did not know was that later in the night she would tell those men to stay away from me, calling me bad news and a whore, before trying to get their numbers herself. I found out because the men contacted me the next day. We are no longer friends. Letting go of her was a relief. No one needs that kind of negativity in their life.

There is one friendship that deserves its own space in this story because it took me the longest to understand, and it hurt the most to let go.

We were friends for over thirty years. Decades of shared history, shared conversations, shared seasons of life. This was not a friendship built on school or convenience. It grew alongside adulthood. Through relationships, changes, moves, and reinvention. It was the kind of friendship I believed would always be there simply because it always had been.

I held that friendship in high regard. I protected it. I invested in it. I spoke about it with certainty, as though time alone made it unbreakable.

I was the one who kept the connection alive.

I reached out. I called. I messaged. I visited. I made the effort year after year without questioning it. That was just what you did for someone you loved. I never kept score. I never asked for more. I assumed that loyalty meant showing up, even when it was not returned in the same way.

It took me far too long to notice the imbalance.

In more than twenty years, they never visited me. Not once. I travelled. I rearranged my life. I made space. And slowly, painfully, I began to realise that the effort was flowing in only one direction.

At first, I made excuses. Life is busy. Everyone is dealing with their own struggles. I told myself that history mattered more than reciprocity. That love meant enduring the unevenness. That asking for more would somehow make me demanding or ungrateful.

But something shifted as my own life became harder.

Illness has a way of stripping everything back. When your energy is limited and your body is already fighting, you start to notice where your effort goes. I noticed how drained I felt after always being the one to initiate contact. I noticed how quiet things became when I stopped reaching out. Days passed. Then weeks. Then months.

That silence was louder than any argument could have been.

The real grief was not losing the friendship. It was losing the belief that it was what I thought it was. I grieved the version of the friendship I had carried in my heart, not the reality that existed.

Letting go was not dramatic. There was no final conversation. No confrontation. Just a quiet decision to stop abandoning myself.

I stopped calling. I stopped messaging. I stopped being the only one holding the connection together. And nothing changed.

That was the answer.

It hurt more than I expected. Thirty years does not disappear without leaving a mark. I questioned myself. I wondered if I was being too harsh. I wondered if I should try again. But every time I considered reopening that door, my body told me the truth. Tightness in my chest. Exhaustion. A familiar ache I had learned to recognise as self betrayal.

Holding that boundary went against everything I had been taught about loyalty and love. But it was also one of the most important things I have ever done.

That friendship taught me something no book ever could. Love without reciprocity slowly erodes you. History does not excuse imbalance. Time does not guarantee care.

Friendships, like all relationships, must move in both directions. Otherwise, they are not connections. They are obligations.

Letting go of that friendship created space in my life. Space for people who show up without being chased. Space for friendships that feel steady rather than draining. Space for relationships that honour me as much as I honour them.

It took thirty years to learn that lesson.

But it changed everything.

As I have grown and reinvented myself, my circles have changed. I love conversations with people who understand and support what I am building. But in

Australia, we have Tall Poppy syndrome. I have lived it. People pulling away. Subtle shifts. Hard comments disguised as concern. I learned who I could share my goals with and who I could not. Now I stay in my own lane. The people trying to bring you down are not the ones paying your phone or gas bills.

I am often asked how I keep going when so many people have fallen away. The truth is that I did not always cope well. There were days I questioned myself. Days I wondered if I was too much. Too honest. Too ambitious. Too visible. Tall Poppy syndrome has a way of making you doubt your own growth.

For a long time, I tried to soften myself to stay connected. I downplayed my achievements. I avoided talking about my goals. I learned which rooms required me to be smaller. Eventually, I realised the cost of that shrinking was far greater than the cost of standing alone.

Staying in my own lane became an act of self preservation. I stopped seeking validation from people who were uncomfortable with my success. I stopped explaining my dreams to people committed to misunderstanding them. The people who belong in my life now are the ones who celebrate my growth without resentment.

This shift did not make my world smaller. It made it stronger.

Loneliness has shaped many of my decisions. I have made terrible choices because I was afraid of being alone. I once complained to my counsellor about going through chemotherapy by myself. I told her I did not have the strength to do it alone and needed a partner beside me. She replied that it would be better to go through this alone than in one of the terrible relationships I had been in. She was right. From that moment on, I just got on with it.

I find it difficult to ask for help. I will ask, but I insist on paying. Somewhere along the way, I learned that needing help meant being a burden. I know now that asking for help is not weakness. It is strength. You cannot build resilience alone.

I got my dog, Pansy, in 2018. She is my world. I got her because I did not want to feel so alone in my own home. I became an empty nester far earlier than I ever imagined, and the silence was heavy. Pansy filled that space. She follows me everywhere. When she needed back surgery, my world stopped. Thankfully she has made a ninety eight percent recovery. For someone so little, she has had a huge impact on my life.

Meeting new friends as an adult takes time. Every time I moved across Australia, I had to start again. I have learned it takes at least twelve months before friendships form and a place begins to feel like home.

Because I have not lived close to family for most of my life, my friendships have become the family I choose. They have helped me more times than I can count.

Working for yourself can be lonely. Networking became a way to build my tribe. I attend at least one networking event each week. Over time, those connections led to some of my biggest projects, not because I chased opportunity, but because trust came first.

A positive mindset matters, but mindset alone cannot hold you. You need people. You need belonging. You need boundaries.

Life teaches you the difference between fair weather friends and forever friends. Fair weather friends fade when the storm arrives. Forever friends stay.

We were never meant to do this alone.

2023 Pansy with the 6m long Pansy on my side fence

2024 Pansy and me in my art gallery hallway

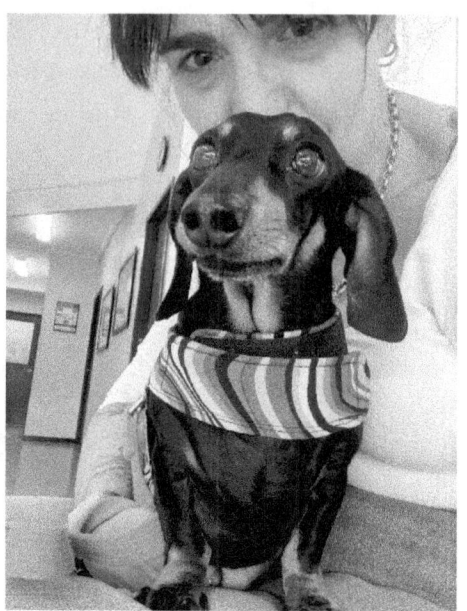
2025 Pansy at the vets

2025 Pansy not impressed being a model for me

CHAPTER 37

The Canvas of Life

This was first written for Dr Tererai Trent's Substack in 2023. I wrote this chapter while staying alongside her in Crome Castle in Ireland.

In 2010, my son Zakariah, 17, enlisted in the Australian Army as a combat engineer. Six months before he was to leave for the army, he asked to get a tattoo on his right leg. The law in Western Australia stated that he could only get one if he had a signed letter from a parent. A permission note. As far as I was concerned, if he was old enough to serve in the army and die for his country, he was old enough to get his first tattoo. It was a shark. It was not something that held much meaning, except that he loves the ocean and, of course, sharks. So, I signed the note, as well as his enlistment papers.

He came home to visit in 2012 for my 41st birthday, and was so proud to give me my present. Something he had paid for with his own money. A voucher. He gave me a voucher for a tattoo, along with a note that said I was booked in to get my first tattoo two days later.

I had always wanted a tattoo, but for a few reasons, I hadn't taken the plunge before now. I panicked — where on my body would I get it? I was previously morbidly overweight and have very little skin that isn't dented by stretch marks or cellulite. I do have a tendency to overthink things.

With Zak's help, I decided on just a simple tattoo of both my children's names positioned between my upper shoulder blades, somewhere that didn't have stretch marks! My cousin, Myalie, held my hand, because I was afraid it was going to hurt a lot. It didn't. A year earlier, I was diagnosed with multiple sclerosis (MS), and as it turns out, parts of my back have now lost feeling from the nerve damage. So I sailed through it. But it did ignite in me a desire to have more — a lot more — ink on my body.

A few months later, I was sitting in an art class for people with multiple sclerosis and drawing a Celtic-inspired, swirling heart. Nola, who was a lot older than me, was sitting to my right, and commented that my drawing would make a great tattoo. I thought to myself, 'yes, it sure would'. It had a lot of meaning behind it. A heart, meaning the love of my children and love of life. I had recently become single when my fiancé declared he was leaving me because my MS diagnosis would affect his dreams and life goals. Wow — what do you say to that?!

A week later, I walked back into the MS group, lifted my top to expose my right ribs and showed Nola my new artwork in black ink. She scoffed that it wasn't real, and I had to convince her that it sure was! I loved it. It then got me thinking about what else I could add to it. I was hooked!

When I had the children's names tattooed on me, I wanted to add swirls around them as I felt it looked unfinished. I sat and drew a few different designs until I found the one I wanted forever.

I had the tattooist ink my design. I was so happy with the end result – framing my children for eternity on my back. But something was missing. The two designs had to meet!

I continued to draw, and drew the middle section so the heart and the frame would join. It then took on a whole new life and new meaning. A new beginning for me. This tattoo also continued the swirls, and looks to me like feathers from the gods and forefathers. New beginnings come from the love of my children and wanting to be around to see what their futures hold.

But it didn't feel finished. There were two more drawings and tattoo sessions before I felt it was where it was meant to be at this time. After 23 hours, my tattoo now extends over my right shoulder to my collarbone and down over my left bicep. Just like a forever hug. Is it finished? I would say 'yes' at this point in time, but who knows what my imagination or tomorrow will bring?

My next tattoo is on my right wrist. This is the triple infinity knot with swirls of freedom around it. The knot represents me at the top and my two children, Zakariah and Alexandra, at the bottom of the knot. We are linked together by blood, love and ink for eternity. Zak has the infinity knot on his left inside ankle; he declared that he wanted to get it "without the girly sh*t on it", and Ally has the same design as mine on her left forearm.

My third tattoo came 12 months later, after my nanna had passed away and Zak was home for her funeral. He wanted to get something to remind him again of me and the special times we have shared. We are both Star Wars fans, so he thought it fitting to get matching lightsabers.

He got Darth Maul's double-ended red lightsaber, and I got Yoda's green lightsaber, on our feet. Zak's on the left foot again, and mine is on the right, along the bottom edge of the right side of the foot. To date, it has been the most painful of all of my tattoos. I have both of these on the right side of my body, as this means the love flows into my heart forever.

By 2015, I got my second colour tattoo. On my left wrist, over my radial artery. It was the 'Kiss Goodbye To MS' lips logo. I originally wanted to get this tattoo on my arse, so that MS could 'kiss my arse'. However, I decided it wasn't such a good idea, as after a few drinks, I'd likely want to show people. So, instead, I opted for the wrist. It also means a kiss of life. My life didn't stop when I was diagnosed with MS; it just took on a better meaning.

My next tattoo, number five, was behind my right ear. I kept seeing a particular symbol pop up on social media, and I looked into its meaning. It is the Zibu angelic symbol for Embrace Life. Something that I do each and every day. I got this tattoo not long after I had finished chemotherapy for having three primary cancers all at once – melanoma, lymphoma and leukaemia, plus two separate blood conditions, all while dealing with MS.

This symbol also reminded me of a time when I loved to compose classical music in my late teens. When I had big dreams to be a classical conductor and composer, but due to my mother's MS, I had to quit my degree and go home to care for her. I always thought I'd get back to it one day, but my own MS has caused an acquired brain injury, and unfortunately, that part of my brain is now gone. I can no longer even read music. But I know I still carry it deep within my own soul.

I was hooked on getting tattoos and couldn't wait to draw my next few. I used a few different artists, including one my son used in Townsville, Queensland. When I would go on holiday to visit Zak, who was stationed in the army there, I would also get a tattoo to bring me closer to him, as we live 3000 km apart.

In 2018, just before my son's wedding, I drew a dragonfly. I have always loved them and would imagine fairies riding on their backs. To me, they represent HOPE and new beginnings. This dragonfly was done in the watercolour technique, just as I painted it, but with a twist. Its body and head are a paintbrush. It is positioned on my left inside forearm, right with the strands of the paintbrush looking like it has painted MS's red lips.

You see, I was told in 2011 that I would never be able to work again, due to my disabilities and brain damage, by a medical professional. He told me to find a hobby as I would have a lot of time on my hands. I had always wanted to learn how to paint. It took me four months to walk into the art studio due to my anxiety, but once I did,

I took to it like a duck to water. I loved it. So, if I hadn't gotten MS, I may never have learned how to paint.

Art gave me back my purpose; when people see my art, they stop and smile and sometimes pass over their hard-earned money to buy my paintings, sculptures, drawings and illustrations. I am now an award-winning artist as well as a children's book author and illustrator.

My story also gives other people hope when they see what I have achieved despite the adversities I continue to face. I share my story as a keynote speaker throughout the world. Spreading the word of Hope.

At the same sitting, I got my left foot tattooed with swirls, as a way of rebelling: my dermatologist told me I wasn't allowed any more tattoos because it would make it too difficult to detect any new melanoma on my body. I'm not one to follow instructions very well. I can tell you that, out of my whole body, my feet have hurt the most. This is because the MS is worse in my feet and legs. So, no more tattoos down there for me.

The final tattoo I got in Bali was probably not my smartest move, as I have little immune system left due to all the treatments I've undergone to stay alive. Getting it done in a third-world country was not smart at all. I ended up with cellulitis, and was worried I would lose the colours from it, never mind all the damage it was actually causing my skin and bloodstream. This tattoo is on my left forearm, next to the dragonfly.

At the bottom of the tattoo is an open book. The book represents the books I have written and am currently writing and publishing to share my story and the stories of others. It gives them a voice and helps other people. One of the pages features the night sky, symbolising my belief that I can make a difference in this universe. Standing upright from the book is a microphone, representing my voice as a keynote speaker and author sharing my story to give people hope around the world.

In the centre of the book, a bird of paradise emerges. This flower was my mother's favourite. Although I never had a great relationship with her, she was still my mom, and I loved her. She passed away from complications related to her MS when I was 26 years old. Birds of paradise symbolise joyfulness, freedom, anticipation, paradise and excitement. They also represent faithfulness, love and thoughtfulness. It is said they also represent having a good perspective on life — all values I hold dear. Additionally, the bird of paradise resembles a phoenix rising out of the book, symbolising immortality, resurrection and life after death. Having survived three primary cancers and two blood conditions, all while living with MS, I have been able to recreate myself and the life I want to live.

My tattoos are not just pretty pictures; they capture the stories of overcoming adversities and positivity – loving things on my body from a spiritual place. They remind me of how far I have come and that I have the strength and courage to continue in this marvellous thing called life.

There is still plenty more canvas to cover!

As I mentioned, when I returned home to Australia after being tattooed in Bali, I became unwell. My arm felt like it was on fire, and I had a red rash working its way up from my forearm to my bicep, then to my shoulder. I had lots of angry blisters. It was like something out of a horror movie — so, another trip to my GP and more antibiotics. I had developed cellulitis from the bugs in Bali, due to having no immune system anymore.

The funny thing was, I was more worried about losing the colour from my new tattoo than the thought that I could actually lose my limb or even my life. I guess I had hardened the fuck up.

My back tattoo

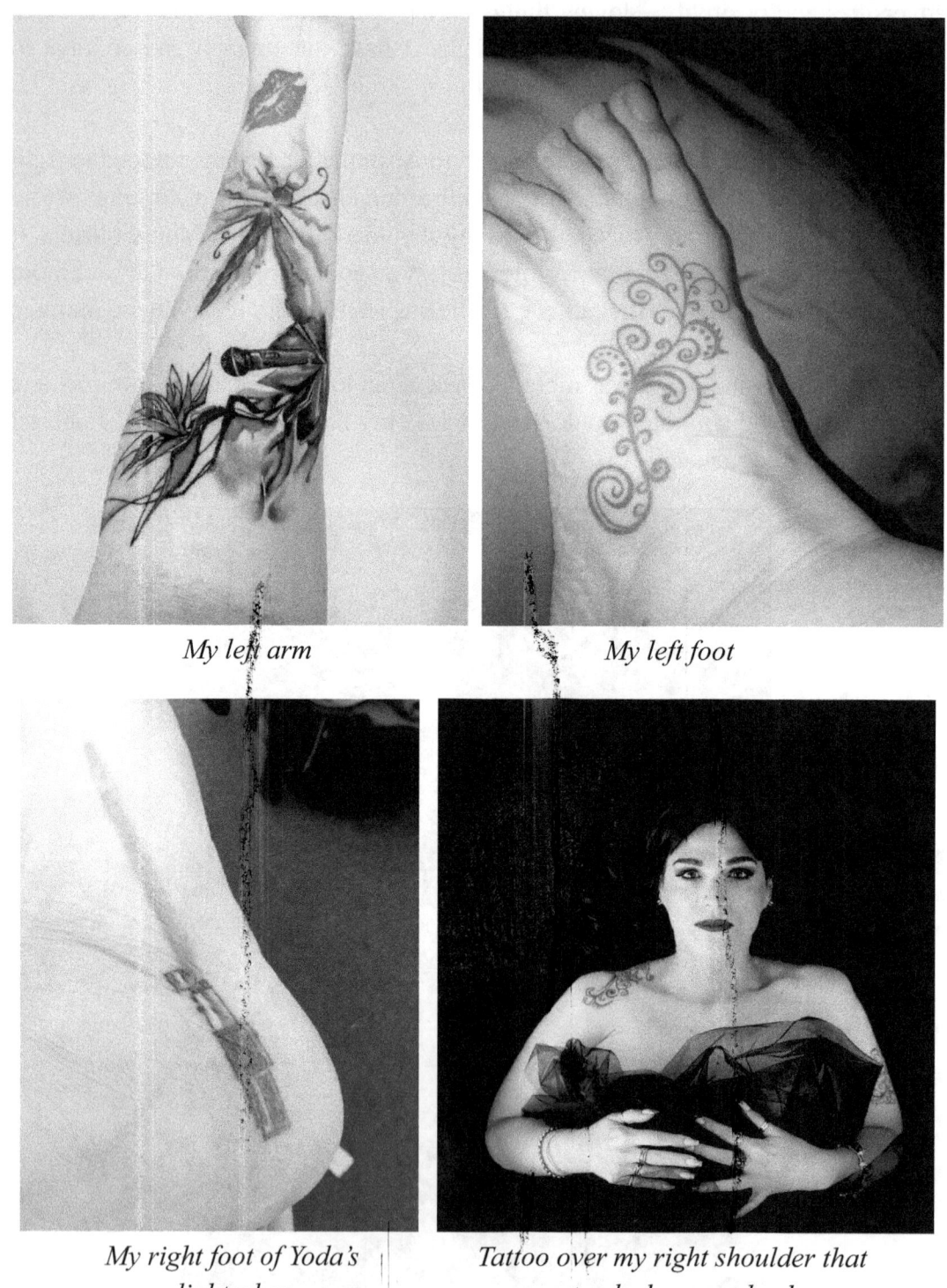

Triple infinity knot that my children also have

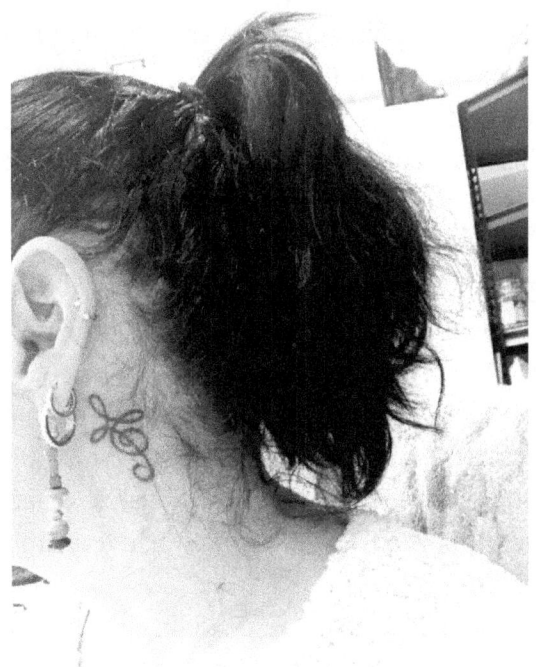

Zibu Angelic symbol for Hope

CHAPTER 38

The Elephant in the Room

Death is one of those things people pretend is far away, tucked out of sight, right until the moment it bursts into our lives and refuses to leave. People avoid the topic as though not naming it will stop it from happening. But death sits beside all of us every day. I have been keenly aware of it walking beside me. Someone once said to me that death follows me, but they were wrong. Death follows all of us. The difference is that I do not look away from it. I do not fear the conversations that others run from. I sit with people in the hardest moments of their lives and sometimes in the very last ones. I suppose that makes me appear to be familiar with death, but it is really loyalty, honesty and love that I follow.

We do not talk about death enough in our culture. It is treated like a forbidden subject, something whispered about or avoided entirely, as if pretending it is not there will keep it from arriving. But every single one of us will face it. No one gets out alive. Not one.

I have faced my own mortality more times than I care to count. My heart surgeries cracked open the illusion that my body was somehow immune to breaking. Lying on a hospital bed with machines charting every beat of your heart makes you suddenly aware that nothing is guaranteed. Then came the cancer. Stage four. The kind of diagnosis that takes the floor out from under you and leaves you in free fall. I remember the fear, the disbelief, the stillness of shock. I had to fight every single day to stay alive. Fight with every cell, every breath, every stubborn piece of me that refused to give in.

And then came the day I found Dean dead on the floor. Nothing prepares you for that. Nothing prepares you for the silence. That kind of loss splits something inside you, and it never goes back the same way again. That loss taught me that life can be here one moment and gone the next.

You might think that facing death so many times would make it easier to understand. It does not. If anything, it makes it stranger, sharper and more surreal. What it has done is deepen my compassion. It has made me soften, not harden. I learnt to soften the hell down. When you fight so hard to stay alive, when you choose life again and again despite pain, grief and trauma, it becomes almost unbearable to watch people throw their lives away. Not in judgement, but in sorrow. I worked so hard to remain here. I fought with everything I had to keep breathing, to keep walking, to keep existing. So watching people waste the very thing I nearly died for is something I struggle to make sense of.

Death has taught me that life is not measured in years but in choices. That every breath is a privilege. That love is the only thing that matters in the end. That connection is what carries us. That speaking openly about mortality does not bring death closer. It simply makes us braver, more honest and more present while we are still here.

I met Kerry in 2019 at a networking coffee catch-up. She came to my home shortly after, trying to sell me a new phone plan for her business. I did not join her multi-level marketing company, but we added each other on Facebook and stayed in each other's orbit. In late 2022, I posted, asking if anyone wanted to be my walking buddy. I needed accountability, motivation and company. Kerry replied immediately, saying she would love to walk with me. She had moved around the corner and was keen to get out each day.

So we started walking. Down to the highway and back, a neat two kilometres. She was living with stage four ovarian cancer. I was living with MS and recovering from domestic violence. Both of us were carrying pain, fear and uncertainty. But with each step, we kept each other afloat. If I did not feel like walking, she would be at my door. If she did not feel like walking, I would be ringing her asking where she was. Sometimes she slowed her pace so I could keep up with my wheelie walker. Other days, I could outpace her, and I knew she was struggling. We learnt each other's rhythms without needing to ask.

Our conversations were nothing like the usual small talk. We talked about death, treatment, pain, fear, funerals, regrets and mortality. All the things other people avoid. I asked her the hard questions because I understood. I had stood in her shoes with stage four cancer myself, staring down the possibility of dying. I think my survival gave her a sliver of hope that she might catch a miracle too.

Kerry's humour was one of my favourite things about her. Dry, sarcastic and whip smart. Once I got used to it, I returned it just as fast. We respected each other because we saw each other clearly. Two women walking through life's brutality and beauty at the same time. We walked hundreds of kilometres together in rain, hail and sunshine. Sometimes we changed scenery and walked along Eastern Beach. Those were some of our best days.

As her cancer progressed, the walks became fewer, but our friendship never shifted. We messaged constantly. I visited her in the hospital often. Some visits were confronting. One day, my good friend Helen and I walked in, and Kerry, frail and exhausted, told us to fuck off. I looked at her and said, "Well, tough luck, we're not going anywhere." She was embarrassed and vulnerable. She had not even told her children she was dying. She thought she was protecting them by keeping the truth hidden. I respected her choice, although it hurt my heart. I gently told her that if she did not tell them, they might resent her later for being robbed of precious time. But it still had to be her decision. Death is a journey we must walk honestly and on our own terms.

When she could no longer walk at all, I would pick her up, and we would drive to Torquay. We would sit in the car looking at the ocean, breathing in the salt air, talking about life and death, two women unafraid of the truth. One day, we could not find gluten-free food anywhere, so I went to IGA and came back with gluten-free crackers and lactose-free dips. We had our makeshift picnic in the car with a million-dollar view and laughed at the absurdity of life.

It was during one of these drives that I asked, "Would you like a living wake?" A chance to hear the words people would normally say after you are gone. A chance to feel that love while you are still here. Her eyes lit up. She said yes. I offered my home. As soon as I created the Facebook event, she invited everyone she had ever known. That was Kerry. All in, every time.

I also asked if she had prepaid for her funeral or thought about what she wanted. She had ideas, especially about music, but nothing organised. I booked an appointment with a funeral director. She cancelled it the morning of. It was too much. Too confronting. Making those choices forces you to stand face to face with your mortality. Most people never do it. We live in a culture terrified of death. We act like naming it brings it closer. Newsflash: none of us are getting out of this alive.

The day of the living wake arrived quickly. I moved furniture, lit candles, tidied the house and hoped people would turn up. You can never really be sure with Facebook events. But people came. More than sixty five. They brought food, hugs, tears and stories. My home was full of laughter, love, nostalgia and heartbreak all at once. I had a book for people to write messages to Kerry. Words she could read in the weeks ahead. She read them many times.

We held a small formal moment in the middle of the chaos. Everyone introduced themselves, because Kerry's circles overlapped in ways people did not realise. We shared memories. We cried. We laughed. The room was full of love. What we did not know was that Kerry had a day pass from the palliative care ward. I saw the hospital band on her wrist and felt the weight of it. She was closer to the end than she had admitted.

Too often, the only time people talk about what someone means to them is when they are already gone. People stand at funerals telling the most beautiful stories, while the person who deserves to hear them lies silent. The living wake gave Kerry what most people never receive. Her flowers while she was alive.

As Kerry's health declined, I supported the family as much as I could. I arranged for the funeral director to come to the ward. Together we planned her funeral. It was heavy but filled with love. She chose her sister and me to do her makeup for the viewing. I was honoured. She asked me to officiate her funeral because she did not want a stranger standing at the front speaking about her life. I agreed immediately. It was one of the greatest honours of my life.

We recorded her final messages. First on a Saturday night. Then again, the next morning, because she had makeup on and wanted to look her best. I laughed and told her she was the only dying woman I knew who would ask for a second take. She smirked and said, "Well I am not going out ugly!" That was Kerry.

During this time, I underwent a general anaesthetic to have nine cysts removed from my scalp. I knew I would be out of action for a few days, so I rang Helen and told her she needed to come. Kerry was slipping away. The stress caught up with me, and I became very ill with bronchitis, but I kept my phone by the bed every night, not on silent, waiting for that call.

Days passed. Then a week. Then two. She was fading. One day, she whispered, "I cannot." I felt something crack inside me. It is a privilege to sit with someone in that stage of life, but it is brutal.

On Friday, 26th July, at two in the afternoon, I received a message from Helen telling me to come. Kerry did not have long. When I arrived, her family stood around her bed. I put my hand on her arm, and she took her final breaths. A moment of absolute stillness. She was finally free of pain. Being allowed to be present in that moment was something I will carry for the rest of my life.

That night, I rang the funeral home to collect her. On Monday morning, Helen and I went in to finalise everything. Choosing her clothes made everything real. It hit me that I now had the most important speaking role of my life.

The viewing was on Wednesday. When I walked into the chapel and saw Kerry lying in the coffin I had chosen, my breath caught. The mortician had placed a lace doily over her face, and it took me back twenty seven years to my mother's viewing. Kerry looked different. Fuller in the face. Her teeth were back in. Her skin was cold to the touch.

Helen handed me Kerry's makeup bag and brushes. They were old and awful. I wished I had known earlier. I tried my best. I learnt very quickly that a normal foundation does not stick easily to dead skin and that Band-Aids do not either. Then there were the little round disks with tiny spikes under the eyelids to keep them closed. That made eyeshadow almost impossible. But we did it. We joked softly to her. Helen put on the bright pink lipstick she found. We looked at each other, horrified and said she will haunt us forever if we leave that on. So we changed it to her favourite red.

She looked peaceful. Beautiful. I lit a candle beside her and said my private goodbye.

On Friday, I officiated the funeral. I arrived early, wearing the brightest dress I own, a colourful Camilla piece covered in pink, purple, yellow and green with sparkles around the neckline. She wanted everyone in bright colours, and the room was a sea of them. When I saw the order of service with my name listed as celebrant, it became real.

The service opened with Disturbed's Sound of Silence. People were not expecting that. As the final seconds played, the funeral director and I walked together down the aisle, bowed in front of her coffin, and I walked to the front. I told everyone who I was and that every detail had been planned by Kerry herself. I played the one-minute video she had recorded saying her final message.

Her life was celebrated with honesty, laughter and colour. And of course, standing beside her coffin was a life-size banner of Chris Hemsworth, because she was obsessed with him. Two of her friends had brought it into the palliative ward, so naturally, he came to the funeral too.

She had personally rung ten people asking them to speak. They were stunned, but who can say no to a dying woman? At one point, the whole room was dancing. I kept myself together until the final closing words. Then I broke. The funeral director and I accompanied her coffin to the hearse and walked in front of it as a final act of respect. Then the wake began.

After the service, six people approached me and said it was the most beautiful funeral they had ever attended and asked if I would officiate theirs when the time came. Six people, all asking the same thing. It humbled me deeply. It made me realise that something meaningful had grown out of this heartbreak.

The following week, I looked into what was needed to become a funeral celebrant. It was simple. Within hours, I was registered and insured. Out of a life moment, something new was born. My services will not be all doom and gloom. They will be celebrations of life. Living wakes included. Exactly the way Kerry wanted hers.

Her death, like so many others before it, changed me. It reminded me that the most profound act of love is simply showing up. Being present. Holding space. And not shying away from the truth that touches every single one of us. Never be afraid of those who are dying, because one day it will be you.

2024 Kerry and me at the beach having our car picnics

2024 Kerry and myself at the living wake I organised for her.

2024 Kerry's funeral as the funeral celebrant

CHAPTER 39

Shame

Brene Brown writes, "I define shame as the intensely painful feeling or experience of believing that we are flawed and therefore unworthy of love and belonging – something we've experienced, done, or failed to do makes us unworthy of connection."

Writing in the impressive castle in Ireland, I realised how and why it had taken me so long to break through in writing MOXIE. It was actually 'shame'. I felt ashamed. I have watched Brene Brown's talks on shame and vulnerability several times, but it never occurred to me until recently that I had been ashamed.

I had always told myself the lie that I've never been ashamed of any of my past actions. But that is a colossal lie. There are so many things I have done that I wish I had never been put in the position of having to do; many of them were acts of survival.

There is no easy way to say any of this. I'm taking ownership of all that I have done. There have been so many men that I have slept with, way too many. I've lost count over the past 40 years, looking for that one repeated thing my whole life. LOVE. What's that old cliché, looking for love in all the wrong places? It just took me a while to work out that love and sex are two entirely different things. You can have love without sex and sex without love, and you can have love and sex together. But the latter is harder to find. Any two people can have sex without love, especially if one has no boundaries.

Poor choices in my past relationships stem from those feelings of never being good enough. Not being thin enough, not being pretty enough, just not being enough. I allowed them to do what they wanted to me, putting myself in harm's way. And, oh boy, it sure put me in harm's way over the years. I have been lied to, cheated on, raped, beaten and even had my bones broken by men who have claimed to love me. I am the first to admit I am lucky to still be alive considering the risks I have taken.

When a man showed me attention, I would wish and hope it would turn into love because, in my mind, I wasn't good enough or perfect enough. If he wanted to sleep with me, he surely must want a relationship with me. I've finally learned it doesn't work that way. It took me a long time to finally set some boundaries and stop being used. Why did he want to sleep with me? For a few reasons: I'm female, I have a vagina, and I had no boundaries. Simple. A winning combination for many men; they had won the lottery with me. But not anymore.

I wanted to be the perfect-looking woman for a man to love. I wanted to have a perfect, small, thin body for a man to fall in love with. I thought that had to be what was wrong with me, why I wasn't good enough. I picked on myself every single day. I bullied myself every single day. I was so hard on myself every single day.

I had lost weight in the past, a lot of weight and got to a place I was almost happy with, only to have my partner cheat on me (again) and not just with a woman but also with a man. How do you ever compete with that? You can't. I still wasn't good enough to keep a man.

I thought that being successful would cause a man to fall in love with me. I have made a success out of myself, only then to discover men tell me I'm intimidating! Really? I now realise I am not intimidating; I'm living my life on my terms. They are merely intimidated, which I now realise is their issue, not mine.

It was time to get some help to find out who I really was. I have been in counselling for over 13 years. Addressing the fear that has plagued me my whole life, of not being good enough, which has led to nearly every decision I have ever made — right and wrong, but mainly wrong ones.

So, let's get back to shame. If I had my life over again, would I do things differently? Yes, in a few cases. I wouldn't let men abuse and use me, believing they were loving me, because they absolutely weren't. They were just using my vagina and never cared about me. Did I allow it? Yes, I did. Was it intentional? No, it wasn't.

After years of counselling, I realised I had been responding from trauma in most situations, had no boundaries, and never protected my inner child. Did I know any different? No, I didn't. But that doesn't mean I let it continue. After M11 broke my arm, I knew I had to change. The common thread with all these men hurting me, was… me.

If I wanted someone different, then I had to behave differently, to protect myself and my inner child. I had to learn how to parent myself. I have done a fantastic job of parenting my own children. Raising them both to be in loving, caring relationships with healthy boundaries. Something that I never had myself growing up. It was time to lay down the baton of shame in the race I was running and start a new race — one where I am in control and aware of my actions — a future where I feel safe and loved first and foremost by myself.

It hasn't been easy at all. I am becoming more self-aware. I am scared, but putting strategies in place, parenting myself, and protecting my inner child so that I will never be in a position of ignoring red flags when they present themselves. Therefore, I will never be on the firing line of domestic violence ever again, both physical violence and coercive control.

Can you imagine what it has been like to live my whole life thus far carrying this burden and this shame?

Yes, I learnt to harden the fuck up. But I've also learnt how to soften the hell down. And in between the hard and the soft, I found my moxie. Not the loud kind. The quiet kind. The kind that keeps you alive when you're drowning inside yourself.

It's time to forgive myself.

I forgive myself.

2024 Her Story keynote Speaking

2023 This bag called me to buy it

2024 Her Story keynote speaking

2024 Momentum Empowerment talk in Perth

2024 Momentum Empowerment talk in Perth

2024 Photoshoot in my boardroom

2025 Disability Expo Speaking

CHAPTER 40

The Weight of a Blue Rosette

For a long time, I thought my story was something to survive, not something to speak about. I carried it quietly, like a weight strapped to my ribs. I did not think it had value. I did not think it made me special. I thought it made me broken. I thought it made me too much. Too messy. Too complicated. Too dark. So I did what a lot of people do when they are drowning. I kept going. I kept working. I kept smiling. I kept pushing through. I hardened the fuck up. I did not realise at the time that I was also building something else, something far more powerful than survival. I was building moxie.

Back then, I did not have a name for it. I just knew I had something inside me that refused to quit. Even when my body was failing. Even when grief was swallowing me whole. Even when my life did not look like anything I had imagined it would. I kept finding a way to stand back up. Not because it was easy, but because I had no other choice. And somewhere along the way, that stubborn grit turned into purpose.

When I first started speaking, my talks were mostly built around the part of my story that began in 2011, when I was diagnosed with multiple sclerosis. That was the obvious starting point. The public version of my pain. The part people could understand because it came with a diagnosis, and scans, and specialists, and medical language that made it sound real enough for the world to believe. It was the chapter of my life that had a name people recognised. MS. Cancer. Disability. Survival. And at the start, that was enough, because it had to be. I was still learning how to use my voice without shaking.

But speaking has a funny way of changing you. The more you say things out loud, the less power they have over you. The more you tell the truth, the less shame can survive in your body. And every time I stood on a stage and saw someone crying in the audience, not because they pitied me but because they finally felt understood, something shifted. I started to realise that my voice mattered. Not because I was special, but because what I had lived through was real, and people needed real. People needed to hear that they were not alone. People needed hope.

Over time, my talks began to evolve, because I began to evolve. I stopped staying in the safe section of my story. I stopped polishing my life to make it palatable. I stopped hiding behind the neat timeline of diagnosis and treatment, and I started talking about the deeper truth. The truth that the MS chapter was not the beginning of my adversity. It was just the chapter where my body finally forced the world to pay attention. As you have just read, my story started long before that. It started in childhood. In trauma. In shame. In survival mode. In believing I was not good enough. In carrying adult-sized burdens as a teenager. In being a young mum doing her best while quietly falling apart.

And this is where the real power of my talks came from, because suddenly it was not just a medical story. It was a human story. It was a story about resilience. About rebuilding. About identity. About loss and grit and determination and passion. About falling down and choosing to rise anyway. That is what moxie is. It is not just bravado. It is not fake confidence. It is not a motivational quote slapped on a mug. Moxie is the part of you that keeps going when you have every reason to stop. It is the part of you that says, not today.

The more my speaking grew, the more I realised it was never just about telling people what happened to me. It was about teaching people what I learnt from it. Because survival is one thing, but meaning is another. And at some point, I stopped speaking just to share my story, and I started speaking to give people tools. Actual strategies. Real life practices. Mindset shifts. Things people could use in their own lives when they were in the trenches, in their own grief, in their own illness, in their own trauma, in their own shame. That is where Resilience Mindset was born, not as a brand, but as a mission.

Coaching became the natural next step, because after a talk people would come up to me and say, "How do you do it?" Not in a surface way, but in a desperate way. They wanted to know how you survive when life is relentless. They wanted to know how you keep going when your body is failing and your heart is broken and the world keeps moving anyway. They wanted to know how you build confidence when you have been torn down for years. They wanted to know how you stop blaming yourself. How you stop carrying shame for things you never had control over. How you forgive yourself. How you soften down, after decades of hardening up. How you find your own moxie.

So I started coaching resilience clients. Not because I had a perfect life, but because I had lived it. I had walked through the fire, and I had learnt what actually works. I had learnt how to create routines that keep you afloat. I had learnt how to build mental strength without becoming emotionally numb. I had learnt how to keep fighting without losing yourself. I had learnt how to turn pain into purpose. And I had learnt how to speak to people in a way that made them feel safe, seen, and capable again.

Then the speaking took another leap. I started being invited to bigger stages, wider audiences, different rooms, and different industries. It stopped being just disability spaces, though those will always be part of my world. It became leadership events, business events, community events, conferences, keynotes and workshops. I also launched the Resilience Mindset podcast, which became another platform to share the tools, stories and strategies behind how I keep getting back up. And with each opportunity, my confidence grew. Not ego. Confidence. The kind that comes from knowing you have earned every word you say.

The wildest part is that my story did not just reach Australians. It went international. I spoke in Bali. I spoke in Ireland. And this year I'm speaking in London and Paris. Sometimes I still cannot believe that sentence belongs to me. Because the truth is, on paper, I should not be here. I lived through stage 4 cancer. I failed English at school. I struggled academically. I grew up with chaos and pressure and pain. I was told in a hundred different ways that I was not enough. And yet here I am, travelling the world with my voice. Not despite what I have lived through, but because of it.

Every time I walk into a room or an auditorium, onto a stage or a platform to speak, I feel the same thing. Pride. Gratitude. Disbelief. And a deep quiet knowing. I am exactly where I am meant to be. Not because life has been kind, but because I did not quit. Because I kept going when it would have been easier to disappear. Because I took everything I have been through and decided it would not end me, it would build me. That is moxie. That is what this book is. That is who I am.

And I want to be clear about something. I am not inspiring because of what happened to me. I am inspiring because of what I chose to do with it. Because I made a decision, over and over again, to keep turning up. To keep finding meaning. To keep transforming trauma into purpose. To keep helping other people. That is why I speak. That is why I coach. That is why I publish books. That is why I build communities. Because I know what it feels like to feel hopeless. And I never want anyone else to feel alone in that darkness.

This is the part people do not always see. Speaking is not just getting on stage and telling a story. Speaking is carrying the emotional load of other people's pain after you step off that stage. It is holding space for their grief. Their triggers. Their memories. Their breakdowns. Their breakthroughs. It is hugging strangers who are sobbing because you put language to a feeling they have carried for years. It is reading messages at midnight from someone saying, "I was going to end it but then I heard you speak." And realising that your life is no longer just yours. It is a lighthouse for others.

And I'll be honest, it's not always easy. There are days my body screams at me to stop. There are days I am exhausted. There are days I feel like I have nothing left to give. But even in those moments, my purpose holds me up. Because I am used to things going wrong. It is my normal. But what I am not used to, what I still marvel at, is that everything going wrong did not destroy me. It shaped me. It sharpened me. It built me into someone who can walk into a room and change energy. Someone who can take pain and turn it into power. Someone who can make people believe in themselves again.

I sought counselling to make sense of my life. To untangle the trauma. To understand my patterns. To rebuild my worth. And through that process, I learnt the biggest truth of all. Shame grows in silence. Healing grows in truth. And moxie is not just hardening up. Moxie is also learning when you do not have to fight anymore. It is learning when you are allowed to soften. It is learning that strength is not always loud. Sometimes strength is rest. Sometimes strength is boundaries. Sometimes strength is saying, "I need help." Sometimes strength is forgiving yourself.

That is why I do what I do now. Because I have lived the burden and shame. I have carried it for decades. And I know what it costs. I know what it steals from you. I know how heavy it is. And I also know this. You can survive it. You can rebuild. You can heal. You can create a life you love, even with scars. Even with disability. Even with trauma. Even with grief. Even with the messy bits still clinging to you.

My story is not a tragedy. It is a testimony.

And every time I speak, every time I coach, every time I publish, every time I stand up and tell the truth, I am choosing moxie again. I am choosing grit, determination, passion. I am choosing to live. I am choosing to be the hope I needed when I was younger.

I am not finished.

I am only getting started.

There is a question I get asked more than almost anything else, especially when people see another finalist announcement pop up on my socials or they walk into my office and spot yet another trophy tucked on a shelf:

"Why do you enter so many awards?"

It is never said with malice. Sometimes it is curiosity. Sometimes it is admiration. Sometimes it is that quiet edge people carry when they have never stood in an arena themselves. But beneath the question sits the same curiosity. They want to know what all this means to me, why I chase them, why I keep showing up, and why I continue to put myself and my businesses in those rooms.

To answer that, I cannot begin in my fifties. I cannot begin with MS in remission, or the resilience coaching, or the speaking gigs, or the business accolades. I cannot begin on stages or at award nights in glamorous gowns. I have to start where it really began. The place most wounds begin. Childhood.

For as long as I can remember, achievements were my language. Not because I wanted to be better than anyone else, but because I was longing for something I did not know how to ask for. Pride. Approval. A simple, 'I am proud of you.' I was not the little girl who was showered with praise. I was the little girl who learnt quickly that if I wanted words of affirmation, I had to earn them. And often even when I earned them, they never came. My father has told me only twice in my life he was proud of me.

In Year 5, in 1981, I won my very first art award. The painting was simple. Pink background, blue vase, flowers. But hearing my name called felt like someone had lit a sparkler inside my chest. First prize. A blue rosette. I wanted my mum to say she was proud of me. I wanted her to tell me I was special. Instead, she was in hospital being diagnosed with MS, and my brother and I were living with our grandparents. Her pride never came. That blue rosette is now forty four years old. I have carried it with me across states, houses, heartbreaks and entire chapters of my life. It is the only surviving piece of my childhood art. Nothing else was saved.

Achievements became the way I coped. The way I tried to fill the gap that silence had left behind. High school added its own wounds. I was in the bottom English class. We had five classes. Number one was the top. The clever ones. The A grade, star students. We called them nerds. They called us worse. We were the 'veggie' class. Imagine being told at fifteen that your intelligence was wilted. That you were already stamped as less capable, less bright, less likely. Words like that burrow themselves under your skin. They become false beliefs that follow you into adulthood. I failed English terribly. I was told I talked too much. Ironic, considering that talking became my career and I am now paid very well to stand on stages and speak.

But back then, none of that felt possible. I was simply the girl who tried very hard for very little acknowledgment. The girl who wanted someone to clap. The girl who wrote down the top one hundred songs from the radio every Saturday afternoon so she could win a free album. Which I did. Twice. Once for Fergal Sharkey. Once for Toni Childs. And once again, I was proud. And once again, it was met with silence.

By adulthood, achievement was woven into my DNA. I did not understand the psychology of it at the time. I simply knew that entering competitions felt natural to me. I entered hobby ceramics shows and won my way from beginner through to professional. I entered photography competitions and brought home ribbons for my portraits. I created the Christmas window competition for the Glen Innes Chamber of Commerce and Jangles Fashion Hut won that recognition that year.

In 2002, I won tug of war trophies and volleyball awards. I began collecting state titles, then national medals. I went on to break world records. I won the LeRêve Founders Day Award in 1994. A WW weight loss award in 2007. Then came the Tupperware awards between 2007 and 2010. In 2013, the art awards began rolling in. In 2021, the business awards followed. Strongman medals. Olympic weightlifting victories. Powerlifting competitions. Disability awards. Author awards. Accolades for every business I have built.

But none of that explains the 'why'. None of it touches the real story.

The truth is, I did not know why I was entering so many awards until a book cracked me wide open:

'Will I Ever Be Good Enough? Healing the Daughters of Narcissistic Mothers', by Dr Karyl McBride.

That book was a mirror I did not know I needed. It put language to wounds I had carried for decades. It explained the narc mother wound. It explained the ache for approval. It explained why achievements felt like oxygen. Why validation meant survival. Why no matter how much I won, it never filled the gap. That book made sense of my entire life. It did not excuse it. But it explained it.

Then came the healing.

Hundreds of counselling sessions over thirteen years. Week after week. Session after session. It was not glamorous. It was not easy. It stripped me back to the rawest version of myself. I had walked into my counsellor's room in 2012 as a woman who was angry, exhausted, hurt, defensive and so tightly armoured that nothing real could get in. I had been through trauma. Illness. Violence. Loss. I had lived with MS. I had survived stage four cancer. I had buried my partner. I had fought so hard to stay alive that I forgot how to simply live.

Counselling softened me. Not into weakness. Into truth. Into clarity. Into peace. Into a softness that only comes from doing the deep work. I learnt to breathe instead of fight. Feel instead of flee. Speak instead of swallow my pain. I learnt that my mother's wounds were hers, not mine. I learnt that love should not be earned. I learnt boundaries. I learnt my worth. And gradually, I softened the hell down.

That softness is not fragility. It is the greatest strength I have ever held.

When that healing settled into my bones, everything shifted. Especially my relationship with awards.

I realised I no longer needed them to fill a void. My validation was no longer external. It was internal. I was finally enough without any trophy telling me so. Awards no longer gave me worth. They reflected the worth I already knew I had.

That is the moment the 'why' changed.

Today, I enter awards for very different reasons.

I enter awards because I am proud of myself.

> Because I back myself.
>
> Because my work matters.
>
> Because I want disabled people to see what is possible.
>
> Because my businesses change lives.
>
> Because my story gives hope.
>
> Because awards increase visibility for my authors.
>
> Because standing in excellence encourages others to rise.
>
> Because joy is allowed to be celebrated.
>
> Because achievement deserves acknowledgement.
>
> Because success is not a dirty word.
>
> Because representation matters.
>
> Because advocacy needs a microphone.
>
> Because when I win, others win too.

I do not enter awards hoping for someone to finally clap. I clap for myself now. And that internal shift has changed everything.

Of course, not everyone understands that. Some people project their own insecurities. I learnt that the hard way with Miss X, a woman I had considered a friend. Someone I had fed at my table. Someone who decided that my awards were a personal offence to her. When I made it into the top applications out of nearly five thousand entries for the 2023 Australian Small Business Champion Awards, she messaged my staff, abusing us for how we marketed ourselves. She did not have the courage to message me. Suzie and I were sitting on the runway waiting to fly home after one of the best nights ever when the message came through. We ignored it. Six months later, when I won the Geelong Business Excellence Awards 'Business Leader of the Year', she had the audacity to congratulate me for winning something with purpose. The hypocrisy was astounding.

But it taught me something vital. The people who criticise you the loudest are often the ones doing the least. My Aunty Lynny always says, "Stay in your own lane, Justy." And she is right. When I stay in my lane, life feels peaceful. Purposeful. Aligned. Miss X was not paying my power bill. She was not putting food on my table. She was not contributing to my joy. Why should her opinion matter?

That was not the first time I had experienced jealousy disguised as critique. Years earlier, a fellow art student came for a cuppa and casually informed me that people at another art group were asking who I thought I was. They did not like that I was creating art that did not fit their expectations. It gutted me at the time. I carried the hurt longer than I should have. Then it clicked one day. They were jealous. My art made them question their own choices. Their own courage. Their own potential. People lash out at what they do not understand, and at what they secretly wish they had the bravery to do. I realised then that their opinion was none of my business. And I let it go.

Then came Bali.

In July 2023 I enrolled in a writer's retreat in Ubud. It was the first time I had ever travelled overseas alone. I talked myself through every stage so my anxiety would not win. Travelling with disabilities takes extra planning, especially with SCIG therapy, but I did it. I took the 'no love' bus to the airport. It is really the Gull Bus, but we have named it the 'no love' bus, for when you have no family or friends to take you or pick you up from the airport. I packed my matching rose gold luggage. I arrived in Bali terrified and excited. The retreat was life changing. Five days of writing, reflection, connection and clarity. I felt closer to God than ever before. I extended my stay for some well deserved rest. I spent my days writing by the infinity pool in a bikini. And then came the fall. My foot slipped on wet slate by the pool and my legs went flying. I landed flat on my front in front of a crowd drinking cocktails at happy hour. Humiliating, yes. Painful, yes. Dangerous, absolutely. I lay there thinking I had broken something. And then I reminded myself that even if I had, I was not alone. I had travel insurance. I had people I could call. And I was still here.

That fall bruised my leg but strengthened my resolve. I knew I wanted to finish my book. I knew I wanted to step deeper into being an author and a publisher. I knew I wanted to keep rising. That retreat cemented it.

And through all of this, the awards kept coming.

Here is the complete list, in date order, because I am proud of every one of them:

1994
Le Rêve Founders Day Award

1992 to 1999
Hobby Ceramics Champion of the show, 1st, 2nd and 3rds

2002 to 2005
Tug of War Medals, National and State level

2002 to 2003
Volleyball trophies

2004 to 2011
World records in All-round Weightlifting

2013 to 2016
Olympic Weightlifting State and National medals and titles

2007
Weight Watchers weight loss award

2007 to 2010
Tupperware Team and Management Awards

2015
Learn Local Awards runner-up out of 55,000 people

2019
- Barwon Health Volunteer Of The Year Consumer Representative: Winner
- Geelong Women In Community Life Living with a Disability Award: Winner
- Disability Services Commissioner Award: Winner

2021
- Geelong Awards for People with a Disability Achievement Award
- Roar Success Awards
  - GOLD Australian Creative Artist of the Year
- Ausmumprenuer Awards
  - GOLD Coach Of The Year

- SILVER Disabled Business Excellence
- SILVER Creative Entrepreneur
- BRONZE Business Pivot
- BRONZE Overcoming The Odds

2022
- International coach/speaker of the year -Judges' choice award
- Ausmumprenuer Awards
  - BRONZE Disabled Business Excellence

2023
- Geelong Business Excellence Awards
  Winner GBEA Business Leader of the Year
- Ausmumpreneur awards
  - GOLD - Disabled Business Excellence
  - BRONZE - One to Watch Award
  - SILVER - Overcoming the Odds Award
  - SILVER - Podcast Award

2024
- Geelong Awards for People with Disability 2024
  - Winner Business Leadership Award
- International STEVIE® Awards
  - GOLD Social Change Maker of the Year - Disability
- ABLE Golden Book Awards 2024 Winner
  - Gold for Best in Anthology Book - Whispers of Resilience
- Ausmumpreneur Awards 2024 Winner
  - GOLD for Disabled Business Excellence
  - SILVER for Creative Entrepreneurs
  - Honourable Mention for Business Coaching
- Top 10 Voices - Women's Business Voice Award and Tamsin's Choice Award
- Women Changing the World Awards - Disability Leadership Awards (Silver)
- Momentum Empowering Woman Of The Year Award - Winner

2025

- International STEVIE® Awards
  - Silver Award for Social Change Maker of the Year - Disability.
- ABLE Golden Book Awards Winner
  - Silver Award in Anthology Book for "Breaking The Barriers : Story Through The Lens"
- FLARE of the Year
- Ausmumpreneur Awards
  - Gold for Podcast Award
  - Gold for Disabled Business Excellence
  - Silver for Creative Entrepreneur
  - Silver for Author award
  - Bronze for Business Pivot Award
- Heart of Women Awards
  - Entrepreneur of the Year,
  - Runner-Up – Health & Disability Award
  - 2nd Runner-Up – Woman of the Year Award
- Women Changing the World Global Awards Winner
  - SILVER in Disability Leadership

And that is not even all of them.
Because I still enter awards.
And I will continue to enter them.
Not because I need validation.
Because I deserve to be in those rooms.

Awards have become the echo of the life I have built. The life I fought for. The life I never thought I would live. For a disabled woman to stand on a stage and be applauded is not just a personal win. It is a message. It says, 'Look at what is possible.' It says, 'Your story is not a limitation.' It says, 'If I can, you can.'

Awards no longer define me. But they amplify me.

They amplify my advocacy.
My authors.
My message.
My resilience work.

THE WEIGHT OF A BLUE ROSETTE

My creativity.
My courage.
My softness.
My story.
My impact.

The little girl with the blue rosette once stood wondering if she would ever be enough.

The woman writing this chapter knows she is.

Not because of the awards.

But because she has finally chosen to clap for herself.

Awards reflect the woman I have become. Strong but soft. Brave but grounded. Purpose driven. Healed. Enough.

Each award is not a replacement for love. It is a celebration of the life I have built from the ashes of the one I lost. Each ceremony is not an attempt to prove anything. It is a moment to stand in my truth. Each nomination is not a plea to be seen. It is an act of visibility that shows what disabled women can achieve when they refuse to give up.

Awards are not my identity. But they are the glittering by-product of a woman who finally knows her worth.

1981 Spring Flowers Painting that won

2021 Ausmumpreneur Awards

MOXIE

2021 Geelong Disability Award for Achievement

2022 National newspaper article

2023 Front page Glen Innes Examiner

2023 GBEA with Les Watson the Time Lord

2024 ABLE book awards with my children's book Finding Hope

2024 Business mentoring

2024 GBEA with Matthew, Ally, Myself, Jo Jo, Corey and Les.

2024 My name in lights at Emmaville Central School

2024 Vision board

2025 Ausmumpreneur Awards

2025 Ausmumpreneur Conference with Ally and Maycee

2025 Flare of the Year award

2025 Geelong Advertiser newspaper

2025 Geelong Times front cover

2025 HOW Entrepreneur of the Year

2025 Morpheus Publishing

2025 Proud mumma moment with Ally winning awards at Ausmumpreneur awards

2025 Speaking at the Ausmumpreneur Conference

2026 All my awards

Geelong Times article

CHAPTER 41

I Forgave Her

Every time I go back to Glen Innes, I forget one thing. It takes me about an hour to walk two blocks.

It does not matter how many times I return; I still underestimate it. I step out thinking I am just going to duck down the street quickly, stretch my legs, breathe in that cold New England air, maybe grab something small, then jump back in the car. But that is not how it works in a country town. You do not simply duck down the street. The moment you appear on the footpath, it starts.

Childhood friends. Schoolmates. People who used to work with Mum. People who remember Simon. People who remember me as a young mum with two kids hanging off my hips. People who look you in the eye and say your name like you never left. And so yes, it takes me an hour to walk two blocks. Every trip home.

That is the magic of Glen Innes. You cannot hide, even if you wanted to. And the truth is, I do not want to. There is something grounding about being seen. Being remembered. Being part of a place that still holds the history of who you were. Every familiar face reminds me of something important. People do not forget you as quickly as you think they will. They remember your kindness. They remember your family. They remember your laugh. They remember your wins and they remember your losses. They remember you as part of the fabric of the town.

For a long time, I thought leaving meant disappearing. As though, if I drove far enough away, the past could not reach me. But Glen Innes does not work like that. It carries you whether you live there or not.

One of the trips home that hit me the hardest was in 2023.

I had gone back to speak at the RSL. Not about some polished, sugar-coated version of my life either. I spoke about my story. About the adversities. About the chaos. About the things most people do not say out loud. I spoke about what I survived and what I built. I spoke about how far I had come since leaving Glen Innes, and I did it for a reason. To show people that where you start does not determine where you finish. To prove that your past does not get to write your ending.

Standing there in front of familiar faces was surreal. In Glen Innes, people remember you as the version they knew. They remember you when you were little. They remember you when you were struggling. And there I was, back in my hometown, standing up the front, sharing the truth, not just the shameful bits, not just the broken girl version. The whole story. The woman version. The survivor version. The version that built something out of nothing.

When I finished speaking, people did not just clap politely and head for the exit. They came up to me. They hugged me. Proper hugs. The kind that squeezes the air out of you. People held my hands. People looked me straight in the face and told me they were proud. Some of them cried. Some of them shared their own stories. Some just said, "Thank you." And that is when I realised something.

My story does not just belong to me anymore.

It belongs to everyone who needs proof that when life is brutal, you can still rise.

Walking out of the RSL after that talk, I felt the nerves leave my body and something else replace them. Not arrogance. Not ego. Just a quiet certainty that my voice was never the problem. Maybe it was the tool. Maybe everything I had lived through was not pointless suffering. Maybe it was the training ground for what I do now. That night did not just reconnect me with the town, it reconnected me with myself. It reminded me that moxie is not something you are born with. It is something you build, layer by layer, every time life tries to flatten you and you refuse. My talk made the front page of the Glen Innes Examiner, the town's local paper.

And then of course, I did what I always do in Glen Innes. I tried to walk down the street quickly and it took me forever. One person turned into five. Five turned into ten. And the whole time I kept thinking, this town holds the entire timeline of my life. It holds the old me. It holds the young me. It holds the memories I have tried to avoid. But it also holds something else too. Proof. That I existed. That Mum existed. That my life was real. That my story mattered.

Emmaville Central School contacted me to come and speak to the high school students on 27th November 2024. When I pulled up outside the school, on a big digital notice board, written in flashing lights was 'Justine Martin, Author and Public Speaker, 27-11-24'. What a surreal moment. 42 years ago, I walked into this school. It was the fourth primary school I had been to in just over 12 months! It was fantastic to be able to share some wisdom on how to gain resilience, self-awareness and what MS does to your body to the high school students.

That same trip home saw me invited to the Glen Innes Library's 70th Birthday celebrations as their guest keynote speaker. This meant more to me than I can explain. Not because I spent time in the library when growing up (I didn't), but because it symbolised something much bigger. It was recognition. It was being invited back, not as the girl who struggled, but as the woman who survived, built a life, and turned adversity into something meaningful.

Until that point, most of my talks had focused on 2011 onwards, when I was diagnosed with multiple sclerosis. That was the chapter people knew. The public chapter. The part of my story that made sense to the outside world because it had a clear starting point, a diagnosis, a reason. But that day, standing in my hometown, I finally spoke about what came before it. The part of my life I had spent years trying to bury. The part where I was still a kid, still trying to survive school, still carrying responsibilities that never should have been mine in the first place.

That day I told my story properly for the first time in Glen Innes, out loud, in a room full of people who knew my face, my family name and my past, or at least pieces of it. I spoke about how hard school was for me, how low my English grades were, how much I struggled, and how much shame I carried for years, thinking I wasn't good enough. I spoke about how hard it was at home with Mum, what we were living with behind closed doors, and how much Simon and I were trying to manage with no one really seeing it. But I also spoke about what I have built since leaving. Becoming an author. Becoming a publisher. Creating Morpheus Publishing and helping other people tell their stories. Building businesses, building a platform, and somehow turning all the pain into purpose.

And then something happened after my talk that I will never forget. One of my teachers was in the audience. She came up to me afterwards, emotional, and she apologised. She told me the school and the system had let Simon and me down. She said she had no idea what was happening at home. That moment hit me like a wave, because it validated what I lived through. It wasn't all in my head. I wasn't weak. I wasn't being dramatic. I was a kid surviving things no kid should have to endure.

I donated every book I have written and illustrated to the library that day, and that felt like my way of closing a loop. Not rewriting my past, but honouring it. Giving back to the town that shaped me, and proving to myself just how far I have come.

My trip home in June 2025 saw me repeat what I do each visit home, 'chuck a lap up the main street', but this trip I also drove up to Martins Lookout. That place holds a special memory etched permanently in my mind. In 1987, my brother Simon and I walked all the way up there in the dark, at about 4 am, to watch Halley's Comet fly across the sky. Mum insisted we see it, because it only appears once every seventy-five years. She was already sick by then, but she made sure we did not miss that moment. I can still see Simon and me lying on the massive boulders, staring up at the night sky in absolute wonder. For a brief moment in our messy childhood, everything felt magical.

Standing there again in 2025 brought tears to my eyes. For the lost years. For the broken years. For the beautiful ones, too. I looked across the New England hills and felt that strange mixture of grief and gratitude that only comes with age.

When I go 'home', I stay at my brother's farm. One thousand acres of rolling New England country. Open skies. Wind that hums through the grass. A peace that sits heavy and soft at the same time. There is something about that land that settles me in ways I cannot explain. Maybe it is because it feels stable. Solid. A place where memories live without hurting. Whenever I am there, I feel grounded. Safe. Connected. Like the land itself is holding me.

Simon and I talked about Mum. About childhood. About life now. About how far we have come. Being with my brother and sister-in-law brings a comfort that only family can. It is the closest thing to home I have left.

By the time I returned again in mid-October 2025, the full circle moment was waiting for me.

I wanted to visit the Loloma Tin Mine in Emmaville. It is the reason we moved to Glen Innes in the first place. Sitting in the car looking out at that landscape, I had one of those moments where your life suddenly makes sense in reverse. I thought to myself, what if Mum had never become sick with MS? What if she had never struggled? What if she had lived without the pain and limit of her illness? What if we had never moved? My life would have been unrecognisable. I never would have met the people who shaped me. I never would have ended up in Melbourne. I never would have built the life I have today. Everything truly does happen for a reason, even when the reason does not reveal itself until decades later.

I was invited to be the keynote speaker at my old school, Emmaville Central School's 150th birthday reunion celebration dinner.

That was not a small thing. That was a huge thing.

Because school was not where I shone. School was where I felt dumb. Where I felt ashamed. Where I felt like failure was stamped onto my forehead. Where I was trying to survive what was happening at home while pretending everything was normal. The place where I struggled through classes, struggled with confidence, and could not see a future bigger than Glen Innes.

Attending the birthday reunion dinner as the woman I am now felt almost unreal. Like I had stepped into an alternate universe. I was no longer the teenager trying not to be noticed. I was the speaker. I was the one standing at the front. I was the one showing the ex-students that their circumstances do not get to define them.

I spoke to the former students about resilience, courage and finding a place in the world even when life feels like it is pulling you in the opposite direction. They listened. They connected. Some of them cried. Some hugged me afterwards. I walked out of there feeling ten feet tall, not because of ego, but because I could feel the connection between my past, their present and the future they are walking into.

And it hit me, while standing there, that this is what moxie looks like.

Not the trophies. Not the titles. Not the awards.

Moxie is returning to the place that once made you feel small… and taking up space anyway.

Moxie is looking at the version of you that used to feel trapped, and saying, 'Look. You made it.'

After the school talk, it happened again. The one hour to walk two blocks. I tried to walk down the street and people kept stopping me. People who remembered me from school. People who knew Mum. People who had watched my whole story from the outside. People who could not believe I had come back as a speaker. Hugs. Tears. Hands on my arm. The disbelief on their faces turning into pride.

That is Glen Innes. You cannot hide.

And I did not want to.

During that October trip, and previously in June 2025, I did something else I had avoided for years. I drove past every childhood home we ever lived in. I do not know what made me do it. Maybe I needed to prove to myself those houses did not own me anymore. Maybe I wanted to see if the walls still held power. Maybe I wanted to reclaim them. Or maybe part of me needed to remind myself that I survived every room, every fear, every night I lay awake wondering what would happen next.

Driving slowly past each house felt like flipping through the pages of a book I once tried to close forever. Each home held a version of me I had not spoken to in a long time. The version who learnt to be an adult far too early. The version who was always bracing for the next disaster. The version who carried responsibility that never belonged to a child.

And then I went to the home I built. The one I poured everything into. The one I lost.

Sitting outside it with the engine running, I felt a sadness that sat heavy in my chest. Not regret. Not pain exactly. More like a quiet acknowledgement of what that

I FORGAVE HER

home represented. The stability I tried to build. The life I tried to create. The version of me who still believed that if you just tried hard enough, everything would be ok.

15th October was Mum's birthday. She would have been 78 years old.

Being in Glen Innes at that time meant I could visit her grave on her birthday, which then brought up emotions I had not allowed myself to fully feel in decades. Leaving Glen Innes all those years ago had been its own grief. Not just leaving the town, but leaving Mum's grave behind. Knowing I could not simply drive up the hill when I needed her. Knowing I could not visit when I was overwhelmed, lonely or in need of guidance. Knowing I had to grieve from afar. That distance created a wound I had never acknowledged.

But on that October day in 2025, I drove straight to the cemetery.

It was warm. Still. Quiet. The kind of New England day where the sun sits softly on your skin and the air carries a faint smell of eucalyptus. I parked beside the tap, the way I have always done. My body walked the familiar path as if it were yesterday, not more than twenty-seven years since she passed. I went to the exact spot without even looking at the plaques. I know that lawn too well.

Row AC. Number six.

I lowered myself onto the grass, right above her. The scorched peanut bar I had left months earlier was still sitting there. Not even touched by ants or birds. Perfectly preserved. I laughed through tears, thinking about how Mum used to hide her chocolates in the pantry and count them to make sure Simon and I had not stolen any. Violet Crumbles were her favourite. I left chocolates instead of flowers because flowers remind me of sickness and death. They die too quickly and feel wasteful. I much prefer a living plant. But chocolates felt right for Mum. Something she would have smiled at.

As I sat there, I felt the grass dampen my clothes. It must have rained recently, but I did not care. I felt closer to her than I had in years. Maybe ever. The cemetery around me was colourful as always. Fresh bouquets on almost every headstone. A place full of love and endings sitting together quietly. There was no one else there. Just me and Mum. Just us.

And that is when I said the words aloud.

The words that said I had forgiven her in my heart long before this day, but had never spoken out loud to her resting place.

I forgave her.
> For the things she said in anger.
> For the things she could not say.
> For the emotional distance she could not bridge.

For the mother she could not be because of her illness.

For the mother she tried so hard to be but never felt she succeeded.

For the years she suffered with no support.

For the loneliness she must have felt every single day.

For the pain she carried quietly.

For the mistakes she made that left marks on my growing heart.

I forgave her because I finally understood.

She was young.

She was sick.

She had no disability pension.

No counselling.

No medications like we have now.

No NDIS.

No support worker to give her respite.

No one to lean on.

She was drowning while trying to raise us.

As I sat on that grass, I said it all. I told her I loved her. I told her I forgave her. I told her I wished she had been given more support, more love, more compassion. I told her that despite everything, she was still my mum. And the truth is, she was my hero long before I ever found the words for it.

Something inside me shifted that day. The tightness I had carried across my chest when thinking about her loosened. A heaviness that had lived inside me quietly began to melt. It felt like releasing a breath I had been holding for decades.

And I realised something sitting above her grave.

Every time I return home, I leave with more peace.

Because the houses do not own me. The town does not own me. The past does not own me.

It shaped me, yes.

But it did not finish me.

And that is moxie.

Not the glossy quote version. The real version.

The kind built in silence. In survival. In heartbreak. In illness. In fear. In loneliness.

The kind that dragged me out of Glen Innes when I thought I would never escape.

And the kind that carried me back again years later, not as a broken girl, but as a woman who turned her pain into purpose, and her story into hope.

2025 Visiting Mum at her grave on her birthday

2026 In my gallery with Pansy — Marshall, Victoria

CHAPTER 42

More Than My Fair Share

I sometimes sit back and genuinely marvel at how much shit one human body can go through before it starts sending eviction notices to the soul living inside it. When I hear people say things like, "It was my first time ever in a hospital," or "I have never needed surgery," or "I have never even broken a bone," my brain glitches. I cannot even comprehend that kind of life because mine has been the exact opposite. Hospitals have been my second home. Specialists have become my extended family. Waiting rooms are now my natural habitat. Needles, blood tests, scans, pain, exhaustion, recovery and resilience have woven themselves into the fabric of my existence before I even understood what the word illness meant.

My medical timeline reads like an encyclopedia, which would almost be funny if it were not my actual life. Illness never knocked politely for me. It barged in, kicked the door off the hinges and made itself comfortable.

And this is where moxie started for me, long before I ever called it that. Not the glossy, motivational kind. The real kind. The kind you build when your body keeps falling apart, and you still have to turn up for your life. Over time, I learnt two skills that sound like opposites, but they are actually the same survival muscle. I learnt when to harden up so I could keep going, and when to soften down so I could heal. That combination is what I mean when I say moxie. Where I developed the grit, courage and determination to keep fighting to stay alive.

This timeline is probably not complete. At the time of writing, this is all I can remember; there is probably more.

1971

I was born.

1974

My very first trauma came when a dog bit me when I was out walking with Mum and Simon. I do not remember it, but my body did. It has led to a lifetime of fear of most dogs.

1975

Tore my leg open on the metal top of a calendar on the doorframe.
Fillings in my baby teeth from weak enamel.

1976

Wore an orthodontic plate for a few years as my teeth were too big for my mouth.

1977

I had my tonsils removed, and at the same time, my adenoids were taken out. I attended speech therapy to learn to talk properly again.
I also had German measles.

1978

I had chicken pox, then the mumps and also aseptic meningitis at the same time — something no one should experience, but especially not a child.
I was taken to the hospital with chronic bowel pain. I discovered years later it was due to an intolerance to lactose.
In those early years, I stacked up illnesses as if they were school badges; albeit, ones that no one would have wanted.

1981

I had impetigo in both my armpits.

1983

I sprained my right ankle.
Had my appendix removed.
I got my period for the first time.

1984

I squashed two discs in my neck and spent a week flat on my back, lying on a board in the hospital.
Had 4 mercury fillings put in my teeth.

1985

I had cysts removed from my eyelids on both eyes, and more would follow across the decades. That same year, I had six teeth removed due to my mouth being small and my teeth too big.

I fell down a flight of stairs at school, and the senior high school boys walked on me as I lay screaming on the ground.

I developed dark facial hair and was diagnosed with polycystic ovary syndrome (PCOS).

1986

Had cysts removed from my scalp.

I got shingles for the first time around my chest.

Hemiplegic migraines arrived and never left.

I had a rosacea flare on my face for the first time and it stayed for the next 40+ years.

Plus, I got a concussion.

1988

Cold sores across my bottom lip.

1989

I had glandular fever and Epstein-Barr virus.

Had 12 moles removed, then developed Keloid scars.

I started on the contraceptive pill for birth control and to regulate my periods.

My childhood and teenage years were basically a medical circus without applause.

And then came the nineties, and the universe clearly decided it had not had enough fun yet.

1990

Bulimia — an eating disorder — started.

1991

A dentist removed the wrong back molars. He was drunk!

I got Human Papillomavirus (HPV).

I had my first abortion, the kind of experience no one forgets, no matter how young they are. Became intolerant to caffeine and gluten.

1993

I gave birth to my first baby, Zak, through a caesarean section, where the epidural did not work properly, and I felt more than any woman should ever feel, and at the same time I tested positive for HSV-1 and HSV-2, better known as genital herpes.

1994

I got septicemia from tonsillitis.

1995

I slipped down my front steps and damaged all the ligaments in my right ankle.

1996

I slipped down the steps again but this time I broke my leg and the top of my foot, and to be honest, by then, injuries were almost expected.

1997

I gave birth naturally to Ally.

Between those births, losses, injuries and illnesses, the nineties gave me no relief, and that same year, depression crashed into my life for the first time. Postnatal and full-blown depression. Proper, deep, suffocating depression that steals your breath and blinds your hope.

1998

I had my second abortion due to a medical mistake by a doctor.
I had a white-tailed spider bite me, and felt as though the universe was throwing in bonus injuries just to keep the momentum going.

I had an abscess removed from my underarm 6 weeks before my wedding, and then 4 days before my wedding had two large abscesses drained from my groin under general anaesthesia.

I got boils all over my body, which I couldn't get rid of for the next two years.

1999

I lived inside a body that was morbidly obese. I carried 46 kilograms more than my frame carries now. When I finally lost those 46 kgs and reached my goal weight in 2007, it was one of the most profound physical and emotional victories of my entire life. My body had battled me for years, but that was one fight I won in spectacular fashion.

2002

I was king hit and spent a few days in hospital.

I broke my tailbone and my back while participating in national Tug of War.

Second and third degree burns on my face from IPL for hair removal.

My vision went blurry.

2003

I had a cone biopsy after CIN1 and CIN2 were found on my cervix. I had a dermoid cyst on my right ovary, the size of a grapefruit, removed.

2005

I got my ovaries drilled, which is burning them, in an attempt to manage PCOS. I developed mild Hashimoto's and was put on HRT troches.

2006

Had cysts removed from my scalp.

Chondral disease in my knees.

2007

I couldn't lift my left arm very high due to acute pain.

2008

I developed myofascial pain syndrome in my face, and I had dry needling to help with the pain.

2009

I had my tonsils removed for the second time, and also tonsil crypts removed.

2010

I suffered an acquired brain injury (ABI) that changed me forever, stripping me of executive functions I once took for granted and forcing me to build entire new systems just to function.

I developed bursitis in my left shoulder as well as a ganglion on my right foot.

Each ailment stacked upon the next like a cruel Jenga tower that somehow refused to collapse.

Then came 2011, the year everything changed.

2011

A cyst behind my right eye in my brain.

I was diagnosed with multiple sclerosis (MS). It is what caused the ABI.
I started on disease modifying treatment (DMT). First trying Copaxone, where I gave myself a needle every second day. It failed. Then onto 4 weekly infusions of Tysabri. I tested positive for the John Cunningham virus (+JCV) which drastically limited my treatment options. Tysabri and JCV do not go well together. I did 37 infusions and then had to stop.

The MS brings its own special brand of torment. People who do not live with multiple sclerosis will never truly understand the bizarre, unpredictable sensations it can create. I get what they call the MS hug, which is the most ironic name for something that feels nothing like a hug. It is a crushing band that wraps around my ribs so tightly it feels like my body is trying to strangle itself from the inside. Some days it feels like a python squeezing the air out of me. Other days it feels like a tight, burning pressure that flares without warning. There is no gentle comfort in it at all. It is a reminder that my nervous system is misfiring, that my body sends the wrong messages, that pain can appear in places no one can see.

Then there is Lhermitte's sign. A shooting electric shock that zips down my spine whenever I bend my neck. It is quick, sharp and unnerving, like my body has been plugged into a socket. The first time it happened, I thought I had done something catastrophic to my spine. But no. It was just another delightful symptom of MS. Another strange, invisible cruelty that I had to learn to live with, to breathe through, to carry.

These symptoms come and go like unexpected storms. Some days I barely notice them. Other days they stop me in my tracks. They are not dramatic enough for most people to notice, but they are constant enough to shape how I move, how I stretch, how I breathe and how I exist inside my own skin.

And yet even in those moments, when my ribs are being crushed by an invisible force or lightning bolts shoot down my spine, something inside me still refuses to fall apart. Something inside me steadies itself. Something inside me whispers, not today. Something inside me taps into the part that has survived everything else. Something inside me reaches for that familiar grit, that stubbornness, that spark that refuses to dim. That is the moxie talking. The part of me that endures even when my body has had enough.

And of course, the MS does not stop at the hug or the lightning bolts down my spine. It has a whole bag of tricks it likes to pull out whenever it wants to remind me who is really running the show. My feet spasm without warning, twisting, tightening and cramping in ways that make it impossible to pretend everything is fine. It can happen when I am resting, walking, lying in bed or even in the middle of talking to someone. One moment my body is still, the next it behaves like it has been struck by an electrical surge. My hip flexor joins the rebellion too, constricting so violently at times that it feels like the entire muscle has turned into concrete. It grabs, locks, pulls and becomes so tight that even taking a normal step feels like dragging a leg made of stone.

Then there is the optic neuritis that comes and goes like a thief in the night. One day my vision is clear, the next it blurs or clouds or burns, and I am reminded again that my optic nerve has taken hits that will never fully heal. It feels like looking through dirty glass. Sometimes like someone dimmed the lights. Sometimes the world has lost depth or clarity. And every time it happens, even for a moment, that fear stirs in my chest, the fear of losing something I know I cannot afford to lose. But just as unpredictably as it comes, it settles again, giving me space to breathe until the next round.

One of the hardest symptoms is the ABI — simple things like counting and telling the time, I simply couldn't do anymore.

2012

I developed atrial fibrillation (AF).

I started counselling every two weeks for the next 13 years.

2013

Internal ultrasound of my heart.

I came off the pill.

I had my first pulmonary vein ablation, where they burn your heart. I haemorrhaged after the surgery.

I had an IUD Mirena inserted for birth control. Turns out I have a posterior cervix, meaning I now have to be put under anaesthesia to have them removed and new ones inserted.

2014

The AF returned. I also had atrial tachycardia (AT), and I had my second pulmonary vein ablation after a resting heart rate of 217 beats per minute. I also haemorrhaged again.

Broke my front tooth on a nail polish bottle, and had the piece glued back on.

I was put on Gilenya, got shingles again this time on my face and had to stop taking Gilenya before it killed me. Then was put on Aubagio, which scared the shit out of me as it takes over 2 years to come out of your body naturally.

My immune system was a battlefield, and every treatment carried risks that most people will thankfully never have to face.

But the medical avalanche was not done with me yet.

Started on NDIS.

2015

Pitting on my eyeballs has been caused by the medications to control everything else.

I had premature atrial contractions (PAC). I was missing 1 in every 5 beats. I had a front wall ablation on my heart. As a result of the surgery, I developed pericarditis. My heart literally misfired its way through the decade, and yet somehow I kept going.

Started laser hair removal on my whole body.

2016

I was diagnosed with livedo reticularis, and my skin was going purple. I looked like a zombie. Then they found melanoma on my lower right leg when they were looking for the cause of livedo. I had that cut out with a 10cm scar left in its place.

2 x asymptomatic moles burnt from my face.

My blood gave me IgM, which is mixed cryoglobulinaemia. Too much protein in my blood. I developed necrosis on my left hand from the livedo.

I also had my first bone marrow biopsy on the right side of my pelvis.

2017

I ruptured my ear drum.

I was told over the phone I had chronic lymphocytic leukaemia (CLL) and small lymphocytic lymphoma (SLL). These are two different types of cancer, and the SLL was stage 4.

I had a new Mirena put in.

I had my second bone marrow biopsy, this time on the left side of my pelvis. I was awake, pain medication didn't work, and the procedure failed as they couldn't break off the 1cm bone. Later that year, I also had a third bone marrow biopsy under general anaesthesia. I had four skin biopsies on my lower legs.

I had a Hickman line inserted into my chest, straight into my heart. Chemotherapy of Bundamustene and Rituximab caused allergic reactions, and I spent the next 18 months on steroids.

I had neutropenia and had to have a needle into my stomach to grow white blood cells in my bone marrow.

At the end of that year, I woke up one morning unable to walk, had chronic laryngitis and spent weeks in the hospital. I learnt to walk again.

I was assaulted in the hospital by another patient.

3 x asymptomatic moles removed from my legs.

2018

I was started on infusions of other people's antibodies called Intravenous Immunoglobulin (IVIG). It took me a long time to get my head around having bits of other people in me. This was to help with the risk of infections that I was getting at a rapid rate due to them wiping out my whole immune system.

I was diagnosed with lipoedema — inflammation of the fat — a condition I had unknowingly carried most of my life. My legs and arms had always troubled me and finally there was a name for it. That diagnosis shaped my daily routine, my mobility, my self-image and my pain levels.

I also discovered my left leg is 12mm shorter than my right leg; I now have to wear a heel wedge and can't walk barefoot, or I put my back out.

I went into remission from the cancer late in that year.

I injured my back and spent three days in the hospital.

I had the plastic cuff removed from my chest that remained when they yanked the hickman line from my chest while I was awake.

Put on 20kg from being on steroids, but at least I was alive.

2019

Broke my big toe on my right foot from a fall.

Broke my rib from another fall.

2020.

Due to the COVID-19 pandemic, I had to switch from IVIG to Subcutaneous Immunoglobulin (SCIG). I was taught to give myself the infusions at home on a weekly basis in my belly or in my legs.

So far this treatment alone has cost over one million dollars. And if we added everything else I have endured, the treatments, surgeries, admissions, doctors, scans and procedures would easily hit several million more. The cost of staying alive is extraordinary in every sense.

2021

Broken right arm with a radius broken through, cracked ulna, torn cartilage, broken tail bone and concussion from domestic violence.

Haemorrhoids.

Laser treatment for the rosacea on my face.

20+ keratoses on my skin frozen off.

2022

I went into the Andrew Love Cancer Centre, hoping my doctor would tell me I was now on 6 monthly visits. Instead, she told me the cancers were back. I went on 'wait and watch' for the next eight months, having levels checked regularly, hoping they would go back under that magic level they call remission.

The same year, I was officially diagnosed with mast cell activation syndrome (MCAS). I am histamine intolerant. This diagnosis answered many questions and filled in some of the missing pieces of the puzzle that is me.

Bacterial vaginosis.

I had my third Mirena inserted.

I was bitten by another dog.

I got COVID-19 for the first time, and I was given antivirals.

Had my right wrist repaired with surgery.

2023

Went back into remission for CLL and SLL.

I got COVID-19 for a second time.

My right lung collapsed.

And because my body seems determined to collect medical plot twists like souvenirs, 2023 delivered yet another one. What should have been a simple, joyful moment of getting a tattoo turned into cellulitis. My skin blew up. The pain was like fire. I ended up on another round of antibiotics, which my system barely tolerates anymore.

And that became the turning point, the moment I learnt that I am now antibiotic-resistant for UTIs. Years of infections, treatments, reactions and complications have left my body unable to rely on medications most people take for granted. A UTI for me is not a quick fix. It is a medical negotiation. It is fear. It is hoping that the infection does not crawl into my kidneys. It is hoping that the doctors can find one last antibiotic that still works. It is yet another reminder that surviving this long has come with a cost that sits quietly under the surface until it flares.

Discovered cysts in my thyroid.

I discovered that I have TMJ — Temporomandibular Joint (TMJ) dysfunction — when the jaw joint and muscles go haywire, causing grinding, clenching and face pain.

2024

I got COVID-19 for the third time.

I developed an ulcer on my eyeball from having my eyelashes tinted! Menopause slammed into me with the subtlety of a freight train; vaginal atrophy was something I didn't know was possible! But here I am, living with that hell!

I had vaginal surgery to repair damage caused by domestic violence from three years earlier, with 7 stitches and a permanent scar to remind me.

As if all of that were not enough, my hormones decided to join the rebellion.

I developed a fistula from my bowel to my bladder thanks to vaginal atrophy. My oestrogen levels have dropped to almost nothing, creating a cascade of problems that would make anyone else crawl into bed and not come out. Low oestrogen means hormone replacement therapy (HRT), trying to rectify vaginal dryness, pain, tearing of the vaginal skin, urinary issues, increased infections, mood swings, insomnia, hot flushes, and an emotional rawness that blends with all the physical battles I am already fighting. It affects my bones, my muscles, my cognition, my skin, my bladder and my energy. It is another invisible load tucked behind everything else, yet I still get up, still work, still speak, still write, still show up in the world with a strength most people will never fully grasp.

Botox in my eyebrows to stop the twitching from MS.

I discovered my front big tooth needs to be removed due to trauma from domestic violence over the years.

2025

My vision was blurry, and I became photosensitive. I was diagnosed with bilateral cataracts and also blepharitis on my eyelids.

Two benign tumours were found on my spine.

A venous lake on the inside of my mouth.

8mm tear of my right subscapularis in my shoulder.

I was diagnosed with hypermobile Ehlers-Danlos syndrome (hEDS). Finally, a lot of the pieces to the puzzle of my body had answers. Lipoedema, MCAS, and possibly MS are all comorbidities with each other.

Influenza A at Christmas time, and had to take antivirals.

More keratoses were frozen off.

Three skin blemishes frozen off on my face.

2026

I now wear an occlusal splint on my bottom teeth so I do not bust a tooth off in my sleep due to TMJ. When something else happens, I have no idea if it is MS,

MCAS, lipoedema or something else. That is the exhausting reality of living inside this body. It is a constant interpretation. Constant guessing. Constant management. Constant adapting.

This is the truth of my body.

A body that has been cut open, broken, stitched, burnt, biopsied, scanned, medicated, infused, shocked, repaired, bruised, battered and scarred.

A body that has learnt how to function even when almost every system inside it has given up at one point or another.

A body that has tried to quit on me so many times yet still carries me forward with a kind of exhausted loyalty.

A body that demands more resilience than most people will ever need to summon in their entire lifetime.

I only have one body and I put self-care at the top of my list just so I can function daily. Hypermobile joints. Hormonal facial hair. Keratoses. Chronic pain. Muscle spasms. Concussions. Boils. Pimples. Haemorrhoids. Stretch marks. Keyloid scarring. Allergic reactions to medications. Allergies and intolerances to penicillin, codeine, Tegretol, Bendamustine, caffeine, lactose, gluten, strawberries, tomatoes, chocolate, cacao and sulphur.

Local anaesthetics rarely work. Pain medications barely touch me. And through all of this, I have had over 27 MRI scans, PET scans, CAT scans, ultrasounds, internal heart ultrasounds, nasoendoscopy, colonoscopies, endoscopies, transvaginal ultrasound, more x-rays and blood tests than I could ever count, and at least eleven general anaesthetics.

And in the middle of my medical storm, I have carried a team of specialists. GPs. Neurologists. Cardiologists. Gynaecologists. Urologists. Physiotherapists. Occupational Therapists. Speech Therapists. Psychologists. Counsellors. Chiropractors. Massage Therapists. Bowen Therapist. Dentists. Orthodontists. Podiatrists. Hand Therapists. Support Coordinators. Plan Managers. The list is endless, and somehow necessary. My life is a full-time medical project.

NDIS: I am grateful beyond words, but I also hate that I need it. I hate begging for funding every plan review. I hate proving my illnesses and disabilities again and again at every single plan review. It is the most stressful time of the year, worse than dealing with Centrelink. But without it, I would not survive; I have accepted that reality with the same reluctant grit I have learnt to apply everywhere else in my life.

They pay for therapies to help me move my body, such as neurophysiotherapy, mobility devices, and home cleaning. Be careful what you wish for. I always thought that if you had a cleaner, you had made it in life. In order to get mine, I had to become disabled. Be really clear on your goals! LOL.

Yet despite all of it, with every hit, every diagnosis, every surgery, every fall, every setback, every needle, every night spent awake in pain, every time my body broke, every time my life paused, something inside me refused to quit. Something inside me grew louder, fiercer, wilder, stronger. Something inside me said, 'absolutely not'. Something inside me learnt to harden the fuck up. Something inside me learnt to soften the hell down. And that alchemy of strength and softness is what carried me through. I finally understood how moxie was me.

Yes, I have had far more than my fair share. But I am still here. Still rising. Still fighting. Still creating. Still building a life I love. Still daring to live even when my body tries its hardest to drag me down. Still laughing. Still turning trauma into purpose. Still giving hope to others. Still living a life that makes sense only when you understand the moxie it took to survive it.

I am used to things going wrong. It is not dramatic to me. It is familiar. Crisis, illness and disruption have been the baseline of my life for so long that calm feels suspicious. When other people say they have had a bad year, I nod politely, knowing my nervous system has been trained on a completely different scale.

For a long time, I thought that meant something was wrong with me. That I was cursed. Broken. Too much. Then I realised something important. This was not a flaw. It was conditioning. My body learnt early how to adapt. My mind learnt how to problem-solve under pressure. My spirit learnt how to stay strong when everything else was falling apart.

I sought counselling, not because I was weak, but because I wanted to understand myself instead of being consumed by my story. I wanted to stop surviving on instinct alone and start making sense of the pattern. Counselling gave me language for what I had lived. It helped me separate what happened to me from who I am. It gave me permission to soften where I had hardened too much, and to strengthen where I had been worn thin.

That is where moxie really took shape.

Moxie is not pretending things are fine.

Moxie is not positivity pasted over pain.

Moxie is knowing exactly how bad things are and choosing to stay anyway.

Every diagnosis taught me something. Every recovery demanded something. I learnt how to listen to my body without being ruled by it. I learnt how to ask for help without shame. I learnt how to rest without guilt. I learnt how to advocate for myself when no one else could see what was wrong. I learnt how to build systems around a body that could not be trusted to behave predictably.

And slowly, something shifted.

What broke me did not define me.

It shaped me.

I began to understand that my purpose was never to live a small, protected life. My purpose was to walk through the fire and come back carrying light for others. To sit beside people in pain and not rush them. To speak honestly about bodies that fail and minds that fracture. To tell the truth about resilience; it is messy, exhausting and deeply human.

I give people hope because I am living proof that it can coexist with suffering. Not hope that everything will be fixed, but hope that life can still be meaningful. That joy can still exist alongside pain. That identity does not disappear just because your body betrays you.

This chapter is not a list of what went wrong.

It is a record of what did not defeat me.

Moxie is the quiet decision I made again and again to stay. To adapt. To rebuild. To turn experience into wisdom and pain into purpose. It is the reason I speak, write, mentor and show up the way I do. It is the reason other people recognise themselves in my story and feel less alone.

I did not choose this body.

I did not choose this timeline.

But I chose what I would do with it.

And that choice is moxie.

Above everything else, I am still me.

And that is the greatest miracle of all.

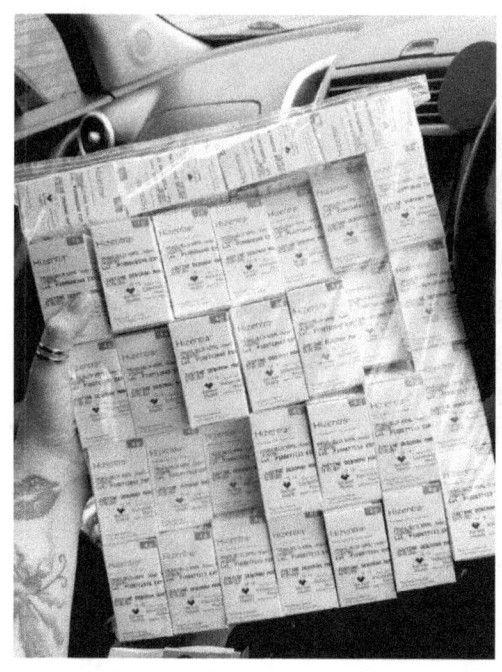

3 months worth of Hizentra (human) antibodies for my weekly infusions

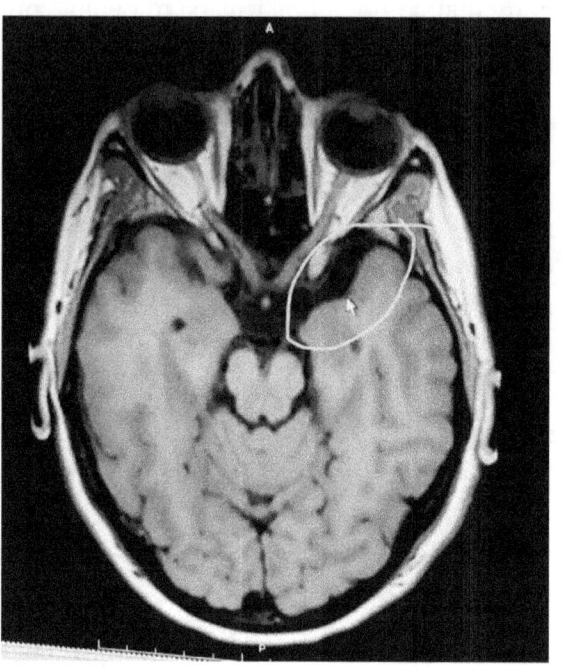

2015 MRI of the cyst behind my right eye

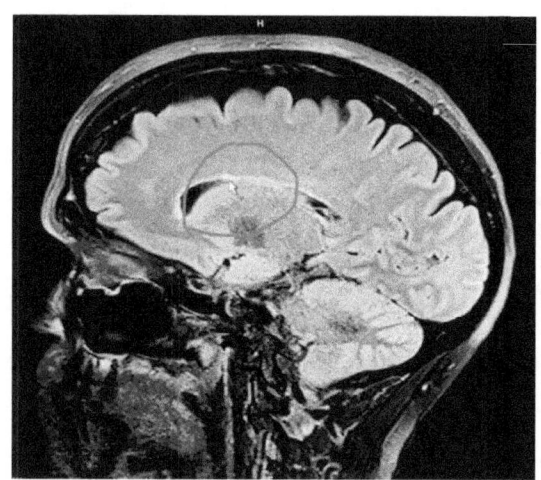

2015 MRI, MS lesion circled

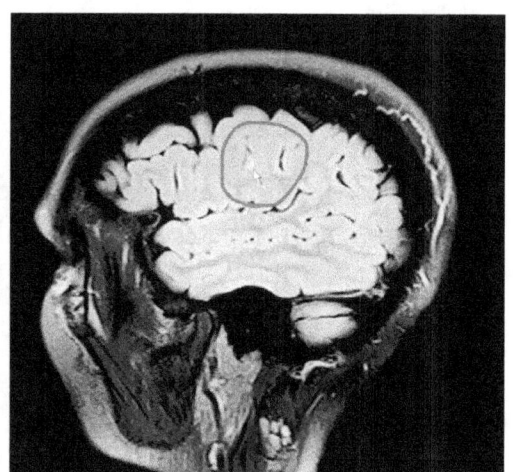

2015 MRI, MS lesion circled

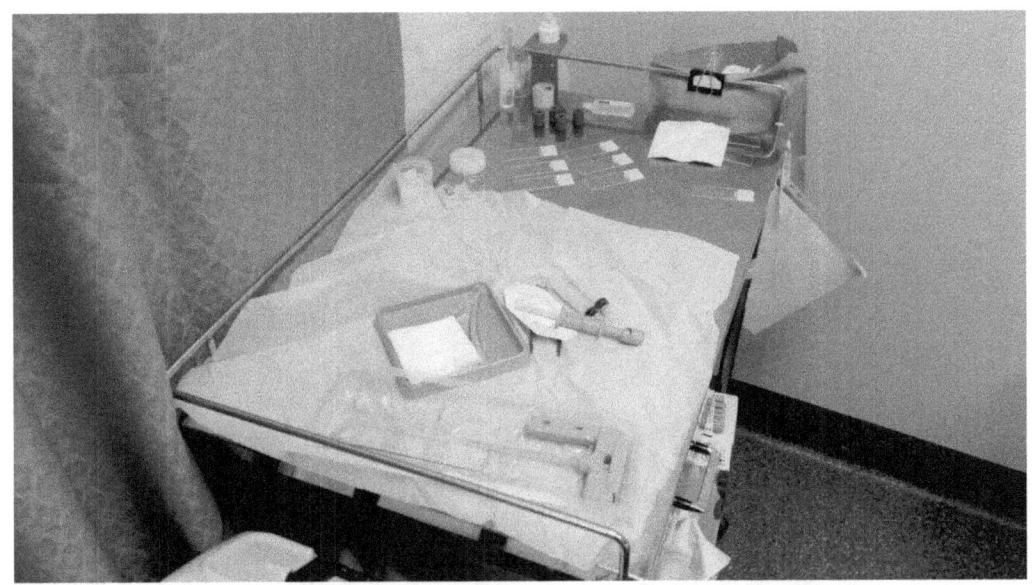
2016 Bone marrow biopsy equipment

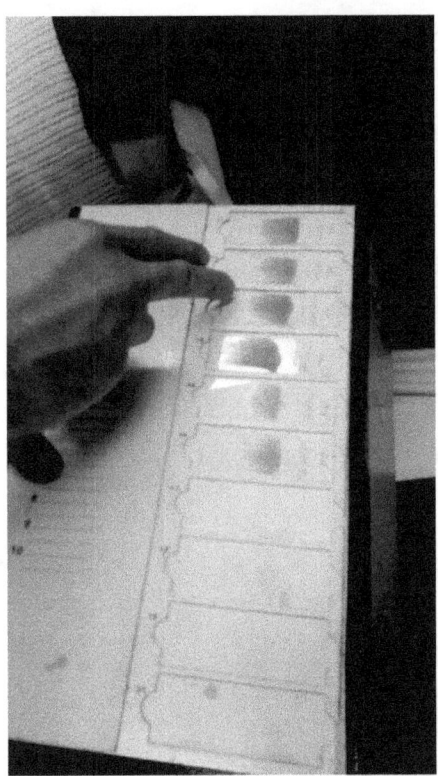
2016 Bone marrow biopsy

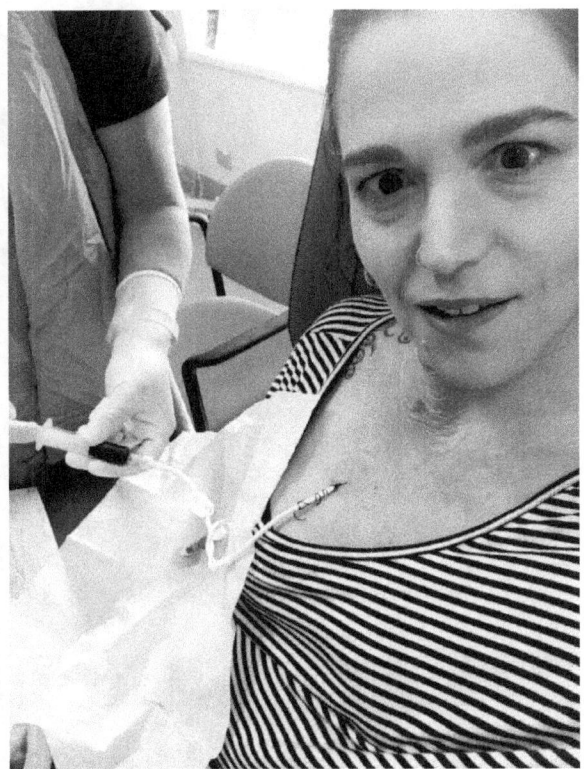
2017 Blood test through my Hickman line

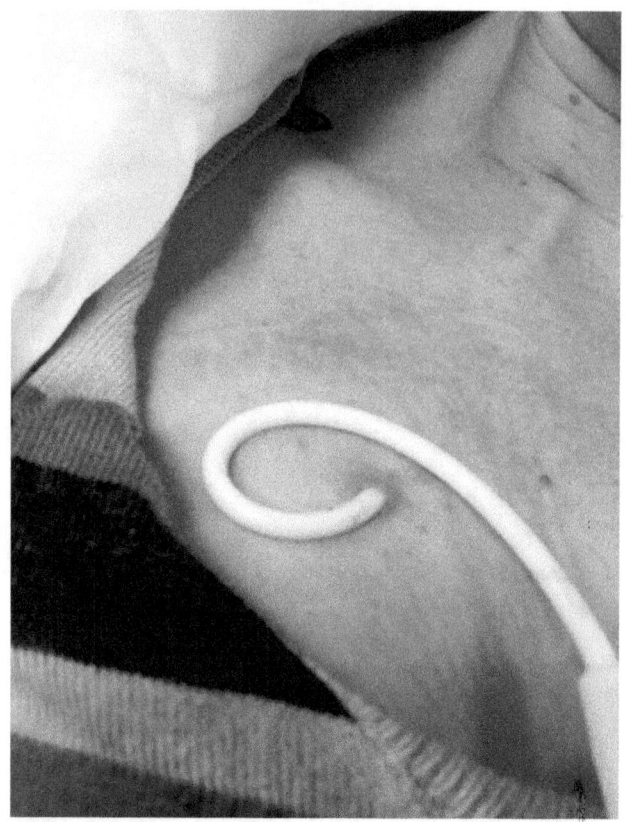

2017 Hickman line straight into my heart

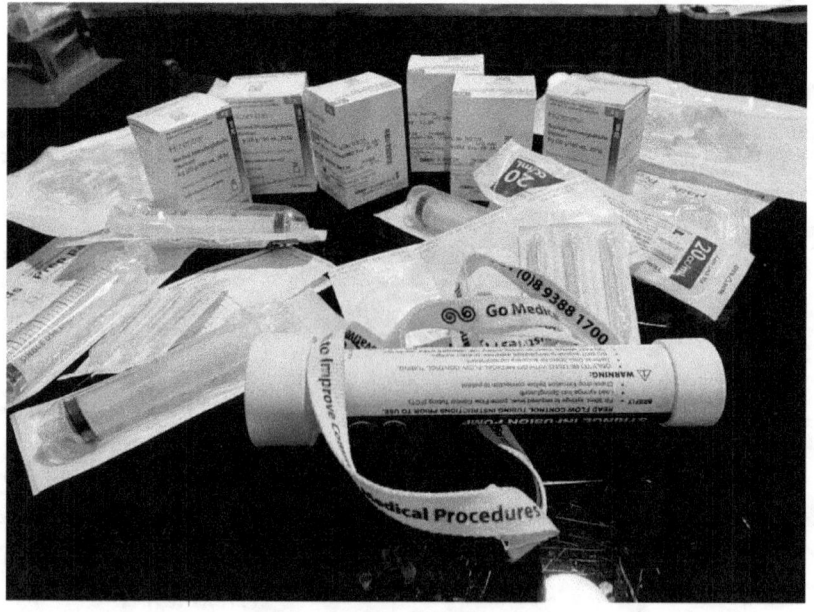

SCIG infusion equipment

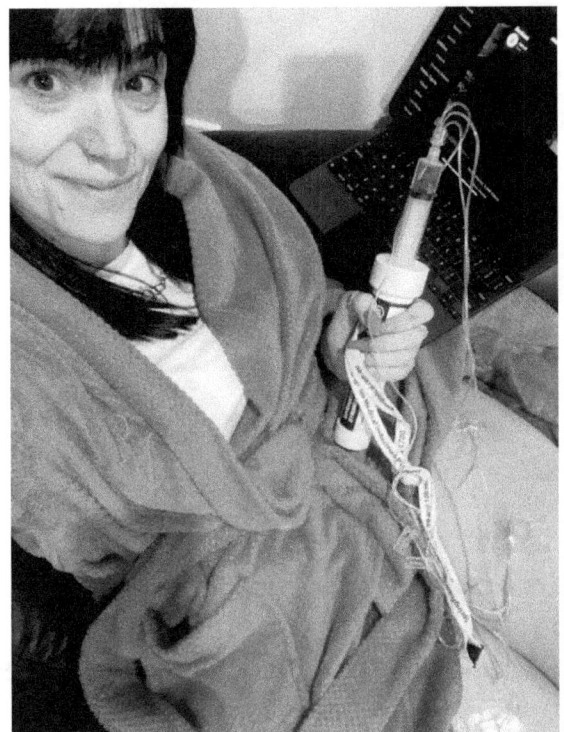

SCIG infusion in my legs

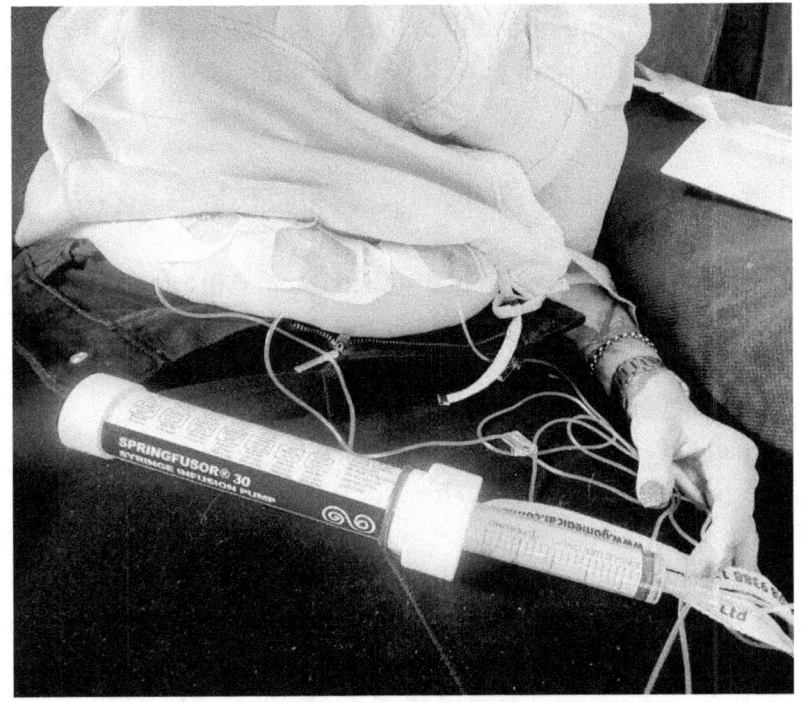

Weekly SCIG infusion of Hizentra in my legs

CHAPTER 43

What If

When I look back across the chapters of my life, it feels like I am watching different versions of myself walk across the same landscape. The frightened young woman, the overwhelmed mother, the fighter battling illness, the advocate, the artist, the business owner, the speaker, the survivor and the soft-centred warrior I have become today. Writing this book has forced me to gather all those versions together, hold them close and honour them. I spent six very long years writing Moxie, stopping and starting, falling and rising, healing and hurting, living and learning. Finishing it on my fifty-fifth birthday feels like a moment the universe planned long before I did, a perfect closing of one life chapter and the opening of another.

And somewhere in the writing of it, one question kept whispering through my mind.

What if?

What if I had never walked through that art studio door?

What if I had let fear win?

What if the woman I used to be had stayed trapped inside the limits life set around her?

What if I had never discovered the strength I hold inside me now?

What if I had never learnt to harden the fuck up?

What if I had never softened the hell down?

These questions are not regrets. They are reflections. They are acknowledgements of just how close I came to missing the life I have now.

Because the truth is, the day I walked into that art studio changed everything. It looked like such a small moment from the outside, barely a ripple. But inside, it was a shift in my entire world. I had been drowning quietly for so long, holding myself together with tape and grit and forced smiles. Art handed me back my breath. It

WHAT IF

showed me that broken things can still create beauty. It gave me a doorway to my own healing.

If I had not walked in that day, I do not know if I would have found myself again. I do not know if JUZT Art would exist. I do not know if Morpheus Publishing would exist. I do not know if I would be speaking on world stages, or lifting others, or holding space for people the way I do now. All of it traces back to one terrified woman walking through one doorway and deciding to try.

What if I had not?

What if I had not become an MS ambassador?

What if I had stayed silent?

What if I had believed that my voice did not matter?

Speaking as an MS Australia ambassador was the first moment someone walked up to me and said, "You should do this for a living." Imagine if they had not said it. Or worse, imagine if I had not listened. My entire speaking career, my entire impact, began with that sentence.

What if I had not run for elections to fight for medical change?

What if CBD oil had never become legal in Victoria?

What if I had never advocated for myself?

What if I had accepted the limitations others placed on me?

I might not be here. At least not like this. Not as a woman writing her story from a place of strength. Not as a woman with remission written across diagnoses that once threatened my life. Not as a woman with purpose so deeply stitched into her bones it hums.

And then there are the 'what ifs' that touch the heart.

What if Zak had never been stationed in Townsville?

What if he had never met Amelia?

What if Ally had never met Matt?

What if my children had not found the loves of their lives?

What if their marriages were not built on respect and gentleness and humour the way they are now?

I must have done something right because the relationships my children are in are steady, warm and safe. The kind of love I once thought belonged in other people's lives, not mine. People often ask me if there is anything I cannot do, and I always answer with humour. Yes. Romantic relationships. That is the one area I have not quite mastered. Maybe one day that will change. For now, I am content to be wrapped in love from every direction, even if romantic love remains the one puzzle piece that came bent in the box.

And then there is the lawnmower.

A small thing to some, but to me it was a declaration of independence.

When my ex-husband took the lawnmower, it felt like one more stripping away of something that was mine. Something practical. Something symbolic. I remember standing there, humiliated and furious and exhausted, thinking, 'No. Not this. Not again.' So I went out and bought my own mower. That moment was not about grass. It was about reclaiming myself.

So the universe must have had a good laugh when I eventually stopped owning lawnmowers altogether and instead ended up owning an entire gardening business. I went from one single lawn mower to running a company with staff and clients, and machines far bigger than anything I could have imagined on that day. That is what moxie looks like. Turning a moment of loss into a lifetime of possibility.

Art is still stitched into my world, not always through exhibitions or long studio hours, but through the children's books I illustrate and the creative projects I bring to life. Art helped me breathe again when I had forgotten how. Now it continues through every child who reads one of my books and every adult who rediscovers hope in the pages of something I helped create.

Somewhere along the way, I found my purpose. Giving people hope. Not in a shallow way, but in the deep soul-anchored way of someone who has survived enough darkness to understand how sacred hope truly is. I give people hope that life can be rebuilt, that adversity can be survived, that a human spirit can be shaped by fire yet somehow rise softer and kinder. That is my purpose. That is my work. That is my legacy.

For most of my life, I believed I had to be tough at all times. I hardened the fuck up because life demanded it. My illnesses demanded it. Trauma demanded it. Survival demanded it. I learnt to armour myself, to dig deep, to claw my way through situations I would not wish on anyone. But what surprised me most in these later years is that strength is not only found in the fire. It is also found in calmness, compassion, softness and peace. I did not see it coming, but somewhere along the way I learnt to soften the hell down.

I did not lose my resilience in that softness. I found it. I bounced forward. My reactions changed. Things that once enraged me or drained me now glide past without landing. The storms that once shook me to the core now pass through me like summer wind. I carry peace now, not because life is perfect, but because I am finally safe in myself.

WHAT IF

Boundaries became the scaffolding of that peace. Not walls. Not defenses. Just clear and honest lines that honour my energy. Boundaries that remind me to protect my time.

And my time is sacred.

Time is the most precious commodity we have.

You cannot buy it, sell it, borrow it or ask for a refund.

You only get to spend it. So be careful on what and on whom you spend it.

When I give someone my time, I am giving them a piece of my life I will never get back.

That awareness shaped my entire existence.

And it is why my life today feels like something I have built with intention. I own my home. A warm, safe place that holds every version of me. I drive my own car — freedom on four wheels. I stand on world stages and speak to thousands from every corner of the globe. As a woman who was once told she would never work again, I now stand as a leader, educator and storyteller.

My MS is in remission. My cancers are in remission. Even writing that brings tears. My body has carried more medical trauma than most will ever face, yet here I am, still breathing, still laughing, still creating, still living.

And above all of that, I am a grandmother to seven beautiful grandchildren, each one a light in my life. Riley, Maycee, Chase, Odin, Cooper, Maxwell and Ripley. They are joy embodied. Their laughter reminds me that life renews itself.

Somewhere inside this life I built, I also became the person who should have protected me when I was a child. I am safe now because I learnt to become my own parent.

I may have lived a lifetime already, but I am nowhere near done. More books. More art. More stages. More adventures. More moxie. Another fifty years of living with intention, joy, strength and softness.

So when I think of all the 'what ifs', I do not feel fear.

I feel gratitude.

Because every 'what if' I chose to say 'yes' to is the reason I am here.

If you take anything from these pages, let it be this.

You can choose your 'what ifs'.

You can harden the fuck up when life demands it.

You can soften down when your soul needs it.

You can reclaim your time.

You can build boundaries.

You can rise again and again.
You can rebuild a life from ashes into something extraordinary.

That is moxie.
And it lives in you too.

3D prints Zak made for me for displaying River's Gift Finding Hope Book

2019 Carols By Candlelight

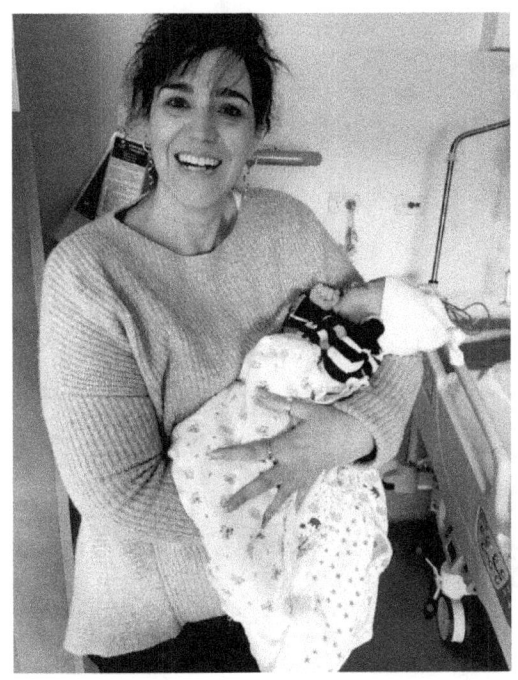

2019 Holding Chase for the first time

2020 My first cuddle with Odin in Townsville

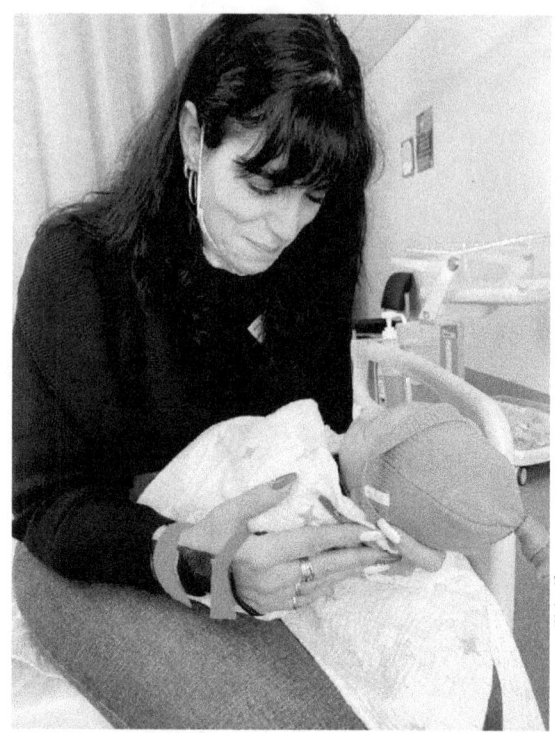

2021 My first time holding Cooper

2023 All my kids at my place

2023 Ally and Zak just before she got married

2023 Ally's wedding with Zak and Maxwell at the Geelong Botanical Gardens

2023 First time holding my grandson Maxwell

2023 Matron of honour at Ally's wedding

2023 Matron of honour at Ally's wedding

2023 Maxwell's Christening

2023 my kids at Zaks shop risingsunfpv.com.au

2024 Finding Hope book launch

2024 Speaking at the Glen Innes Library's 70th birthday celebration

2024 The poster for the Geelong Business Excellence Awards with my photo on it.

2024 Zak and his family on the Strand in Townsville

2024 Finding Hope book launch

2025 Ally, Matt, Riley, Maycee, Chase, Cooper and myself in Melbourne

2025 Breaking the Barriers Exhibition at Geelong Heritage Library

2025 Christmas photo with Zak, Amelia, Odin, Maxwell and Ripley

2025 Deadlifting at Strong Geelong

2025 Disability Expo Geelong

2025 First time holding Ripley

2025 JMC stand at Geelong's Disability Expo

2025 My new car that I had on my vison board for 18 months

2025 Odin, Maxwell and Ripley in Townsville, three of my little men.

2025 Ripley's christening in Townsville

2025 Speaking at the Five Dock Chamber of Commerce

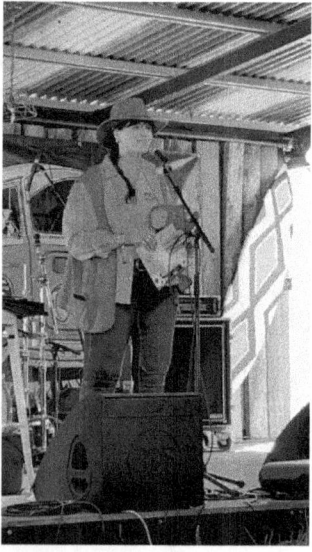

2025 Speaking on stage at the Gympie Music Muster on behalf of River's Gift

2026 My new sign out the front of Justine Martin Corporation, othewise known as my home, with Pansy peeking over the fence

I never travel light

One of the 3D prints Zak made and painted

Resilience Mindset Podcast

Morpheus Publishing Author Spotlight Podcast

JUSTINE MARTIN CONTACT DETAILS

Linktree QR Code
Download QR Here

Linktree:
https://linktr.ee/justinemartincorporation

Email Address:
hello@justinemartin.com.au
hello@morpheuspublishing.com.au

Phone Number:
+61 403 564 942

BRING MOXIE
TO YOUR STAGE

If this story resonated with you, moved you, challenged you or made you feel less alone, Justine can bring that same raw honesty and practical resilience to your audience.

Justine Martin is an international keynote speaker sharing real life resilience, not the glossy version. Her talks combine lived experience, humour, vulnerability and practical tools that help people navigate adversity, change, pressure, illness, grief and rebuilding when life does not go to plan. Audiences do not just leave inspired. They leave equipped.

Her presentations are tailored for:
- Corporate teams and leadership groups
- Business and entrepreneurship events
- Health and community organisations
- Conferences, workshops and keynotes
- Schools and youth audiences.

To book Justine as a speaker

Email: hello@justinemartin.com.au

Website: www.justinemartin.com.au

PUBLISH YOUR STORY THROUGH MORPHEUS PUBLISHING

Everyone has a story. Not everyone knows how to get it into the world. That is where Morpheus Publishing comes in.

Founded by Justine Martin, Morpheus Publishing supports everyday people, especially those with lived experience of adversity, disability or major life challenges, to become published authors. Morpheus believes stories change lives, including the life of the person brave enough to tell it.

Whether you are writing a memoir, a self-help book, a children's book, a poetry collection or a story you have carried for years, you do not have to do it alone.

To learn more about publishing your book

Website: www.morpheuspublishing.com.au

Email: hello@morpheuspublsihing.com.au

www.ingramcontent.com/pod-product-compliance
Lightning Source LLC
Chambersburg PA
CBHW081206230426
43666CB00015B/2668